Psychoanalytic, Psychosocial, and Human Rights Perspectives on Enforced Disappearance

I0131039

Collecting authoritative contributions, *Psychoanalytic, Psychosocial, and Human Rights Perspectives on Enforced Disappearance* combines the life experience of victims with the expertise of scholars and practitioners of human rights, psychoanalysis, and artists to compose a picture that renders the complexity of this crime in its legal, psychological, and social aspects.

Victims offer a glimpse into the bottomless despair of those who lose a family member in such a dramatic and torturous way. Academic scholars give a picture of this crime in contemporary world. Experts in human rights law address the progress and limitations of the different standards applied in international human rights law. The psychosocial framework in the context of forensic investigations and reparations encourages the decision-making process of the victims and the elaboration of their personal and collective stories. Psychoanalytic authors address the problems of perpetrators' states of mind, the profound psychological and unconscious significance of torture and the disappearance of people by the State, and the issues of memory and trauma in its multiple meanings, individual, collective, and transgenerational. Art is part of this collective effort to work through, to question, to understand, and to repair the damages of evil.

The book is aimed at postgraduate students, scholars, and practitioners in politics, psychoanalysis, law, psychology, psychosocial studies, human rights, social work and justice, and related fields.

Maria Giovanna Bianchi, PhD, is an analytical psychologist and psychotherapist. She worked for almost three decades as a United Nations Human Rights Officer.

Monica Luci, PhD, is a Jungian and relational psychoanalyst, and a lecturer in refugee care in the Department of Psychosocial and Psychoanalytic Studies of the University of Essex.

"This outstanding collection weaves its intricate threads to connect human rights work with psychoanalysis. To call it 'interdisciplinary', though correct, is far too dry. The commitment of those who work in the field of human rights rests on the most profound depth psychological motivations. And psychoanalysis, at its base, is committed to freedom. The crime of enforced disappearance presents a challenge at every level. This book is an amazingly vibrant response."

Andrew Samuels, *author of* The Political Psyche

"Really important work on the critical link between psychology and human rights. Both disciplines are about healing, much needed to counter the scourge of enforced disappearances."

Volker Türk, *United Nations High Commissioner for Human Rights*

"This vital new volume both witnesses the suffering and discusses the psychopolitical meaning of the immense human rights violation of disappearing human beings. Assembling an array of authors who are impressively knowledgeable and deeply implicated in this story, Bianchi and Luci's book is a much-needed contribution to the recognition and understanding of one painful and unfortunately representative recent and contemporary political repression."

Jessica Benjamin, *psychoanalyst and author of* Beyond Doer and Done To: Recognition Theory, Intersubjectivity and the Third

"In the 1970s, mothers and grandmothers in Argentina looked for the disappeared, fought for the right to the truth, and obtained the adoption of the International Convention. This book, in a profound juridical and psychological analysis of enforced disappearances, shows the sophistication needed to address, from the point of view of victims, relatives, perpetrators, lawyers, and psychotherapists, a crime that unfortunately is still being committed in many countries of the world."

Federico Villegas, *former President of the Human Rights Council, Ambassador of Argentina to the United Nations*

Psychoanalytic, Psychosocial, and Human Rights Perspectives on Enforced Disappearance

Edited by
Maria Giovanna Bianchi
and Monica Luci

Routledge
Taylor & Francis Group

LONDON AND NEW YORK

Cover image: Anne Blanchet.

First published 2024
by Routledge
4 Park Square, Milton Park, Abingdon, Oxon OX14 4RN

and by Routledge
605 Third Avenue, New York, NY 10158

Routledge is an imprint of the Taylor & Francis Group, an informa business

British Library Cataloguing-in-Publication Data
A catalogue record for this book is available from the British Library

ISBN: 978-1-032-32058-8 (hbk)
ISBN: 978-1-032-32057-1 (pbk)
ISBN: 978-1-003-31264-2 (ebk)

DOI: 10.4324/9781003312642

Typeset in Times New Roman
by codeMantra

To all those who suffered harm because of enforced
disappearance

Contents

About the editors

Maria Giovanna Bianchi, PhD, is Jungian psychoanalyst and psychotherapist in private practice in Geneva, Switzerland. She is the member of the Board of Directors of the C.G. Jung Foundation, Zürich. She worked as human rights officer at the United Nations Office of the High Commissioner for Human Rights for almost three decades. She authors articles, speaks at international conferences, and lectures in academic and professional contexts on the trans-disciplinarity and complementarity between human rights and analytical psychology.

Monica Luci, PhD, is clinical psychologist, Jungian and relational psychoanalyst, and is a lecturer in refugee care in the Department of Psychosocial and Psychoanalytic Studies at University of Essex. She teaches in different professional and academic contexts, speaks at international conferences and is author and editor of publications on the themes of psychoanalysis, human rights, social violence, gender and sexuality, trauma and refugees. Some of her works are *Torture, Psychoanalysis and Human Rights* (Routledge, 2017) *Torture Survivors in Analytic Therapy: Jung, Politics, Culture* (Routledge, 2022), and *Lockdown Therapy: Jungian Perspectives on How Pandemic Changed Psychoanalysis* (Routledge, 2023).

About the contributors

Michelle Bachelet is former United Nations High Commissioner for Human Rights. She has a medical degree in Surgery, with a specialization in Paediatrics and Public Health. She also studied military strategy at Chile's National Academy of Strategy and Policy and at the Inter-American Defense College in the United States. From 2018 to 2022, she served as United Nations High Commissioner for Human Rights. In 2011, she was named first Director of UN Women. Ms Bachelet was elected President of Chile on two occasions (2006–2010 and 2014–2018). She was the first female president of Chile. During her presidential tenures, she promoted the rights of all but particularly those of the most vulnerable. Among her many achievements education and tax reforms, promotion of women and girls' rights, recognition of LGBTQ rights, as well as the creation of the National Institute for Human Rights and the Museum of Memory and Human Rights stand out. She served as Health Minister (2000–2002) as well as Chile's and Latin America's first female Defence Minister (2002–2004). She was awarded several honorary degrees, styles, honours, and arms.

Maria Giovanna Bianchi, PhD, is Jungian psychoanalyst (CGJIZ-IAAP and ASP) in private practice in Geneva, Switzerland. She obtained a master's in political science from the University of Bologna, a PhD in international relations from the University of Padova, and a diploma in Jungian psychoanalysis and psychotherapist specialized in adults, adolescents, and children from the C.G. Jung Institute in Zürich. She worked as human rights officer at the United Nations for almost three decades, including as Secretary of the United Nations Working Group of Enforced and Involuntary Disappearances from 2008 to 2012 and as Secretary of the Committee on Enforced Disappearances from 2012 to 2018. In both these capacities, she coordinated the work of experts during field missions in different countries and helped in determining the fate or whereabouts of disappeared persons. Since 2019, she is a member of the Board of Directors of the C.G. Jung Foundation, Zürich. She is supervisor for analyst trainees pursuing the Router Training of the International Association for Analytical Psychology. She authors articles, speaks at international conferences, and lectures in academic and professional contexts on the trans-disciplinarity and complementarity between human rights and analytical psychology.

Anne Blanchet is an artist from Switzerland. Her artistic career began in the United States in 1983. She produces large outdoor installations such as choreographed barriers (1999, 2000, 2005) or doors (1997, 1998), a long question mark in a park against enforced disappearance (2010), clouds (2013, 2015, 2017, 2021), prepared benches (tactile installations 2008, 2013, 2014). Since 1994, Anne Blanchet has been producing her Light Drawings. Sheets of plexiglass are cut to delimit variable fields of light. In 2022, she composed a choreography of light for a Light Drawing. During the past 15 years, she took part in many prestigious exhibitions, including the Beyeler Gallery in Basel (CH) 2003–2004; "Homage to Denise René", 2013 and "Constructive Art Kinetic", Miami (USA) 2014; Fondation Croÿ-Roeulx, Le Roeulx (BE) 2015; Institut d'Art Contemporain, Villeurbanne (F) 2016; Stiftung Konzeptuelle Kunst, Soest (D) 2017; Ensemble Contrechamps, Geneva (CH) 2022. She works with Gallery Denise René, Paris, since 1995; Gallery Linde Hollinger, Ladenburg, since 2013; and Luca Tommasi Contemporanea, Milano, since 2014; Gallery Alice Pauli, Lausanne (2003). Anne Blanchet received the Prix Gustave Buchet in 2000. Her outdoor and indoor works have been bought for private and public collections all over the world. For further information visit www.anneblanchet.com.

Andrea Paula Bleichmar, PsyD, Faculty of the Massachusetts Institute for Psychoanalysis, United States, writes on issues related to mourning and memorializing. Originally from Argentina, she graduated as a psychologist from Sorbonne University in Paris and William James College in the United States. Dr Bleichmar has a private practice in Boston, Massachusetts.

Pauline Boss, PhD, Professor Emeritus at the University of Minnesota, United States, is a Fellow in the American Psychological Association, the American Association for Marriage and Family Therapy, and the National Council on Family Relations. She practised family therapy for over 45 years. With ground-breaking work in research and practice, she coined the term *ambiguous loss* in the 1970s and since, developed and tested the theory of ambiguous loss, for guiding work with families of the missing, physically or psychologically. She summarized her research and clinical work in the now classic book, *Ambiguous Loss: Learning to Live with Unresolved Grief* (Harvard University Press, 2000), and in over 100 peer-reviewed articles and chapters. Her other books include *Loss, Trauma, and Resilience: Therapeutic Work with Ambiguous Loss* (W. W. Norton, 2006); *Loving Someone Who Has Dementia* (Jossey-Bass, 2011), and most recently, the widely acclaimed book, *The Myth of Closure: Ambiguous Loss in a Time of Pandemic and Change* (W. W. Norton, 2022). Her work is known around the world, and thus her books are available in 19 different languages. For more information about Dr Boss, her writings, and the ambiguous loss online training program, see www.ambiguousloss.com

Ghislaine Boulanger is a psychologist and psychoanalyst in private practice in New York City, United States, a member of the Relational faculty at New York University's Postdoctoral Program in Psychotherapy and Psychoanalysis, and the faculty of Adelphi University's Specialization in Trauma Studies. She is on the editorial boards of the Division/Review and the *International Journal for Applied Psychoanalytic Studies*. The topics of particular interest to her concern the psychodynamic treatment of immigrants, psychoanalytic politics, and massive psychic trauma. Since the publication of *Wounded by Reality: Understanding and Treating Adult Onset Trauma* (Routledge, 2007), Dr Boulanger has taught and published extensively on the psychodynamic dilemmas facing adults who have survived violent and life-threatening events, and the clinicians who work with them.

Manon Bourguignon is a senior researcher at the Institute of Psychology of the University of Lausanne in Switzerland (UNIL). She obtained her master's degree at the Free University of Brussels in Belgium in 2013 and her PhD in 2020 at the University of Lausanne. She is also a clinical psychologist in an institution for teenagers.

Santiago Corcuera Cabezut obtained a degree of law from the Universidad Iberoamericana, Mexico City, Mexico, in 1982 and a master's in law from the University of Cambridge, Queens' College, in 1983. He is currently a member of the Board of Trustees of the Voluntary Fund for the Financial and Technical Assistance in the Implementation of the Universal Periodic Review and of the Voluntary Fund for Technical Cooperation in the Field of Human Rights, appointed by the United Nations Secretary-General since 2019. From 2018 to 2021, he was a member of the National Citizen Council of the National System for the Search for Disappeared Persons of Mexico. From 2013 to 2017, he was a member of the Committee on Enforced or Involuntary Disappearances and served as its Chair between 2016 and 2017. From 2004 to 2010, he was a member of the United Nations Working Group on Enforced or Involuntary Disappearances and its Chair between 2006 and 2009. He also served as Chair of the Coordination Committee of the Special Procedures of the United Nations Human Rights Council in 2009 and 2010. He provides advice to organizations of relatives of victims of enforced disappearance.

Gabriella Citroni, PhD, is an adjunct professor of International Human Rights Law, University of Milano-Bicocca, Italy, and teaches "Enforced Disappearances in International Law" course at the Geneva Academy of Humanitarian Law and Human Rights. She is the Vice-Chair of the United Nations Working Group on Enforced or Involuntary Disappearances. She is international legal advisor of the Federación Latinoamericana de Asociaciones de Familiares de Detenidos Desaparecidos (FEDEFAM) and of the NGO TRIAL International. From 2003 to 2005, Ms Citroni was a member, as legal advisor, of the Italian delegation during the negotiations of the International Convention on the

Protection of All Persons from Enforced Disappearance. She researches and has published extensively on subjects related to international human rights law. She has been appointed as expert witness before the Inter-American Court of Human Rights in three prominent enforced disappearance cases. She has been an external consultant in charge of researching and drafting studies on issues related to enforced disappearance for different international institutions, including the Commissioner for Human Rights of the Council of Europe; the Office for Democratic Institutions and Human Rights of the Organization for Security and Cooperation in Europe; and the International Committee of the Red Cross.

Emmanuel Decaux is President of the René Cassin Foundation (International Institute for Human Rights), France, since April 2021. He is Professor Emeritus of the University of Paris II – Panthéon-Assas, where he taught public international law and international human rights law. He has published on topics of public international law and international organizations, with a focus on the peaceful settlement of disputes and human rights. In addition to his academic career, Prof. Decaux has held several functions within the United Nations. He was a member of the Committee on Enforced Disappearances between 2011 and 2019 and presided its beginnings during five years. Prior to that, he was a member of the United Nations Sub-Commission on the Promotion and Protection of Human Rights (2002–2007) and a member of the Advisory Committee of the Human Rights Council (2007–2010). He was rapporteur on the issue of the administration of justice by military Courts. In 2019, Prof. Decaux was elected President of the Court of Conciliation and Arbitration within the Organization for Security and Co-operation in Europe (OSCE). He served as an expert as part of the Moscow Mechanism on the Human Dimension of the OSCE on behalf of which he acted as Rapporteur twice in 2003 (Turkmenistan) and 2011 (Belarus).

Alice Dermitzel is a junior researcher at the University of Lausanne in Switzerland (UNIL). She obtained her master's degree at UNIL in 2019. She is also a psychologist in a support service for families coping with illness. Her work focuses on the subjective, familial and group repercussions of social disasters from a psychoanalytical perspective. Her current research, funded by The Swiss National Science Foundation, explores the impact of enforced disappearance on families. This qualitative research focuses on the specificity of the work of memory and transmission between generations among families affected by enforced disappearance. The undermining of the grieving process is also part of her questioning as well as the impact of exile on the way relatives cope with the loss of a loved one.

Bernard Duhaime is a full professor of international law at the Faculty of Law and Political Science of the University of Quebec in Montreal (UQAM, Montreal, Canada), where he specializes mainly on international human rights law. He is also a visiting professor at Université Paris II Panthéon-Assas and an associate research fellow at the Geneva Academy. He has served as a member of the Working Group on Enforced or Involuntary Disappearances reporting to the United Nations Human Rights Council (2014–2021). He is the author of more than 60 peer-reviewed publications and has presented more than 200 conferences worldwide. Duhaime was a Trudeau Foundation fellow, a Canada-US Fulbright visiting chair at the University of Southern California, a visiting fellow at the European University Institute, at Harvard Law School, at NYU School of Law, and at the University of Victoria. He was also Visiting Professor at the National University of San Martin and the University of Palermo, at Université Aix Marseille, and at the Fondation René Cassin. He contributes to the defence and promotion of human rights since 1996, representing victims before international judicial and quasi-judicial institutions. Prof. Duhaime is a senior counsel of the Quebec Bar, in Canada.

Baltasar Garzón is a magistrate judge, lawyer, and President of the International Foundation Baltasar Garzón (FIBGAR), in Spain. He is the Director ILOCAD Law Firm (International Legal Organization for Cooperation and Development). Earlier, he was Counsel for the Prosecutors Office of the International Criminal Court in 2010 and 2011, member of the Committee for the Prevention of Torture of the Council of Europe in 2011 and 2012, and external consultant of the Organization of American States Mission to Support the Peace Process in Colombia in 2011 and 2012. Also, he served as advisor to the Human Rights Commission of the House of Representatives of Argentina until December 2015 and President of the UNESCO International Center for the Promotion of Human Rights (CIPDH) in Argentina, between 2012 and 2016. His other roles include Coordinator of the International Oversight Committee for the judicial reform carried out in Ecuador (2012), human rights law professor at the University of Washington in Seattle, USA (2011–2015), member of the Latin American Council for Justice and Democracy - CLAJUD-Puebla Group (2019), and President for Europe of the World Jurist Association. Currently, he is a trustee of PPLAAF, the Platform for the Protection and Defence of Whistle-blowers in Africa. He has authored 16 books and his latest publication is *Los Disfraces del Fascismo* (2022). He has been awarded as an honorary doctor by 30 universities.

Muriel Katz is a senior lecturer in clinical psychology at the Institute of Psychology of University of Lausanne in Switzerland (UNIL) since 2001from where she obtained her PhD in 1999. She is also a psychotherapist.

Monica Luci, PhD is a clinical psychologist, Jungian and relational psychoanalyst (AIPA-IAAP and IARPP), and lecturer in refugee care in the Department of Psychosocial and Psychoanalytic Studies of University of Essex (UK). She is consultant and supervisor for NGOs and international organisations in the psychosocial interventions and psychotherapeutic work with vulnerable refugees, especially survivors of torture, human trafficking, gender-based violence and other human rights violations. She is teaching in professional courses and to analyst trainees within the International Association for Analytical Psychology

Developing Groups. And she is the author, translator, and editor of publications on the themes of trauma, torture, displacement, collective violence, gender, and psychoanalysis among which the monographs *Torture, Psychoanalysis, Human Rights* (Routledge, 2017), *Torture Survivors in Analytic Therapy: Jung, Politics, Culture* (Routledge, 2022), and *Lockdown Therapy: Jungian Perspectives on How the Pandemic Changed Psychoanalysis* (Routledge, 2023). Since 2020 she has been a member of the Editorial Board of the *Journal of Analytical Psychology* and member of the Center for Trauma, Asylum and Refugees of University of Essex.

Richard Mizen worked for many years in NHS and Social Services hospitals and clinics as both a clinician and a manager in the fields of child, adult, and forensic mental health. He has practised as an analyst for over 30, having trained with the Society of Analytical Psychology in London. He has been a psychotherapist for 40 years, the last 18 of which have been at Exeter, in the southwest of England. For the last 18 years, he has also worked at the University of Exeter, as a portfolio director for the studies in psychoanalytic psychotherapy programmes, part of the Psychology School, in the Faculty of Health and Life Sciences, where he is an Associate Professor. Here he directs a doctoral training programme to become a clinical researcher and a further doctoral programme that provides British Psychoanalytic Council accredited clinical trainings as a psychodynamic psychotherapist or a pyschoanalytic psychotherapist. He is a training analyst and works as a consultant and clinical supervisor to both trainee and qualified analysts and psychotherapists and also supervises post-graduate research. He has taught and published widely, nationally and internationally.

Angkhana Neelapaijit is a member of the United Nations Working Group on Enforced or Involuntary Disappearances since 2022, from Thailand. Ms Neelapaijit became a human rights activist after her husband who was a prominent human rights lawyer was abducted by a group of police officers and disappeared since 12 March 2004. She is the founder and former chairwoman of Justice for Peace Foundation. Mrs Neelapaijit worked relentlessly to help victims of human rights abuses in Thailand. The mission has made her one of Thailand's most prominent human rights defenders. Her dedication has won her many several international human rights awards, including the Gwangju Prize for Human Rights in 2006, the honour of "Chevalier de l'Ordre de la Légion d'Honneur" from the French President in December 2010 for her outstanding work in the human rights protection, and The Ramon Magsaysay Award in 2019. Ms Neelapaijit used to be the member of Constitutional Drafting Committee in 2007 and member of Ad Hoc Committee on Drafting Prevention and Suppression of Torture and Enforced Disappearances Act, B.E. 2022. She was the Commissioner of the National Human Rights Commission of Thailand (NHRCT) from November 2015 to July 2019.

Simon Robins is a practitioner and researcher with an interest in humanitarian protection, human rights, and transitional justice. For the last decade, he has combined academic research with a consulting practice focusing on evaluation and programme support with international agencies, including the United Nations and NGOs, with an emphasis on states emerging from conflict and violence. His consulting work has sought to provide policy and programmatic support to a range of humanitarian and human rights related programming, including extensive engagement with monitoring and evaluation, and in particular of protection and rule of law. His academic work is driven by a desire to put the needs of victims of conflict at the heart of efforts to address its legacies, and this has led to his engaging with victim-centred and therapeutic approaches to histories of violence. He is a Senior Research Fellow at the Centre for Applied Human Rights at the University of York and Research Advisor to the Red Cross Red Crescent Missing Persons Centre. His recent publications include *Transitional Justice in Tunisia: Innovations, Continuities, Challenges* (Routledge, 2022), and *From Transitional to Transformative Justice* (Cambridge University Press, 2019), both of which he co-edited.

Morris Tidball-Binz is Special Rapporteur on Extrajudicial, Summary, or Arbitrary Executions since 2021; Adjunct Clinical Professor in Forensic Medicine, Monash University, Australia; and Visiting Professor, University of Coimbra, Portugal, and University of Milan, Italy. He is a medical doctor specialized in forensic science, human rights, and humanitarian action. Over the past 35 years, he has conducted fact-finding, technical assessments, and capacity building missions to over 70 counties in all regions. He worked for the Grandmothers of Plaza de Mayo in Argentina. He participated in the creation of the first-ever genetic database to locate victims of enforced disappearances and their relatives. In 1984, he co-founded the Argentine Forensic Anthropology Team which he then directed until 1990. From 1990 until 2003, he directed regional and global human rights programmes for Amnesty International (UK); the Inter-American Institute of Human Rights (Costa Rica); Penal Reform International (UK), and the International Service for Human Rights (Switzerland). From 2004 to 2020, he worked for the International Committee of the Red Cross, where he established and served as the first director of the Forensic Services Unit. He has published extensively and is a member of several scientific entities and publications, serving on boards of directors and editorial boards. He is the recipient of two Honoris Causa Doctorates.

Foreword by Michelle Bachelet

I am pleased to write this Foreword for a book that I consider original in its focus and interdisciplinary approach to psychoanalysis and enforced disappearance. The volume offers multiple perspectives on different aspects of the topic and aims at contributing to a deep and comprehensive understanding of this crime and its related psychological, societal, and legal aspects.

I write this Foreword as a person who has dealt with the crime of enforced disappearance and its consequences from different angles. I was born and raised in Chile. In 1973, a military golpe immersed my country in a climate of gross human rights violations, including enforced disappearances. My family and myself experienced some of these violations, as victims and survivors. When I returned to Chile after a period of exile, through my political engagement and most of all my work as paediatrician, I bore witness of the extreme psychological damage suffered by individuals and by the society as a whole by the scourge of human rights violations. Particularly moving to me was to witness the devastation of children and the transgenerational transmission of trauma, in particular for relatives of those who had been disappeared.

In my life I was honoured with the opportunity to be elected as President of Chile on two different occasions, to serve my country also as Minister of Defense and of serving the international community as head of UN Women and United Nations High Commissioner for Human Rights. In my different professional capacities, I witnessed the many facets of enforced disappearance, its repercussion on the victims and, by rippling effect, on entire nations. Nothing can justify an enforced disappearance, and nothing can justify the extent of trauma, including on future generations, that it causes. In my latest posting as United Nations High Commissioner for Human Rights, I called for the search for the disappeared to continue in countries in different regions such as Bangladesh, Bosnia and Herzegovina and Mexico and for their families' right to truth and access to justice to be fully respected, no matter how much time has passed. I have been particularly moved by the resilience, courage, and perseverance of family members and wish to pay tribute to them in this Foreword.

When I flipped through the pages of the book, I appreciated the breadth of its approach and the complete picture on the topic that it offers to practitioners both in the field of human rights and in psychoanalysis. The book gathers contributions by authoritative authors, personal testimonies of victims, lawyers, forensic experts, psychoanalysts, and human rights officers. I am also very conscious of the vicarious trauma lived by many United Nations officers, in assisting victims of gross human rights violations, in particular related to disappearances.

This book fills a gap and represents a concrete contribution to the fight against enforced disappearances and to the psychological support of victims and society at large, while they come to terms with their terrible experience, trying to give it a meaning and rebuild individual lives and the fabric of society. It attempts to find common ground in the work of practitioners of human rights law, psychosocial assistance and psychoanalysis. All of them deal with human rights violations from their own perspective which should be further integrated in the goal of providing support to the victims.

This book attempts to foster exactly that: a fruitful dialogue, still not sufficiently explored and practised, a meeting halfway between human rights as a field that tries to respond to the deep need for dignity of human beings, and psychoanalysis as a field with the potential to investigate the deep reasons of evil perpetrated by human beings. I am profoundly convinced that such dialogue will represent an enormous resource to combat gross violation of human rights.

There are many "musts" in the work for human rights: We must prevent and raise awareness on enforced disappearances; continue searching the disappeared, giving priority to the search in life; in cases of death, return the identified remains to their family; support victims and those left behind in their coming to terms with their loss; and obtain justice and reparation, including and foremost in the form of psychosocial support. We must remember and not forget as an investment in the mental health of future generations who must be protected from the transgenerational transmission of trauma.

However, often in this field we are confronted with the frustration and insufficiency of a 'must approach'. We need more and deeper understanding. I am convinced that the new perspectives opened up by the contributions included in this volume can help us all to better understand the challenges faced by victims of enforced disappearance, and find lasting means to build their resilience, capacity of find meaning in their personal experiences, and putting human dignity at the core of our societies.

Michelle Bachelet

Acknowledgements

We would like to sincerely thank all the people who have put their trust in this project: first and foremost, the authors (ourselves included) who have written this book, Michelle Bachelet, Maria Giovanna Bianchi, Anne Blanchet, Andrea Paula Bleichmar, Pauline Boss, Ghislaine Boulanger, Manon Bourguignon, Gabriella Citroni, Santiago Corcuera Cabezut, Emmanuel Decaux, Alice Dermitzel, Bernard Duhaime, Baltasar Garzón, Muriel Katz, Monica Luci, Richard Mizen, Angkhana Neelapaijit, Simon Robins and Morris Tidball-Binz. We thank them all for their enthusiasm and for sincerely adhering to the general idea that guided the book, that of an advancement in knowledge as the result of a collaborative effort between two – human rights and psychoanalysis – and more disciplines, which seem to be different and distant but are in reality close, related, and extremely interconnected. Their skilful and valuable expertise, their inspired ideas, and the *soul* they have put into this work and their will to face the challenges in it have opened up and illuminated the way forward for us. Even in facing difficulties, their presence and trust in the common effort never failed.

We would particularly like to thank among the authors those who had the generosity to write from their personal story and direct, tragic, and differently difficult experience: Michelle Bachelet, Andrea Paula Bleichmar, Angkhana Neelapaijit and Baltasar Garzón. We owe to Ugo Cedrangolo and Albane Prophette-Palasco for their professionalism, expertise, generous personal contribution behind the scenes, and support to this book since the very beginning of its conception. They all have contributed in different ways to make these texts embodied, living, authentic, and truly courageous.

We would like to acknowledge the generosity of Andrea Paula Bleichmar, thanking her also for flying from her home to Buenos Aires on the occasion of the XXII International Congress of the International Association of Analytical Psychology in Buenos Aires to meet us and to share with us a moment of grieving, something that will remain in our hearts as a testimony to the fact that the energy put into this book reaches people and their lives. And we would like to acknowledge the professionalism of the *Fundación Garzón* staff, for their work in facilitating our contacts with Baltasar Garzón and for their precious help coordinating the three of us, addressing language, time, and text issues.

We would like to thank our fantastic endorsers, Jessica Benjamin, Andrew Samuels, Volker Türk, and Federico Villegas who made flattering comments that we did not expect and that sounded to us like sincere appreciation.

A special thank you as friends and colleagues goes to Alessandra di Montezemolo, who introduced us, Maria Giovanna and Monica, at the opening event of Stillpoint in Paris in 2017, for her smart intuition about our affinities and to whom we also owe our friendship.

Heartfelt thanks also go to the publishing house and in particular to the always impeccable and encouraging professionalism of the editor Susannah Frearson together with the editorial team, who believed in this unusual project, and for having offered the space to develop it, taking care of it.

Maria Giovanna would like to thank Bianca, her daughter, for having turned her life upside down for the better, from the very first moment she set foot on this earth, for being such an amazing, intelligent, tenacious, and committed human being as well as a continuous source of challenge and inspiration to reach higher standards.

Monica would like to express as always endless thanks to Leonardo, her lifelong partner, and husband, who unconditionally supports her endeavours, an everyday gift for which there are not enough words but only looks full of understanding and small and big gestures. Last but not least, she wants to thank from the bottom of her heart her father who is no longer here but who is benevolently watching over her and she knows he will do forever. Without these two supports, nothing could have been so beautiful and tender.

Introduction

Maria Giovanna Bianchi and Monica Luci

Genesis of the book and approach to the theme

This book had a long genesis that started almost six years ago when we first met at a conference in Stillpoint Paris where we had been invited to present our respective work at the same roundtable.

We come from different backgrounds: a human rights officer who became psychoanalyst because of her work with victims of enforced disappearance, and a psychoanalyst working clinically with torture survivors who researched and studied human rights because of her fieldwork. Both of us were looking for explanations for the horror we witnessed in our own work and, at the same time, for ways to deal with the sustained trauma stemming from it.

Those who work in the human rights field never bring only their professional expertise; there is always a human and personal element and motivation that comes into play. On this personal question, and with different but complementary professional skills, the editors of this book met: Maria Giovanna Bianchi with her skills and work experience as Secretary of both the United Nations Working Group on Involuntary or Enforced Disappearances and the Committee on Enforced Disappearances and Monica Luci with her skills and experience of clinical work and research as a psychologist and psychotherapist with people who survived torture and other human rights violations.

The common interest and the respect for each other's work became a long-distance friendship between Geneva and Rome, where we live, mainly based on written communications, calls and participation in initiatives organized by the analytical psychology community. During our conversations, it was recurrent the idea of editing a book on enforced disappearance, human rights, psychoanalysis and psychosocial support. It seemed to us that, notwithstanding the vast and excellent literature existing on enforced disappearance, there was still a gap to bridge on this topic in terms of interdisciplinarity and multiplicity of perspectives that could have contributed to the understanding of such a complex crime and subsequently of the consequences on the victims and on society at large.

Conversation after conversation, email after email and call after call, our idea was taking shape. More than editing this book, we weaved it, as if human rights and

DOI: 10.4324/9781003312642-1

psychoanalysis were two threads, the warp and the weft, one vertical and the other horizontal, to be crossed and intertwined incessantly so that each discipline could contribute to the meaning of the other and create a tapestry, a bigger picture, to help grasping the essence of enforced disappearance, the extent of the tear caused by it in the society and the possibility that exist to mend and repair that damage. To that aim, we invited contributions from experts in both fields of psychoanalysis and human rights, academics, clinicians, practitioners, artists and most valuably from relatives of persons who disappeared. Some of the experts are old colleagues and friends, others we met with astonishing synchronicity when the project was already on its way.

Once we took the first step, the way showed by itself: every pace was like a leap of faith and every time a board would appear from somewhere, in the form of an encounter, a conversation, a piece of news, an artwork, that would support the weight of our work and sustain our efforts.

We like to think of this book as a 'project from the soul and of the soul' because we put our souls in it and attracted other 'like-souled' individuals in a common effort that is far from being an intellectual exercise but rather a tribute to all those who suffered harm because of enforced disappearance. Without detracting from the standing of scholars of this subject to our authors, the approach to the subject of this book intends to be practical and humane. We wished to understand and have an impact, not as narcissistic gratification but as a contribution, however minimal, to improving our human world and to develop more ideas about how to alleviate the suffering of victims and societies and prevent situations in which this crime occurs.

Enforced disappearance: Definition of the crime and its presence in the world

Enforced disappearances consist in the arrest, detention, abduction or any other form of deprivation of liberty by agents of the State or by persons or groups of persons acting with the authorization, support or acquiescence of the State, followed by a refusal to acknowledge the deprivation of liberty or by concealment of the fate or whereabouts of the disappeared person, which place such a person outside the protection of the law (Article 2 of the International Convention for the Protection of all Persons from Enforced Disappearance and Preamble of the Declaration on the Protection of all Persons from Enforced Disappearance). It is characterized by three cumulative and constitutive elements: (a) Deprivation of liberty against the will of the person; (b) Involvement of government officials, at least by acquiescence; (c) Refusal to acknowledge the deprivation of liberty or concealment of the fate or whereabouts of the disappeared person.[1]

A disappearance has a doubly paralyzing impact: on the victim, who is removed from their life, their family and from the protection of the law, frequently subjected to torture and in constant fear for their lives; and on their families, ignorant of the fate of their loved ones, their emotions alternating between hope and despair, wondering and waiting, sometimes for years, for news that may never come. It has frequently been used as a strategy to spread terror within society. Trends and manifestations of enforced disappearances have also evolved in the last decades, as explained in various reports of the Working Group on Enforced or Involuntary Disappearances and interpretations of the Convention by the Committee on Enforced Disappearances, the mechanism that monitors the implementation of the Convention.

We can assume that enforced disappearance always existed in history as a practice to eliminate political opponents although not with the level of institutionalization and sophistication that was first recorded in 1941 when the Nazi regime proclaimed the decree *Nacht und Nebeln*. The decree instructed Nazi troops to forcibly disappear persons explaining how spiriting away people in the "night and fog" would have created uncertainty and suspicion and would have subjugated the entire society. Latin American military regimes, in the 1960s, 1970s and 1980s, became then iconic examples of the widespread and systematic practice of this crime. However, enforced disappearance is far from being confined to a geographic area or to a point in time: governments worldwide and in all ages, including nowadays, recurred and continue to recur to enforced disappearance as a very efficient and effective way to eliminate political opponents and control society through terror.

In its report covering the period between May 2021 and May 2022, the United Nations Working Group on Enforced or Involuntary Disappearances (WGEID) registered 375 new cases occurred in 26 States; of those cases 54 were treated under the urgent action procedure, which means that the victim was disappeared within the previous three months, and transmitted to the 13 States where the disappearances occurred, namely to Azerbaijan, Bangladesh, Egypt, Kenya, Lebanon, Libya, Mozambique, Nicaragua, Pakistan, Russian Federation, Saudi Arabia, Turkey and Venezuela. Since its inception in 1980, the Working Group has transmitted a total of 59,600 cases to 112 out of the 193 State members of the United Nations, meaning that almost 60% of those States at some point in time perpetrated enforced disappearance. As at May 2022, the number of cases that remained unresolved, and those under active consideration by the WGEID, stood at 46,751 in a total of 97 States.[2] These numbers, as horrific as they can be, are only the tip of the iceberg considering the phenomenon of underreporting of cases due to the lack of knowledge about the crime, the lack of access to justice and recourses, as well as the well-founded fear of intimidation and reprisals. Those numbers do not represent reality nor speak about the devastation behind them, because indeed these are not cases or numbers but persons that somebody continues to love and wait for against all odds. This is what all authors tried to convey in this book.

The international community responded to the despair of the victims slowly and late, but it did respond and in 1992 the United Nations General Assembly adopted the Declaration on the Protection of All Persons from Enforced Disappearance calling on States to prevent, eradicate and punish acts of enforced disappearance under criminal law. A specific international legal framework began to take shape at the regional level with the entering into force of the Inter-American Convention on Forced Disappearance of Persons in 1996, and at global level with the entering into force of the International Convention for the Protection of All Persons from Enforced Disappearance in 2010. They address enforced disappearances perpetrated by States according to the three constitutive elements mentioned earlier; the inclusion of non-state actors as perpetrator was discussed during the drafting process of the Convention and, to avoid diluting the States' responsibility in the commission of the crime, it resulted the recognition of the existence of acts that 'tantamount to enforced disappearances' but without any specific provision. As a result of this compromise, for a long time neither the Working Group nor the Committee on Enforced Disappearances took up cases perpetrated by non-State actors. The adoption of the Rome Statute of the International Criminal Court added new elements: Article 7, paragraph 1, i) of the Statute includes enforced disappearance among the list of crimes against humanity, making it punishable by the Court, when the act is perpetrated in the context of a widespread or systematic attack directed against a civilian population, moreover the act can be perpetrated also by a "political organisation' and not only by a State (Article 7, paragraph 2(i)).

The reality of international relations being much more complex, it is now recognized that both States and non-State actors recur respectively to enforced disappearance and acts that tantamount to enforced disappearance both in internal conflicts and in armed conflicts and in a variety of other grey areas difficult to define: in Algeria (with Islamist armed groups), in Colombia (with Fuerzas armadas revolucionarias de Colombia/FARC and other guerrillas), in Sri Lanka (with the Liberation Tigers of Tamil Eelam/LTTE) and, more recently, in Iraq/Syria (with the Islamic State of Iraq and the Levant), Libya (with the de facto authorities after the fall of Gaddafi), Mexico (with various armed groups and cartels and gangs), Nigeria (with Boko Haram) and Ukraine (with the self-proclaimed « Donetsk People's Republic » and « Luhansk People's Republic »).[3] In the absence of adequate domestic criminal laws, those acts are often treated as villain kidnappings and abductions which they are not as *de facto* they tend to include all the constitutive elements of enforced disappearance other than formal state involvement. The combination of these factors results in the difficulty to hold perpetrators accountable and for victims to receive remedy and reparation amplifying, if possible, their pain.

Enforced disappearance is also a military tactic in armed conflicts. Hundreds of thousands of people disappeared in Afghanistan, Chechnya, Colombia, Crimea, Iraq, Sri Lanka and the former Yugoslavia. Eight months into the armed conflict facing the Russian Federation and Ukraine, the United Nations Human Rights Monitoring Mission in Ukraine (HRMMU) documented 457 cases of arbitrary detention and enforced disappearance of civilians.[4] In the case of international armed conflicts, the potential movement of victims across international borders makes extremely difficult to investigate enforced disappearance, a crime that, by definition, leaves behind little evidence.

As far as the Committee on Enforced Disappearances is concerned, it considers the Convention a living instrument to be interpreted in light of present-day conditions and of the evolution of international law and is drafting a general comment on the way to include some cases of disappearances carried out by non-State actors, albeit under very strict conditions, in the context of the Convention.[5] There is therefore an effort from the United Nations mechanisms to expand their tools to face 'the state of the art' of disappearances in the real contemporary world. Even if the applicability of these new tools will depend on strict factual circumstances, it will be much more difficult for Boko Haram or organized crime in Mexico to enjoy total impunity.

We hope in this book to provide a 'reality check' of the global, ageless and collective dimension of this crime which intertwines with other crimes such as torture, arbitrary detention, secret detention and extra-judicial or summary executions; is practised in a variety of contexts well beyond military dictatorships, such as in counter-terrorism operations, trafficking, organized crime operations, and international armed conflicts ; and targets not only political opponents but also their families, key witnesses, human rights defenders, journalists, lawyers, migrants and civilians in armed conflicts.

The rationale of this book

Like other abhorrent crimes enforced disappearance calls the human conscience to gather its energies and intelligence in order to counter it by affirming the dignity of human beings. The need for a trans-disciplinary approach among different disciplines is postulated here. While a mono-disciplinary approach deals with an issue autonomously, a multi-disciplinary approach addresses it in parallel; and an inter-disciplinary approach addresses it with a certain level of integration between the different fields. The trans-disciplinary approach presupposes that the knowledge and experience, derived from the disciplines in question, be organized around the construction of a meaning to respond to problems and themes as complex as they are in their reality, fostering collaboration and providing multiple layers of support and connection (Bianchi, 2020). To combat enforced disappearance, transdisciplinarity is required at a minimum among psychoanalysis, international human rights law, forensic science, sociology and politics, the meaning of which is given by the fulfilment of an innate sense of justice and the therapeutic treatment of victims of human rights violations in support of a common goal centred on respect for human dignity. We believe that the depth of insight of psychoanalysis into human soul, the normative and containing framework of international and human rights law, the practice of the psychosocial approach to human rights violations, each in their own stand and especially engaging each other can contribute substantially to develop new perspectives on the issue and new tools of interventions in both the individual and social domains. This book aims to be a contribution, however small, through the ability of multiple perspectives, to broaden the horizon of understanding and intervention, and improve our human world by preventing the occurrence of enforced disappearances (and torture) and to contribute to think how to alleviate the suffering of families and of society as a whole.

Although psychoanalysis has never been a major force in the world to fight for human rights, or opposing war, human rights violations and crimes, several recent developments in psychoanalytic theory have made it more axiomatic for individual analysts to take position for social justice and respect of human rights (Bianchi,

2020, 2023; Luci, 2017, 2022, 2023a, 2023b; Montagna & Harris, 2019; Seu, 2015; Varvin, 2021, among others). And in the last few years even the politics of analytical societies has become more aware and sensitive to problems of social justice and even of justice. One of the drives of this development has been an ever-expanding and increasingly refined appreciation of the impact of trauma on mental functioning and even the transmission of trauma through generations and how much this affects our social life. Even the moral dimension of psychoanalysis as a theory and practice distinctly emerged, an aspect that was disavowed by Freud in his insistence that psychoanalysis was a science and not a worldview or a moral philosophy (Abel, 1989) and despite Jung's complex and sometimes contradictory positioning regarding ethics (Colacicchi, 2020). Today, intersubjective approaches of relational psychoanalysis are the guiding lights for this kind of research, with Jessica Benjamin's work on intersubjectivity and recognition as a main prominent reference (2017). However, also analytical psychology has been more and more sensitive to themes of political relevance, and there are groups working in the many areas of social and political sphere (e.g., see Carta & Khiel, 2020; Kiehl et al., 2016; Samuels, 1993, 2001, 2015).

The struggle for human rights and justice is far from being a linear historical process. On the contrary, at any given time, all visions of human rights and fights for justice constellated powerful opposition forces fundamentally because they raise profoundly disturbing issues about what it means to be human. From an analytical psychology viewpoint, human rights compel us to confront the shadow. Jung wrote:

> With more foreboding than real knowledge, most people feel afraid of the menacing power that lies fettered in each of us, only waiting for the magic word to release it from the spell. This magic word, which always ends in "ism" works most successfully with those who have the least access to their interior selves and have strayed the furthest from their instinctual roots into the truly chaotic world of *collective consciousness*.
>
> (Jung, 1954, para. 405, italics in original)

He expressed his preoccupation for the political and security situation which led to the II World War observing how the intertwining between collective shadow and unconscious material altered mass consciousness in a mutual reinforcing spiral with authoritarian political regimes with disastrous consequences for human rights and wrote surprisingly words that still sound as valid today:

> Mass degeneration does not only come from without, it also comes from within, from the collective unconscious. Against the outside some protection was offered by the *droits de l'homme* which at present are lost to the greater part of Europe, and even where they are not actually lost we see political parties, as naïve as they are powerful, doing their best to abolish them in favour of the slave state, with the bait of social security.
>
> (Jung, 1946, para. 502, italics in original)

Jung referred to human rights as "die ewigen Menschenrechte", the eternal human rights, linking them to a higher order (Jung, 1942, para. 444). The eternal human rights transcend time, culture, social and political orders, and any other contingent situation. Human rights, before being a codification of law, are at the innermost kernel of the Self and belong to all of us, as human beings.

While psychoanalysis has been increasingly interested into societal and cultural processes in the past three decades (Altman, 2009; Beebe, 2003; Frosh, 2010; Grand, 2000; Samuels, 1993, 2015; Singer & Kimbles, 2004; Soldz, 2008; Summers, 2009; Zoja, 2017), and a psychosocial approach has established itself as the most appropriate for the reparation and rehabilitation of the closest relatives and victims in general of enforced disappearances (Lira et al., 2022), psychoanalysis has rarely expressed itself on this specific subject even if with very interesting examples paving the way. The work of Nancy Caro Hollander (1997, 2013) or the contributions of Janine Puget (2002, 2004), Rojas Baeza (2009) and Marcelo Viñar (2017) are invaluable in this sense for their illuminating reflections on the effects of enforced disappearances and social violence and dictatorship has had on people's thinking in Latin America. Some more recent psychoanalytic works focus on the mourning process in the case of enforced disappearances (De la Fuente-Herrera & Soria-Escalante, 2021; Taiana, 2014), others treat the trauma from the point of view of psychosocial interventions (Preitler, 2015) or in the perspective of the trans-generational transmission of trauma (de Viñar, 2012). Some examples involve psychoanalysis and human rights at the same time and do so with regards to social violence, torture or human rights violations, war and militarism (Harris & Botticelli, 2010; Hollander, 2016; Mandelbaum et al., 2021). However, no one, at least according to our knowledge, addresses the actual process that individuals and society systematically go through in their life and history to process the specific trauma of enforced disappearances, combining psychoanalytic thinking with a psychosocial approach and the understanding of human rights. More in particular, we would like to start filling, at least tentatively, this gap in psychosocial studies between psychoanalysis and human rights on this specific topic, so that each discipline can benefit from the experience of the other and can each collaborate and glean from field experience and perspectives of the other, understanding and expanding the domain to benefit the victims, their families and affected societies, and hopefully to build a future freer from this aberrant violence.

To give a concrete example, searching the whereabouts of victims of enforced disappearances is not only a right enshrined in international law. From a psychoanalytic perspective, research efforts are also remedial acts aimed at contributing to the restoration of social ties and mutual trust among members of a society and within institutions. And in this process, it becomes crucial to consider the needs of families during the reparation process and the great social significance that this reparation has both at an individual, family and social level. How do human rights law and psychoanalysis understand what happens during and after an enforced disappearance, and how does society attempt to redress such crimes? What is the significance of such reparation for the individuals involved and for society as a whole?

How should the procedure be shaped depending on the meaning attributed by the victims and the different phases of this process for individuals and society? What does it mean, from an individual and social point of view, to promulgate laws that ensure impunity to perpetrators? Why is it so difficult for the relatives of the disappeared persons to consider the possibility, and maybe at a later stage surrender to the evidence, that their beloved ones may never come back? What does this mean in their lives, and what does it mean for society? Has this a meaning and even a value? These are just a few of the thousands of questions worth seeking an answer to, of course not all of which are addressed in the book. However, the point is not exhaustiveness.

Our point here is to broaden the horizons of our understanding of the crime of enforced disappearances through multiple perspectives of academics, lawyers, humanitarian officials, United Nations officials, psychoanalysts, psychotherapists, researchers and artists, to promote the trans-disciplinarity of psychoanalysis and human rights, linking practice and theory, experience and thought, individual and collective, psyche and law, in a cooperative work that is not only possible but also necessary, at the service of a style of co-living ethically higher, in which truth and justice are also a cure for the soul (Luci, 2023b).

The structure of this book

The book is organized in three parts. Part 1 (Chapters 1–3) collects academic contributions and testimonies of the victims of enforced disappearance, which show how it is sadly a contemporary crime still used and unfortunately present in our societies. Part 2 (Chapters 4–8) comprises articles by academics, United Nations experts and practitioners specialized in human rights and on the legal aspects of enforced disappearance. Part 3 (Chapters 9–15) includes articles by psychoanalysts and psychosocial experts and an artist, who explore the deep psychological impact of the crime both at individual and collective level. All the contributions included in the book systematically highlight the interaction between the individual and collective spheres at all stages of the enforced disappearance and its consequences.

In Chapter 1, Bernard Duhaime, through a retrospective of his past seven years at the United Nations Working Group on Enforced or Involuntary Disappearances (WGEID), analyses how this heinous human rights violation is unfortunately still used worldwide by State agents today. Enforced disappearance, commonly perceived to be essentially a tool used by former Latin American repressive regimes to eliminate political dissents, is not a crime of the past but is, on the contrary, very contemporary. While some of its features may vary in different contexts, including in the fight against terrorism or in the context of migrations, its devious purpose and disastrous impact on victims remain the same. Instances of abductions carried out by non-State actors may also tantamount to acts of enforced disappearance as argued in recent debates.

No matter the legal qualifications of an enforced disappearance or an act that tantamount to an enforced disappearance, and no matter where and in which period it took place, the suffering for the relatives is equally unspeakable. In Chapter 2, Angkhana Neelapaijit writes about the 'ambiguity' between 'existence' and 'non-existence' that an enforced disappearance causes in all victims involved, the disappeared and their families, including hers after the disappearance of her husband. Ambiguity annihilates their 'sense of self', their identity and their reputation and is used by the perpetrators to conceal the truth and fabricate allegations against the victims. The author also elaborates on the gendered impact of an enforced disappearance with surviving wives unable to support their families economically and confused about their own status of 'widows'.Ambiguity is at the basis of the difficulties met by the relatives in the mourning process, making it an abstract task, deprived of the recognition of the loss in the form of ceremonies and rituals performed in presence of the community.

Drawing on her personal experience, in Chapter 3, Andrea Paula Bleichmar describes the lifelong process of mourning the loss of her mother, who disappeared in Argentina in 1976, when the author was a teenager. She walks the reader through mourning in the different stages of her life: from the difficulties in explaining and acknowledging the grief, to the search for the truth through DNA testing and the responsibility towards her children to transform what could potentially be a transgenerational transmission of trauma into an intergenerational transmission of experience. She also stresses how the recognition of her loss, in the form of testimonies delivered in a series of trials against the perpetrators, and a *baldosa*, a memorial placed in front of her mother's practice, helped the mourning process.

The recognition of the suffering of the relatives of the disappeared is one of the most salient features of the International Convention for the Protection of All Persons from Enforced Disappearance that defines them victims at the same level of the disappeared persons. In Chapter 4, Emmanuel Decaux, while acknowledging the limitations that the law may have in front of the extent of human devastation caused by enforced disappearance, comments the most relevant articles of the Convention as examples of rigorous law coupled with compassion and attention for the 'human factor'. The Convention succeeded in defining in legal terms the undefinable horror of an enforced disappearance, by spelling out its components, as an individual crime and as a crime against humanity. It qualified the unqualifiable in the broadest terms: the authors of the crime are all those who participate and cannot hide behind due obedience, and the victims are the disappeared and all those who suffered harm. It spelled out the obligation of States to ensure the right to obtain collective and individual reparation even if the ultimate damage is unrepairable.

The analysis of binding and non-binding norms of international human rights law provides important elements that address the psychological impact that enforced disappearance has on the victims and the community. In Chapter 5, Santiago Corcuera Cabezut elaborates on the right to search, locate and release the person who disappeared and postulates the mirroring right of the victim to be searched. Persons who disappeared have also the right to be presumed alive, until and unless there is proof of the contrary. To this end, the author affirms the outmost importance, both from the legal and the psychological point of view, of the issuance of a declaration of absence as a result of enforced disappearance to allow relatives to exercise their rights without obliging them to request a death certificate. The author illustrates the economic effects of the disappearance of family members and explores the provisions relating specifically to children. He highlights the importance of the right to obtain reparations, in particular rehabilitation and satisfaction, as forms of compensation for the mental and moral damage suffered by the victims and notes the importance of social and State support to victims. The important psychological repercussions of disappearances result in specific psychosocial needs, including in the approach to forensic investigations aimed at clarifying the fate of the victims.

In Chapter 6, Morris Tidball-Binz provides a short overview of the origins and developments in the domain of the psychosocial contribution to forensic interventions in Latin America and presents some of the international recommendations of best practices with particular significance for the implementation of a psychosocial approach in forensic investigations into human rights violations, in particular enforced disappearances and extrajudicial, summary or arbitrary executions. The search, the recovery, the identification and the proper disposition of the bodies of victims of extrajudicial, summary or arbitrary executions, including those who do not survive enforced and involuntary disappearances, are framed by obligations under international human rights and humanitarian law but should also be guided by the primary need to alleviate suffering and maintaining human dignity, with the victims and their families at the core. The importance of including a psychosocial perspective, including work with affected families and communities, as an integral part of planning and implementation of forensic investigations into disappearances and potentially unlawful killings, is at the core of a worldwide consensus of international experts and practitioners, which also provides guidance for their implementation.

Relatives of disappeared persons are recognized as victims of a violation in their own right, because of the anguish and stress caused by the enforced disappearance of their loved ones, the continuing uncertainty on their fate and whereabouts and the attitude of indifference shown by authorities in the face of their pain. Albeit the principle is relatively straight-forward, Gabriella Citroni demonstrates, in Chapter 7, through an analysis of international jurisprudence, that significant discrepancies exist on rather major issues, beginning with who could validly claim the victim status. The answers given by international human rights mechanisms depend largely on the position taken on another crucial issue, i.e., the rationale to recognize specific persons or groups of persons as victims in the first place. The burden of proof applied weighs significantly on the subjects at stake. Lastly, for those who overcome all the procedural hurdles and are recognized as victims, what is the name given to the violation(s) endured? Moving from an analysis of the jurisprudence of the European and Inter-American Courts of Human Rights, as well as of the Human Rights Committee and the Committee on Enforced Disappearances, the chapter aims at illustrating the main existing discrepancies and their ramifications, including on the measures of reparation awarded.

When it comes to a state crime such enforced disappearance, innumerable trials and obstacles are posed to victims and investigators as well.

In Chapter 8, Baltasar Garzón reflects on the challenges that arose when he investigated and prosecuted cases of enforced disappearance, in his former capacity of former Spanish investigating judge. Towards the end of the 1990s, applying the principle of universal jurisdiction, he carried out several investigations the violations of human rights, including cases of enforced disappearance, perpetrated by the military regimes of both Chile and Argentina, including in the framework of the Operation Condor, a coordinated effort by the several South American countries to exterminate and disappear thousands of political opponents. Ten years later, the author opened the first, and so far, the only investigation of the crimes committed during the Spanish Civil War and the Francoist dictatorship, in which more than 140,000 people were forcibly disappeared. In all these cases, the author was able to experience first-hand the challenges of tackling impunity for the most heinous human rights violation which condemns the disappeared person never to be found and his or her families to a state of never-ending suffering.

In Chapter 9, Maria Giovanna Bianchi addresses the memories of enforced disappearance as a place for the interplay of psychological needs and political aims. Memories surrounding enforced disappearance are traumatic and affectively charged both for the persons who disappear and for their relatives. The majority of relatives, after an undetermined period, realize cognitively, although they may never accept it emotionally, that their beloved ones may not return alive and their remains may never be found. It is then that the role of memory becomes preponderant both at individual level, and at collective level. Enforced disappearance always engendered resistance including through a community of memory and the creation of collective memory. International law preserves collective memory against the passing of amnesty laws or the development of revisionist and negationist arguments and provides for reparations which include memorialization. Memorials carry both messages and warnings to prevent the repetition of such atrocities and the transgenerational transmission of trauma. Thus, memory is not only the link between past and present but also the link between present and future.

In Chapter 10, Monica Luci pursues the hypothesis that tortured bodies are the sites of 'knowing' for torturous societies, i.e. the 'places' into which unprocessed social contents are stored and interrogated through torture by the ruling group and/ or made disappear through enforced disappearances. The combination of crimes such as torture and enforced disappearance perpetrated by States represents an extreme social case that illustrates the processes leading to the social dynamics of massive denial ('knowing and not knowing') of what is happening in a society slipped into a *monolithic societal state* for perpetrators, bystanders and victims. The concept of embeddedness expresses the notion that social actors exist within relational, institutional and cultural contexts and cannot be seen as atomized decision-makers. The body of the victim of torture and enforced disappearance seems to be the site where, in case of severe social violence, the 'truth' is stored and can be regained, together with the possibility of collective healing that repairs social ties, be it a body that survived torture, or one that succumbed, like in the case of the many who were disappeared.

A hypothesis of the affective basis of violence in the case of enforced disappearance is proposed by Richard Mizen in Chapter 11. This essay explores the unconscious, implicit emotional forces, in both perpetrators and victims that are brought to bear at intrapsychic, interpersonal and societal levels. In particular the way that enforced disappearance plays upon early-life anxieties, for example, those that precede the achievement of narrative memory and the capacity to manage the loss, even temporarily, of primary objects. The psychological, cognitive and emotional developmental processes involved are described and how vulnerabilities and deficits in these developments are exploited by perpetrators as a means of controlling at individual, political and social levels.

In Chapter 12, Ghislaine Boulanger considers the role of the UN officers and others who work for intergovernmental, nongovernmental or humanitarian organizations. This role places the officers in direct contact with the families of the disappeared. Listening to details of painful and ambiguous losses confronts the officers with many personal and professional challenges. The author proposes that the officers fit Margalit's (2002) description of "moral witnesses," someone whose testimonial mission has a moral purpose, whose authority is based on being an eyewitness to evil, and who ascribes intrinsic value to his testimony, no matter what the consequences will be.

In Chapter 13, the topic of the trans-generational transmission of trauma in case of enforced disappearance is analysed by Manon Bourguignon, Muriel Katz and Alice Dermitzel. Enforced disappearance is a crime against humanity that impacts the direct victim as well as their relatives and society through generations. Relying on psychoanalytic theory, the authors explore the theme illustrating the complexity of this process with a family case study: a mother and her child coping with the disappearance of her brother during a period of dictatorship in a Latin American country. They demonstrate how the traces of the trauma endured by the relatives of the disappeared are caused by the state violence and the ambiguous loss of the person who was disappeared. These traumatic traces make the communication within the family very complex, because of an unconscious pact within the family group, and the way traces of state violence can be passed down through generations. The persistent impunity hinders the recognition of the crime but also the work of elaboration and reparation for victims and for the second generation. Unresolved questions remain through the generations and are passed on.

In Chapter 14, Pauline Boss and Simon Robins, with their different and complementary experience in family psychotherapy and psychosocial interventions in humanitarian context, address the complex topic of supporting the families of the disappeared, who with no evidence or proof about the whereabouts or fate of the disappeared, find themselves in a limbo of confusion and uncertainty. The theory of ambiguous loss provides a psychosocial map for understanding and intervening with the individuals, families and communities left behind after disappearance. As they wait for an answer, a balance is urgently needed between psychosocial support and advocacy for truth and justice. The tension is not between human rights and family survival, but rather, seeking to ensure both support for the latter early on and delivering the former in due time. The framework of ambiguous loss is effective for understanding this here-to-fore unnamed loss and for shaping interventions for building the resilience to live with it, as long as the ambiguity lasts.

Finally, to conclude the volume, Chapter 15 offers the performative perspective of an artist on the topic. Anne Blanchet explains her artwork for the *Jardin de Dispaurs* in the city of Meyrin and what drove her to creating it like it is. She states that she chose to create a place and not an artwork. A place for the sorrow to be expressed and a place for action. A space that is simultaneously private and public in nature. She chose to install a question mark, i.e. a sign that is used in countless languages. To draw a question mark is to start with a circular shape that does not close in on itself, but that opens and continues with a straight line with a full stop affixed below. A disappearance raises innumerable questions: about life and death, about justice, trust in humankind, possibilities and means of action. The white question mark is clearly legible on the grass by Google Earth or from the planes landing or taking off from the Geneva airport, and by all the decision-makers who fly over the city. With this question mark, which keeps questioning us, we like to close our endeavour in order to pass it on to the readers hopefully for more and more effective responses to be searched.

Notes

1 A/HRC/51/31.
2 Ibidem.
3 de Frouville (2021).
4 Office of the High Commissioner for Human Rights, Update on the situation in Ukraine 31.10.2022.
5 See https://tbinternet.ohchr.org/_layouts/15/treatybodyexternal/Download.aspx?symbol no=INT%2FCED%2FINF%2F22%2F33923&Lang=en.

References

Abel, D.C. (1989). *Freud on Instinct and Morality*. Albany: SUNY Press.
Altman, N. (2009). *The Analyst in the Inner City: Race, Class, and Culture through a Psychoanalytic Lens*, 2nd Edition. New York: Routledge.
Beebe, J. (2003). *Terror, Violence and the Impulse to Destroy: Perspectives from Analytical Psychology*. Einsiedeln: Daimon Verlag.
Benjamin, J. (2017). *Beyond Doer and Done To: Recognition Theory, Intersubjectivity and the Third*. NewYork: Routledge.
Bianchi, M.G. (2020). Il potere curativo della giustizia: un'esplorazione dei rapporti tra psicologia analitica e diritti umani. Polis e psiche: politica e prospettive analitiche nella contemporaneità. *Studi Junghiani*, 26(2), 38–52.

Bianchi, M.G. (2023). Victims of Enforced Disappearances: Absent Bodies, Inner Presences. *Journal of Analytical Psychology*, 68(2), 327–336. doi: 10.1111/1468-5922.12901.

Carta, S., & Kiehl, E. (Eds.) (2020). *Political Passions and Jungian Psychology. Social and Political Activism in Analysis*. Abingdon and New York: Routledge.

Colacicchi, G. (2020). *Psychology as Ethics: Reading Jung with Kant, Nietzsche and Aristotle*. London and New York: Routledge.

de Frouville, O. (2021). "Criminalizing or Trivializing Enforced Disappearances? The Issue of 'Non-state Actors,'" in O. de Frouville & P. Pavel Sturma (Eds.), *La pénalisation des droits de l'homme*. Paris: Pedone, coll. "Publications du C.R.D.H." http://doi.org/10.2139/ssrn.3798450

De la Fuente-Herrera, J.J., & Soria-Escalante, H. (2021). The Ravages of Enforced Disappearance: A Psychoanalytic Perspective of Traumatic Events and Encrypted Mourning. *Omega (Westport)*. http://doi.org/10.1177/00302228211019208

de Viñar, M.U. (2012). Political Violence: Transgenerational Inscription and Trauma. *International Journal of Applied Psychoanalytic Studies*, 9, 95–108. https://doi.org/10.1002/aps.1310

Frosh, S. (2010). *Psychoanalysis Outside the Clinic: Interventions in Psychosocial Studies*. London: Palgrave Macmillan.

Grand, S. (2000). *The Reproduction of Evil: A Clinical and Cultural Perspective*. Hillsdale, NJ: The Analytic Press.

Harris, A. & Botticelli, S. (eds). (2010). *First Do Not Harm: The Paradoxical Encounters of Psychoanalysis, Warmaking, and Resistance*. New York: Routledge.

Hollander, N.C. (1997). *Love in a Time of Hate: Liberation Psychology in Latin America*. New Brunswick, NJ: Rutgers University Press.

Hollander, N.C. (2013). Social Trauma, Politics and Psychoanalysis: A Personal Narrative. *Journal for the Psychoanalysis of Culture and Society*, 18(2), pp. 167–183. https://doi.org/10.1057/pcs.2013.8

Hollander, N. C. (2016) The Freedom to Speak: Psychopolitical Meanings in Argentine History. *International Journal of Applied Psychoanalytic Studies*, 13, pp. 224–232. doi: 10.1002/aps.1500.

Jung, C.G. (1946). "The Psychology of the Transference", in *The Collected Works of C. G. Jung*, vol. 16, G. Adler (Ed.), (trans. R.F.C. Hull). Princeton, NJ: Princeton University Press, pp. 163–321.

Jung, C.G. (1954). "On the Nature of the Psyche" in *The Collected Works of C. G. Jung*, vol. 8, H. Read, M. Fordham, G. Adler & W. McGuire (Eds.) (trans. R.F.C. Hull). Princeton, NJ: Princeton University Press 1969, pp. 159–234.

Jung, C.G. (1942). "Transformation Symbolism in the Mass", in *The Collected Works of C. G. Jung*, vol. 11, H. Read, M. Fordham & G. Adler (Eds.) (trans. R. Hull). Princeton, NJ: Princeton University Press, pp. 296–448.

Kiehl, E., Saban, M., & Samuels, A. (2016). *Analysis and Activism: Social and Political Contributions of Jungian Psychology*. London and New York: Routledge.

Lira, E., Cornejo, M., & Morales, G. (2022). *Human Rights Violations in Latin America: Reparation and Rehabilitation*. Cham: Springer.

Luci, M. (2017). *Torture, Psychoanalysis & Human Rights*. London and New York: Routledge.

Luci, M. (2022). *Torture Survivors in Analytic Therapy: Jung, Politics, Culture*. London and New York: Routledge.

Luci, M. (2023a). Enforced Disappearances and Torture Today: A View from Analytical Psychology 2. Torture Survivors and the Unthinkable: A Hyper-Present Body in the Therapeutic Process. *Journal of Analytical Psychology*, 68(2), pp. 337–347. doi: 10.1111/1468-5922.12902.

Luci, M. (2023b). In Search for Soul: The Contribution of Analytical Psychology to Heal Human Rights Violations. *British Journal of Psychotherapy*. https://doi.org/10.1111/bjp.12855

Mandelbaum, B., Frosh, S., & Lima, R.A. (2021). *Brazilian Psychosocial Histories of Psychoanalysis*. London: Palgrave Macmillan.

Margalit, A. (2002). *The Ethics of Memory*. Cambridge, MA and London: Harvard University Press.

Montagna, P., & Harris, A. (Eds.) (2019). *Psychoanalysis, Law, and Society*. New York: Routledge.

Preitler, B. (2015). *Grief and Disappearance: Psychosocial Interventions*. Los Angeles, London, New Delhi, Singapore, Washington DC, Melbourne: Sage Publications.

Puget, J. (2002). The State of Threat and Psychoanalysis: From the Uncanny that Structure to the Uncanny that Alienates. *Free Association*, 9D(4), pp. 611–648.

Puget, J. (2004). Penser la subjectivité sociale. *Psychothérapies*, 24, pp. 183–188. https://doi.org/10.3917/psys.044.0183

Rojas Baeza, P. (2009). *La interminable ausencia*. Santiago de Chile: LOM.

Samuels, A. (1993). *The Political Psyche*. London: Routledge.

Samuels, A. (2001). *Politics on the Couch: Citizenship and the Internal Life*. London: Routledge.

Samuels, A. (2015). *A New Therapy for Politics?* London: Karnac.

Seu, I.B. (2015). A Double-Edge Sword: The Role of Psychoanalysis in Public Responses to Human Rights Violations – Denial, Justifications and Passivity. *Psychodynamic Practice*, 21(1), 5–18. https://doi.org/10.1080/14753634.2014.989712

Singer, T., & Kimbles, L.S. (Eds.) (2004). *The Cultural Complex: Contemporary Jungian Perspectives on Psyche and Society*. London and New York: Brunner-Routledge.

Soldz, S. (2008). Healers or Interrogators: Psychology and the United States Torture Regime. *Psychoanalytic Dialogues*, 18(5), pp. 592–613.

Summers, F. (2009). Violence in American Foreign Policy: A Psychoanalytic Approach. *International Journal of Applied Psychoanalytic Studies*, 6, pp. 300–320.

Taiana, C. (2014). Mourning the Dead, Mourning the Disappeared: The Enigma of the Absent-Presence. *International Journal of Psychoanalysis*, 95, pp. 1087–1107.

Varvin, S. (2021). *Psychoanalysis in Social and Cultural Settings Upheavals and Resilience*. London and New York: Routledge.

Viñar, M.N. (2017). The Enigma of Extreme Traumatism: Trauma, Exclusion and Their Impact on Subjectivity. *American Journal of Psychoanalysis*, 77, pp. 40–51.

Zoja, L. (2017). *Paranoia: The Madness that Makes History*. London and New York: Routledge.

Part I

Enforced disappearance in the contemporary world

Chapter 1

Enforced disappearances in the contemporary world

The recent contributions of the United Nations Working Group on Enforced or Involuntary Disappearances

Bernard Duhaime

Introduction

On 2 October 2018, Washington Post Journalist Jamal Khashoggi entered the Saudi consulate in Istanbul and never came out. Khashoggi had been in exile for several years because of the critical opinions that he held towards his country's regime. For weeks, his fate and whereabouts were unknown and the Saudi authorities denied having detained him. Two weeks later, after pressures from his family and civil society, as well as denunciations by the United Nations special procedures, including by the WGEID (A/HRC/42/40, paras. 45 and 56), the authorities of the Kingdom of Saudi Arabia finally admitted that he had been captured, detained and executed in the consulate, but indicated that the operation had been led by so called rogue agents. While certain individuals were swiftly convicted by the Saudi judiciary, many have suggested that this outcome has targeted the wrong individuals and prevented shedding the light on the intellectual authors of this crime. More concerning is the fact that, to this day, the full truth about the enforced disappearance and killing of Jamal Khashoggi is not known and his remains have not been located nor returned to his family.

While enforced disappearances are often perceived to have been a tool used by former Latin American repressive regimes to eliminate political dissent, they are still being used today all over the world for a variety of reasons in a large spectre of contexts. As recently indicated by the WGEID, "the Atrocious Crime of Enforced Disappearance Continues to Happen and Takes New Shapes and Forms" (OHCHR Press Release of 21 September 2021). This chapter proposes to first review traditional conceptions regarding this heinous human rights violation, it then discusses what some may consider as new forms of enforced disappearances. The author then addresses how the WGEID has adapted to contemporary problems related to enforced disappearances and finally reflects as to whether past and present forms of this human rights violation share similar characteristics and how this should feed current debates regarding how the international community should tackle this heinous crime in the future.

DOI: 10.4324/9781003312642-3

Enforced disappearance: A Latin American atrocity of the past?

In international human rights law, enforced disappearance is generally understood as

the arrest, detention, abduction or any other form of deprivation of liberty by agents of the State or by persons or groups of persons acting with the authorization, support or acquiescence of the State, followed by a refusal to acknowledge the deprivation of liberty or by concealment of the fate or whereabouts of the disappeared person, which place such a person outside the protection of the law.
(Convention article 2; Declaration preamble)

While enforced disappearances have earlier historical origins, their judicialization is generally associated with the post–World War II Nuremberg Trials, particularly with the trial of Field Marshal Keitel. The Tribunal addressed inter alia the adoption and implementation of the 'Night and Fog Decree' by the German High Command, which required the secret detention of captured alleged members of the resistance in the occupied territories (Duhaime and Painter, 2022; Finucane, 2010).

This being said, the crime is commonly associated with abuses committed by authoritarian regimes or during internal armed conflicts, often in implementation of the counterinsurgency policies and of the national security doctrine which characterized Latin-America during the darkest years of the Cold War (Cavallaro, 2019, Chapter 5). Indeed, cases of widespread use of this practice to repress political opponents were well documented in the Guatemalan and later in the Salvadorian civil wars. Similar cases were reported during the years which followed the coup in Chile and in Argentina, as well as under the repressive regimes in Brazil, Paraguay and Uruguay, as part of a broader regional plan of oppression called the Operation Condor (Dulitzky, 2018, p. 436 and following).

In response, Latin-American victims and relatives, civil society organizations, multilateral organizations and later States have been very active locally and internationally to tackle this phenomenon. Indeed, at the end of the 1970s, courageous advocacy lead by the Latin-American Federation of Associations for Relatives of the Detained-Disappeared (FEDAFEM) and the Grandmothers of Plaza de Mayo, for example, have had considerable successes in bringing the Inter-American Commission on Human Rights to address the issue in country reports and individual cases (e.g. see IACHR, Report on the Situation of Human Rights in Argentina, 1980), as well as the United Nations to create the United Nations Working Group on Enforced or Involuntary Disappearances in 1980 (Guest, 1990; UN Commission on Human Rights, Resolution 20 (XXXVI)). Similarly, the Inter-American Court of Human Rights adopted in 1988 its standard-setting case of *Velásquez Rodríguez v Honduras*, addressing thoroughly the legal concept of enforced disappearances as prohibited by international human rights law. In addition, Member States of the Organization of American States adopted, in 1994, the Inter-American Convention on Forced Disappearance of Persons, the first binding instrument on the matter, which obviously influenced greatly the development of the International Convention for the Protection of All Persons from Enforced Disappearance adopted by the United Nations General Assembly in 2006.

While it is true that many emblematic historic disappearances have occurred in Latin America between the 1960s and mid-1980s, one should recall that the practice has been used widely in other regions and contexts. Indeed, such a crime was extensively implemented as a tool of repression against suspected political opponents in the Soviet Union (Baranowska, 2017; Dulitzky, 2018). Similarly, in the colonial context, the "Organisation de l'Armée Secrète" a special unit of the French military forces enforcedly disappeared many anticolonial militants during the Algerian war of independence (Rahal and Riceputi, 2021; Thénault, 2019).

In its 2021 Annual Report, the WGEID indicated that, since its inception in 1980, it has transmitted a total of 59,212 cases to 110 different States (A/HRC/48/57, p. 1). While one should be very careful with those numbers, as they obviously represent only a very small portion of the actual number of cases, one can observe that disappearances have been documented officially in roughly 57% of the United Nations Member States that only 23% of the Working Group's total number of cases are said to be attributable to Latin American States (*Ibid.*, p. 30 and following).

Indeed, governments have used enforced disappearances to repress political opposition in a multitude of contexts. Emblematic cases were documented during the *années de plomb* in Morocco's 1970s and early 1980s (Loudiy, 2014), as well as in the course of the infamous 1988 prison massacre in Iran (Shahrooz, 2007) for example. Similarly, important numbers of disappearances occurred during armed conflicts, including during the war in Cyprus (Kyriakou, 2011), the Iran-Iraq war (E/CH.4/1983/14, paras. 118–120) and the Bosnia war (E/CN.4/1993/25, paras. 38–42) for instance. During non-international armed conflicts, important number of cases were documented as well, as in the Lebanese civil war (Comaty, 2019) or the Chechen civil war (Barrett, 2009). Finally, the practice of enforcedly disappearing people in the course of fighting terrorism was implemented worldwide well before 9/11, as attest the cases widely reported during the mass violence perpetrated against alleged communist terrorists in Indonesia and in the Philippines during the Cold War (Van der Kroef, 1987) or during Algeria's "dark decade" (Howell, 2016).

As indicated by the WGEID and recently, "enforced disappearances continued to happen, taking new shapes and forms", and are "not a crime of the past but continue to be used across the world" (OHCHR Presse release, 21 September 2021). Indeed, while the phenomenon is still very present in certain parts of Latin America, as in Mexico, Colombia or El Salvador for example, the crime is currently being denounced daily in all regions of the world in different contexts. In addition, contemporary enforced disappearances have many faces. During the author's mandate as Member of the Working Group, he has encountered this type of human rights violation in different settings including as a strategy of political oppression, in the context of armed conflicts, as part of counter-terrorism measures, including during transnational transfers, or in the context of migration.

Enforced disappearances as a tool of repression of opponents

Indeed, enforced disappearances are still among some governments' prime tools to silence political opposition today. The crime's main objective of deterring large numbers of opponents thought terror, as was expressly provided in the German High Command's 'Night and Fog Decree', is still present in contemporary repressive strategies. As in that case, in certain circumstances, recent enforced disappearances were conducted as part of a massive and systematic attack against the civilian population and could very well constitute crimes against humanity (Statute of the International Criminal Court, art. 7).

For instance, the WGEID has repeatedly noted its concern at the numbers of enforced disappearances allegedly undertaken against perceived opponents of the regime in the Democratic People's Republic of Korea. In this regard, it has called on the Security Council to consider referring the situation in the Democratic People's Republic of Korea to the International Criminal Court because of the extent and scale of enforced disappearance in the country, as also highlighted by the work of the commission of inquiry on human rights in the Democratic People's Republic of Korea which has revealed the nature of crime against humanity of enforced disappearances that have been committed and are ongoing in the country (A/HRC/27/49, para. 72). The WGEID has reached similar conclusions regarding the widespread and systematic human rights violations, including enforced disappearances, committed throughout Eritrea over the past 25 years. Again, it endorsed the call made by the UN Commission of Inquiry on Human Rights in Eritrea for the Security Council to consider referring the situation in Eritrea to the International Criminal Court (A/HRC/39/46, para. 100).

Analogous concerns were formulated by the WGEID regarding the situation in the Sudan and the allegations of increased numbers of enforced disappearances of protesters and opposition activists and critics committed in the context of the large-scale protests in the country (A/HRC/WGEID/118/1, para. 102). This was also the case regarding the important number of cases of enforced disappearances committed during the protests and unrest which occurred during the political violence which took place in Burundi between 2015 and 2018, as denounced by the WGEID (A/HRC/42/40, para. 65) and the UN Commission of Inquiry on Burundi (A/HRC/39/63, paras. 35–36), which led the Prosecutor of the International Criminal Court to launch an investigation into the situation of Burundi, including regarding the alleged crimes against humanity of enforced disappearances (ICC-01/17-X-9-US-Exp, 2017).

Similarly, in Myanmar, the WGEID has repeated its preoccupation about the consistent and reliable reports of grave and systematic human rights violations in Rakhine State, including enforced disappearances, targeted in particular at the Rohingya minority (A/HRC/WGEID/112/1, A/HRC/36/39, para. 92; A/HRC/42/40, para. 76). Similar conclusions were formulated by the Independent International Fact-finding Mission on Myanmar (A/HRC/39/64, paras. 2, 63 and 88), which together with the Special Rapporteur on the situation of human rights in Myanmar and the WGEID called on the Security Council to refer the situation in Myanmar to the International Criminal Court or, alternatively, create an ad hoc international criminal tribunal (A/HRC/39/64, para. 105; A/HRC/42/40, para. 76).

In addition, the Working Group has also denounced important numbers of enforced disappearances conducted in the context of political repression in certain countries, without characterizing them as crimes against humanity. For instance, it has documented enforced disappearances undertaken in Pakistan by Rangers, Frontier Corps and other security forces targeting political opposition groups or minorities in the region of Balochistan, of Sindh or the Pashtun areas of Pakistan (A/HRC/22/45/Add.2, paras. 38 and 39; A/HRC/WGEID/117/1, Annex 1, para. 9–12; A/HRC/42/40, para. 81). Comparable methods of repression against political opposition groups have also been reported to the Working Group concerning the frequent use of enforced disappearance in Bangladesh as a tool by law enforcement agencies, paramilitary and armed forces to detain and even to execute individuals extrajudicially (A/HRC/42/40, para. 63).

Enforced disappearances in the context of armed conflicts

Many contemporary disappearances occur in the contexts of armed conflicts, at least this is the case of the great majority of countries for which more than 1,000 cases were processed by the WGEID (A/HRC/42/40, 2019) regarding Algeria, Argentina, El Salvador, Guatemala, Iraq, Peru, Sri Lanka, Colombia and Pakistan). Indeed, since 1980, the Working Group has addressed enforced disappearances occurring in non-international armed conflicts (E/CN.A/1A35, paras. 84–101, 131–144). In doing so, it has traditionally only considered allegations of disappearance committed by State forces, in accordance with the definition of the crime, and not of disappearances attributed to rebel forces (Duhaime and Painter, 2022).[1] It is only since 2011, however, that the WGEID has dealt with enforced disappearances occurring in international armed conflicts (A/HRC/19/58/Rev.1, para. 4, 2012).

While it has then addressed disappearances in a series of conflicts, including those which took place in the Former Yugoslavia (Report of the: Mission to Bosnia and Herzegovina, para. 1; Mission to Serbia, including Kosovo, para. 2; Mission to Montenegro, para. 6; Mission to Croatia, para. 2) and in Chechenia (E/CN.4/2005/65, para. 237; A/HRC/WGEID/110/1, para. 109; A/HRC/WGEID/111/1, para. 109; A/HRC/WGEID/112/1, para. 82), as well as during and after the last war Iraq (A/HRC/WGEID/110/1, paras. 54–55; A/HRC/WGEID/113/1 paras. 135–136; A/HRC/WGEID/116/1, para. 76), it has dealt more recently with such allegations in the context of the conflicts in Sri Lanka, in Turkey, in Ukraine, in Libya, in Syria and in Yemen.

Indeed, after its visit to Sri Lanka in 2015, the Working Group addressed patterns of enforced disappearances, which occurred during the internal armed conflict opposing the Sri Lankan armed forces and the Liberation Tigers of Tamil Eelam

(LTTE) (A/HRC/33/51/Add.2). The WGEID documented important numbers of disappearances taking place during or after the May 2009 surrender of the LTTE. It also referred to clandestine detention centres and mass graves on military premises in the North-East of the country.

Similarly, in its report regarding its 2016 visit to Turkey, the Working Group also dealt with disappearances in different contexts of armed conflicts. It first addressed the military operations which had been lead in the South-East of the country, opposing the Turkish army and armed members of the Kurdistan Workers Party (PKK). It referred, in particular, to the alleged disposal of bodies during security operations in Diyarbakir and how this impedes families from identifying the disappeared (A/HRC/33/51/Add.1, para. 12.). It also discussed the issue of pushbacks and of *refoulement* of migrants entering the Turkish-Syrian border and fleeing the war in Syria (A/HRC/33/51/Add.1, para. 55; see also A/HRC/36/39/Add.2, paras. 25, 32, 33, 59). The WGEID also took this opportunity to refer to how Turkey should fulfil its obligations regarding the search and identification of the missing from the 1974 Cyprus conflict (A/HRC/33/51/Add.1, para. 79).

After its 2018 visit to Ukraine, the Working Group denounced the existence of clandestine detention facilities as well as instances of enforced disappearance of detainees of various durations by military and security forces agencies on both sides of the conflict in the Donbas region. It also discussed how families and victims face obstacles to obtain information and to establish the truth because of the conflict, the division of the territory the difficult access to military archives. The WGEID issued a series of recommendations to the authorities of Ukraine, but also to those of Russia and of the self-proclaimed "Donetsk People's Republic" and "Luhansk People's Republic" (A/HRC/42/40/Add.2), reiterating the States obligation to investigate and prosecute instances of enforced disappearances, though the civilian judiciary, taking into consideration the doctrine of command responsibility, the inapplicability of the defence of superior orders and the prohibition of amnesty laws for such crime.

In addition to those visit reports, the Working Group also reiterated its denunciations of disappearances occurring in Libya by military forces on both sides of the conflict (A/HRC/42/40, para. 75). In 2019, after an attack on a detention centre in Tripoli, it urged Libya to

> search for and locate the disappeared migrants, using all the means at its disposal, including forensic investigative resources, and to incorporate ante-mortem information in a centralized database to allow families of the deceased to have information on the fate of the victims.
>
> (A/HRC/42/40, para. 75; A/HRC/39/46, para. 109)

In the Middle East, the WGEID denounced abuses occurring in the Syrian conflict A/HRC/42/40, para. 84–86), referring, in particular, to tens of thousands of disappearances reported to correspond to specific patterns of capture by State authorities and militias, to resort to clandestine detention installations, and followed by mass executions (A/HRC/WGEID/117/1, at p. 28). The Working Group also urged the Security Council to consider referring the situation in Syria to the International Criminal Court (A/HRC/42/40, para. 85; A/HRC/39/46, para. 132; A/HRC/27/49, para. 99; A/HRC/33/51, para. 103). Regarding the conflict in Yemen, the WGEID similarly denounced enforced disappearances allegedly undertaken by agents of the government of Yemen, the de facto authorities, as well as by agents of the United Arab Emirates and of Saudi Arabia (A/HRC/42/40, para. 91; A/HRC/33/51, para. 109; A/HRC/36/39, para. 111; A/HRC/39/46, para. 139).

Enforced disappearances in the fight against terrorism, including during transnational transfers

A very common area where enforced disappearances increasingly occur worldwide is that of certainly law enforcement or security operations, in particular, those related to the fight against terrorism (A/HRC/48/57, para. 38, 39, 43, 37, 54, A/HRC/45/13, para. 46, A/HRC/42/40, para. 56). On this matter, the 1992 Declaration provides that "no circumstances whatsoever, whether a threat of war, a state of war, internal political instability or any other public emergency, may be invoked to justify enforced disappearances."

One should recall that the 2010 Joint Study on Global Practices in Relation to Secret Detention in the Context of Countering Terrorism, produced by the WGEID, the Special Rapporteur on the Promotion and Protection of Human Rights and Fundamental Freedoms while Countering Terrorism, the Special Rapporteur on Torture and Other Cruel, Inhuman or Degrading Treatment or Punishment, and the Working Group on Arbitrary Detention discussed this reality in considerable detail (A/HRC/13/42).

More recently, the Working Group has called on many countries to halt the misuse of counter-terrorism, including as a measure persecution of civil society activists, lawyers, journalists and human rights defenders, which often leads to their enforced disappearance. An emblematic case is the enforced disappearance by the State of Pakistan of leading human rights defender and minority civil society activist Idris Khattak who was abducted by security agents in November 2019 and was subjected to seven months of enforced disappearance. In June 2020, authorities acknowledged that he was being detained, without revealing his place of detention, and he has been held incommunicado ever since. In December 2021, he was sentenced to 14 years imprisonment following an apparent unfair trial by a military court in Pakistan. The WGEID indicated that "Khattak's detention and sentencing is part of an alarming pattern of silencing human rights defenders and outspoken civil society leaders through systematic abuse of counter-terrorism and security legislation, intimidation, secret detention, torture and enforced disappearance" (OHCHR Press Release of December 15th, 2021).

Similarly, the Working Group denounced Egypt's Anti-Terrorism Law provisions as going beyond the scope necessary to counter terrorism and as limiting civic space and the exercise of fundamental freedoms in Egypt. It expressed concern regarding the Law and the Terrorism Circuit Courts, considering that the systematic use of overly broad and vague definitions of terrorism that target human rights defenders are detrimental to human rights and fail to comply with international human rights law, international humanitarian law and international refugee law (OHCHR Press release of December 1st, 2021). More recently, it called for an immediate moratorium on the use of Sri Lanka's Prevention of Terrorism Act (PTA), urging the Government to review and revise the legislation to comply with international human rights law, as this act has been used for decades enabling prolonged arbitrary detention and enabling enforced disappearances, allowing the detention of suspects for decades without charge (OHCHR Press release of March 2nd, 2022).

In addition, in its last Annual Report, the Working Group recommended to States to "cease justifying enforced disappearances on the grounds of protecting national security, combating terrorism, and tackling extremism" (A/HRC/48/57, para. 60 a). A full section of the report then addressed extensively the issue of enforced disappearances in the context of transnational transfers (A/HRC/48/57, para. 38–60), in which it documented numerous instances of extraterritorial abductions and forced returns, including expulsions, often undertaken in undercover operations in cooperation between two or more States, on the pretext of combating terrorism and protecting national security. The WGEID referred to a series of cases which allegedly involved numerous countries. The most emblematic cases have concerned the capture of individuals suspected of belonging to the Hizmet/Gulen movement by Turkish authorities, captured from Afghanistan (AL TUR 5/2020),[2] Albania (UA ALB 1/2020, UA ALB 2/2020), Azerbaijan (AL AZE 1/2019), Cambodia (AL KHM 7/2020), Gabon (AL GAB 2/2018), Kazakhstan (AL TUR 5/2020), Kenya (A/HRC/WGEID/124/1, para. 59), Lebanon (AL TUR 5/2020), Malaysia (A/HRC/WGAD/2020/51), Pakistan (A/HRC/WGAD/2018/11), Panama (UA PAN 2/2020) and Uzbekistan (A/HRC/WGEID/123/1, para. 163), as well as from Kosovo (AL KSV 1/2018) and sent to Turkey (AL TUR 5/2020) to face terrorism related charges. Similarly, other cases related to the capture of Chinese nationals of Uighur ethnicity from Egypt (UA CHN 7/2017), Myanmar (UA CHN 12/2015), and the United Arab Emirates (A/HRC/WGEID/114/1, para. 155) who are sent to China where they are often sent to alleged re-education camps.[3]

According to this thematic section of the WGEID's 2021 Annual Report, States have signed bilateral security cooperation agreements, often referring to broad and vague justifications of combating terrorism and transnational crime. In many cases, transfers appear to have taken place shortly after the entry into force of such cooperation agreements. In compliance with the latter, lists of individuals are circulated and surveillance operations are conducted, followed by house raids often lead during covert operations. Individuals are captured without warrant or explanation, carried in unmarked vehicles, and detained for varying periods of time in clandestine detention facilities, without contact with relatives or legal representatives, and often face interrogation and torture to extract confessions. They are then transferred to other another country, often their country of origin, in the margins of regular expulsion procedures,[4] or as part of covert extraterritorial operations, including so-called extraordinary renditions. Civilian or military intelligence services are said to have unmarked aircraft or commercial flights for these operations. Many abducted individuals are reported to have been indicted upon arrival in the host State and remanded in pretrial custody pursuant to counter-terrorism legislation and emergency decrees. Some are maintained in secret detention, including under residential surveillance (A/HRC/48/57, para. 41–49).

Finally, one should recall that some enforced disappearances may be transnational in nature, even if there is no consent of the host State or transnational transfer of the victim per se, as was the case of the sadly famous disappearance of journalist Jamal Khashoggi at the Saudi consulate in Istanbul (A/HRC/WGEID/117/1, paras. 8, 109 (b), 110, 116 and 118–119, A/HRC/WGEID/118/1, para. 95, A/HRC/42/40, paras. 45 and 56).

Enforced disappearances in the context of migration

In recent years, increasing numbers of disappearances have been documented by civil society in the context of the "migratory crisis" (Citroni, 2017; Duhaime and Thibault, 2017). This includes, for example, the famous case of the migrants who went missing in San Fernando, Tamaulipas Mexico, in 2011 (FJED, 2014, p. 7; IA-CHR, 2013, p. 81) or of those who disappeared in the Mediterranean while trying to cross from Tunisia to Italy (A/HRC/WGEID/112/1) or from Turkey to Greece (Amnesty International, 2014; EUAFR, 2015, pp. 87–88).

In 2017, the WGEID completed its thematic Report on enforced disappearances in the context of migration (A/HRC/36/39/Add.2.), after having made a call for inputs and held consultations with experts on the matter. It first discussed how enforced disappearances can be a cause for migration, for example when individuals migrate to escape threats of being subjected to enforced disappearance, either as persons close to victims which already disappeared or persons who are harassed because of their initiatives to seek truth and justice in such contexts (paras. 8–10, 13). Similarly, relatives of disappeared migrants may also migrate to the country of transit or destination where the disappearance allegedly occurred, in order seek more directly truth and justice, as doing so from home can be more difficult, if not impossible (paras. 11–12; FJED, 2014, p. 8; IOM, 2016, p. 36).

It mainly addressed the phenomenon of enforced disappearance as a result of the abduction of migrants for political or other reasons, where victims are captured by agents of the State of origin in the territory of the transit or the destination State, with the authorization or complicity of the latter, or where they are captured by agents of the transit or destination State and then transferred to the authorities of the victims' State of origin. These operations may involve the exchange of intelligence between the concerned States so that "political" migrants can be located within the host State's territory (A/HRC/36/39/Add.2., para 16). This type of situation includes, for instance, disappeared nationals of the Democratic People's Republic of Korea who had crossed the border into China to avoid persecution were reportedly captured by Chinese officials and repatriated (A/HRC/WGEID/107/1, para. 25), in certain cases where both States had allegedly exchanged information on the matter (A/HRC/25/CRP.1, para. 446).

The WGEID also indicated that migrants may disappear during detention or deportation, in great part because of the lack of transparency, the fact that migrants are often detained in unofficial detention centres with little or no registration systems, of the very limited access of migrants to the justice system and of the lack of an independent monitoring mechanism for such detentions (A/HRC/36/39/Add.2., para. 23; UNHCR, 2014, p. 20), as was documented, for example, in detention facilities operated jointly by State agents and non-State actors in Libya (UNSMIL, 2016, pp. 1 and 14 ff). It also referred to the arbitrary expulsions where migrants are returned or removed either outside legal procedures or in accordance with legal processes and procedures which do not comply with international law, in particular with the human rights principle of non-refoulement or the prohibition of collective expulsion, as does the practice of pushbacks which may lead to enforced disappearances and which contravene article 11 of the Declaration which provides that

> all persons deprived of liberty must be released in a manner permitting reliable verification that they have actually been released and, further, have been released in conditions in which their physical integrity and ability fully to exercise their rights are assured.
>
> (A/HRC/36/39/Add.2., paras. 25–33)

Previously, in its report on its visit to Turkey, the WGEID had referred to important number of mass returns of Syrian refugees from Turkey and the use of violence by border guards to prevent Syrian nationals from entering Turkey (A/HRC/33/51/Add.1, para. 55).

Enforced disappearances of migrants may also occur at the hands of corrupted State officials who act as smugglers or traffickers, organize the smuggling or trafficking of migrants, facilitate undocumented migration, enable their stay, etc. Similarly, the disappearances of smuggled or trafficked migrants by non-State actors may also generate State responsibility for instance when smuggling or trafficking is closely linked to corruption or collusion of State officials, or occur with their implicit or explicit authorization, support or acquiescence (A/HRC/36/39/Add.2., paras. 34–43).

Factors that contribute to the enforced disappearances of migrants are said to include the fact that migrations often occur in contexts of armed conflicts and violence, the fact that migrants are often exposed to greater socioeconomic challenges, face discrimination and impunity, and are often the object of harsh state migratory and counter-terrorism policies. Also, very little statistical data address enforced disappearances of migrants, contributing to their invisibility (A/HRC/36/39/Add.2., paras. 46–56).

Adapting enforced disappearances to new realities?

As it did in 2011 when it decided to change is practice regarding enforced disappearances occurring in international armed conflicts, the WGEID continues to adapt to pressing problems related to this heinous crime. Accordingly, the Working Group indicated in its 2019 Annual Report,

> For a number of years, [it] has been receiving information about increasing instances of abductions carried out by non-State actors, which may be tantamount to acts of enforced disappearances. In light of its humanitarian mandate and the fact that the victims of these acts do not have any remedy to address their plight, the Working Group has decided to document cases concerning enforced or involuntary disappearances allegedly perpetrated by non-State actors that exercise effective control and/or government-like functions over a territory.
>
> (A/HRC/42/40, para. 94)

This new position, on a very delicate and controversial issue (de Frouville, 2022), is the result of long consultations and discussions that the WGEID has held in recent years (A/HRC/33/51, para. 51). While the Working Group wanted to address somehow the issue of disappearances committed by non-State actors, it clearly was not ready to modify the legal definition of this very specific form of human rights violation, where the public apparatus is perverted to abuse human dignity, in contexts of State terrorism or of corrupt impunity. Nevertheless, this middle ground position appears to be a good approach to a very present reality. This development may indeed contribute to the WGEID's humanitarian mandate of assisting relatives obtain information as to the fate or whereabouts of their loved ones. This practice will also allow for some international record to be kept of these instances of disappearances. Finally, as non-State actors sometimes later become agents of the State, in transitional contexts for instance, this new practice will assist the State in its obligation to provide the relatives with the information that former non-State actors now State agents may have as to those crimes.

This development is quite recent and the WGEID's practice still burgeoning: so far, the WGEID has documented 36 such cases regarding to the Libyan National Army, the self-proclaimed "Donetsk People's Republic," the de facto authorities in Sana'a – Yemen and to Hamas (A/HRC/45/13, para. 24, A/HRC/48/57, para. 23). In doing so, the Working Group recalled that it was acting

> pursuant to its humanitarian mandate to address a growing protection gap affecting disappeared individuals and their relatives who have been denied information on the fate and the whereabouts of their loved ones. In implementing this practice, the Working Group underscores that the cases transmitted to non-State actors do not in any way imply the expression of any opinion concerning the legal status of any territory, city or area, or of its authorities.
>
> (A/HRC/45/13, note 3)

It will be interesting to see how the Working Group will proceed with this matter in the future and, possibly, reflect this new practice in its Methods of Work (A/HRC/WGEID/102/2).

Conclusion

While this chapter has tried to demonstrate that contemporary enforced disappearances occur worldwide and in a variety of settings, including as a strategy of political oppression, in the context of armed conflicts, as part of counter-terrorism measures or during transnational transfers, or in the context of migration, one should of course recall that similar crimes took place in the Latin America of the 1970–1980s (Dulitzky, 2018, pp. 436 and following). Indeed, massive disappearances occurred during the armed conflict in El Salvador and Guatemala (A/HRC/48/57, pp. 41–42) for instance. Similarly, the enforced disappearances which occurred as a result of the infamous Operation Condor (Lessa, 2015), were also instances of disappearances part of a strategy of political oppression pretexting to fight terrorism, involving transnational transfers in the context of the abductees' migration (Duhaime and Thibault, 2017, pp. 576–577).

As it did in 2011 when it decided to change its practice process cases dealing with enforced disappearances occurring in international armed conflicts, the WGEID has again adapted to current realities and decided, as part of its humanitarian mandate, to start documenting instances of abductions carried out by non-State actors, which may be tantamount to acts of enforced disappearances.

As time passes, and enforced disappearances persist beyond borders, so does impunity and so does the relatives' suffering. Today, the prohibition of this heinous crime is considered a norm of *jus cogens*, and States have an *erga omnes* obligation to prevent and sanction it (Trindade, 2012). This obligation knows no limit in space or time, as the crime is indeed sadly continuous in nature (A/HRC/16/48, para. 39). The international community needs to continue supporting the victims of enforced disappearances, including their relatives who, by their courageous and vital efforts, are every day relentlessly at the forefront of a crucial battle for human dignity.

Notes

1   But see *infra* Section 6.
2   To access the UN Special procedures communications mentioned here see https://spcommreports.ohchr.org/Tmsearch/TMDocuments.
3   Other reported cases include transfers from Cambodia, the Lao People's Democratic Republic and Viet Nam to Thailand; from Thailand to the Lao People's Democratic Republic; from Malaysia to Egypt; from Egypt to Yemen; from Lebanon to the Syrian Arab Republic; from Ukraine to Uzbekistan; from France and Germany to the Russian Federation; from the United Republic of Tanzania to Burundi; from Kenya to South Sudan; from Afghanistan and Pakistan to the United States of America and subsequently to the United Arab Emirates; from Senegal via Tunisia to Libya; and from the United Republic of Tanzania via Afghanistan and Djibouti to Yemen (A/HRC/48/57, para. 40).

4   In certain circumstances, the authorities orchestrating the transfers have revoked the citizenship or annulled the passport of targeted individuals with the aim of facilitating expeditious arrests abroad (A/HRC/48/57, para. 48). In the Report on its visit to Kyrgyzstan, for example, the Working Group said having received information indicating that many migrant workers from Xinjiang autonomous region of China lost their work permits once their passports expired, were allegedly not informed about their rights, including the right to seek asylum, were deported – frequently upon the request of the Chinese authorities – and were subsequently subjected to enforced disappearance (A/HRC/45/13/Add.2, para. 38).

References

Amnesty International. (2014). *Greece: Frontier of Hope and Fear – Migrants and Refugees Pushed Back at Europe's Border*. London: Amnesty International.

Association for the Prevention of Torture, International Detention Coalition, United Nations High Commissioner for Refugee. (2014). *Monitoring Immigration Detention: Practical Manual*. Geneva: UNHCR.

Baranowska, G. (2017). *Wymuszone zaginięcia w Europie. Kształtowanie się międzynarodowych standardów zapobiegania i egzekwowania odpowiedzialności państwa* (Enforced Disappearances in Europe. The Shaping of International Standards of Preventing and Enforcing State Responsibility). Warszawa: Wydawnictwo C.H. Beck, pp. 267.

Barrett, J. (2009). "Chechnya's Last Hope-Enforced Disappearances and the European Court of Human Rights." *Harvard Human Rights Journal*, 22, pp. 133–143.

Cavallaro, J.L., Vargas, C., Sandoval-Villalba, C., Duhaime, B., Brewer, S.E., Bettinger-Lopez, C., Naddeo, C.C. (2019). *Doctrine, Practice, and Advocacy in the Inter-American Human Rights System*. Oxford: Oxford University Press, p. 968.

Citroni, G. (2017). "The First Attempts in Mexico and Central America to Address the Phenomenon of Missing and Disappeared Migrants." *International Review of the Red Cross*, 99(905), pp. 735–757.

Comaty, L. (2019). *Post-conflict Transition in Lebanon: The Disappeared of the Civil War*. London: Routledge.

Declaration on the Protection of All Persons from Enforced Disappearance, UN Doc. A/RES/47/133, 18 December 1992.

de Frouville, O. (2022). "Criminalizing or Trivializing Enforced Disappearances? The Issue of 'Non-State Actors.'" In de Frouville, O., Sturma, P. (eds.), *La pénalisation des droits de l'homme*. Paris: Pedone, pp. 147–196.

Duhaime, B., Painter, R. (2022). "International Convention for the Protection of All Persons from Enforced Disappearance (ICPPED)." In Binder, C., Nowak, M., Hofbauer, J.A., Janig, P. (dir.), *Elgar Encyclopedia of Human Rights*. Cheltenham: Edward Elgar Publishing.

Duhaime, B., Thibault, A. (2017). "Protection of Migrants from Enforced Disappearance: A Human Rights Perspective." *International Review of the Red Cross*, 99(905), pp. 569–587.

Dulitzky, A.E. (2018). "The Latin-American Flavor of Enforced Disappearances." *Chicago Journal of International Law*, 19(2), p. 423.

European Union Agency for Fundamental Rights. (2015). *Fundamental Rights: Challenges and Achievements in 2014 – Annual Report 2014*. Luxemburg: EUAFR.

Finucane, B. (2010). "Enforce Disappearance as a Crime under International Law: A Neglected Origin in the Laws of War." *Yale Journal of International Law*, 35(171). New Heaven: Yale Law School. http://hdl.handle.net/20.500.13051/6607.

Foundation for Justice and the Rule of Law. (2014). *Disappeared Migrants: The Permanent Torture*. Mexico City: FJED. https://www.fundacionjusticia.org/disappeared-migrants-the-permanent-torture/.

Guest, I. (1990). *Behind the Disappearances: Argentina's Dirty War against Human Rights and the United Nations*. Philadelphia: University of Pennsylvania Press.

Howell, J. (2016). "Investigating the Enforced Disappearances of Algeria's 'Dark Decade': Omar D's and Kamel Khélif's Commemorative Art Projects." *The Journal of North African Studies*, 21(2), pp. 213–234.

Inter-American Commission on Human Rights, OEA/Ser.L/V/II Doc 48/13, 30 December 2013.

Inter-American Commission on Human Rights, *Report on the Situation of Human Rights in Argentina*, OEA/Ser.L/V/II.49, Doc. 19 corr.1, 11 April 1980.

Inter-American Convention on Forced Disappearance of Persons, Organization of American States Treaty Series (OASTS), No. 60, 9 June 1994.

Inter-American Court of Human Rights, *Velásquez Rodríguez v Honduras*, Ser. C No. 4, judgment of 29 July 1988 (Merits).

International Convention for the Protection of All Persons from Enforced Disappearance, 2716 UNTS 3, 20 December 2006.

International Criminal Court, Public Redacted Version of "Decision Pursuant to Article 15 of the Rome Statute on the Authorization of an Investigation into the Situation in the Republic of Burundi", ICC-01/17-X-9-US-Exp, 25 October 2017.

International Organization for Migration. (2016). *Fatal Journeys: Tracking Lives Lost During Migration*. Geneva: IOM.

Kyriakou, N. (2011). "Enforced Disappearances in Cyprus: Problems and Prospects of the Case Law of the European Court of Human Rights." *European Human rights Law Review*, 2, pp. 190–199.

Lessa, F. (2015). "Justice Beyond Borders: The Operation Condor Trial and Accountability for Transnational Crimes in South America." *International Journal of Transitional Justice*, 9 (3), pp. 494–506.

Loudiy, F. (2014). *Transitional Justice and Human Rights in Morocco: Negotiating the Years of Lead*. London: Routledge.

Rahal, M., Riceputi, R. (2021). *La mémoire de la disparition forcée durant la Guerre d'indépendance algérienne. Mémoires en jeu*. Association Mémoire des signes - Editions Kimé.

Shahrooz, K. (2007) "With Revolutionary Rage and Rancor: A Preliminary Report on the 1988 Massacre of Iran's Political Prisoners." *Harvard Human Rights Journal*, 20, pp. 227–262.

Statute of the International Criminal Court, United Nations, Treaty Series, vol. 2187, No. 38544, 17 July 1998.

Thénault, S. (2019). « Les disparus de la guerre d'Algérie ». *L'Histoire*, 466, pp. 12–19.

Trindade, A.A. (2012). "Enforced Disappearances of Persons as a Violation of Jus Cogens: The Contribution of the Jurisprudence of the Inter-American Court of Human Rights." *Nordic Journal of International Law*, 81(4), pp. 507–536.

UN Commission on Human Rights, *Question of Missing and Disappeared Persons*, 35th Sess, UN Doc. E/CH.4/1983/14, 1983.

UN Commission on Human Rights, *Question of Missing and Disappeared Persons*, 37th Sess, UN Doc. E/CN.A/1A35.

UN Commission on Human Rights, *Question of Missing and Disappeared Persons*, 49th Sess, UN Doc. E/CN.4/1993/25, 1993.

UN Commission on Human Rights, Resolution 20 (XXXVI), 29 February 1980.

UN Human Rights Council, *Communications, Cases Examined, Observations and Other Activities Conducted by the Working Group on Enforced or Involuntary Disappearances*, 107th Sess (14–18 September 2015), A/HRC/WGEID/107/1.

UN Human Rights Council, *Communications, Cases Examined, Observations and Other Activities Conducted by the Working Group on Enforced or Involuntary Disappearances*, 110th Sess, HRC Doc. A/HRC/WGEID/110/1.

UN Human Rights Council, *Communications, Cases Examined, Observations and Other Activities Conducted by the Working Group on Enforced or Involuntary Disappearances*, 111th Sess, HRC Doc. A/HRC/WGEID/111/1.

UN Human Rights Council, *Communications, Cases Examined, Observations and Other Activities Conducted by the Working Group on Enforced or Involuntary Disappearances*, 112th Sess, HRC Doc. A/HRC/WGEID/112/1.

UN Human Rights Council, *Communications, Cases Examined, Observations and Other Activities Conducted by the Working Group on Enforced or Involuntary Disappearances*, 113th Sess, HRC Doc. A/HRC/WGEID/113/1.

UN Human Rights Council, *Communications, Cases Examined, Observations and Other Activities Conducted by the Working Group on Enforced or Involuntary Disappearances*, 116th Sess, HRC Doc. A/HRC/WGEID/116/1.

UN Human Rights Council, *Communications, Cases Examined, Observations and Other Activities Conducted by the Working Group on Enforced or Involuntary Disappearances*, 117th Sess, HRC Doc. A/HRC/WGEID/117/1.

UN Human Rights Council, *Communications Transmitted, Cases Examined, Observations Made and Other Activities Conducted by the Working Group on Enforced or Involuntary Disappearances*, 118th Sess, HRC Doc. A/HRC/WGEID/118/1.

UN Human Rights Council, *Joint Study on Global Practices in Relation to Secret Detention in the Context of Countering Terrorism of the Special Rapporteur on the Promotion and Protection of Human Rights and Fundamental Freedoms while Countering Terrorism, the Special Rapporteur on Torture and Other Cruel, Inhuman or Degrading Treatment or Punishment, the Working Group on Arbitrary Detention*, A/HRC/13/42, 20 May 2010.

UN Human Rights Council, *Report of the Commission of Inquiry on Burundi*, 8 August 2018, A/HRC/39/63.

UN Human Rights Council, *Report of the Detailed Findings of the Commission of Inquiry on Human Rights in the Democratic People's Republic of Korea*, A/HRC/25/CRP.1, 7 February 2014.

UN Human Rights Council, *Report of the Independent International Fact-Finding Mission on Myanmar*, 12 September 2018, A/HRC/39/64.

UN Human Rights Council, *Report of the Working Group on Enforced or Involuntary Disappearance, General Comment on Enforced Disappearance as a Continuous Crime*, 26 January 2011, A/HRC/16/48.

UN Human Rights Council, *Report of the Working Group on Enforced or Involuntary Disappearances, Mission to Bosnia and Herzegovina*, 16th Sess, HRC Doc. A/HRC/16/48/Add.1.

UN Human Rights Council, *Report of the Working Group on Enforced or Involuntary Disappearances, Mission to Croatia*, 30th Sess, HRC Doc. A/HRC/30/38/Add.3.

UN Human Rights Council, *Report of the Working Group on Enforced or Involuntary Disappearances, Mission to Montenegro*, 30th Sess, HRC Doc. A/HRC/30/38/Add.2

UN Human Rights Council, *Report of the Working Group on Enforced or Involuntary Disappearances, Mission to Serbia, including Kosovo*, 30th Sess, HRC Doc. A/HRC/30/38/Add.1.

UN Human Rights Council, *Report of the Working Group on Enforced or Involuntary Disappearances, Post-Sessional Report*, UN Doc. A/HRC/WGEID/112/1, 25 July 2017.

UN Human Rights Council, *Report of the Working Group on Enforced or Involuntary Disappearances*, 19th Sess, HRC Doc. A/HRC/19/58/Rev.1, 2012.

UN Human Rights Council, *Report of the Working Group on Enforced or Involuntary Disappearances*, 39th Sess. HRC Doc. A/HRC/39/46, 2018.

UN Human Rights Council, *Report of the Working Group on Enforced or Involuntary Disappearances*, 61st Sess, UN Doc. E/CN.4/2005/65.

UN Human Rights Council, *Report of the Working Group on Enforced or Involuntary Disappearances*, 28 July 2016, A/HRC/33/51.

UN Human Rights Council, *Report of the Working Group on Enforced or Involuntary Disappearances*, 30 July 2019, A/HRC/42/40 (WGEID 2019 Annual Report).

UN Human Rights Council, *Report of the Working Group on Enforced or Involuntary Disappearances*, 4 August 2014, A/HRC/27/49.

UN Human Rights Council, *Report of the Working Group on Enforced or Involuntary Disappearances*, 7 August 2020, A/HRC/45/13.

UN Human Rights Council, *Report of the Working Group on Enforced or Involuntary Disappearances*, 4 August 2021, A/HRC/48/57.

UN Human Rights Council, *Report of the Working Group on Enforced or Involuntary Disappearances on Enforced Disappearances in the Context of Migration*, 2017, 36th Sess, HRC Doc. A/HRC/36/39/Add.2.

UN Human Rights Council, *Report of the Working Group on Enforced or Involuntary Disappearances on Enforced Disappearances*, 42nd Sess. HRC Doc. A/HRC/42/40/Add.2.

UN Human Rights Council, *Report of the Working Group on Enforced or Involuntary Disappearances on Enforced Disappearances*, Visit to Kyrgyzstan, 24 August 2020, A/HRC/45/13/Add.2.

UN Human Rights Council, *Report of the Working Group on Enforced or Involuntary Disappearances on Its Mission to Pakistan*, 26 February 2013, A/HRC/22/45/Add.2.

UN Human Rights Council, *Report of the Working Group on Enforced or Involuntary Disappearances on Its Mission to Sri Lanka*, 2016, 33rd Sess, HRC Doc. A/HRC/33/51/Add.2.

UN Human Rights Council, *Report of the Working Group on Enforced or Involuntary Disappearances on Its Mission to Turkey*, 2016, 33rd Sess, HRC Doc. A/HRC/33/51/Add.1.

UN Human Rights Council, *Revised Methods of Work of the Working Group on Enforced or Involuntary Disappearances*, 7 February 2014, A/HRC/WGEID/102/2.

United Nations Support Mission in Libya (UNSMIL) and OHCHR, "'Detained and Dehumanised': Report on Human Rights Abuses against Migrants in Libya," 13 December 2016.

UN OHRCHR Press Release, *Sri Lanka: UN Experts Call for Swift Suspension of Prevention of Terrorism Act and Reform of Counter-Terrorism Law*, 2 March 2022. https://www.ohchr.org/en/press-releases/2022/03/sri-lanka-un-experts-call-swift-suspension-prevention-terrorism-act-and.

UN OHRCHR Press Release, *UN Experts Condemn Conviction of Pakistan Human Rights Defender and Minority Activist Idris Khattak*, 15 December 2021. https://www.ohchr.

org/en/press-releases/2021/12/un-experts-condemn-conviction-pakistan-human-rights-defender-and-minority.

UN OHRCHR Press Release, *UN Experts Urge Release of Rights Defenders in Egypt, Condemn Misuse of Counter-Terrorism Measures*, 1 December 2021. https://www.ohchr.org/en/press-releases/2021/12/un-experts-urge-release-rights-defenders-egypt-condemn-misuse-counter.

UN OHRCHR Press Release, *Working Group on Enforced Disappearances: The Atrocious Crime of Enforced Disappearance Continues to Happen and Takes New Shapes and Forms*, 21 September 2021. https://www.ohchr.org/en/press-releases/2021/09/working-group-enforced-disappearances-atrocious-crime-enforced-disappearance.

Van der Kroef, J.M. (1987). "Terrorism by Public Authority: The Case of the Death Squads of Indonesia and the Philippines." *Current Research on Peace and Violence*, 10(4), pp. 143–158.

Chapter 2

The curse of ambiguity
The traumatic memory of victims of enforced disappearance

Angkhana Neelapaijit

Background

My life as a professional nurse and mother of five children turned into the life of a survivor and woman human rights defender after my husband, Somchai Neelapaijit, a prominent human rights lawyer and vice chairperson of the Committee on Human Rights, Lawyers Council of Thailand, was disappeared by police officers during the night of 12 March 2004. Somchai was disappeared because of his role in the defense of victims of torture, enforced disappearance and ill-treatments in the low-intensity conflict in the Southern Border Provinces (SBPs) of Thailand, which flared up in 2004.[1] As a son of poor farmers, Somchai knew about suffering, exploitation and other social injustices. That is what inspired him to become a lawyer – to help marginalized people. Somchai had a genuine and strong belief in the justice process. On 27 February 2004, just 13 days before he was disappeared, Somchai Neelapaijit gave a speech that was, described by a journalist as a "powerful, bitter, outraged speech" (International Commission of Jurists, 2014), at a panel discussion at the Santichon (Peace People) Foundation in Bangkok. Somchai said: "I have struggled in the court for almost 20 years and the judiciary, lawyers and others have said that I am the Muslim bandits' lawyer. But I am not discouraged".

On that day Somchai had strongly criticized the Thai police and military for the alleged ill-treatment and discrimination against the Malay-Muslims people in Southern Border Provinces of Thailand. The day before his disappearance, he had referred the allegations of abuse he had received by many State agencies. As a human rights lawyer, Somchai really believed in the justice system.

My eldest daughter Sudprathana Neelapaijit, who is following her father's path, wrote in a book which was distributed in the public event to commemorate the ten years of Somchai Neelapaijit's disappearance, *When [My] Father ... Was Disappeared* (Neelapaijit, 2013). During the commemoration, she told:

> My father had a great deal of trust in justice (it seems difficult to explain why he had this degree of confidence and trust in the judicial process). He always said that the court decided whether one was right or wrong. My father did not unceasingly think that his clients were innocent. If they committed a crime,

DOI: 10.4324/9781003312642-4

then they had to be punished. But the punishment had to be one that fitted the crime, not one that exceeded the crime. Everything is a struggle in the judicial process, from the Court of First Instance to the Appeal Court and then the Supreme Court.

Based on the allegations of abuse, Somchai submitted a petition to the court to move five of his clients who were from the Malay-Muslim minority and accused of acts of terrorism, from police custody to a regular prison, so that they would not be tortured by police. His petition was rejected.

On 11 March 2004, Somchai then submitted a petition, alleging abuses to his clients by the police officers, to the Ministry of Justice, the Ministry of Interior, the Royal Thai Police, the Attorney General's Office, the National Human Rights Commission, the Prime Minister and the Office of the Senate. On 12 March, only one day later after having submitted that petition, Somchai was disappeared by five police officers and nobody has seen him since then. For some State officials, Somchai was just an enemy of the State, a rebel or a bandit lawyer who chose to help wrongdoers.

Pratubjit Neelapaijit, my second daughter, once said that:

Dad was wrongfully accused as Tanai Chon (bandit lawyer) because he provided legal assistance to suspected insurgents who were tortured by state authorities in the Deep South. Such accusations hurt him deeply. Since his disappearance dealt a heavy blow to our family, we have promised to take a good care of one another, and live lives that are useful to other people. On top of that we want to prove that Dad was not a villain. ... After my father disappeared, we had very difficult years in our family but we have to prove his innocence. We try to do our best as he taught us to be good, humble and empathic to all people.

(Neelapaijit, 2017)

On the way seeking for truth and justice

Thailand, like other countries in the region, has a decade long history of State violence and authoritarianism. In this broad political context, human rights violations often take place. Very serious human rights violations, such as extra-judicial killings, arbitrary detention, torture, enforced disappearance, threats and intimidation were documented in the country at least since the 1950s. Enforced disappearances should therefore be viewed as one manifestation of the violent methods employed by the Thai State to stamp out dissent or to eliminate suspected criminals, outside of the rule of law (Justice for Peace Foundation, 2012). The abduction of the human rights lawyer Somchai Neelapaijit occurred in the context of the national policy on anti-terrorism in the Southern Border Provinces of Thailand. In 2006, the Royal Thai government appointed the National Reconciliation Commission to investigate and reconcile the human rights violation in SBPs. One of the key findings of the

Commission was the connection between the lack of accountability in the Somchai Neelapaijit case and the lack of trust between the Malay-Muslim community and State authorities in Southern Border Provinces of Thailand;

> The violence that claimed Somchai had a direct impact on state-citizen relations. In particular, the lack of trust among the several affected ethnic minorities, who felt that there was someone who always put his faith in the state's justice process, yet even he was not safe. It goes without saying how important faith in the country's justice process is to state-citizen relations.
>
> (National Reconciliation Commission, 2006)

The disappearance of Somchai was the first and only case of enforced disappearance in Thailand which could be brought to court by the family of the disappeared. It has been described as emblematic of the challenges encountered in the attempt of achieving justice in cases of serious human rights violations in Thailand.

On 8 and 29 April 2004, the Criminal Court issued arrest warrants for five police officers for their alleged participation in robbing Somchai Neelapaijit and forcing him into a vehicle (charging them with coercion[2] and gang-robbery but not of abduction or enforced disappearance).[3]

Proceedings

Court of First Instance

The Court of First Instance handed down its verdict on 12 January 2006. It convicted the first defendant – Police Major Ngern Thongsuk – of the relatively minor charge of coercion and sentenced him to three years in prison, but released him on bail pending his appeal. The other accused were acquitted.

Appeal Court

After the verdict of the Court of First Instance, my children and I filed an appeal to the Appeal Court. Five years later, on 11 March 2011, the Appeal Court issued its decision, finding that: (a) Somchai Neelapaijit's wife and his children could not be considered joint plaintiffs[4] in the proceeding because there was insufficient evidence to prove that Somchai was seriously injured or dead so it must be himself to file the complaint to the court and the family cannot act on his behalf; (b) the conviction of Police Major Ngern Thongsuk should be overturned and; (c) with respect to the remaining four accused, there was insufficient evidence to convict them.

During the time of the appeal, the newspapers reported that Police Major Ngern Thongsuk, released on bail pending the appeal, had disappeared in a flood caused by a break in a dam in Northern Thailand.

Supreme Court

On 10 May 2011, my children and I appealed to the Supreme Court for both the decision on my family's standing as joint plaintiffs and the substantive issues in the case.

Four years and a half later, on 29 December 2015 at 9.30a.m., at the courtroom number 809 of the Bangkok Criminal Court, the Supreme Court acquitted the five police officers charged with abduction and thievery, on the basis of weak evidence that lacked verification from the proper authorities. The ruling also rejected a petition from the family to be a co-plaintiff, thus effectively setting a norm that the families of those forcibly disappeared cannot represent their loved ones. The Supreme Court further ruled that: "the facts do not demonstrate that Somchai Neelapaijit was assaulted and murdered or grievously injured and unable to represent himself".

This also meant the two appeals[5] that we wrote, respectively to the Appeal Court and to the Supreme Court, were left unexamined by the Court. These decisions denied the right of the family to be co-plaintiffs and were an explicit attack on the rights of victims of State violence to seek justice and redress.

The 2015 ruling means that there have been no damaged party, no wrongdoers, no culprits and that the family cannot access a rehabilitation process: it is just a dead-end for us. The ruling reinforces a culture of impunity whenever State officials are involved in wrongdoings. This is a major flaw in Thailand justice system, one in which State officials involved in enforced disappearances and other human rights violations can get away with the crime.

After the Supreme Court issued its verdict, one of my children wrote:

> The verdict on our father's case came out in 2015, the case ended and we had nothing left. Dad disappeared without anyone making him disappear, without any reason for him to disappear, and without knowing where he is right now. We didn't get any truth at all from the judicial process that started in 2005, for the reason that no corpse was found; his fate was not proved. It resulted in our family losing our rights as joint plaintiffs in place of Lawyer Somchai, since the verdict stated that since there was no corpse, it cannot be affirmed that Lawyer Somchai is not able to file charges himself, and there is no law stating that enforced disappearance is a criminal offense. So enforced disappearances still happen and have the chance of happening again.
>
> (Sutthichaya, 2018)

The changes in my life and family's life

If my husband had not been disappeared, I would have continued my life as an ordinary woman with barely any knowledge of law. On the contrary, my life changed, with no possibility to return to the one I had. After my husband disappeared, I had to struggle to raise my children through difficult and upsetting times while trying to figure out a way to expedite justice for the father of my children. My human rights journey continued throughout these years. I became a voice for the relatives of the disappeared and for the most marginalized in Thailand who are the victims of human rights violations.

Before the disappearance of Somchai I did not clearly understand the word "disappearance" and how it affected the life of victims and their families until I faced it myself. This tragedy made me understand how someone could "be absent forever" and destined to "vanish". The disappearance of someone does not affect only the victim's body but it totally changes the lives of their family.

In 2016, Pratubjit Neelapaijit – my second daughter and her colleagues – made a resonant argument that the crime of enforced disappearance is one that generates *"ambiguity"* which at once distinguishes it from other forms of State violence and makes it difficult to resolve. The ambiguity is a result of the inability to determine with clarity whether the person who has disappeared remains alive or is dead or whether was murdered or intended to flee (Neelapaijit & Pitukthanin, 2016). The humanity of the disappeared person is made ambiguous, the role of the perpetrators is ambiguous and the relatives of the disappeared persons face ambiguity in resolving the crime as well as in building their futures. The ambiguity due to enforced disappearance marked the history of Thailand, with all its implications of even greater degree of partiality and uncertainty than other forms of State violence (Haberkorn, 2018). The ambiguity is amplified by the legislation that does not recognize enforced disappearance as a crime in the criminal code and by the impunity that does not allow that the perpetrators of enforced disappearances can be held accountable even against the charges of far less serious crimes.

What kind of society allows people to disappear?

After Somchai disappeared, the atmosphere in our house was lonely and shrouded in fear. It's hard to describe how I felt on 12 March 2004. Since that day many close friends and relatives have been keeping at distance from our lives because of fear. It was the day that my family was called "the bandit's lawyer family". I think one could imagine the trauma and suffering that we faced. All that was left was a house where a woman and her children were left alone. For me, as a mother – the most difficult thing was, and still is, how to explain to my children what happened. How can we find the truth and justice for our loved one? How can we continue with our lives? And how can we look for a better future?

I often ask myself, what kind of society allows people to disappear without doing anything to stop this serious crime. Why do we allow it to happen again and again without any responsibility? And why impunity still remains in our country?

One year after Somchai's disappearance, I began to talk to my children about what to do next. We had the choice of either spending our lives, as other people did, accepting money and favors in exchange of our silence, or standing up and struggling for truth and justice. Choosing the latter meant the possibility of facing

Figure 2.1 Angkhana Neelapaijit in front of a series of posters, portraying her husband Somchai Neelapaijit, displayed in Bangkok on the 18th anniversary of his disappearance. Photo by A. Neelapaijit.

threats and intimidation: our lives covered with fear and insecurity and in the end with no certainty to obtain any justice or remedy for ordinary people like us. We also had to consider the possibility of being abandoned by some relatives, colleagues and friends who might be unable to cope with the threats and intimidations or just being afraid of them.

In the end, after I had explained the alternatives, all of my children agreed that we must not have allowed their father to vanish without us doing nothing. We would have not been happy in receiving any help and many offerings in exchange for the suffering and pain of our loved one … and when I was sure the children had understood, I started to think what I could do more besides fighting the case in the court of justice (Figure 2.1).

The curse of ambiguity

Desaparecido is someone who is "absent forever", whose "destiny" was to "vanish". Officially, a "desaparecido" is neither alive nor dead, neither here nor there. The explanation is at once totally vague and resoundingly final. The combination of the vague and final nature of the violence is what makes disappearance devastating to those who are left behind. The families of those who are disappeared rarely know the details of the last moments of the lives of their loved ones and are rarely able to bury them (Haberkorn, 2018).

Enforced disappearance creates "ambiguity" between "existence" and "non-existence" to all the victims involved. It affects the disappeared person through captivity, often torture and inhuman and degrading treatment and very often death and disappearance of the body. It also annihilates their "sense of self" and their reputation and the memory of them in those who survive and in the community, degrading the victim's sense of self, their human dignity and identity, directly and indirectly. This causes tremendous chaos and fear among families of the victims and inflicts a trauma on them which is much more complicated and aggravated than the one inflicted by other kinds of human rights violations. Moreover, "ambiguity" is used as a tool to conceal the truth and it made victims lose their identity and self-confidence. In many cases, the victim's memory is destroyed by the creation of new memories by the perpetrators. These often include a legislation to protect officials while victims are blamed as the wrongdoer, such as the bandit's lawyer, the "drug dealer" or the "terrorist", which is extremely degrading for victims' dignity.

Enforced disappearance may lead to extensive impacts on the victims' family physical and mental health. Such "ambiguity" makes the families constantly engrossed in excessive imagination on the disappearance and haunted by the images of their loved ones subjected to torture, inhuman and ill treatment, pains, and even of the destruction and concealment of their bodies. The families of the victims, as a result, have to live with the traumas and grossly inhuman and cruel memories that define their life perpetually.

As a family member of a disappeared person – I can say that it is hard to imagine all the implications of enforced disappearance, and how immense is their impact on the victims themselves, including their economic and cultural rights, on their social status. And this has repercussions on their family, their community and society as a whole.

I remember well the first week after my husband disappeared. We received both good and bad news interchangeably. Some days, we smiled with hope but after a while our hope vanished with tremendous fear taking its place. We were continuously exposed to contradictory feelings and thoughts, and we did not know what to hope or whom to trust.

Many families face the same situation. This continuous and sustained mental uncertainty provokes in some children aggressive behaviors or depressed personalities, some others lose their trust in other human beings becoming pessimist and dispirited.

Ambiguity stops your life at the point where your loved one was disappeared. Whatever you choose to do, it stops your life. A Karen woman I know, she was 29-year old with five children when her husband was disappeared after he was arrested by public officials, five years later she married a man in the village. Instead of supporting her, some of the villagers ridiculed the fact that she sought for her own happiness without seeking justice for her previous husband, implying a grave moral judgment on her.

This violation has a gendered-specific impact. For example, when it is a man to be disappeared, his wife is left to struggle with the economic, psychological and social distress as a result of his loss. The surviving wife may suffer the burden of not being able to support the family economically due to lack of employment opportunities for women. Such deep impact has made the daily lives of the families of the victims challenging, as they experience pressure when interacting with their society and find it difficult to reconnect with it. Many family members suffer from post-traumatic stress disorder (PTSD) as a result. Some are constantly consumed by fear and anxiety that make them lose trust in persons close to them or become pessimistic. Some children are growing up with anger and depression also because their mothers cannot explain to them the meaning of "disappearance", and how and why this happened. The truth is difficult to explain both because you do not know it and can just imagine or reconstruct it from the information you have and the facts you know, and because it is emotionally difficult and ambiguous. It is unspeakable truth.

However, for families, the right to the truth, to justice and to effective remedy is immensely important. Even though sometimes truth might make us suffer, it helps to understand what has happened and it release us from "ambiguity", while justice will restitute dignity to victims and their families.

A mother in Southern Border Provinces of Thailand said:

> They took our children alive so we want them to return alive or at least, return their bodies to us. What everyone wants is the "truth". Because of the need to know the truth, the struggle of families, especially of women, continues. But if God does not want they would not able to do anything. For, as families of the disappeared, we are bound by traumatic memories and can't look forward for a better future.
>
> (private communication)

Letter without recipient

Some families of the disappeared try to heal themselves by writing a message to their loved one – the "letter without recipient".

N.Y. is one of the wives of a disappeared person in the Southern Border Provinces of Thailand. Her husband was disappeared in 2007 when he was 31 years old and she was 27. N. said that she now turns 37 but her husband – M. – is still 31. In the letter to her husband in 2017, N. wrote:

> Dear M., you know, during the first years that you disappeared if there was an anonymous corpse appearing in our village I would go there with the hope that the nameless corpse was you. But it was not you, your body has never been found. The Muslim fortune teller told me that you are still alive but you never come back, I am still waiting for the truth with hope but there is no positive news about you. It's like there's the dark cloud obscuring my hope, my tears like it's raining in my eyes every day and my life continues slowly without light. You probably know how much I suffer. I can't sleep alone in our bedroom without you. Your clothes are still hanging in the wardrobe. Do you want to know why?

I keep all of your belonging as if you still be with us, everything stays the same even though you're not with us. If I throw them away it's like you don't exist in this world anymore. Sometime I think I'm fooling myself but I do not want to change anything about you, just only changes my life.

Suicide is a sin in Islam but sometime I want to disappear from this world, I do not want to live without you but I have to stay" – N. reminds her suffering.

(Way magazine, 2017)

Krongtham Neelapaijit – a daughter of Somchai Neelapaijit once said:

Dad, after you disappeared, you've been accused as "bandit lawyer". You may not be disappointed as you probably heard this before and I know this caused you so much pain. After you disappeared, they were very difficult years for our family but we have to prove your innocence. We try to do our best as you always taught us, humbly and with empathy for all people.

We still miss you, we are still sad when thinking of you but as the time passes, we know that we have to go on and we have to continue our lives. For some people, years may pass by quickly, but for us, time has been so slow. After you disappeared, all your belongings remained in their places -- your clothes are in the wardrobe, your books and notebooks, a desk calendar and other items on your desk -- as if they were waiting for the owner to come back, like us who are still waiting for you.

We still have hope and if we have a chance to meet you, we want to tell you that our family has a good life and we live humbly, as you wish us to do.

N.J., a 68-year-old Lahu widow, from an ethnic minority in Northern Thailand,[6] is still tormented by the unknown fate of her husband *J.J.* who was disappeared during the height of the "war on drugs" in 2003. N. never saw even a glimpse of her husband's shadow for more than a decade – and she said:

"I still have hope that one day he might return" while casting her eyes downwards, staring at a beam of light through a crack in the bamboo floor.

(Areerat & Kummetha, 2015)

Between the lines

After the 2015 verdict, my family faced even more ambiguity. The judicial system did not reply to our questions: where is Somchai? Is he alive or dead? Who made him disappeared? Who is the perpetrator or is there no perpetrator?

In 2016, one year after the Supreme Court emitted its verdict, the Department of Special Investigation (DSI) sent me an official letter informing that the Special Investigation Committee resolved to suspend the investigation into Somchai's case because "no culprits could be found", thus putting an end to almost 12 years of judicial proceedings without truth and justice: 12 years of our loss and pain.

On one fine day I privately talked to a member of the DSI, whom I trusted, and asked about the disappearance of my husband as I wanted to know the truth, just and only truth, no official documents. The story I heard was that after Somchai was pushed into the perpetrators' car, he was brought to a secret detention center, he was tortured, seriously tortured until he died. His body was brought to a province near Bangkok on that night, they burned him in a 200-liter barrel and threw the fragments of his bones into the Meklong river, in Ratchaburi province, about 100 kilometers from Bangkok, nearby. Everything was finished before dawn, nothing remained and Somchai was completely disappeared.

I decided to tell my children what had happened to their father although I understand how traumatizing and heartbreaking it was for the children, but it is the truth that we have to accept. Yes, it's really painful and heartbreaking, but it releases us from the ambiguity that we have faced for more than a decade.

It's difficult to convey how traumatic the experience can be to bear witness to the fact that a person who did so much for so many people is not even remembered with a gravestone where his descendants can hold a service in his memory.

Pratubjit Neelapaijit once said in a public discussion on enforced disappearance in Thailand:

> For survivors of enforced disappearance, the best remedy is to be confronted with the truth. Once, an officer at DSI replied to an inquiry made by my mom about the fate of my dad that: after my father was shoved into the car, he was brought to a safe house near the Crime Suppression Division. There, he was tortured to death. Then, his body was burned and the ashes were scattered in the Meklong River. Upon arriving home, my mom shared the story with us. We started to cry and asked how she felt about that. She said we had to thank them for telling us how our father had died. The most important thing is to know the truth. Before this, we had different phantasies as to how our dad would have been. Eventually, we heard that he was tortured to death and we at last knew who were involved.
>
> (Sayuntrakul, 2013)

For me, if the Meklong River was the last place where Somchai's body was buried, there could be many other lives which had been shed unjustly and buried in various other rivers, too. The question of how many disappearances occurred in Thailand, and how we can stop this crime against humanity from happening should not challenge all those in power?

Traumatic memory

No one knows how traumatized a family can be because of an enforced disappearance, except those who suffered from it. This crime does not only harm the integrity of the victim's body, identity and reputation, but it also affects their families. Families often experience difficulties because of their inability to connect to and find support in their communities, society and culture at large and they also suffer violations of their economic rights. Most families have to live in constant fear, threatened and intimidated. Many children refuse to go to school to avoid criticism or questions from teachers and friends about the disappearance of their loved ones, some of them, in addition to adult family members, shows long-term symptoms of PTSD in addition to anger, fear and paranoia.

Most children often have nightmares while their mother faces serious stress and re-traumatization by narratives of grievances. In addition, the ambiguity of enforced disappearance induces victims to imagine the disappearance with images of torture, abuse, destruction or disguise of dead bodies which greatly affect the mental health of families. Family members still suffer, even after many years have passed from the disappearance, some of them relegate themselves in the shadow of a lifelong traumatizing memory. This makes the nature of enforced disappearance more complex than other forms of human rights violations.

The confrontation with government officials seriously scares the families, especially women and children, because they have power, weapons, guns, the authority to imprison and some of them are not afraid to use all of these means against those who dare to confront them with their responsibilities and hold them accountable. However, the families' ultimate fear can turn into the courage to face everything fearlessly. And people have recorded their own story in order to preserve memories that cannot be erased by any power. As long as those stories remain written, the memory of victims will be preserved and they will be remembered and mourned forever. For victims, these memories are part of the healing process from their mental suffering. If remembering is healing, most of the victims fear that over time they might forget what happened. For this reason, generally, these memories, though bitter, heartbreaking and defeated, will be passed down from generations to generations, in order to prevent that this crime against humanity might be perpetrated again in the future – *Never again.*

For the victim's family, the external wounds may fade with the passing of time but the inner traumatic wounds and scars in their hearts and minds cannot easily be cancelled or healed. Because of these wounds, some families still continue their struggle for truth and justice not only for their loved one but for all the disappeared persons. That traumatic experience motivates them, or better us, to fight against any injustice.

Some State officials may have thought that the problem would have disappeared by disappearing its messenger. That is a grave error in judgment. While the messenger disappeared, his disappearance triggered a tidal wave ripping through the deepest levels of our community and society. It unleashed a movement that has changed the political landscape of a country where horrendous human rights abuses are no longer ignored and violators can no longer hide. Cries for truth and justice are resounding loudly and clearly from the local to the global level.

The story of the family of a disappeared person may sound traumatizing, hopeless, despairing, and distressing but that is the truth and, and however horrible or frightening, we cannot close our eyes in the face of it. It casts a shadow on society, but to learn and to remember the stories of the disappeared is the way to preserve the truth and to preserve the possibility to change that society.

It is a memory that we want to keep to remind ourselves and those around us and to tell the perpetrators that we are not afraid and life can be healed and repaired for us, the so-called victims, to become strong again by ourselves, sooner or later.

Many times, I have wondered is it worth for us to trade everything we have just for the sake of justice which, until the end of my life, I may not have a chance to reach. What keeps me working today is the love, the encouragement, the kindness, the friendship, the caring concern from all friends and colleagues near and far, especially the courage, the sacrifice, the patience and the love of all children. These things strengthened my heart to endure adversity and to continue the struggle.

Last but not least, I would like to thank all those colleagues and friends who are always beside me. My special thanks to the United Nations Working Group on Enforced or Involuntary Disappearances (WGEID) that continues to pursue further information until the fate of the disappeared persons is known. I remember very well when I first met the WGEID during its 75th session held in Bangkok in June 2005 when it took on Somchai Neelapaijit's case and later a lot of other cases of enforced disappearance in Thailand.

My whole heartedly thank you goes to my family and relatives of all the disappeared who inspire me to continue my struggle to stop enforced disappearance and to find truth for all families. I wish to encourage all relatives of the disappeared to continue their struggle until we find truth and justice and end impunity.

I salute all victims' families for their hard work: these extraordinary people in their courage, determination and commitment, they serve as evidence that every one of us can make a difference to stand for what is right and just. It is this, ultimately, that represents the hope of a country that was buried in the silence of the past years.

If the pursuit of justice was a road, then my family and I would be almost at the end of it. We faced numerous obstacles and hardships over the past 19 years that have blocked us from reaching truth and justice. Even though to me the evidence in Somchai's case is more than enough and so clear that I can see the faces of the culprits, it was not enough to obtain justice and sometime I feel that all I have done was useless.

For myself, for the rest of my life, even if I may lose or I may not be able to find truth from a court, I would say that I have done my best. And no matter how the story of Somchai Neelapaijit's disappearance ends, I believe that one day the truth will be revealed, the offenders will have nowhere to hide and justice will be restored. This culture of impunity needs to be stopped. Not just for me, or for my family, but for hundreds of others who have suffered similar injustices.

I believe that no one is too small to live with honor and dignity. I also believe that even if the wounds in our hearts are invisible and intangible, they do tell us all stories of trauma, pains and so many injustices inflicted on us all. And owing to the wounds, we shall fight for justice and I believe that in the midst of losses and pains, through the course of our fight, we have woven our fabric of friendship, solidarity and mutual sympathy, something that will certainly last and be inerasable over the time.

This chapter is a testimony of the courage that ordinary people and women have. Ultimately, the story of Somchai Neelapaijit and of the victims of enforced disappearance in Thailand, and worldwide, while it is not unique, had an extraordinary impact and changed the life of many women and families of an entire nation.

Notes

1 The SBPs of Thailand are Yala, Pattani and Narathiwat provinces, and its near Thai-Malaysia border where the majority of people are Malay Muslim people.
2 Section 309 of the Thai Criminal Code B.E. 2551 (2009): "Whoever, compels the other person to do or not to do any act, or to suffer any thing by putting him in fear of injury to life, body, liberty, reputation of property of him or another person, or commits violence so that he does or does not do such act, or suffers such thing, shall be punished with imprisonment not exceeding three years of fined not exceeding six thousand Baht, or both" (Official translation).
3 Section 340 of the Thai Criminal Code B.E. 2551 (2009): "Whoever with three persons upwards participate in committing robbery, such persons are said as offenders of gang-robbery and shall be punished with imprisonment of ten years to fifteen years and fined of twenty thousand to thirty thousand Baht" (Official translation). [As Thailand has no "Enforced Disappearance Act" so the crime of enforced disappearance did not exist in the Criminal Code of Thailand, therefore it would have not been possible to charge the defendants of enforced disappearance.]
4 The family's co-plaintiffs are the wife and the four daughters of Somchai Neelapaijit (Angkhana Neelapaijit, Sudpratna Neelapaijit, Pratubjit Neelapaijit, Khobkusol Neelapaijit and Krongtham Neelapaijit). Somchai's youngest son cannot be the co-plaintiffs as he's under 18-year-old.
5 The appeal to the Appeal Court and Supreme Court.
6 State authorities believe that the border districts are part of a drug trafficking route from Wa State in Myanmar and that some hill tribe people are involved. According to Lahu Association President Sila Jahae (Mr.), more than 20 Lahu people were victims of enforced disappearance at the hands of army rangers and police officers. The Lahu people, mostly living in districts bordering Myanmar in Chiang Rai and Chiang Mai provinces, have been living in a climate of fear since the Thaksin Shinawatra administration announced the War on Drug policy in 2003.

References

Areerat, K. & Kummetha, K. (2015) Rubbing Salt on Open Wounds: Enforced Disappearance, Torture and Discrimination among the Lahu People. *Prachatai.* Available from: https://prachatai.com/english/node/5488 [Accessed 23th September 2015].

Haberkorn, T. (2018) *In Plain Sight: Impunity and Human Rights in Thailand.* Madison: The University of Wisconsin Press.

International Commission of Jurists. (2014) *Ten Years Without Truth: Somchai Neelapaijit and Enforced Disappearances in Thailand.* Available from: www.icj.org/wp-content/uploads/2014/03/Ten-Years-Without-Truth-Somchai-Neelapaijit-and-Enforced-Disappearances-in-Thailand-report-2014.pdf [Accessed 12th March 2014].

Justice for Peace Foundation. (2012) *Enforced Disappearance in Thailand.* Bangkok: Justice for Peace Foundation Report.

National Reconciliation Commission. (2006) *Overcoming Violence through the Power of Reconciliation, Prognosis of Violent Phenomenon*. National Reconciliation Commission Report, 45–46.

Neelapaijit, A. (2013) *Ten Years on, Somchai's Family Refuses to Give Up*. Available from: www.bangkokpost.com/opinion/opinion/387221/ten-years-on-somchai-family-refuses-to-give-up [Accessed 30th December 2013].

Neelapaijit, P. (2017) Memory of Pratubjit: Letter without Recipient. *Way Magazine*. Available from: https://waymagazine.org/forced_disappearance03/ [Accessed 30th December 2013].

Neelapaijit, P. & Pitukthanin, A. (2016) Enforced Disappearance and the Implications of Ambiguity. In *Nonviolence Space Thailand and Future: Knowledge, Secrecy, and Memories*, Chaiwat Satha-Anand (eds.), 1st ed., p. 29 Bangkok: House of Commons (PROTESTISTA).

Sayuntrakul, R. (2013) Pratubjit Neelapaijit: Enforced Disappearance in Thailand. *Isaranews Agency*. Available from: https://www.isranews.org/content-page/item/22442-1-sp-534.html [Accessed 20th July 2017].

Sutthichaya, Y. (2018) *Pratubjit Neelapaijit: Enforced Disappearance Still a Void, Human Rights at the Discretion of the State*. Available from: https://prachatai.com/english/node/7670 [Accessed 15th March 2018].

Way Magazine. (2017) Memory of Pratubjit: Letter without Recipient: Nureeya. *Way Magazine*. Available from: https://waymagazine.org/forced_disappearance-01/ [Accessed 28th August 2017].

Chapter 3

Mourning the disappeared

A personal account

Andrea Paula Bleichmar

This essay is my contribution to the literature on mourning the disappeared. I will relate my personal experience and describe the process that helped me mourn a specific type of loss: the loss of my mother, who was a victim of enforced disappearance in Argentina during the last military dictatorship. She is one of 30,000 Argentineans who became known by the euphemism of "the disappeared." People do not just disappear. The State made her disappear from her own life, from the lives of people she loved, and from the lives of people who loved her.

The acknowledgment, by the Argentinean government, of the crimes committed by the State, helped me, as Marion Oliner (2006) writes, to "relocate past events into the external world from which they originated" (p. 883). The recognition that something horrendous truly happened and that I could memorialize my mother's life by installing a plaque in front of our home also helped me in the lifelong process of disentangling myself from the complex feelings that mourning of this type entails.

My mother, Rosa Mitnik, disappeared in Argentina on November 13, 1976. During the military dictatorship in power from 1976 to 1983, enforced disappearance was a mechanism of State terrorism to instill widespread fear within society. The military established a national underground network of torture centers where those who were disappeared were secretly detained, tortured, subsequently killed, and their bodies disposed of – either dumped into mass graves or hurled out of airplanes into the river Rio de la Plata to conceal the State crime. The disappeared came from all walks of life: students, factory workers, journalists, farmers, lawyers, artists; my mother was a psychoanalyst.

Before I continue, a disclaimer: I will not describe horrifying details. I have chosen not to describe those details because I am hoping to create an atmosphere where you can read, and feel, and think, without being apprehensive that, at any moment, you will read words that would horrify you to the point of getting in the way of your being able to think, feel, and calmly read. There is a difference, I think, between being moved, even upset by a story, and being startled in a way that makes thinking and feeling impossible because of the violence of the story. I am protecting you and protecting myself from the impact that learning the facts had on me. I don't want, and I don't think that it is necessary, to experience – you the reader and I – moments of breakdown in thinking because of the brutality of a story.

DOI: 10.4324/9781003312642-5

I was 15 years old when my mother disappeared in November 1976. My parents were divorced; I was my mother's only child and I had always lived with her, while seeing my father on a weekly basis.

At the end of 1975, because of the violence and financial instability of the months before the military coup, my father had decided to leave Argentina together with his wife and my two half-siblings. I did not want to leave. I had my friends, my school, my boyfriend, my home, and my mother. At the time, I was a sophomore at the *Colegio Nacional de Buenos Aires*, a public-exam high school with a long tradition of student political engagement, and my parents feared for my safety. When I finally agreed to leave, my father cried with emotion. My mother, who had also encouraged me to leave, started preparing and packing what she felt I could need abroad and away from her. So, there I was, on February 27, 1976, less than a month before the military coup, flying to Caracas with a suitcase containing three big bottles of Revlon shampoo, beautiful new clothes, and my mother's approval, which meant so much over the years in dealing with my guilt for having left.

We left Buenos Aires in February 1976. The military came to power on March 24. Five months after we left, four close friends from my high school disappeared. Then, in November, my mother became a victim of enforced disappearance herself.

In exile in Mexico, my aunt had learned of my mother's forced disappearance from the Argentinean newspaper *La Opinión* and called my father. Wanting to wait for more information and probably finding it heart-wrenching to give me the news, he did not tell me at the time. Nevertheless, I learned the news three weeks later because my mother's brother called my father to tell him that he was unable to find any information about my mother from the sources he had searched: the police, hospitals, or morgues. I was around, I heard it was my uncle. I asked what was happening, and I understood that my mother was in jail as a political prisoner. The figure of a political prisoner was familiar to me because, at 15, my family and I had mostly lived through military regimes, and we always knew of somebody who was a political prisoner.

I soon learned some details: my mother's friend, Silvia, also an analyst, had called from another province, where she was living, and asked my mother for help. Silvia's daughter, Irene, who belonged to the *Montoneros* guerrilla group fighting the military government, was in danger. Some of Irene's comrades had disappeared, and Silvia feared for her daughter's life. She asked my mother to hide Irene and Irene's eight-month-old baby. In a horrendous sequence of events, Irene and my mother disappeared. The baby was not taken. That was the narrative I had from age 15; it was what her friend Silvia told me at a dinner party in Caracas, where she came after my mother and her daughter had disappeared. I do not remember how I transitioned from thinking that she was in prison to learning about, and somehow making sense of, the concept of "disappeared." I don't remember either when I stopped waiting for news of her and, instead, started thinking that she was dead. Today, I do not have more information about what specifically happened to her, but some of what I did learn, I learned in the company of others who acted as witnesses. These witnesses provided a new holding space, a container that allowed me to create a psychic space within myself where I could mourn my mother. Dori Laub (2012) says:

> The new holding space is found within oneself in the presence of an intimate, listening other. This other is able to be present internally, along with representations of family and community. In this space, the process evolves and progressively deepens. There is a subject who holds it and a direction in which to proceed; at the same time, it is directed to an "other" – a listener inside oneself and also in one's immediate proximity.
>
> (p. 74)

Also, I learned what happened to her from official sources that confirmed an element of reality that I hadn't had until then. Friends, my aunt, uncle, and cousins, human rights organizations, and the acknowledgment of the democratic government of Argentina were the witnesses that, with their dedication and authority, allowed me to move forward in this never-ending-always-a-work-in-process of mourning. I will come back to this.

Over the years and with my aunt's love and encouragement, my father and I were able to have conversations on how difficult it was for him to talk about my mother's disappearance and of loss in general. Yet, for me, it was different. I had a wider and richer emotional range. I had the capacity to experience loss and to fully go through a process of mourning without submitting to the trauma. What was helpful was to see my family limitations in an historical context. When I presented a version of this chapter at the 2015 annual meeting of the International Psychoanalytic Association, my father, also an analyst, was in the audience. At one point during my reading, he started crying, sobbing really. I stopped and offered him water. When the presentation ended, we left the building and we took a taxi back home. We were in silence for a long time when he finally said:

> "Now I know why my father never talked about Lithuania." My grandfather had come to Argentina during the pogroms at the age of fifteen. He had left his mother in Lithuania and never again knew what had happened to her. I wish my father had been able to work through the demons of my grandfather's truncated mourning, but we are all part of a traumatic history, my father and I included.

In December 1979, when I was 18, and almost four years after we left Argentina, I moved to Paris for undergraduate and post graduate school. Up to that point, it was difficult for me to talk about my mother; very few people around me knew what had happened to her. I was not purposely hiding something from them; what had happened to my mother, and hence, to me, was just un-sharable. During my first year in Paris, at a medical appointment, a Parisian doctor asked for my family medical history. I replied that my mother had died young in a car crash. I was aware I was not telling the truth, but I was not aware of how quickly, and automatically, I was assuming that it was too long, too much, too impossible to explain that, no, my mother had not died of a medical illness that could statistically predict if I would get that illness. It seemed apparent to me that the way she had died and how I felt about it was not possible to describe. I was constantly discarding the possibility that what had happened could be comprehended by other mortals.

In Paris in the early 1980s, there was a large community of people from South America who had escaped the military regimes. I had an ambivalent relationship with that group. I felt understood when I was with them, but I also felt that I did not belong, that they had suffered much more than I had, and that little of what had happened to them had a relationship to me. I could not, at first, let myself feel that if I was in Paris at that moment, and if most of my new friends had those light-blue refugee passports that the United Nations had given them, it was because something real and terrible had happened – to me, as well as to my friends. When I finally started to feel and accept this reality, the validation and sharing of experiences allowed me to start feeling my mother's death with what at the time felt like interminable sorrow. Today, I am grateful I had the capacity to experience those feelings because, as Dori Laub (2012) writes:

> *[T]he price we pay for the denial of one's past by far exceeds the price of mourning.*
> (p. 576)

In this group, I met Daniel. He was a refugee whose father and sister had disappeared in Argentina. He was 22, and I was 19. I liked him a lot, and I liked his commitment to doing more than just surviving, and, through the next four years, we stayed engaged with life and with each other. I also became close to Daniel's mother and Gabriel, his younger brother. The four of us became each other's witnesses and developed into a sort of community, in the way Anna Ornstein (2010) describes Holocaust survivors staying together after the war. She states that they

> develop special bonds and provide each other what at first they most need: not help in mourning and remembering, but help in creating a community that supports their efforts to pick up the threads of their disrupted lives.
> (p. 643)

The experience of alienation and isolation that I had felt until then started to subside, at least a little. Daniel, his family, the community of South American friends, and my Parisian friends had become the empathic other, the witness and the community that I needed next to me to start mourning.

When democracy came back to Argentina in 1983, I was 22. Three years later, I was ready to go back to Buenos Aires for the first time. My mother was not going to be there. Did the city of Buenos Aires still exist, or had it too disappeared? Were the streets and coffee places still there? The whole project felt dream-like.

I had organized my plans to stay in Buenos Aires for two months. I lived with my two cousins who had come back to Buenos Aires from their exile in Mexico to start college. My dear aunt and uncle stayed back in Mexico, but they would join my cousins soon. My cousins and I lived under the care of our grandmother. At night we all watched T V snuggled in a big bed while eating Dulce de Leche with soup spoons. This sweet milk has the consistency of peanut butter, but – and I am biased – it tastes much better. Back then, you could buy Dulce de Leche only in Argentina. It represented Argentina and childhood; people traveling to Caracas, Madrid, or Mexico City brought it as a precious gift to their friends and families in exile. Ten years ago, when I learned more details about my mother's disappearance, I learned that the neighbors who hid the baby, Silvia's grandson, while the military command was looking for his mother, kept giving the baby Dulce de Leche to keep him silent. Like mother's milk, that sweet milk helped all of us.

After that first trip to Argentina in 1986, I went back to Paris to finish my studies. I was engaged to Martin, whom I had met the previous year, and we planned to get married in Madrid, where my father and the rest of the family had moved in 1984. Martin was American, Jewish, and 20 years my senior. His father, together with Martin's grandparents, had come to the United States from Berlin in 1933. While his parents were working, he was raised by his German grandmother, who was mourning the loss of her two daughters who had stayed back in Berlin and were killed by the Nazis. Martin always understood loss, mourning, and recovery from it; his *grossmutter* Sophie was a vital woman actively engaged in the community and the family business. Martin remembers her with love and gratitude. Martin and I got married and I moved to Boston. We had a child, I went back to school for my doctoral degree, and I started my first analysis. I also had kept my apartment in Paris, which allowed me to go back again and again to a place that had become familiar and dear to me, which contributed to a smooth transition to my life in Boston.

Later on, Martin and I got divorced but we remained close friends. Over the years, I remarried and had a second child. I had the opportunity of a second analysis, this time with a woman who had come from Germany before the war. I feel grateful to her. In fact, the first letter I wrote to Argentina to start the process of knowing what happened to my mother I sent from my laptop, in her office.

In the spring of 2011, I turned 50. A childhood friend contacted me through Facebook to congratulate me. He knew about my mother's disappearance and asked me if I knew what exactly had happened to her. I said that I had some information and that what I knew was enough for me. What I knew had an eerie phantasmagoric quality that made me run away from it. That sinister feeling is still present when I imagine how things happened. However, I now know that the more I learn, or do, concerning her disappearance, the easier I find it to live with the wound.

My childhood friend described in detail what had been happening with human rights in Argentina since 2003. Democracy had returned to Argentina in 1983, but only recently, since 2003, was a democratically elected president, Néstor Kirchner, willing and able to bring justice and confront the military structure. The recognition by the Argentinean government of the violations of human rights that the military dictators had perpetrated represented for me the opposite of the feeling of helplessness. It encouraged me to get out of the internal sphere that over the years I had maintained to deal with my mother's disappearance and death and put what had been done to her into a broader social and political context.

With my analyst and friend's help, I contacted the *Equipo Argentino de Antropología Forense* (EAAF, Argentine Forensic Anthropology Team). The EAAF was created in the mid-1980s by the American anthropologist Dr. Clyde Snow. The organization investigates human rights violations by applying forensic and archaeological methods. In August 2011, I met twice with a member of this organization. The first meeting with the team was at the Consulate General of Argentina in New York to meet with the forensic anthropologist Mercedes Doretti. I traveled from Boston to New York with Martin. Although Martin and I had been divorced for many years, he had always been present with anything related to the mourning of the loss of my mother. The goal of the appointment was to give the forensic anthropologist a DNA sample and to tell the team what I knew about the circumstances of my mother's disappearance. The DNA sample was used to see if there was a match with any of the remains of disappeared people that had been found over the years. There was no match. However, by telling the group what I knew about the disappearance, they were able to put together some new information with what they already had, and from there reconstruct the facts, as much as they could. They said they would consult with the team in Buenos Aires to put all the facts in order, and we agreed that we would meet the following week for the debriefing.

Five days later, Martin and I went back to New York, this time with Seth, our then 22-old son. The report they gave us had more details than the ones we already had, some of them intolerable to hear. At some points, I asked them to pause before going on. I was for moments overwhelmed, dissociated, and I could not follow all the information. I was protecting myself, protecting my son, protecting myself by protecting my son, and trying to make sense of what they were saying and of what was happening. For us, just the practical act of mobilizing our family to meet with the forensic anthropologists and finally being able to read, together, official documents about my mother's disappearance and to have a reconstruction, a narrative to the sequence of horrific events, was an act of truth. For our family, this second meeting was charged with reparatory meaning and healing. The presence of Martin, my son's father, and the members of the forensic team provided me with the necessary witnesses that Dori Laub had written about. Those were whom I needed to have a narrative built with objective facts – a narrative that I could assimilate. The narrative still has many questions: How exactly did she die, and when? But this was a new opportunity to continue to transform what was unspeakable some years earlier at the doctor's office in Paris, into a symbolized reality that could be shared with others. It is in this sharing of a narrative that part of the never-ending healing happens. Dori Laub (2013) writes:

> Re-externalization of the event can occur and take effect only when one can articulate and transmit the story, literally transfer it to another outside oneself and then take it back again, inside.
>
> (p. 576)

I wish my father had had the same opportunity my son and I had: to meet in a holding environment to talk about Lithuania with his father, my grandfather, about my grandfather's mother, whom he had left behind at the age of 15. I also feel responsible to make this mourning different for my children, and I hope that by working through the mourning of my mother, I will help my two boys not to have a ubiquitously present, unknown, and unsymbolized void in lieu of their grandmother.

Soon after meeting with the EAAF, I started corresponding with other families of the disappeared. I learned that since 2006, some families of the disappeared had been installing *Baldosas*, plaques in the streets in their honor. The *Baldosas* are the equivalent of the European *Stolpersteine*, which are cobblestone-sized memorials installed on the ground, with a bronze top on which is written the name and basic information about the persons taken from their homes, brought to concentration camps and killed during the Holocaust. The *Stolpersteine* in Europe are small, discreet, and identical, but this is South America. Our *Baldosas* are 20-by-16-inch mosaics made from colorful little stones, and the families participate in decorating them. A friend who had installed a plaque for her brother said, "I needed to put him somewhere so he would stop being everywhere." I needed to do the same.

There is a reason for cemeteries and a wisdom in religious rituals for death. Faced with their impotence and lack of control over death, people put their loved ones where they want to locate them. I wanted the sense of agency that comes with all that: a physical, concrete place that represented my feelings and where I could symbolically localize my mother. I wanted to do it in the presence of people. With that purpose, I contacted *Barrios x Memoria y Justicia* (Neighborhoods for Memory and Justice), an organization that makes and coordinates the installation of the plaques. The organization does more than help the families build the plaques. They also collect and prepare a file with the information about the disappearance, testimonies, and biographical information of the disappeared. Their goal is to bring the memory of the disappeared back to the neighborhoods where the person lived, worked, or studied and, by doing that, helping to make it tangible and part of the community's memory. I worked with them for almost a year, planning every detail of the ceremony.

The actual making of the plaque happens a month before the installation, so the plaque can solidify and go through some treatment with varnishes. With the help of two friends, I designed the plaque in Boston. We made an actual-size maquette of the plaque and arranged the colorful stones according to our design; we took pictures and sent them to my family in Buenos Aires. I FedExed the colorful stones

Figure 3.1 The Baldosa commemorating Rosa Mitnik, placed outside her home and practice, decorated with flowers on the day of its inauguration. Photo by A. Bleichmar

in little envelopes that were marked by areas: upper right corner, top left, etc. Along the top center, the plaque design has two little blue stones representing my eyes, and on the sides, two little blue and two little green stones representing my children's eyes. With the addition of those eyes on the plaque, I became symbolically able to see what was until then unbearable to see and to bear witness to my own mourning process.

During the actual making of the plaque, I followed through Skype how my cousins and a neighbor, together with members of the organization, prepared the mix and made and decorated the plaque. I corresponded with my friends and my mother's friends and colleagues, letting them know about the ceremony for the installation of the plaque. During those months, I was convinced something would go wrong and that all this work was going to be in vain. I could not even fantasize that something related to my mother's disappearance would go well, that I could have some control over an event I had always felt powerless over.

Finally, in August 2014, we traveled to Buenos Aires for the ceremony. I had decided to place the *Baldosa* at the entrance to the building where I had grown up with my mother. She had a home office, so this was also the place where she saw her patients. Many people attended the ceremony: my father, many of my mother's friends and family, one of her former patients, some of my classmates from nursery school to high school, my fifth-grade teacher, my childhood analyst, many neighbors, and Daniel, who came from Uruguay for the day. I made the installation of the plaque coincide with the annual meeting of the Latin American Psychoanalytic Federation. Doing that allowed some of my mother's colleagues who had stayed abroad after going into exile in the 1970s, but who were planning to come to the conference, to participate in the ceremony. I also wanted to be sure that my father, with his clumsy, enraging, endearing, and well-known difficulty dealing with mourning, would be in Buenos Aires with me.

By an uncanny coincidence, the day I installed the plaque was the Catholic celebration of Santa Rosa, my mother's name, as well as International Day of the Victims of Enforced Disappearances. Daniel, who was the editor of the journal *Brecha* of Montevideo, told a colleague about the ceremony. The article that appeared in the paper commemorating those who had disappeared described the ceremony for my mother and said: "*Rosa volvió a su barrio para ya no irse más*" ("Rosa came back to her neighborhood never to leave again")

At the installation of the plaque, I spoke about my mother and the meaning of the ceremony for us and for our country. I explained why I was wearing a beautiful, colorful jacket: it represented vitality and the capacity to enjoy the pleasures of life, traits that had characterized my mother and that I know she wanted to pass on to me. I expressed my thanks for the many years of work and the help of most of those who were present that day. I specifically thanked a friend of my mother who had told me, years before, that after I had left Argentina, my mother spoke with gratitude about my father for having taken me out of danger, and, although she missed me, she was happy for the opportunity I had to spend time close to my father in Venezuela. I thanked my mother's friend for that conversation, which recurred again and again in my two analyses while I was trying to disentangle myself from the power of my conflicting loyalties and identifications with my mother and my father. My mother had given me permission and encouraged me to leave, and by that act, she dreamt for me and gave me a life for a second time.

To every participant at the ceremony, I handed out colored stones like those found on the plaque. At the ceremony, and with the installation of the plaque, we had created a memorial – a memorial that, as Jeanne Wolff Bernstein (2000) writes, creates a space in which "the past is not simply remembered but is instead actively mourned" (p. 347).

After ten days in Buenos Aires, I felt torn apart when leaving the city. By installing the plaque, I had put "my mother" in this city, and now I had to leave "her" there. It was difficult – but possible – to leave her there, to separate from what was now symbolized as her and her destiny. My mother had stopped being omnipresent everywhere. Marion Oliner (2006) captures this sentiment by saying:

Externalization, through memorialization, facilitates the use of objects in external reality to limit fantasies that, despite a person's knowledge of historic facts, dominate his or her unconscious mental life.

(p. 884)

In April 2015, I was called to give testimony in the trial regarding the *Escuela Mecánica de la Armada*, E.S.M.A., the detention center where my mother had been seen by a survivor. The trial had been in process for three years, and thousands of people had already given testimony. The judges gave me the choice to do it by Skype, but, since so many of the acts of mourning my mother were symbolic, I wanted to immerse myself in the real experience and be there. Even though giving testimony was in itself a symbolic act of remembrance, I wanted, at least, to do it in person. I traveled to Buenos Aires, prepared the testimony with the prosecutor, and spoke in court. During my deposition at the trial, the judges were interested in what I knew about my mother's disappearance and also in knowing about my mother as a person. They were now recognizing her as an individual; she was not just part of the 30,000 disappeared. That humanization of her took me by surprise, but I had clearly gone to the court to bring her "to life" as much as possible. I had brought pictures with me. I asked the court to project pictures of my mother and of both of us at birthday parties that she loved to organize for me. I also asked them to show pictures of my children since those were the grandchildren my mother never met. I spoke about my mother as a mother and about her commitment to social justice and making mental health available to all sectors of Argentinean society.

The official documentation of her disappearance was one more step towards healing, but the act of talking about what had happened in front of that audience felt movie-like. It was probably the only mind state in which I could do it: to feel like I was acting in a movie and that the audience that came to the court to hear the trial was watching a crime T V show. When we were leaving the court, I said to my uncle, "What we just did is unreal; to talk about the things we described here today is unreal!" And he responded, "It is not unreal; it's an excess of reality."

Four years later, in that same court, the same judges read the sentences to the assassins. Thanks to the thousands of people who testified at the trial, there was recognition of what had happened and, finally, accountability for the atrocities the State had committed.

After that trip to give testimony, I came back to Boston. I felt, for the first time in all these years, that I could be the same person in both places and in any place, for that matter: the same person whether I am speaking Spanish, or French, or English. I thought: Buenos Aires is not as far away as it used to be. Thomas Ogden (2000) writes:

> Successful mourning centrally involves a demand that we make on ourselves to create something – whether it be a memory, a dream, a story, a poem, a response to a poem – that begins to meet, to be equal to, the full complexity of our relationship to what has been lost and to the experience of loss itself. Paradoxically, in this process, we are enlivened by the experience of loss and death, even when what is given up or is taken from us is an aspect of ourselves.
>
> (p. 65)

I understand Ogden's writing as a description of the many valid ways, the vast range of options, that those who are bereaved have available to navigate the mourning process. All options are valid when they allow for the continuity of remembrance but, also and foremost, for the presence of curiosity, enjoyment in life, and an engagement in a creative process. This process of mourning also allows us to recapture ourselves, but, this time, ourselves minus who we were with the person we lost. This me – minus my mother and who I was with her – is not an impoverished me. I will always feel nostalgia for her, and I'm also enriched by the process I have gone through in order to mourn her. My being has expanded in my capacity to feel the pain of loss and hence to delight in the joys of life.

Afterword

November 13, 2021, was the 45th anniversary of my mother's disappearance. In the past, and for many years, I had placed a remembrance note in a Buenos Aires paper to mark the day. Many families of the disappeared do this, and the newspaper offers the space free of charge. What I did for the 45th anniversary was to post a note on the Facebook page of the neighborhood where I grew up and where the plaque is installed. I posted a note specifically for the neighbors. My Facebook's posting had a picture of the plaque and a description of how and why my mother disappeared: hiding her daughter and the grandson of one of her friends. I also wrote that she had been a loving mother and I asked people to stop by the plaque for a minute in her memory. In less than 48 hours, I had 1,000 "likes," 300 "comments," and people were sharing my post on their own Facebook pages. The majority of the comments were customary sayings that human rights organizations have used over the years: "*presente*," "*nunca más*," and "*memoria y justicia*" ("present," "never again," and "memory and justice"). This speaks about the profound work done by the Argentinean human rights organizations over the years to keep the memory of the disappeared alive. Many comments were personal feelings expressed by neighbors, people whom I had never met: "Andrea, we'll never forget your mother." "Andrea, I have a store across the street, and I remember when the plaque was installed. I always keep an eye on it." "I'm a doorman, I work one block away. I'll make sure it's always clean. I'll also tell other colleagues to watch for it." Not unusual in Buenos Aires, a neighbor told her analyst about the Facebook posting, and the analyst replied by saying that my mother had been her analyst.

After some hours, neighbors started posting pictures of themselves with the plaque, or pictures of the plaque with flowers that they had brought, or pictures of the plaque with some stones on top as is the Jewish tradition on a gravestone. Only two people wrote defamatory posts. They both wrote about what had happened in the 1970s as a "war" between two "armies" that were equally at fault, the theory of the "two demons." The group became infuriated with them, responding with detailed historical and political explanations of why what they were saying was inaccurate. Others condemned them for being "offensive" and "disrespectful": "Andrea is doing a tribute to her mother, and it is what we are all doing here! If you don't like it, have the courtesy to stay in silence!" "This *señora* lost her mother during one of the worst periods in our country! It's a duty for all of us to stand in solidarity with the families of the disappeared."

References

Bernstein, J. W. (2000) Making a memorial place: The photography of Shimon Attie. *Psychoanalytic Dialogues*, 10, 347–370.

Laub, D. (2012) Testimony as life experience and legacy. In Goodman, N. R., & Meyers, M. B. (eds.), *The power of witnessing: Reflections, reverberations, and traces of the Holocaust*. London: Routledge, p. 74.

Laub, D. (2013) On leaving home and the flight from trauma. *Psychoanalytic Dialogues*, 23, 568–570.

Ogden, T. H. (2000) Borges and the art of mourning. *Psychoanalytic Dialogues*, 10, 65–88.

Oliner, M. M. (2006) The externalizing function of memorials. *Psychoanalytic Review*, 93, 883–902.

Ornstein, A. (2010) The missing tombstone: Reflections on mourning and creativity. *Journal of the American Psychoanalytic Association*, 58, 631–648.

Part II

Enforced disappearance and human rights

Chapter 4

The law in front of the denial of the law[1]

Emmanuel Decaux

The law is too often cold, distant and icy, precepts carved in stone, keeping emotions and feelings at bay. Without doubt, this is necessary for justice to be fair, independent and impartial, "dispassionate" one might say. However, this should not be to the detriment of the human dimension of any true justice. There is no right "on a human scale" without a measure of compassion, empathy and pity for the misery of men. This irreducible human factor is even more necessary when "crimes against humanity" are involved, when men have denied the humanity of the victims, plunged into anonymity, oblivion and denial.

However, a whole tradition inherited from Roman law aims to establish an "objective law" recorded in "codes" with logical rigor, in search of a fair balance, being all the warier of the multiplication of subjective rights, such as human rights. A great legal theorist, such as Jean Carbonnier (1996), considered that the preamble to the 1989 Convention on the Rights of the Child abandoned the field of legal obligations for that of good feelings, by affirming "that the child, for the full and harmonious development of his or her personality, should grow up in a family environment, in an atmosphere of happiness, love and understanding".[2] In criminal law, psychology is often dismissed and the words of its experts discredited with regard to the discernment of the perpetrator. *A fortiori*, the voice of the victims, reduced to the role of civil parties, remains marginal in the criminal trial where the State defends the public order.

These discrepancies are flagrant when it comes to taking into account dramatic situations, such as those constituted by enforced disappearances, whether on an individual or collective level. Not only because human rights are called into question, as the subjective rights of individuals, or the foundations of criminal justice, with the risk of "re-victimization" of particularly vulnerable victims, but even more because the crime of enforced disappearance immediately seems unspeakable and inaudible, upsetting all the classic benchmarks of law, with their reassuring routine, the habit of precedents, trust in institutions, the slowness of procedures and the limit of prescriptions.

In a way, the International Convention for the Protection of All Persons from Enforced Disappearance is not a human rights convention like the others dealing with vulnerable groups. It opens a new era of international rights law by offering

DOI: 10.4324/9781003312642-7

a different reading framework that takes as its starting point the perspective of victims. In a sense, it can be said to operate a Copernican revolution, which began with the Declaration of Principle adopted by consensus by the General Assembly of the United Nations in 1992 which was transformed into a treaty, from soft law into hard law, in 2006.[3]

It is also the result of the mobilization of non-governmental organizations (NGOs) and in particular associations of families of the disappeared, as well as the experience of independent experts from the Sub-Commission on the Promotion and Protection of Human Rights, such as Louis Joinet and Théo Van Boven. Far from starting from preconceived abstract ideas, the experts in fact started from their experience in the field, closely connected with the struggles of civil society to challenge "reason of State" and obtain an end to impunity. This fundamental reflection on the gross violations of human rights, within the collegial framework of the Sub-Commission, through a permanent dialectic between law and practice, found its continuation in the specialized experience of the Working Group on Enforced or Involuntary Disappearances (WGEID) established in 1980 by the Commission on Human Rights. The Working Group has been confronted with the most diverse situations, through its urgent appeals and its visits in the field, starting from an empirical approach to draw up guidelines at its turn. Without chasing feelings or affects, the law gradually built up on an indispensable empathy, with the concern to provide concrete solutions and to deliver general principles.

This was also because of the awareness of the limits of a purely legal response. Thus, unlike the WGEID, whose mandate concerns all the Member States of the United Nations, on the basis of the resolutions of the General Assembly as well as of the then Commission on Human Rights and later of the Human Rights Council, the Committee on Enforced Disappearances (CED) is competent only for States which have expressly ratified the 2006 Convention, i.e. 71 States Parties to date – just a little bit more than a third of the Member States of the United Nations. Moreover, when drafting the Convention, the States took great care in limiting its application in time and to exclude the competence of the Committee for any disappearance that occurred before its entry into force. This principle of non-retroactivity is found at the domestic level and the French courts have long hesitated to extradite an Argentine officer recognized as the author of enforced disappearances, insofar as the incriminating acts pre-dated the entry into force of the Convention in French legislation.[4]

These limits, inherent in the law of treaties, are difficult to explain to relatives of the disappeared who expect everything from the "international community". I felt a deep sense of helplessness and shame when meeting at the Palais des Nations in Geneva, Ms Shui-Meng Ng, the wife of Sombath Somphone, a peasants' rights activist who "disappeared" in 2013 in Laos. The only institutional response that I could offer, beyond a few personal words of compassion, was to say that the CED was not competent for her husband's case because Laos did not ratify the Convention, but that the WGEID could perhaps make a move, without rocking illusions a woman on the verge of despair. Five years later, I saw Mrs Shui-Meng Ng again, during a round table organized at the French National Assembly, in Paris, her determination and her courage commanded admiration. The word resilience is too simplistic to evoke this unshakeable will, not to forget in order to survive, but to live to fight, with the strength of who has nothing left to lose, despite all the intimidations, all the threats and all the manoeuvres.

A major challenge of the Convention is to take into account the urgency, the time of the victims both of the disappeared persons for whom everything must be done to find them as soon as possible, while the chances of finding them alive are the strongest, but also of the families of the disappeared for whom every day is an anguish, every night a nightmare. Some, uncertain of the fate of their loved one, imagine a different tragedy each time, others cling to the idea that their child will come back one day, like a Uruguayan mother who continued to buy him ties that he would have liked. But the time conceived by human beings in terms of numbered days is confronted with the time of the States which drag their feet to ratify the Convention – whereas it constitutes an "all-risks insurance" with prevention and protection mechanisms – then multiply the tergiversation to escape the monitoring procedures, by delaying the submission of their reports or the acceptance of the visits requested by CED in accordance with Article 33 of the Convention. It is therefore with a mix of patience and impatience that the members of the Committee bring together the short term and the long term, the urgency and the imprescriptible.

Faced with the limits of the law, the Convention must overcome several impasses to deal with a "complex phenomenon", a catch-all formula whose inherent banality can only shock. Instead of the simple definitions of classical law, which has an answer for each question, in the case of enforced disappearance there are so many contradictions, questions and uncertainties that arise from the clash between law and reality. Like the philosopher Vladimir Jankélévitch (1986) speaking of the *Imprescriptible*,[5] it is necessary to consider other moral paradoxes in the attempt to approach, as closely as possible, the legal responses offered by the 2006 Convention.

Defining the undefinable

The first challenge is to define a crime whose purpose is to erase all traces of the victims and to rely on the lies and denial of the perpetrators. Lawyers speak of a "complex phenomenon", without measuring the weight of the formula, for lack of being able to put words to the realities. In fact the crime of enforced disappearance is the accumulation of the violation of all human rights as it consists in the denial of the legal personality of the human person, to make it a simple "object". In other words, the individual loses their inherent quality of "subject of law", with all the guarantees of the rule of law and the due process of law, to be suddenly plunged into non-law, into a legal vacuum conducive to all mental and physical torture, a blind world of worry and anguish.

While in a State, worthy of this name, legal certainty aims to protect citizens with precise rules of procedure including for searches and arrest warrants, time limits, guarantees and remedies, contact with relatives, the right to a lawyer and the visit of a doctor, the victim of enforced disappearance suddenly switches into a world of violence, finding themselves defenceless in the face of the unknown. "Strangers" come to pick them up at their home or intercept them at the corner of a street, without leaving any traces or evidence, even if witnesses have watched helplessly at the scene. We remember the kidnapping of Mehdi Ben Barka, a Moroccan politician, in the heart of Paris where he was exiled, in front of a brasserie in Saint-Germain des Prés, on 29 October 1965. Today, with the proliferation of surveillance cameras, the images testify. We can find images like that of Jamal Khashoggi entering the Saudi Arabian consulate in Istanbul without ever coming out. The attack on the five coaches of Mexican students from Ayotzinapa on the night of 26 September 2014 in front of the Iguala courthouse was the subject of a video which was later destroyed.

But on another scale, this crime, the primary purpose of which is to make the victim disappear, also aims to leave traces, by instilling a climate of fear in society. The threat is becoming omnipresent, fuelled by rumours but also by manipulation, as with Argentinian torture centres, such as ESMA, which also served as 'telephone centrals' to transmit coded messages to relatives or to infiltrate the networks of opponents. The victim thus becomes an unconscious accomplice or is guilt-ridden by their executioners. Desperate families also multiply the steps to try to obtain news of the disappeared and to try to save them, even if most often they come up against a wall of indifference or hypocrisy, in systems based on denial. The tireless tour among police stations, prisons, hospitals and morgues, in search of the slightest clue, becomes the substitute for a proper investigation, while the administration lies and justice is silent.

It is against this backdrop of State lies that the definition of enforced disappearance has gradually emerged. To the fragmented vision of a series of specific violations of human rights, the Convention offers an overall vision, closely associating the negation of the rule of law and the negation of humanity.

An individual crime

The definition of enforced disappearance, as an autonomous crime, emerged gradually. It appeared first in the preamble to the Declaration on the Protection of All Persons from Enforced Disappearance adopted by the General Assembly by consensus in 1992,[6] following the first reports of the Working Group on Enforced or Involuntary Disappearances, before being taken up in Article 2 of the 2006 Convention. Both the Working Group and the Committee place great emphasis on the existence of three constitutive objective elements that define the crime of enforced disappearance and reject any attempt to dilute them with other elements such as an intentional or temporal element. Article 1 specifies that: "no exceptional circumstances whatsoever, whether a state of war or a threat of war, internal political instability or any other public emergency, may be invoked as a justification for enforced disappearance". In accordance with article 2, enforced disappearance is considered to be:

i. "the arrest, detention, abduction or any other form of deprivation of liberty" this is the first constitutive objective element, including for those acts that some call "short-term" or "temporary" disappearances.[7] This is all the more important since the urgent procedure to find a disappeared person must start immediately, in accordance with Article 30 of the Convention which is a sort of international *habeas corpus*, while some States ask for "delays" before launching an investigation;

ii. "by agents of the State or by persons or groups of persons acting with the authorization, support or acquiescence of the State" this is the second constitutive element, making disappearance a "State crime" including when the State acts with the complicity of paramilitary forces, mercenaries or death squads. This is the great distinction with common, villainous kidnappings as foreseen in ordinary law. But on this point, Article 3 of the Convention opens up a new perspective by providing that "Each State Party shall take appropriate measures to investigate acts defined in article 2 committed by persons or groups of persons acting without the authorization, support or acquiescence of the State and to bring those responsible to justice." In my opinion, it is not only an option which is given to the State but also an obligation which implies the responsibility to carry out effective investigations concerning the missing persons who are in the hands of non-state actors and to prosecute the perpetrators of such acts. For a long time, the Working Group maintained a clear dichotomy between actions attributable to the state and those of its adversaries, particularly in the context of armed movements, but the Group's thinking has evolved, and so did the main NGOs. The priority seems to me to be the fate of the victims and it is impossible to oppose "good" victims and "bad" victims, as the situations on the ground are often confused. It is enforced disappearance as such that must be fought and to do so all the victims must be taken into account.

iii. Finally, the third constitutive element is the denial, the conspiracy of silence which makes the crime particularly cruel: the arrest, detention, abduction or any other form of deprivation of liberty is "followed by a refusal to acknowledge the deprivation of liberty or by concealment of the fate or whereabouts of the disappeared person, which place such a person outside the protection of the law." For the Committee, the removal from the protection of the law is an autonomic consequence of the denial, which deprives victims of all legal guarantees, without having to look for a criminal "intention" behind each secret arrest. In this sense, even a person imprisoned after a legal trial can very well become a victim of enforced disappearance, when they are held *incommunicado* and their fate remains concealed. The Convention also provides for a whole series of preventive measures, such as the keeping of prison registries, the contact with families, the visits by lawyers and doctors, to prevent detainees from disappearing into the black hole of a secret jail.

The Committee is very vigilant about the transposition of this strict definition when it verifies that the state party to the Convention has indeed criminalized enforced disappearance as an autonomous crime in its domestic legislation, in accordance with Article 4 of the Convention. Some States invoke incriminations by equivalence with other crimes or by amalgamation of a plurality of different crimes but this neglects the added value of having a single definition of enforced disappearance as a complex and composite crime, with all the resulting consequences for the legal system.

At this stage, it is necessary to emphasize the added value of the 2006 Convention which, by stating in article 1 that "no one shall be subjected to enforced disappearance", creates a new human right, that of not being subjected to enforced disappearance, whereas earlier instruments, such as the International Covenant on Civil and Political Rights or the European Convention on Human Rights made it possible to deal with enforced disappearances only in a fragmentary way, by aiming at the prohibition of torture and inhuman and degrading treatment, the violation of the freedom of movement, legal personality, security, the right to effective remedies and ultimately the right to life. For a long time, the European Court of Human Rights had taken refuge behind procedural violations, "positive obligations" such as the absence of an investigation, instead of confronting "negative obligations" as fundamental as the protection of the right to life. Since the adoption of the 2006 Convention, the jurisprudence of the Human Rights Committee and of the European Court has endeavoured, on the example of the Inter-American Court of Human Rights, to have a global vision of "enforced disappearance", but the possibility to invoke directly the 2006 Convention constitutes a shift in the legal paradigm of particular importance.

A crime against humanity

The definition of enforced disappearance as a crime against humanity is more complex because it is indirect. Article 5 of the Convention states that: "The widespread or systematic practice of enforced disappearance constitutes a crime against humanity as defined in applicable international law and shall attract the consequences provided for under such applicable international law."

Thus, a reference is expressly made to general law but also implicitly to the Rome Statute which in its Article 7 on "crime against humanity" mentions in paragraph 1 (i) "enforced disappearance of persons" before giving the following definition in paragraph 2 (i)

"Enforced disappearance of persons" means the arrest, detention or abduction of persons by, or with the authorization, support or acquiescence of, a State or a political organization, followed by a refusal to acknowledge that deprivation of freedom or to give information on the fate or whereabouts of those persons, with the intention of removing them from the protection of the law for a prolonged period of time.

This definition creates a number of problems, with a risk of shimmering. Firstly, by mentioning a "political organization" alongside, or rather opposite to, the State, the Rome Statute aligns with humanitarian law which applies to "parties to the conflict", according to the criteria of the two Protocols to the Geneva Conventions of 1949, which were adopted in 1977. In other words, in a civil war or a non-international armed conflict, all the parties involved can be accused of "crime against humanity", even if one must undoubtedly distinguish between the notion of "political organization" and that of belligerent taking part in hostilities, within the scope of Protocol II to the Geneva Conventions of 1949 which refers to "organized armed groups (…), under responsible command".

However, the Rome Statute introduces a new constitutive element in the definition of enforced disappearance, namely an additional intentional element combined with a rather vague temporal dimension: "with the intention of removing them from the protection of the law for extended prolonged period of time". Admittedly, an incrimination before the International Criminal Court requires a "generalized" or "systematic" nature of the crime as part of a concerted plan perpetrated over time. However, the Committee, like the Working Group, sticks to a stricter definition, without looking for the intentions behind the crime which reside in the psychology of the perpetrators. The denial of the protection of the law is already in itself the negation of the legal personality of the victims and the foundation of the criminal enterprise: it is as such the negation of the rule of law. In domestic law, a State Party to the Convention can stick to its own definition of crime against humanity which best corresponds to its history, as many Latin American States do. Beyond these considerations of principle, it must be recognized that a State which has transposed the definitions of the Rome Statute into its domestic legislation, will not call them into question to comply with a strict interpretation of the Convention. Equally the recent work of the International Law Commission resulted in a draft Convention on the prevention and punishment of crimes against humanity, that systematically aligns with the definitions of the Rome Statute, and which is currently the subject of discussions before the 6th Committee of the United Nations General Assembly.[8] Another multilateral legal assistance project (Mutual Legal Assistance) in the area of crimes against humanity, steered by Slovenia, also aims to seek the lowest common denominator among States when it comes to these crimes.[9]

These hesitations in the very definition of crimes against humanity are particularly worrying, with the risk of a regression by ruling out any development of *jus cogens* and could lead to the multiplication of procedural difficulties in terms of international cooperation and the implementation of the principle of complementarity, through universal jurisdiction.

Qualifying the unqualifiable

Faced with these multiple legal definitions, it is necessary, to get out of denial, to qualify the crimes by determining the perpetrators as well as the victims. The Convention adopts a broad notion of chains of responsibilities, as well as of bonds of solidarity, in order to embrace the systematic, and to put it bluntly, social dimension of enforced disappearance.

The authors of the crime

It should be emphasized from the outset that the accountability for international crimes operates at two levels. It is first of all an international responsibility of the State, vis-à-vis of other States, under the principles of public international law, such as obligations assumed under the Rome Statute or treaties relating to human rights, be it the International Covenant on Civil and Political Rights or the Convention on Enforced Disappearances. In this sense, Article 32 of the Convention provides, on the basis of voluntary recognition "the competence of the Committee to receive and consider communications in which a State Party claims that another State Party is not fulfilling its obligations under this Convention." We find again this inter-State dimension, in Article 42 which covers "Any dispute between two or more States Parties concerning the interpretation or application of this Convention", according to various methods, involving negotiation, arbitration and ultimately the jurisdiction of the International Court of Justice. This involvement of the State as such is particularly important, as in the cases relating to the 1948 Genocide Convention, because the international responsibility of the State can be called into question alongside with the criminal responsibility of individuals, including the personal responsibility of the Head of State the originality of the Convention, compared to other human rights treaties, is that it also includes a particularly elaborate criminal section. According to Article 2, if the crime is committed "with the authorization, support or acquiescence of the State", it is the act of "State's agents" even if the authors are persons and groups of persons acting on its behalf. In Article 3, the Convention goes as far as targeting "acts ... committed by persons or groups of persons acting without the authorization, support or acquiescence of the State" and it stresses that "each State Party shall take appropriate measures to investigate [those acts] ... to bring those responsible to justice". Therefore, the international responsibility of the State finds its extension in the obligation to prosecute and punish the perpetrators of enforced disappearances within the domestic framework. This is also the basis of international judicial cooperation, provided for by Articles 13–15 of the Convention: for an effective cooperation, a common language is needed, through parallel incriminations.

In this field too, the Convention marks a great advance by qualifying very precisely various offences. This concerns all levels of the chain of command from the principal, at the highest level of the hierarchy, to the performer of the dirty work. Thus, Article 6, paragraph 1(a) targets "any person who commits, orders, solicits or induces the commission of, attempts to commit, is an accomplice to or participates in an enforced disappearance". Article 6, paragraph 1(b), also insists on the responsibility of the hierarchical superior in a very broad way, since it concerns the superior who "knew, or consciously disregarded information which clearly indicated, that subordinates under his or her effective authority and control were committing or about to commit a crime of enforced disappearance" and "failed to take all necessary and reasonable measures within his or her power to prevent or repress the commission of an enforced disappearance or to submit the matter to the competent authorities for investigation and prosecution". At the limit, it may be a question of objective responsibility, in terms of the "higher standards of responsibility applicable under relevant international law to a military commander or to a person effectively acting as a military commander" (Article 6, paragraph 1(c)). This responsibility in principle of hierarchical leaders is closely linked to the systemic nature of the crime which, from the commission to the covering up and denial of the disappearance, implies a collective failure that the political or military authority must assume. Ignorance or powerlessness cannot serve as an alibi in the face of the systematic manipulation and the generalized denial.

The Convention does not go into detail about the forms of complicity or participation but, through the mitigating or aggravating circumstances, one can see the consideration of the human factor in front of the crime. Thus, according to Article 7, paragraph 2 (a), mitigating circumstances may be foreseen

in particular for persons who, having been implicated in the commission of an enforced disappearance, effectively contribute to bringing the disappeared person forward alive or make it possible to clarify cases of enforced disappearance or to identify the perpetrators of an enforced disappearance.

The Convention disregards to seek the deep motivations for such an attitude, whether it's sincere remorse in an admission of guilt or denunciation of accomplices to minimize one's own responsibility. Here again, the darkness of the human soul escapes the law. *A fortiori*, regarding the aggravating circumstances, the Convention introduces a scale in the horror of the crime in paragraph 2 (b): "in particular in the event of the death of the disappeared person or the commission of an enforced disappearance in respect of pregnant women, minors, persons with disabilities or other particularly vulnerable persons". The tragic experience of recent history, notably that of the dictatorships in Latin America, appears behind the enumeration of persons in different situations of vulnerability. Both the Committee and the Working Group went further, highlighting the plight of indigenous peoples, at the forefront of "vulnerable groups", just like the migrants who become "doubly anonymous" as missing and disappeared persons.

Over time, the scope of the Convention broadens, encompassing phenomena as different as non-international armed conflicts, with the involvement of "Parties to the conflict" within the meaning of the Protocols to the Geneva Conventions, in crimes such as recruitment of child soldiers, the abduction of young girls, or the trafficking in human beings by the organized cross-border crime. While the starting point of the Convention was the experience of military dictatorships through the Condor Plan in Latin America, today enforced disappearance is both the work of strong States, remaining a cynical instrument of repression and terror, and that of failed States, in an anarchy conducive to all crimes. In this sense, the Convention is not only turned towards the past but also indispensable to respond to the new challenges where "missing persons" and "disappeared persons" combine and multiply.

The victims of the crime

Here too, the Convention marks a conceptual step forward by going beyond the traditional distinction between direct and indirect victims, a distinction brutally illustrated by the case law of the European Court of Human Rights or the practice of States. For the purpose of the Convention, as specified in Article 24, paragraph 1: "'victim' means the disappeared person and any individual who has suffered harm as the direct result of an enforced disappearance." The parents and relatives of the disappeared person are thus recognized as victims, instead of being relegated to second rank, without any real legal title to act neither in the name of the disappeared, for the impossibility of being the mandatary, nor in their own capacity. The Convention seeks to overcome this vicious circle of lawlessness, which redoubles the denial through the indifference, while the families are in search of the slightest information, the slightest sign of hope. Moreover, the Convention goes beyond this isolation of the families in a solitary struggle to recognize the dimension of the solidarity of their commitment. The Convention is the only human rights treaty, together with the Convention on the Rights of Persons with Disabilities also adopted in 2006, to fully integrate the role of non-governmental organizations by stipulating in Article 24, paragraph 7: "Each State Party shall guarantee the right to form and participate freely in organizations and associations concerned with attempting to establish the circumstances of enforced disappearances and the fate of disappeared persons, and to assist victims of enforced disappearance." The systemic nature of the violation must be addressed by the collective mobilization of civil society. More concretely, the Committee monitors the protection of persons or organizations that cooperate with its procedures, whether by providing information within the framework of the drafting and follow-up of reports, or of "communications" related to an urgent appeal or of a complaint. Apart from the strict rules of confidentiality applied by the Committee and its Secretariat, the Committee may request States to apply "measures of protection", alongside with "interim measures", when a person who is the subject of an urgent appeal is threatened. The Committee, by this mean, was informed of the case of the mother of a disappeared person who was summoned to the very same military barracks where her son had been seen for the last time. These empirical tools, which are specific to each Committee monitoring a human rights treaty, were codified in guiding principles known as the "San José Guidelines against intimidation and reprisal"[10] and endorsed by the Meeting of Chairpersons of Treaty Bodies. They provide a coherent framework for understanding and articulating basic principles and good practices with the priority of the safeguard of persons at risk and the respect of their rights. The San José Guidelines are evaluated annually by the Office of the High Commissioner for Human Rights and the Secretary-General of the United Nations. More broadly, victims often become human rights defenders, going beyond their individual situation to lead a collective struggle. Meeting the relatives of a disappeared person, a daughter, a son, a spouse, is always an emotional shock. Beyond the tireless telling a personal story, there is also a long journey to overcome despair, passivity and resignation, with a "science of law" acquired on the ground that commands respect. Alfredo López Casanova, a Mexican sculptor, collected the worn shoes of these parents, in search of a loved one, accompanied by a photo and a date, to translate into images this itinerancy of beings brought close together by the solidarity of misfortune and the incapacity or refusal of mourning as well as of giving up the search.

Also in the field of rights and guarantees, the Convention broadens the traditional approach. Thus, urgent appeals under Article 30, paragraph 1, may be submitted "by relatives of the disappeared person or their legal representatives, their counsel or any person authorized by them, as well as by any other person having a legitimate interest." This reference to a "legitimate interest" seems very open, going beyond the legal formalism, in the case of a report made to trigger an "urgent action". The same is logically true of Article 18, paragraph 1, which "shall guarantee to any person with a legitimate interest in this information, such as relatives of the person deprived of liberty, their representatives or their counsel" access to essential information on their situation in the event of detention.

This approach is broader than the right to submit individual petitions which, as foreseen in article 31, paragraph 1, only concerns "communications from or on behalf of individuals (…) claiming to be victims of a violation". However, in its views on the Yrusta case,[11] the Committee went beyond the formalistic argument, used by Argentina to oppose the Committee by considering that the sisters of Mr Yrusta, a disappeared person, could not intervene in the legal proceedings and be the authors of the individual communication since only the victim's mother could do so having the status of *beneficiary*. In the case of an old lady, suffering from depression due to the tragic death of her son, it seems a cynical argument to delay full reparation when the Committee had clearly established the responsibility of the State.

One finds a great openness in the qualifications necessary for the information to be received by the Committee under Article 33, paragraph 1, which refers only to "reliable information" to enable the Committee to exercise its competence when "a State Party is seriously violating the provisions of this Convention". Here again, it is for the Committee to assess the reliability of its confidential sources, in a sometimes tense "dialogue" with the State, when relying on allegations specific enough to demonstrate the "serious" breach of the Convention. The same applies to Article 34, which refers to "well-founded indications" on the widespread or systematic practice of enforced disappearance and aims at their referral to the General Assembly of the United Nations.

This easy access for the victims is at the heart of the Convention. Firstly, because the primary purpose of the Convention is the protection of their rights through the prevention and punishment of the crime of enforced disappearance. As such, the Convention has, as I have often repeated, the originality of being a "victim-oriented" treaty, based on the concrete experience of the associations of families of the disappeared who have played a decisive role in the preparatory work for the Convention and continue to do so for its promotion. But victims' associations, like non-governmental organizations of a more general nature, also play an irreplaceable role in providing information to the Committee, which would otherwise be blind and mute. This can be seen in those paradoxical situations where no contribution from civil society or even national human rights institutions comes to feed the file of a State, during the examination of its report under Article 29. To tell the truth, this silence is more disturbing than reassuring.

Repair the unrepairable

The prioritization of victims' rights is a particularly important advancement of the Convention, which codifies on this point many developments of the *soft law*. The Convention is the culmination of a whole work of reflection launched within the United Nations by two special rapporteurs of the Sub-Commission on Human Rights, Louis Joinet on the fight against impunity[12] and Théo Van Boven on the reparation for gross violations of human rights and humanitarian law,[13] with guiding principles that have been enshrined by the then Commission on Human Rights[14] or the General Assembly.[15] It is no coincidence that Louis Joinet was the author of the first draft convention on enforced disappearance. This whole body of guiding principles found its full consecration with the 2006 Convention.

The *pro victima* approach of the Convention is emphasized, since the Preamble by "Considering the right of any person not to be subjected to enforced disappearance [and] the right of victims to justice and to reparation" and "Affirming the right of any victim to know the truth about the circumstances of an enforced disappearance and the fate of the disappeared person, and the right to freedom to seek, receive and impart information to this end".

Collective reparation

It is Article 24, one of the most important of the Convention, which clarifies the legal obligations arising from these principles, giving an inclusive definition of the victim, as has just been seen. Article 24 is too dense to be cited in its entirety, but it details the components of the right to the truth in paragraph 2: "Each victim has the right to know the truth regarding the circumstances of the enforced disappearance, the progress and results of the investigation and the fate of the disappeared person". For its part, as provided in paragraph 3, the State must take "all appropriate measures to search for, locate and release disappeared persons and, in the event of death, to locate, respect and return their remains".

Furthermore, Article 24, paragraph 4, elaborates on the nature of the right to reparation: "Each State Party shall ensure in its legal system that the victims of enforced disappearance have the right to obtain reparation and prompt, fair and adequate compensation" adding, in paragraph 5 and following the thread of the van Boven principles, that this right "covers material and moral damages and, where appropriate, other forms of reparation such as (a) restitution; (b) rehabilitation; (c) satisfaction, including the restoration of dignity and reputation; (d) guarantees of non-repetition". To Louis Joinet's trilogy, aimed at truth, justice and reparation, is thus added a fourth term, essential for the future, with the guarantees of "non-repetition", which implies a consolidation of the rule of law, with the separation of powers, political alternation, the independence of the judiciary and the end of military courts.[16] The Committee cooperates closely in this field with the Special Rapporteur on the promotion of truth, justice, reparation and guarantees of non-recurrence since the creation of the mandate in 2011 by the Human Rights Council.[17]

Individual reparations

The Convention, in Article 24 paragraph 6, aims at the protection of the relatives of the disappeared persons, in particular at their legal status "in fields such as social welfare, financial matters, family law and property rights" and requests that States take "appropriate steps with regard to the legal situation of disappeared persons whose fate has not been clarified". In some States, particularly in Latin America, these appropriate steps took the form of 'declarations of disappearance' instead of requiring families to give up all hope by filing the request for a 'declaration of death'. The Convention devotes the entire Article 25 to the fate of children victims of falsification of identity. The Working Group issued general comments on women and enforced disappearance, and on children and enforced disappearance, which the Committee endorsed. Too often to the social precariousness of the family of a disappeared person, deprived of income, a collective stigmatization is added, when it is not a question of political banishment. To address the risks of harassment, intimidation and "re-victimization" of the families, the Convention, in its Article 24 paragraph 7, provides that the State "shall guarantee the right to form and participate freely in organizations and associations concerned with attempting to establish the circumstances of enforced disappearances and the fate of disappeared persons, and to assist victims of enforced disappearance." If we consider these elements combine, for example, with the provisions on personal information "including medical or genetic data", as foreseen in Article 19 of the Convention and advances in forensic medicine, then we can affirm that the Convention truly marks a considerable step forward in the protection of all persons against enforced disappearance.

The fate of the children of the disappeared, themselves disappeared, is one of the most tragic legacies of the past, as shown by the quest of the grandmothers of the Plaza de Mayo in Buenos Aires. The aim is to find children born in detention and entrusted to families of police or military officers, while the mothers were executed after their delivery. This quest involves technical means, such as DNA banks, but also particularly strong psychological stakes, insofar as the revelation of a hidden identity constitutes a brutal shock to the child, most of whom are now adults, taken out of their family environment as they used to know. The testimonies show that each case is individual, ranging between the refusal to face reality, or even instinctive solidarity with an adoptive parent going so far as to deny the crime and the natural family and, on the contrary, a reunion, assuming the complexity of a double identity, symbolized by the juxtaposition of two first names. Beyond the documented cases of Argentina, one may wonder if the framework of Article

25 should not also apply to situations revealed more recently, such as the fate of children in orphanages in Ireland, separated from their families and anonymous victims of ill-treatment, or the forced assimilation of indigenous people cut off from their families and roots in Australia or Canada. We also know the case of the "children of Creuse", young Reunionese forcibly move to the metropolitan France as a policy to repopulate rural areas between 1963 and 1982, claiming that their families had abandoned them.

Finally, it is necessary to return to the key issue of the temporal implementation of the Convention, which has been the subject of a declaration on the *ratione temporis* competence of the Committee. The drafters of the Convention were careful in stating, in Article 35 paragraph 1, that "The Committee shall have competence solely in respect of enforced disappearances which commenced after the entry into force of this Convention", which expressly excludes the concept of "continuing crime", that is the principle according to which a case of enforced disappearance is occurring until the fate and whereabouts of the disappeared person are clarified, when considering individual communications submitted under Article 31. However, it seems to me that the obligations of States parties under the Convention are not limited regarding the rights of victims, such as the right to know the truth about the corpse in mass graves or the right of the children to have their identities re-established, that have just been mentioned. The consequences of the past are the tragic present of the victims.

Moreover, in the field of general law, the Declaration on the Protection of All Persons from Enforced Disappearance laid down, in Article 17, principles on limitation periods and, in Article 18, principles on amnesty which have been clarified by the Working Group and which apply all States. Article 37 of the Convention, proposed by Switzerland, also contains an original provision referring *to* "any provisions which are more conducive to the protection of all persons from enforced disappearance and which may be contained in [...] international law in force for that State." Even if we remain cautious about the concept of *jus cogens*, this provision covers not only conventional norms but also customary norms.

These technical indications, probably too technical, are there to remind us that the law is not only a "cold monster", like States, it is also an instrument of progress and liberation. It is also the fruit of the long chain of struggle of generations and the affirmation of their human solidarity. Time can be an ally, if we know how to combine patience and impatience, to make it a creative energy.

Notes

1 Translated from original French text by Maria Giovanna Bianchi.
2 For a critical perspective, Decaux (2012) in Verdier (2012).
3 Resolution A/47/133 of 18 December 1992 and resolution A/61/177 of 20 December 2006. The Convention was open for signature on 6 February 2007, (Scovazzi and Citroni, 2007), (Decaux and de Frouville, 2009).
4 On the case Sandoval, see the opinion by Olivier Cahn, *Droits fondamentaux*, n°14 (2016) and n°17 (2019).

5 Jankélévitch (1986).
6 General Assembly Resolution A/47/133 of 18 December 1992.
7 Committee on Enforced Disappearances, decision of 11 March 2016, in *Yrusta vs. Argentine*.
8 See 4th report by Sean Murphy, A/CN.5/725.
9 See the opinion on the draft Convention on Prevention and Punishment of Crimes against Humanity, adopted by the French National Commission on Human Rights on 27 March 2018, *Journal officiel de la République Française*, 1 April 2019.
10 See https://digitallibrary.un.org/record/820400?ln=en.
11 CED/C/10/D/1/2013 at https://juris.ohchr.org/Search/Details/2141.
12 E/CN.4/Sub.2/1997/20/Rev.1. The draft by Louis Joinet was subsequently updated by Diane Orentlicher and published as E/CN.4/2005/102/Add.1.
13 E/CN.4/1997/104. The draft by Théo van Boven was subsequently updated by Chérif Bassiouni and published as E/CN.4/2000/6.
14 Commission on Human Rights resolution 2005/81 adopted on 21 April 2005. Cf. *Updated set of principles for the protection and promotion of human through action to combat impunity*, E/CN.4/2005/102/Add.1. Subsequently the Human Rights Council, as a follow-up to this work on "transitional justice" establishes the mandate for a Special Rapporteur on the right to justice, truth, reparation and guarantee of non-repetition, by resolution 18/7 of September 2011.
15 General Assembly resolution 60/147 adopted on 16 December 2005: *Basic principles and guidelines on the right to a remedy and reparation for victims of gross violations of international human rights law and serious violations of international humanitarian law.*
16 On this point, see the *Principles on the proper administration of justice by military tribunals* adopted by the Sub-Commission on Human Rights in 2006, E/CN4/2006/58, following my reports. Under no circumstances should military courts be competent to try human rights violations and in particular crimes of enforced disappearance committed by military personnel. It should be added that under no circumstances can military courts try civilians by removing them from their "natural judge".
17 The Committee maintained an excellent collaboration with both Pablo De Greiff, the first mandate holder, and Fabián Salvioli, the present mandate holder.

References

Carbonnier, J. (1996). *Droit et passion du droit sous la V° République*. Paris: Flammarion.
Decaux, E. (2012). 'L'ordre qui déplace les lignes, Jean Carbonnier et le droit international' in Verdier, R. (ed.), *Jean Carbonnier, l'homme et l'œuvre*, pp. 571–612.Paris: Presses universitaires de Paris Ouest.
Decaux, E., de Frouville, O. (eds.) (2009). *La Convention internationale pour la protection de toutes les personnes contre les disparitions forcées*. Bruxelles: Éditions Bruylant.
Jankélévitch, J. (1986). *L'imprescriptible. Pardonner? Dans l'honneur et la dignité*. Paris: Éditions du Seuil.
Scovazzi, T., Citroni, G. (2007). *The Struggle against Enforced Disappearance and the 2007 United Nations Convention*. Leiden and Boston: Martinus Nijhoff Publishers.
Verdier, R. (ed.) (2012). *Jean Carbonnier, l'homme et l'œuvre*. Paris: Presses universitaires de Paris Ouest.

Chapter 5

The psychological impact of enforced disappearance on victims in light of international human rights law

Santiago Corcuera Cabezut

The concept of victim

The Declaration on the Protection of All Persons from Enforced Disappearances, adopted by the General Assembly of the United Nations on 18 December 1992, (the "Declaration"), in its Article 1, paragraph 2, provides:

> Any act of enforced disappearance places the persons subjected thereto outside the protection of the law and inflicts severe suffering on them and their families. It constitutes a violation of the rules of international law guaranteeing, inter alia, the right to recognition as a person before the law, the right to liberty and security of the person and the right not to be subjected to torture and other cruel, inhuman or degrading treatment or punishment. It also violates or constitutes a grave threat to the right to life.

The provision above is a clear reference to the psychological effects, the "severe suffering", generated by the disappearance of persons, not only on the disappeared person, who is completely helpless and without any legal protection, but also on their family and loved ones.

Thus, according to the Declaration, not only is the disappeared person a victim, but their relatives and loved ones are victims as well.

Enforced disappearance, according to the aforementioned provision, violates several rights: it is a multi-offensive and multi-violation conduct of human rights, which inflicts pain and suffering equivalent to acts of torture, or at least cruel, inhuman or degrading treatment. As it is known, unfortunately, disappeared persons, while at the mercy of their captors, suffer physical abuse and, of course, psychological harm often amounting to torture. Their relatives and loved ones are victims of severe suffering not knowing the whereabouts of their loved one, imagining what they are suffering or the violence that is being inflicted on them. The testimonies of the relatives of the disappeared persons in this regard demonstrate this clearly and forcefully.

The Inter-American Court of Human Rights

> has held on several occasions that the relatives of the victims of violations of human rights may, in turn, be victims. In particular, in cases involving the forced

DOI: 10.4324/9781003312642-8

disappearance of persons, it can be understood that the violation of the right to mental and moral integrity of the victims' next of kin is a direct result, precisely, of this phenomenon, which causes them severe anguish owing to the act itself, which is increased, among other factors, by the constant refusal of the State authorities to provide information on the whereabouts of the victim or to open an effective investigation to clarify what occurred.[1]

The Convention on the Protection of All Persons from Enforced Disappearances, adopted by the General Assembly of the United Nations on 20 December 2006, (the "Convention"), in its Article 24, paragraph 1, contains a definition of "victim" that reads as follows: "For the purposes of this Convention, 'victim' means the disappeared person and any individual who has suffered harm as the direct result of an enforced disappearance."

As can be seen, the definition of "victim" of enforced disappearance is not only the disappeared person, but also the persons who suffer harm as a direct result of the enforced disappearance.

The Working Group on Enforced or Involuntary Disappearances, one of the Special Procedures of the United Nations Human Rights Council, in its Methods of Work, paragraph 9, defines victims as follows:

While the Declaration does not define explicitly the concept of victims of enforced disappearance, a definition may nonetheless be inferred from it and by taking into consideration the evolution of international law. For the purpose of the implementation of its mandate, the Working Group considers that victims include a disappeared person and any individual who has suffered harm as the direct result of an enforced disappearance.

As it can be noted, the Working Group on the one hand recognizes that the disappearance affects both the disappeared person and their relatives and loved ones and, on the other hand, it takes into account the development of international law on the matter; that is, the Convention itself which does explicitly contain a definition of "victim", that the Working Group takes up literally.

Enforced disappearance is one of the most serious violations of human rights and, certainly, constitutes a gross violations of international human rights law. For this reason, it is important to refer to the Basic Principles and Guidelines on the Right to a Remedy and Reparation, adopted by the General Assembly of the United Nations on 16 December 2005 ("Victims Basic Principles and Guidelines"). Section V, paragraph 8, contains the following definition of "Victims of gross violations of international human rights law and serious violations of international humanitarian law":

For purposes of the present document, victims are persons who individually or collectively suffered harm, including physical or mental injury, emotional suffering, economic loss or substantial impairment of their fundamental rights, through acts or omissions that constitute gross violations of international human rights law, or serious violations of international humanitarian law. Where appropriate, and in accordance with domestic law, the term "victim" also includes the immediate family or dependents of the direct victim and persons who have suffered harm in intervening to assist victims in distress or to prevent victimization.

From this very brief review, it is clear that the concept of victim, in international human rights law and its interpretation by different international and regional bodies, has been progressively broadened to include, beyond the disappeared person, formerly referred to as the "direct victim", also all persons who have suffered harm whether as members of the immediate family and dependents, or in their role as advisors, companions or assistants to the disappeared person. Moreover, in the Victims Basic Principles and Guidelines, the definition is further expanded to clarify that the victims may suffer individual or collective harm, and that this harm can take many forms and can be physical or mental, emotional suffering, economic loss, or substantial impairment of their fundamental rights.

The rights of victims

While the Convention stipulates for the rights of victims in its Article 24, many other provisions of the Convention refer to their rights as well.

For the purposes of this chapter, I will focus on some of those rights that, in my opinion, are most relevant to the psychological effects that enforced disappearances causes, and the way in which the respect, fulfilment and guarantee of those rights may have a healing effect on the victims of enforced disappearance.

Right to search, be searched, locate, release and restitute

As we will see below in the section on the continuous or permanent nature of the crime of enforced disappearance, one of the most terrible moral, emotional and psychological effects on the relatives of disappeared persons is the feeling of uncertainty and anguish generated by not knowing where the disappeared loved ones are or what is happening to them.

That is the rationale of the right to search, and be searched for, as a principle of the utmost importance in this context.

The right of the victim of enforced disappearance to be searched is clear from the various obligations that the Convention and other international instruments impose on State authorities. If to every obligation corresponds a right, and if the authorities have the obligation to search for the disappeared persons, it must be logically inferred that the disappeared persons have the right to be searched for. In this same vein, the loved ones and relatives of the disappeared persons have also the right to have these search obligations fulfilled by the State authorities. In addition, the relatives of the disappeared persons have the right to search by themselves and, in this case, the authorities have the obligation to accompany and protect them in the performance of their search.

The Guiding Principles for the Search for Disappeared Persons drafted and adopted by the Committee on Enforced Disappearances ("Search Guiding Principles"),[2] very clearly refer to the above-mentioned rights, the respect for human dignity, the situation of vulnerability in which migrants, women, children and other groups may be exposed to, as well as to the impact on the psychological and emotional sphere of all those victims of enforced disappearance.

One of the purposes and effects of these search guiding principles is precisely the protection of the family members of the disappeared persons, in order to avoid their re-victimization, that is, further moral and psychological damages.

The desperation caused by the inefficiency and lack of coordination and cooperation of the authorities in fulfilling their search obligations is recurrent in the testimonies of the relatives of the disappeared persons. The mistreatment of the relatives by the authorities, the to-and-fro to different government offices in search for information, not to mention the harassment and threats to which they are often subjected to, causes profound psychological damage. For this reason, the second of the search guiding principles refers to respect for human dignity, a principle that should nourish all other principles related to the search for missing persons.

The Victims Basic Principles and Guidelines, in section VI, paragraph 10, refers to the treatment of victims and provides the following:

> Victims should be treated with humanity and respect for their dignity and human rights, and appropriate measures should be taken to ensure their safety, physical and psychological well-being and privacy, as well as those of their families. The State should ensure that its domestic laws, to the extent possible, provide that a victim who has suffered violence or trauma should benefit from special consideration and care to avoid his or her re-traumatization in the course of legal and administrative procedures designed to provide justice and reparation.

The provision above deals with the same aspects that were already mentioned, and underscores, on the one hand, the psychological well-being of the victims, including family members, and on the other, the special consideration and care of those who have suffered trauma, in order to avoid re-traumatization.

Considering that enforced disappearance inflicts severe suffering at least equivalent to cruel, inhuman or degrading treatment, to avoid re-traumatization, it is advisable that those who provide psychological care to all the victims of this crime, take into account Chapter VI of the Manual on the Effective Investigation and Documentation of Torture and Other Cruel, Inhuman or Degrading Treatment or Punishment, called the Istanbul Protocol of 1999, concerning the psychological signs of torture and, in particular, Section C on the ethical and clinical aspects and the recommendations and considerations on the interview process.

In its most positive outcome, the fulfilment of the right to search and be searched could result in the discovery of the disappeared person alive. In this case, the person could have been arbitrarily deprived of their liberty in an unofficial clandestine detention place or in an official detention facility, but in violation of the rules of information on the location of the person deprived of liberty.[3] In both cases, right to release (i.e. that the disappeared person regains their liberty) must therefore be fulfilled. The multiplicity of positive psychological effects of the situation described in this paragraph is obvious, not only for the disappeared person who regains their freedom but also for their loved ones for whom the State of ambiguity ceases. In this context, rehabilitation and satisfaction measures are of the utmost importance as it will be illustrated at a later stage.

In its most tragic, and unfortunately most frequent, outcome, the realization of the right to search and be searched could lead to the discovery of the dead body or remains of the disappeared person. The testimonies of the victims who participate in the search for corpses, are marked by the frightening and contradictory hope that, among the bodies or the scattered human remains that are found, could be those of their loved one. The psychological accompaniment to the relatives of the victims of disappearances who participates in search brigades in urban or remote areas, in clandestine graves, in drainage channels, rivers or lakes, is absolutely necessary, due to the extremely difficult emotional and psychological experiences that the activity itself implies, which are generated when the graves with human remains are found, and by the subsequent anguishing wait for the results of the forensic medical studies, for the identification, or not, of the disappeared persons. One of the expressions that has impacted me the most was pronounced by the mother of a disappeared person whose mortal remains were found in a clandestine grave, when she said: "at least I had the joy of having found the remains of my son". How desperate she must have been not to knowing where her son was, that she thought it was a joy, at least, to have found his remains!

This psychological feeling, of having found the remains of a disappeared loved one is known as "closure" and it corresponds to a real psychological "need for closure". The effect is that, at least, the uncertainty and anguish ceases by the certainty of the death of the person that was searched.

In the event that the human remains of a person, who is being searched by their relatives, are found, the highest precautions should be taken as to how news is communicated, and the remains are returned, to the relatives. Careful consideration must be given to these aspects, so that the family is not further traumatized and can instead proceed in the work of "closure" and mourning even by treating the body or remains according to their cultural traditions or religious believes.

Right to reparations: The psychological importance of rehabilitation and satisfaction. Compensation of mental and moral damage

The violations of human rights derived from enforced disappearance can generate different types of harm. The definition of the Victims Basic Principles and

Guidelines already suggests what they can be and, in Section IX entitled "Reparation for harm suffered", they are described in detail. Section IX refers to material and non-material damage, including moral, emotional or psychological damage, indicating the types of reparations that are appropriate and adequate, depending on the type of damage caused.

Thus, the Victims Basic Principles and Guidance refers to "compensation" as one of the of the types of reparation for the various damages that may be caused, which include, according to paragraph 20, the following:

(a) Physical or mental harm;
(b) Lost opportunities, including employment, education and social benefits;
(c) Material damages and loss of earnings, including loss of earning potential;
(d) Moral damage;
(e) Costs required for legal or expert assistance, medicine and medical services, and psychological and social services.

For the purposes of this chapter, the moral damage referred to in subparagraph (d) and the mental harm provided for in subparagraph (a), are particularly relevant.

The other types of reparations referred to in the Victims Basic Principles and Guidelines coincide with those mentioned in Article 24(5) of the Convention, that is:

(a) Restitution;
(b) Rehabilitation;[4]
(c) Satisfaction, including restoration of dignity and reputation;
(d) Guarantees of no repetition.

The Victims Basic Principles and Guidelines define each of the above forms of reparation in detail.

The concept of restitution in the field of disappearances, particularly for those victims of enforced disappearance who are never found which, unfortunately, is the vast majority, is merely theoretical. "Restitution" as defined in paragraph 19 of the Basic Principles

Restitution should, whenever possible, restore the victim to the original situation before the gross violations of international human rights law or serious violations of international humanitarian law occurred. Restitution includes, as appropriate: restoration of liberty, enjoyment of human rights, identity, family life and citizenship, return to one's place of residence, restoration of employment and return of property.

This is not really a form of reparation which is realistic.

Even in the best-case scenario in which liberty, identity, family life can be restored, restitution as restoring the victim to the original situation before the enforced disappearance occurred is, from a psychological viewpoint, simply impossible.

However, for purposes of this chapter, the definitions of "rehabilitation" and "satisfaction" are particularly relevant. They read as follows:

21. Rehabilitation should include medical and psychological care as well as legal and social services.
22. Satisfaction should include, where applicable, any or all of the following:

    (a) Effective measures aimed at the cessation of continuing violations;
    (b) Verification of the facts and full and public disclosure of the truth to the extent that such disclosure does not cause further harm or threaten the safety and interests of the victim, the victim's relatives, witnesses, or persons who have intervened to assist the victim or prevent the occurrence of further violations;
    (c) The search for the whereabouts of the disappeared, for the identities of the children abducted, and for the bodies of those killed, and assistance in the recovery, identification and reburial of the bodies in accordance with the expressed or presumed wish of the victims, or the cultural practices of the families and communities;
    (d) An official declaration or a judicial decision restoring the dignity, the reputation and the rights of the victim and of persons closely connected with the victim;
    (e) Public apology, including acknowledgement of the facts and acceptance of *responsibility;*
    (f) Judicial and administrative sanctions against persons liable for the violations;
    (g) Commemorations and tributes to the victims;
    (h) Inclusion of an accurate account of the violations that occurred in international human rights law and international humanitarian law training and in educational material at all levels.

While the relevance of "rehabilitation" for the purposes of this chapter is evident, since it specifically refers to medical and psychological care, the relevance of the reparatory measures listed under "satisfaction" may be less immediate, even if some of those elements have a direct influence on the psychological, and specifically on the psychosocial, impact that this measure intends to repair.

Such is the case of the verification of the facts and full public disclosure of the truth. The right to the truth constitutes here, in itself, a measure of reparation, and a balm for the moral and emotional damage caused by the events that led to the disappearance, for the benefit of the relatives and loved ones of the disappeared person, and, of course, for the benefit of the community itself. Hence, the search for the disappeared persons, whether alive or dead, and for their identity, also has profound implications on the psychological and psychosocial aspects that impact the cultural traditions of the victim's family and community.

The public apology as well as the commemorations and tribute to the victims are elements of restitution as a reparatory measure, which undoubtedly also has healing effects on the psychological and emotional aspects that families and communities suffer as a result of disappearances.

"Compensation" or financial reparation, although not mentioned in the Convention, has also an element aimed at remedying economic damages, or even repairing immaterial damages by means of monetary compensation. Paragraph 20 of the Victims Basic Principles and Guidelines refers to the remedying of economic damages, such as mental harm, moral damages, and the costs of psychological and social services.

As can be seen, international human rights law on enforced disappearances contains a definition of victim, in connection with the damages suffered, and the reparation measures to which the victim is entitled to, that takes into account the individual psychological and collective psychosocial effects that the dreadful practice of disappearances causes.

The right to be presumed alive

One of the most emblematic and significant slogans of the relatives of the disappeared is "because they were taken alive, we want them alive" *("porque vivos se los llevaron, vivos los queremos")*. This demand should be reflected in both laws and public policies. In the search efforts, the disappeared person must be presumed alive; in the legislative measures, the governing principle should be the right of the disappeared person to be presumed alive, so to avoid, at all costs, the need for the relatives to obtain a declaration of presumed death in order to exercise certain rights.

The first among the Search Guiding Principles refers precisely to this issue and is entitled "the search for a disappeared person should be conducted under the presumption that he or she is alive". It states the following: "The search should be conducted under the presumption that the disappeared person is alive, regardless of the circumstances of the disappearance, the date on which the disappearance began and when the search is launched."

The above principle and right has an important impact on the psychological situation of the loved ones of the disappeared person. They always maintain the hope of finding their loved one alive. All authorities and persons involved must behave in a congruent manner to respect this principle.

On countless occasions, I have heard testimonies from relatives of disappeared persons that the authorities in charge of victim assistance, or those who have the obligation to carry out a search or criminal investigation, insinuate or flatly affirm, without evidence, that the missing person has surely already died. In a particularly revealing testimony, at the mother of a disappeared person described that a psychologist, who was supposed to be specialized in victim assistance, told her that he would have helped her overcome her hope to find her son alive. Such behaviour provoked tremendous indignation in the mother, and a sense of lack of empathy and understanding and, therefore, of re-victimization.

While it is true, as mentioned above, that finding the remains of a missing loved one can have a "closure" effect, alleviating the uncertainty of not knowing where the disappeared person is or what happened to them, this does not mean that the "closure" effect can be achieved without having absolute certainty that the disappeared person has indeed lost their life.

The continuous nature of the crime of enforced disappearance and the continuous anguish and despair during all the time that the fate or whereabouts of the disappeared person remains unknown

According to the Methods of Work of the Working Group on Enforced and Involuntary Disappearances and of the Committee on Enforced Disappearances, cases of enforced disappearance cannot be considered clarified until the fate or whereabouts of the disappeared person is known beyond doubt.

Article 21 of the Methods of Work of the Working Group reads as follows: "The Working Group considers cases outstanding until they have been clarified, archived or discontinued in accordance with the present methods of work."

It should be noted that archiving of cases or discontinuation of cases, would not mean that the cases have been clarified as provided for in paragraphs 27 and 28 of the Methods of Work. In those cases, they can always be reopened under paragraph 29.

With respect to the Committee, Article 41 of the Rules of Procedure and Working Methods provides the following:

> The Committee shall continue its efforts to work with the State party concerned for as long as the fate of the person sought remains unresolved. The Committee will maintain both, the State party concerned and the author(s) of the request, updated about any information received from the other and will regularly remind the State party concerned that the fate of the person remains unresolved. The Committee will consider that the fate of the person sought has been resolved if it receives reliable information in that regard.

According to what was mentioned above, the disappeared person must be presumed alive until it is proven with absolute certainty that he or she has lost their life.

Thus, the disappearance begins with the detention or deprivation of liberty from the moment in which the person was last seen and continues all the time until it concludes or ceases at the moment in which either the whereabouts of the person is determined by their indisputable identification, or human remains are found which, through the necessary forensic scientific tests, can be attributed beyond any doubt to the person sought.

It is for this reason that enforced disappearance is a crime of a continuous or permanent nature. This is expressed in Article 8, Section 1, subsection (b) of the Convention.

The continuous nature of the crime of enforced disappearance has important legal implications, which are not relevant to explain in this article as its main focus is on the psychological effects of enforced disappearance. However, the continuous nature of enforced disappearance is demonstrated not only legally, but above all, experientially, in the life and experience of the victims. For the relatives of the disappeared persons, the continuous nature of the crime of disappearance is a permanent experience. The anguish, the uncertainty, the profound pain of not knowing where their loved ones are, are permanently felt. That is why another of the most recurrent slogans of the loved ones of the disappeared persons says: "where are they? where are they? where are our children!?" (¿dónde están? ¿dónde están?¿¡nuestros hijos, dónde están!?).

The economic effects of enforced disappearances in the family members of the disappeared person

In relation to the above, as well as to the principle and right of the disappeared person to be presumed alive, it is relevant to address the issue related to the economic, patrimonial and other effects that the enforced disappearance produces in the life of the relatives of the disappeared.

Disappearances cause a pauperization effect in families when the main breadwinner in the family disappears. When they disappear, the family is left in economic distress. Then, the rest of the family members when faced with the disappearance of their family member not only go out to look for him in every corner but also have to go out to look for the economic support of their families.

The disappearance of their family member brings with it many problems. For example, if the disappeared person is the father of minors, the mother faces various legal problems related to the exercise of parental authority or guardianship of the children. If the missing person is the owner of the property rights, or as a tenant of the family home, the wife faces multiple legal problems, for example, for the renewal of the lease, the sale of movable or immovable property in the name of the disappeared person, the exercise of social security rights, welfare, pensions, and similar aspects. It is also practically impossible for the relatives of the disappeared persons to dispose of the monetary resources deposited in banking institutions. All this causes innumerable situations of psychological distress, which the States must attend to, in order to somehow solve or mitigate such circumstances.

The declaration of absence as a result of enforced disappearance

For the aforementioned reasons, the Convention, in Article 24, paragraph 6, establishes the following:

> Without prejudice to the obligation to continue the investigation until the fate of the disappeared person has been clarified, each State Party shall take the

appropriate steps with regard to the legal situation of disappeared persons whose fate has not been clarified and that of their relatives, in fields such as social welfare, financial matters, family law and property rights.

This provision contains several elements relevant to the subject we are dealing with now and also to what we have already said above.

First, the continuous nature of the crime of enforced disappearance is reiterated by establishing the obligation to continue the investigation (understood in its dual nature of criminal investigation and search investigation), until the fate or whereabouts of the victim is clarified. As already stated above, the Working Group on Enforced and Involuntary Disappearances and the Committee on Enforced Disappearances do not consider a case clarified until the fate or whereabouts of the victim is proven beyond doubt. These bodies periodically send communications to the governments of the States concerned, reminding them to continue their investigations until they find the persons sought.

Secondly, this provision refers to the issue we are dealing with now, in the sense that, as long as the whereabouts of the person remains unknown, the State must adopt the necessary measures related to the legal situation of the person whose fate has not been clarified, in order to enable their relatives to deal with issues concerning social welfare, financial matters, family law and property rights.

In various legal systems, there is the legal concept of "presumption of death", so that persons whose whereabouts are unknown for a certain period of time, may be declared dead, in order to open the probate or succession proceedings, with which the heirs will be able to exercise rights and dispose of assets of the absent person. For such purpose, the legislations normally establish very long periods of time to obtain such declaration of presumed death.

Furthermore, in the minds of the relatives of the missing persons, it is repugnant to have to ask a judge to declare their relative presumably dead when, as far as they are concerned, the person should be presumed alive.

Hence, the Convention establishes the obligations for States Parties to adopt legislative measures, other than the presumption of death. In short, they are obligated to create legal instruments that allow family members to receive the benefits and consequences equivalent to presumption of death, but without the need to make such a declaration. On the contrary, the declaration should be that the disappeared person is presumed alive, so that the judicial authorities can issue a certificate of declaration of absence due to disappearance, which allows to resolve all legal, economic, labour, commercial and any other relevant aspects.

In Latin America, several countries have issued laws establishing the legal instrument of the "declaration of absence due to enforced disappearance". Argentina was the first of these Latin American countries to do so on 8 June 1994, and it has been followed by several others, such as Brazil (4 December 1995),[5] Peru (24 November 2004), Uruguay (19 December 2005), Chile (10 December 2009), Colombia (24 May 2012) and Mexico (22 June 2018).

The Working Group on Enforced or Involuntary Disappearances adopted a general comment in 2011, which refers to the recognition as a person before the law in the context of enforced disappearance. In paragraphs 7 to 11 of this general comment, the Working Group addresses the issue of the declaration of absence mentioned above.

Among other things, the Working Group states the following:

9. Such a declaration should allow the appointment of a representative of the disappeared person, with the mandate to exercise his/her rights and obligations for the duration of his/her absence, in his/her interests and those of his/her next-of- kin. The latter should be allowed to manage temporarily the disappeared person's properties, for as long as the enforced disappearance continues, and to receive due assistance from the State through social allowances. In most cases, the disappeared persons are men and were the family breadwinners and special social support should be provided to dependent women and children. The acceptance of financial support for members of the families should not be considered as a waiver of the right to integral reparation for the damage caused by the crime of enforced disappearance, in accordance with article 19 of the Declaration.

10. In parallel to the issuance of a system of declaration of absence as a result of enforced disappearance, States should continue to investigate all cases to determinate the fate and the whereabouts of the disappeared and to ensure accountability of those responsible for the commission of enforced disappearances. That is, such declaration should not interrupt or close the investigations to determine the fate or the whereabouts of the victim, but should allow his/her next-of-kin to exercise on their behalf certain rights.

The Working Group addresses several of the points that we have underscored above, such as the fact that during the absence of disappeared persons, a representative should be appointed to handle their legal matters; the fact that when the disappeared person is the family breadwinner, the State should provide support to the members of the family, and that these actions should not cause the interruption of the investigations to determine their fate or whereabouts of the disappeared person. Moreover, the support to the family members of the disappeared should not be limited to financial support but integral and, thus, should include psychological treatment whenever necessary or convenient.

Children as victims of enforced disappearances

Article 25 of the Convention specifically refers to the issue of children as victims of enforced disappearance:

1. Each State Party shall take the necessary measures to prevent and punish under its criminal law:
   (a) The wrongful removal of children who are subjected to enforced disappearance, children whose father, mother or legal guardian is subjected to

enforced disappearance or children born during the captivity of a mother subjected to enforced disappearance;

(b) The falsification, concealment or destruction of documents attesting to the true identity of the children referred to in subparagraph (a) above.

2. Each State Party shall take the necessary measures to search for and identify the children referred to in paragraph 1 (a) of this article and to return them to their families of origin, in accordance with legal procedures and applicable international agreements.

3. States Parties shall assist one another in searching for, identifying and locating the children referred to in paragraph 1 (a) of this article.

4. Given the need to protect the best interests of the children referred to in paragraph 1 (a) of this article and their right to preserve, or to have re-established, their identity, including their nationality, name and family relations as recognized by law, States Parties which recognize a system of adoption or other form of placement of children shall have legal procedures in place to review the adoption or placement procedure, and, where appropriate, to annul any adoption or placement of children that originated in an enforced disappearance.

5. In all cases, and in particular in all matters relating to this article, the best interests of the child shall be a primary consideration, and a child who is capable of forming his or her own views shall have the right to express those views freely, the views of the child being given due weight in accordance with the age and maturity of the child.

This article refers to various issues that engender profound psychological effects, both for the disappeared victims themselves when they are minors, as well as for their parents and relatives. It applies to situations in which a minor is born in captivity, or the affliction suffered by children when their father, mother or guardian is the direct victims of the disappearance. In both cases, psychological care is of paramount importance.

There are innumerable and heartbreaking testimonies of cases of children born in captivity because their own mothers were victims of enforced disappearances. In countries such as Argentina and El Salvador, organizations of relatives have been formed in search of their children or grandchildren that, on many occasions, have been successful in locating them.[6] The testimonies that these by now adults give, once they manage to have their identity re-established, are truly shocking. They narrate the profound impact on their lives when they realize that the people they had always considered their parents, who had watched over them and cared for them, fed them and educated them throughout their lives, were in fact criminals who had appropriated them and had, perhaps, collaborated in the disappearance or execution of their real mother. In this sense, the psychological treatment provided by organizations of mothers, grandmothers and relatives of disappeared children is commendable beyond description.

The Convention underlines the precautions to be taken in this regard, always putting above all, the best interest of the child.

The importance of collective support of families of victims. The responsibility of the State to participate in such support

In the previous sections of this chapter, we have tried to describe the international provisions and standards related to the victims of enforced disappearance which are directly or indirectly connected with the psychological effects that this heinous crime generates in its victims, both, individually and collectively.

The Convention and other international standards in this area are very clear in establishing the obligations of the State for the care of and the provision of reparation to the victims, in terms of their personal needs, including those related to medical and psychological care.

Thus, the State must establish governmental agencies and provide them with the technical and material resources, as well as qualified personnel, to achieve these goals.

Unfortunately, many governments do not show compassion for the victims under their jurisdictions, nor are they committed to adopting measures and policies conducive to the fulfilment of the international obligations contracted by their states.

All too often victims themselves are left to carry out those activities, that the State should actually be performing. We see mothers of the disappeared conducting search caravans, digging in the earth with their own hands, hiring technical personnel with their own resources, providing the elements for their protection and security, when they have to go into territories controlled by highly dangerous criminal organizations.

Mothers and relatives of the disappeared establish collective organizations to accompany each other. This community accompaniment serves in itself as a first spontaneous collective psychological therapy, which lacks medical and scientific knowledge, but which nevertheless, intuitively, provides to its members, with unquestionable benefits. The empathy and solidarity that the members of these organizations offer each other strengthens them and allows them to move forward, tirelessly in their struggles in the search for truth and justice. It is therefore of crucial importance that States comply with their obligation under Article 24, paragraph 7, of the Convention, which establishes that: "Each State Party shall guarantee the right to form and participate freely in organizations and associations concerned with attempting to establish the circumstances of enforced disappearances and the fate of disappeared persons, and to assist victims of enforced disappearance."

These victims' organizations also understand the importance of having specialized psychological counselling for victims. The State and academic institutions of higher education, both public and private, must include in their curricula in psychology, medicine and related sciences, subjects that provide adequate training in the area of care for victims of gross human rights violations.

This should be done all over the world, but especially in those countries where the scourge of enforced disappearance strikes the population with greater intensity. The absence of academic programmes in this area is surprising, especially in those countries where the tragedy of disappearances is deeply present.

Article 23 of the Convention provides for the States to ensure that the training of officials including "medical personnel [...] who may be involved in the custody or treatment of any person deprived of liberty includes the necessary education and information regarding the relevant provisions of this Convention".

This obligation should also apply not only to the medical personnel assisting persons deprived of their liberty, but also to the medical and paramedical personnel, as well as psychotherapists, involved in the assistance to all victims of enforced disappearance, in the terms of Article 24, paragraph 5, of the Convention, specifically with respect to the right to rehabilitation, as explained earlier in this chapter.

Conclusion

Enforced disappearance causes a wide range of severe sufferings to the disappeared persons and their relatives and inflicts serious violations of various human rights.

International human rights law takes this into account and, from different angles, proposes measures that States should adopt in order to recognize the psychological effects suffered by the victims and the measures that should be adopted to address them.

Nonetheless, there are important shortcomings in this area, especially in those countries where disappearances are frequent.

From a pro-victim perspective, attention to the psychosocial effects derived from the commission of disappearances should be one of the highest priorities for governmental policies.

Notes

1 Inter-American Court of Human Rights, Case of *"Anzualdo Castro v. Peru"*, Judgment of September 22, 2009, (Preliminary Objection, Merits, Reparations and Costs), paragraph 105.
2 A/CED/7; https://undocs.org/CED/C/7.
3 Such as in the case of *Yrusta vs. Argentina* resolved by the Committee on Enforced Disappearances. See UN Doc. CED/C/10/D/1/2013, IHRL4087 (CED2016), 11 March 2016.
4 It should be noted that the Spanish version of the Convention, when referring to "Rehabilitation", uses the word *"Readaptación"*, which when literally translated into English, would be "Re-adaptation". In our opinion, this is a poor translation, and the word *"Rehabilitación"* should have been used in Spanish. In other words, the word *"Readaptación"* should not be understood as referring to the old concept of social readjustment used in the doctrine of the criminal law of the enemy. The correct term in Spanish should have been "Rehabilitación", as this term is correctly used in the Basic Principles and Guidelines in its Spanish version.
5 This legislation, however, is inconvenient because it does provide for the presumption of death of the disappeared person: *"reconhece como mortas pessoas desaparecidas em razão de participação, ou acusação de participação, em atividades políticas, no período de 2 de setembro de 1961 a 15 de agosto de 1979, e dá outras providências"* ("recognizes

as dead people who disappeared due to participation, or accusation of participation, in political activities, in the period from 2 September 1961 to 15 August 1979, and makes other provisions". (Translated with DeepL Translator). Inter-American Court of Human Rights, Case of *Anzualdo Castro v. Peru*, Judgment of 22 September 2009, (Preliminary Objection, Merits, Reparations and Costs), footnote 119.

6 One emblematic example of these organizations is *"Abuelas de Plaza de Mayo"*. This organization has operated for more than 40 years (since October 1977), and has recovered the identity of 132 children, according to the following publication, https://es.wikipedia.org/wiki/Anexo:Nietos_recuperados_por_Abuelas_de_Plaza_de_Mayo.

Chapter 6

The value and need for incorporating a psychosocial approach to forensic case-work in cases of extrajudicial, summary or arbitrary executions, including those who do not survive enforced and involuntary disappearances[1]

Morris Tidball-Binz

Introduction

For the families of disappeared persons, the trauma of the disappearance becomes a painful part of their daily lives. The yearning to find the person alive, the anguish for what they may suffer, the fear of the confirmation of death: all come together in the hearts and minds of the relatives of the disappeared as a constant and never-ending angst, which only the truth can help put to rest. Families therefore strive to know the facts about the fate and whereabouts of their loved ones, for which forensic sciences are growingly considered necessary. This chapter discusses the intersectionality between forensic investigations and the needs of families of the disappeared, as expressed in a psychosocial approach to forensic action. In the traditional domestic setting of ordinary criminal cases, forensic investigations are mainly oriented towards providing information for the criminal justice system. Only in a lesser degree are they concerned with the families of the victims. When applied to investigating disappearances and potentially unlawful deaths, however, forensic science also aims to alleviate suffering and protect human dignity. In this sense, in contexts of widespread violence, war, and violations of human rights and humanitarian law, forensic investigations take on more social implications. It is the victims and their families who are at the core of the efforts to find the truth, bring perpetrators to justice and ensure full reparations for the victims.

The victims are embedded in society and their suffering, reactions and ways of coping are therefore rooted in their respective communities, with corresponding psychological and social causes and effects.

The psychosocial approach in responding to this reality aims primarily to address and alleviate the psychological reactions and consequences caused by the disappearance of a loved one – considered by international human rights jurisprudence as equivalent to torture and ill-treatment – at an individual and collective levels, for which its intersectionality with forensic investigations is growingly considered indispensable.

DOI: 10.4324/9781003312642-9

The present chapter explains the innovative approach of combining the forensic investigation with a psychosocial approach to find the truth and address the consequences of enforced disappearances and potentially unlawful deaths.

The impact of disappearances

During all these years I knew he could not be alive, but one can never completely give up the dream that he might come home one day. I don't know if there is any worse torture than that. Burying my son, with his name on a gravestone above his tomb, has curiously, paradoxically, rescued him for us. He came out of the fog of persons unknown.

Testimony of Juan Gelman, Argentine poet, after the funeral of his son Marcelo Gelman, who disappeared after his detention by the military in 1976 and whose remains, bearing skeletal injuries consistent with torture and execution-style trauma, were recovered and identified in 1989 (Tidball-Binz, 2006).

The world over, hundreds of thousands of families live in anguish as a consequence of a missing relative, struggling for their *right to know the truth* about the whereabouts and fate of their loved ones. Regardless of their cultural, religious and social background, the relatives of the disappeared usually coincide in expressing that the death of a family member – however painful – can be accepted; but not knowing the fate of a loved one is far worse than almost any other possible experience: its impact is equated to torture (Lenferink, de Keijser, Wessel, de Vries, Boelen, 2017; Perez-Sales, Duhaime, Mendez, 2021).

The disappearance of a person is defined by the lack of information of the fate and whereabouts of this person, and the main emotional impact of the disappearance of a loved one is the uncertainty and ambiguity that it creates.

In cases of enforced disappearance, the State's role and responsibility is paramount, both in the disappearance itself as well as in the consequences that the disappearance produces on individuals and their families and communities. In effect, the practice of enforced disappearance was conceived during WWII by the Nazi regime in the form of the *Night and Fog* directive, signed by A. Hitler in December 1941, as a strategy to spread terror within the victims' family and communities in order to paralyze dissent and resistance to oppression (Mattarollo, 1987). The feeling of insecurity generated by this practice is not limited to the family of the disappeared, but also affects their communities and society as a whole.

Ever since, the practice of enforced disappearance has been used as a strategy to spread terror within societies in a number of contexts around the world, as a result of which millions of people are affected worldwide.

Societies' action or inaction in terms of documentation, sanction, reparations and prevention of disappearances have profound effects on victims' psychological and psychosocial suffering and healing.

Therefore, the State's role and responsibility is also paramount in allowing the truth to be discovered; the justice to be made through investigations, prosecutions and punishment; and appropriate reparation to be provided to all victims of enforced disappearances. These duties are not optional: they are obligations enshrined in numerous international instruments.

According to the United Nations *Basic Principles and Guidelines on the Right to a Remedy and Reparation for Victims of Gross Violations of International Human Rights Law and Serious Violations of International Humanitarian Law*,[2] "victims" are persons that, individually or collectively, have suffered harm, including physical or mental trauma, emotional distress, financial losses or substantial impairment of their fundamental rights, as a result of the States' failure to respect and protect those rights. This includes actions by private individuals and non-state actors.

A person can be considered a "victim" in compliance with this Declaration, without regard to the identification, apprehension, prosecution or conviction of the perpetrator and independently of the family link between the perpetrator and the victim. The term "victim" comprises, in addition and where appropriate, the relatives or persons in charge that have an immediate relationship with the direct victim, as well as with the persons that have suffered harm while trying to intervene to assist the imperilled victim or to prevent victimization.

In the case of unlawful deaths and, in particular enforced disappearances, the psychosocial effects on the victims' relatives and loved ones are diverse and vary in intensity and complexity. They may affect different aspects of a person, and transcend the individual, affecting entire families and communities.

The uncertainty about the fate of their loved ones that many people go through when a loved one disappears can leave a permanent open wound. The American scholar Pauline Boss has defined such a loss as physical ambiguous loss in which the absent person is kept psychologically present because of the lack of the proof of death and of the permanence of the loss (Boss, 2009, 2016).

The impact and long-lasting effects of enforced disappearances on individuals and groups are recognized as being particularly traumatic as the result of a purposeful action to cause suffering on the part of those holding the monopoly of power, such as it was conceived by the Nazis. In effect, the suffering which this causes is recognized as amounting to torture (Albertín, 2006; Perez-Sales, Duhaime, Méndez, 2021; Soria, 2002).

As recognized by Latin American scholars during the 1980s, traumatic ambiguity is the core of the experience suffered by relatives of the disappeared, uncertainty related to not knowing if the person is alive or dead, to the lack of explanations and legal process, and the dissonant experience of the psychological presence of the disappeared who is already non-existent for the society (Agger, Jensen, 1996).

As a result, disappearances generate profound long-term effects, such as anguish, uncertainty, hopelessness, sorrow, fears and trepidation, mistrust, guilt, intrusive recollections, phobic ideas, nightmares, recurrent memories, impotence, nostalgia, despair, frustration and the rupture of life projects (Weinstein, Maggi, Gómez, 1987). In addition, according to Bernstein (2010), other symptoms common to various kinds of traumatic experiences include:

1 A feeling of distress, of being at the mercy of others, of having lost control of life itself;
2 A rupture of existence itself, a breakdown of a vital feeling of continuity; and
3 Unmanageable stress.

Numerous authors state that the paradox of the absence of a loved one without confirmation of his or her life or death; and the resulting ambiguous "presence" of the disappeared person in the life of their loved ones makes it extremely difficult or impossible for families to carry out a normal mourning process, understanding the latter as a normal healing process which follows loss, making it acceptable and allowing the individual to readapt to a reality that no longer includes the lost loved one (Rojas Baeza, 2009). However, in the heart and minds of families of the disappeared, their missing loved ones are neither dead nor alive, making the elaboration of a normal mourning process difficult or impossible.

Within affected families this often leads to an interruption of life projects, the reorganization of the family structure and the investment of all resources into the search efforts while neglecting other needs, economic difficulties. This in turn often leads to a deterioration or disruption of relationships, separations and isolation. In cases of enforced disappearances, social or political stigmatization is often an additional factor, as a result of lack of sympathy or support from the surrounding society for affected families, whose suffering remains hidden in their private sphere and without the benefit of social coping mechanisms. These combined factors may induce a rupture in the social fabric.

According to Albarrán (2002), the families of the disappeared are victims at two main levels:

• Primary victimization, as a direct effect of a loved ones' disappearance, with effects at physical, psychological, economic and social levels of affected relatives, friends and communities and which extends in time;
• Secondary victimization, resulting from the manner in which institutions relate to families of the disappeared, including: depersonalized treatment, lack of information, absence of protection, excessive bureaucracy, slow processes or by casting doubt on the victims' narrative. The system that the victim turns to for support and answers may create a secondary victimization, which constitutes an aggravation of the victims' suffering as a result of the lack of empathy or negative reactions towards their needs.

In cases of disappearance, secondary victimization is all too common. States and their institutions more often than not incur in shortcomings and failures in their attention to families of the disappeared, which combined to a lack of answers and often unclear information, may amount to a re-victimizing interaction. As a result, those affected see themselves further isolated, threatened, lost and misunderstood.

The value of forensic investigations

Forensic investigations can play a fundamental role in the healing process of persons affected by disappearances, if carried out according to applicable standards and guided or framed by psychosocial considerations. By providing families with reliable information of facts about the whereabouts and fate of their missing loved ones and thus ending the uncertainty and ambiguity. However, forensic investigations are not reparatory per se, unless carried out with a psychosocial perspective.

Psychosocial action

As discussed above, the disappearance of a person impacts on both a psychological and social level, so both spheres also need to be addressed when trying to alleviate the impact and the suffering caused.

Psychosocial work is defined as the set of processes of accompaniment on an individual, family, community and social level, aimed at preventing, addressing and confronting the consequences of the impact of a specific event, in this case the death or disappearance of a loved one.[3]

These processes promote wellbeing, social and emotional support for the victims and contribute to re-establishing their integrity, strengthening their dignity and stimulating them in their own actions in the search of truth, justice and integral reparation. Psychosocial work also considers the reconstruction of those social support networks which have been damaged as a consequence of enforced disappearances and other grave violations of human rights or international humanitarian law.

Psychosocial support is indispensable for the integral reparation of families of the disappeared, as it contributes to the recognition of the psychological and social damage and to restoring the dignity of the victims and their families in society. It also enables families of the victims to continue or recreate their life projects.

Working with directly affected individuals and families, as well as with persons that are not directly affected in a community and society, provides the social support needed for comprehensive reparation. The psychosocial sphere is understood as the intersectionality of behaviours, attitudes, emotions and thoughts of individuals or groups, taking into account their historical, social and ideological environment and background, in order to comprehend them. In this regard, the psychosocial effect of a traumatic event is the way in which a phenomenon such as enforced disappearances affect relationships, behaviours and ways of understanding and dealing with the surrounding reality on the part of individuals, groups and communities.[4]

A traumatic event can be defined as an extreme human experience that poses a serious threat to the physical or psychological integrity of an individual and to which the person responds with intense fear, despair or horror. After having experienced a traumatic event of this kind, a series of symptoms may appear and the survivor will not be able to control them and they will generate deep and at times long-lasting psychological suffering (Anderson, 2009).

Damage caused by traumatic events such as enforced disappearances profoundly affect different realms of people's lives, such as individual, family, professional, communal, political, relational, among others. It affects direct victims, their families, organizations and social processes in which they participate. In this sense, psychosocial work aims to empower those affected as subjects of rights, encouraging decision making and action geared towards self-assertion, together with the elaboration of personal stories, collective history and history of the society as a whole.

People are impacted and react differently to similar traumatic events and their needs will vary accordingly. A psychosocial perspective can help identify and incorporate all relevant considerations required for a successful therapeutic intervention on their behalf. Interventions based on a psychosocial perspective can help ensure the intersectionality of the set of actions required at an individual, family, community and social levels, by all institutions, teams and professionals involved, to help ensure the repairing/healing character of these processes, at individual and community levels. A crucial factor in this regard is to establish an empathic therapeutic relationship with those affected by a disappearance as subjects of their own rights, persons with the capacity and possibilities for agency, thus enhancing and empowering their dignity, autonomy and liberty, while preventing re-victimization at all times. Such an approach aims to transform the process of searching for the missing person into a reparatory and healing process for the affected persons and communities.

Background of the psychosocial approach to forensic investigations into the disappeared

In the early days of psychological support to families of the disappeared, most professionals were confronted with novel forms and manifestations of extreme trauma. When families of victims of enforced disappearance in Latin America in the 1970s and 1980s first sought out support from psychologists, they found that these were often unable to relate to and fully understand the situation the families had to deal with. There was no experience regarding the effects that such a disappearance could have on individuals, at the social level and within the families themselves, in other words, at the psychosocial level.

Psychosocial support in the search for missing persons and in forensic investigations carries a number of specific challenges. In many cases, disappearance or loss of a loved one is only one of many traumatic events suffered by the person. Many of the families of the missing persons have also endured themselves enforced displacement, physical trauma, sexual violence and other traumatic experiences.

While psychological support for families in Chile and Argentina was initially not connected or integrated to any forensic search processes, this changed with the creation, supported by the Grandmothers of Plaza de Mayo, an organization of families of the disappeared, of the *Equipo Argentino de Antroplogía Forense* (Argentine Forensic Anthropology Team) in 1984 (see below). In Guatemala, psychosocial work based on social community psychology, was systematically integrated into the forensic search and identification processes from 1997 onwards. In Peru, the need for psychological assistance became evident during the collection of testimonies, as well as during exhumations initiated by the country's *Comisión de la Verdad y Reconciliación* – CVR (Truth and Reconciliation Commission) during the early 2000s.

In the case of the Balkans in Europe, the extensive forensic exhumation projects undertaken by the International Criminal Tribunal for the Former Yugoslavia (ICTY) during the late 90s, were largely carried out without involving the families. However, many of the exhumations which followed during the following years brought the forensic teams closer to the families.

In the case of Guatemala, forensic investigations, particularly large-scale exhumations of victims of past massacres and disappearances, helped to raise awareness of the need for tailored psychological interventions. Initially, the psychological assistance offered to some of the affected families and communities was mainly called for by the forensic teams, who hoped that psychological interventions would help contain and care for extreme emotional manifestations, during what they considered the most traumatic part of the process, i.e. the exhumations or notification of identifications. This led to a strong demand for psychologists' presence particularly during exhumations and it soon became clear that forensic and psychosocial work was a cooperative effort which required close coordination in consideration of the families' needs.

Psychologists soon developed a more comprehensive approach regarding the objectives, scope and timing of their interventions and forensic specialists more aware of the value and need for psychosocial interventions and for incorporating a psychosocial component to their investigations.

As a result, isolated crisis intervention activities turned into sustainable processes of psychosocial accompaniment in full complementarity with forensic processes aimed at strengthening the families' coping strategies and reconstructing the social fabric.

The perception of psychological and psychosocial interventions in forensic investigations into disappearances and unlawful deaths also changed: during the early years, the intervention of mental health professionals carried a certain fear of stigmatization and families were often reluctant to call on their support. Later, the families themselves openly recognized the value of psychological and psychosocial support for helping to cope with loss and to empower their efforts to seek truth, justice and reparations.

As experience expanded in the realm of forensic processes for the search and identification of the disappeared, evidence that the needs of the families went beyond specific psychological and psychosocial therapeutic interventions. This motivated the First World Congress on *Psychosocial Work in Exhumation Processes, Enforced Disappearance, Justice and Truth* in 2007, which led to the elaboration of a set of international recommendations, the *International Consensus on Principles and Minimum Standards for Psychosocial Work in Search Processes and Forensic Investigations in Cases of Enforced Disappearances, Arbitrary or Extrajudicial*

Executions, published in 2010.[5] More than four years of constructive dialogue among the various disciplines involved in the search and identification of missing persons, family associations, authorities and civil society resulted in a consensus of minimum standards necessary for forensic investigations to be restorative for families and communities.

Stemming from a need for international guidelines regarding psychosocial work in forensic processes, rather than describing the therapeutic interventions required, the final document lays out how to incorporate a psychosocial approach in all aspects of a forensic investigation, not just by psychologists, but by all actors involved.

The whole process of developing these guidelines, contributed greatly to an improved articulation between forensics and psychosocial work. The minimum standards in psychosocial support are now part of international recommendations, such as the Organization of American States (OAS) *Resolution on Missing Persons*.

As a result of these developments and practices, there is today ample agreement on the need to articulate forensic and psychosocial work, based on the needs and realities of the families and calls for such articulated work are more and more common, both in armed conflict and other violent contexts, the issue of missing and deceased migrants, as well as in disasters.

This was fully recognized by the *Third Conference on Psychosocial Support in the Search for Truth and Justice for Victims of Enforced Disappearance, Torture and Extrajudicial Execution*,[6] held in 2014 in Manila, Philippines, which identified the need to analyse the socio-political factors that caused the disappearances and the subsequent processes which shaped the victims' experiences, particularly their efforts to search for their missing loved ones, including forensic investigations. This is considered essential for shaping up any therapeutic support required by the affected families.

Forensic investigations of disappearances and psychosocial processes

It is telling that it was the families of the disappeared who pioneered the use of forensic science to help find the whereabouts of their missing loved ones. In effect, the relatives of disappeared and, in particular, the Grandmothers (*Abuelas*) of the Plaza de Mayo (APM), a non-governmental organization of grandparents of disappeared children in Argentina, provided that impulse. The APM was created in 1977, in the midst of the military dictatorship, to find the children (the grandchildren of the APM), kidnapped along with their missing parents. In order to support their search and reliably identify their grandchildren recovered years after their disappearance, the Grandmothers envisioned the use of forensic hemogenetics to assist in these identifications, thus promoting the creation of the world's first forensic genetic data bank. This bank was officially recognized under a national law which the Grandmothers promoted in 1987 and it later incorporated DNA analysis into its investigations, also at the urging of the Grandmothers (Berra, Grinspon,

Liwski, Tidball-Binz, 1986). The Argentine national genetic bank has since become a reference and model of best practice for other contexts, such as the Balkans, and has also inspired the development of applicable standards (Tidball-Binz, Penchaszadeh, Vullo, Salado Puerto, Fondebrider, Carlotto, Gershanik, Villegas Beltran, Albertelli, Toker, Goodwin, 2013).[7]

In addition, the Grandmothers also provided the indispensable support and encouragement for the creation of the world's first forensic organization dedicated exclusively to investigations into the disappeared: the Argentine Forensic Anthropology Team (*Equipo Argentino de Antropología Forense* – EAAF), at a time when the first scientific exhumations carried out by the Team, faced criticism, scepticism and even threats in Argentina. The EAAF was created specifically to search, recover and identify victims ("the disappeared") of the military regime that ruled the country between 1976 and 1983. The EAAF, established in 1984 by a group of young professionals and students supported by the Grandmothers, was the first organization of its kind and used techniques derived from archaeology and forensic anthropology to find and identify some of the thousands of victims of the regime (Celesia, 2019).

The Team greatly contributed to the growing recognition of the value and usefulness of forensic science in finding many of the "disappeared" and providing reliable answers to their families and communities about the whereabouts and fate of their loved ones.

Thus, thanks to the innovative use of forensic investigations advocated by the families of the disappeared, many families all over the world were able to find the truth that they so long sought for; and which had not been provided by traditional forensic systems, often biased by policies and practices of the ruling regimes.

The EAAF has become an internationally recognized institution and continues to carry out these tasks today on a global level. The Team has also become a model for similar initiatives throughout South America and elsewhere, helping to create and train similar teams in Guatemala, Mexico, Peru and South Africa, to mention just some examples. As importantly, the EAAF has contributed to the recognition of the role and value of forensic investigations as part of psychosocial processes on behalf of relatives of the disappeared and to the development of guidelines and standards in this field, including the *International Consensus on Principles and Minimum Standards for Psychosocial Work in Search Processes and Forensic Investigations in Cases of Enforced Disappearances, Arbitrary or Extrajudicial Executions* mentioned above.

Experience in the field has confirmed that the most important contribution of forensic sciences to a psychosocial healing process is the factual information it may provide on request from families, to help overcome some of the main psychological effects of a disappearance derived from uncertainty and ambiguity. In effect, forensic investigations can help clarify the fate and whereabouts of a missing person by providing a reliable forensic identification of the victim and, if dead, evidence-based information on the cause and manner of death of the victim. This information can help resolve ambiguous grief and facilitate a mourning process.

The other more obvious contribution of forensics in cases of dead victims is to enable the reunification of families with the body or human remains of their missing loved one. This is an essential condition for families to be able to carry out the necessary funeral ceremonies, according to their cultural, religious or personal needs (Díaz Facio, 2003).

Another aspect in which forensic experts can also contribute to healing processes is often overlooked. Information is control, and by providing information on the search and identification processes itself, regardless of the outcome, families and communities are enabled to take back some control, to demand their rights, to take action, to take their fate back into their hands, and it also empowers them to actively and very concretely contribute in the search. This is an important element in the psychosocial recovery as it enables persons and communities whom the traumatic events of violence and disappearance have put in the position of helplessness and loss of control, to influence processes which affect them and to recover confidence in themselves, their environment and their future.

Reliable and evidence-based forensic information resulting from participatory investigations can also help rebuild trust in society and authorities. This is of particular importance in transitional contexts where past authorities were responsible for the disappearances, by action or inaction. When proper and reliable forensic investigations are carried out by State institutions, they can help rebuild public confidence in public institutions. This requires however forensic work of impeccable quality, but also a very proactive, honest and empathic communication on the part of the forensic experts to enable families to regain trust into the institutions of the state that they hold responsible for their suffering. The experience of Chile in reforming its medico-legal services during the mid-2000s, in order to provide reliable scientific and trustworthy answers to families of the disappeared, is an example of best practice on this regard.[8]

The value of a psychosocial perspective in forensic investigations

Psychosocial work on behalf of families of the disappeared can contribute significantly to forensic investigations aimed at producing information on the fate and whereabouts of the person and, if dead, the restitution of the body and enabling the families' mourning processes. In other words, they should be regarded as complementary.

In addition, there are some aspects or moments of the forensic process in which the availability of psychosocial support is considered essential, in particular during the interviews of families to collect information and biological reference samples and the handing out of information or results of the investigation and the recovery of the body or human remains of their loved ones.

The interviews of families for purposes of collecting information about their disappeared loved and reference samples for DNA testing, as required for their forensic identification, often represents a potentially traumatic moment for families.

However, if conducted with a psychosocial approach, such an interview may become an empowering experience for the interviewee and also help elicit reliable information, by helping the person to better concentrate on the necessary factual details required from the interview.

For example, the experience of the Community Studies and Psychosocial Action Team (*Equipo de Estudios Comunitarios y Acción Psicosocial* – ECAP, 2010)[9] in the accompaniment of forensic processes in Guatemala, has shown that families and individuals who benefitted from a psychosocial intervention prior to and during ante-mortem data interviews reported these as positive experiences of self-affirmation and personal growth. Typically, during the preparatory interventions, families get acquainted with the questions they will be asked and receive explanations about the purpose of certain questions and their usefulness for identification. They are told which documents to bring to the interview, which photos might be useful, and prepare albums of their missing loved ones, thus approaching the memories slowly and in a protected environment.[10] In cases where such previous work is not possible, a psychosocial approach to the interview itself can include these aspects, leading away from the emotional remembering to specific facts.

Psychosocial support can also help to improve the process of collection of ante-mortem information, in particular with regards to the necessary interviews with families, including to better understand and manage adequately the influence that stress, traumatic experiences and culture have on peoples' memories.

Psychosocial support sessions before and during forensic interventions can also help clarify specific cultural needs, such as ceremonies before or after the recovery of human remains, and to identify specific doubts the families or communities might have about the forensic process. For example, community and spiritual leaders may play an important role in transmitting relevant information and help manage expectations.

A crucial moment of every investigation into a disappearance is informing the family about the findings. The acceptance of the findings or results of an investigation by the affected families, regardless of whether they meet expectations or not, is absolutely essential. Many factors can influence such acceptance: trust in the investigations or not, resistance to the possibility of death on the one hand, or a strong wish to find remains and end uncertainty on the other hand. During the search and identification processes the families will go through varying emotions, fears and expectations. Psychosocial accompaniment helps them imagine different possible scenarios and verbalize their inner questions about what may have happened to their missing loved ones, such as: Are they alive, are they dead? Are they suffering or have they suffered hunger, cold, fear? Have they been tortured?

Verbalizing the various possibilities makes those thoughts more concrete and provides a degree of reality to previously abstract imaginations. As a result, verbalized fears and expectations become more manageable and controllable and can be proven or discarded by confronting them with concrete information received from the forensic investigations, especially when this does not conform to expectations.

For example, families of victims of extrajudicial, summary or arbitrary executions usually expect to recover the complete bodies of their deceased loved ones (imagining a fresh body as known from their everyday experience of deaths and funerals). They therefore find it difficult and often very traumatizing to accept incomplete or badly damaged and unrecognizable remains. When the human remains cannot be found and/or identified, psychosocial support can help the families find alternative solutions for coping, such as communal memorials or symbolical burials. Acceptance by the family of the results of an investigation will also be facilitated by providing concerned families timely, detailed and clear information on the advances of the investigation, explanations of the undergoing methodologies and processes, and by integrating them into the decision-making process throughout.

Best practices for psychosocial interventions in forensic processes

The *International Consensus on Principles and Minimum Standards for Psychosocial Work in Search Processes and Forensic Investigations in Cases of Enforced Disappearances, Arbitrary or Extrajudicial Executions,* referred to earlier, emphasizes the need for an integrated psychosocial approach in every forensic investigation into disappearances.

Every intervention should be framed by human rights law and values, be based on the recognition of victims as right holders and guided by ethical principles, including for ensuring the reparatory nature of any intervention and a differential focus where required, while protecting throughout the mental integrity of victims and their families in a non-discriminatory manner, under the overarching principle of *do not harm.*

The *International Consensus* outlines 16 minimum standards which should guide every forensic investigation into disappearances and extra-judicial, summary or arbitrary executions:

• Every effort should be made to investigate every case of potentially unlawful death and disappearance, regardless of when they occurred or whether any formal denunciation on the part of those affected has taken place.
• The families or relatives of victims should be sought, found, informed and participation in the investigation should be promoted, empowered and protected.
• The active participation of families and relatives should be empowered, promoted, protected throughout.
• The investigation should seek to clarify events, ensure the right to truth and memory.
• The investigation should seek to ensure the right to justice.
• The investigation should seek to ensure the right to full reparations.
• Those participating in the investigation process, particularly families and communities should be assured security and protection throughout, as required by the circumstances and context.

- Families should benefit from constant information and transparency of the process.
- Provisions should be made for the comprehensive physical and psychological care of those participating in the investigation.
- The investigation should take into account and respect the culture and meaning of the affected population.
- The investigation and forensic process and every intervention should be planned and implemented ensuring a gender perspective throughout.
- Special attention and care should be considered in attention of affected children and adolescents.
- Coordination among all participating entities through appropriate mechanisms should be ensured throughout the investigation.
- The independence of participating teams should be ensured to protect the transparency, objectivity and impartiality of the investigation and guarantee the reliability of findings and results.
- Quality assurance and control of forensic processes should prevail throughout, including compliance with applicable international standards.

All the standards should be incorporated into the planning and implementation of any forensic investigation.

For example, security and self-care to help ensure and protect the physical and psychological well-being of the intervening teams and experts. This is important to prevent accidents and burn-out but, as importantly to enable an empathic interaction with victims and their families. The *International Consensus* calls for improved working conditions for experts and public servants, who frequently operate under heavy workloads in challenging environments and in emotionally stressful situations. This also includes continuous professional training to ensure that experts have the knowledge and skills required for their tasks, as well as access to counselling and psychological support.[11] Furthermore, all possible measures must be taken to ensure the safety of families, communities, witnesses and investigators, and to secure the confidentiality and protection of the information collected during the investigation.

At the same time, investigators should be trained and prepared to ensure transparency to victims and families and help ensure that they are properly and satisfactorily informed about objectives, implications, specific steps and technical processes, advances and findings, as well as the limitations and risks of the operation. The transmission of findings and results of the investigation must be done in comprehensible and culturally appropriate terms and format, taking into account the specific needs and sociocultural context of the affected families and communities.

Investigators should ensure strict adherence to professional standards in their forensic investigations. This includes the respectful and dignified treatment of human remains and associated evidence, their appropriate storage and preservation, and the application of the required scientific standards, including international protocols of best practices.

The value of the standards and recommendations from the *International Consensus* are nowadays recognized by the scientific community, have been incorporated into the regular practice of teams involved such investigations, including the EAAF; and are also reflected in international standards applicable to investigations into potentially unlawful death and disappearances. For example, *The Minnesota Protocol for the Investigation of Potentially Unlawful Death* (2016)[12] includes most of the above considerations in the sections on applicable ethical principles and codes and on the participation and protection of family members during an investigation, respectively. This builds from the first edition of the *Minnesota Protocol*, published in 1991 and the United Nations *Principles on the Effective Prevention of Extra-Legal, Arbitrary or Summary Killings*, adopted in 1989.[13] The first United Nations Special Rapporteur of extrajudicial, summary or arbitrary executions, Mr Amos Wako, oversaw the drafting of these documents which have served as landmarks, for which he closely took into consideration recommendations from families of the disappeared, including the Grandmothers of Plaza de Mayo. Similarly, the *Guiding Principles for the Search for Disappeared Persons*, adopted by the UN Committee on Enforced Disappearances and published in 2019,[14] is also in line with the best practices contained in the *International Consensus*.

Conclusion

Forensic investigations into disappearances, extrajudicial, summary or arbitrary killings aim to expose the truth, find and identify the disappeared, dead or alive and help ensure truth, justice and full reparation to victims, their families and affected communities. These goals also guide psychosocial interventions towards victims and their families, the goal of which is not simply to offer emotional support to those in need but to empower them in affirming their rights and the elaboration and reconstruction of their personal histories and the collective history as a whole.

Within this innovative framework, forensics and psychosocial sciences are fully complementary in working for the benefit of the victims, their affected families and communities.

There are however some basic conditions for forensic investigations into disappearances and unlawful deaths to be restorative: respect, quality and transparency of information and coordination are the main pillars for forensic action with a psychosocial approach, for which the 2010 *International Consensus on Principles and Minimum Standards for Psychosocial Work in Search Processes and Forensic Investigations in Cases of Enforced Disappearances, Arbitrary or Extrajudicial Executions* offers a framework for action and stands today as a reference. For example, in updating the *Minnesota Protocol*, the former UN Special Rapporteur on extrajudicial, summary or arbitrary executions, Christoph Heyns[15] ensured that the revised edition published in 2016 devotes attention to the rights of families of a person suspected of having been killed or disappeared, including setting out the right to participate in investigations.[16] The rights-based approach of the 2016 *Minnesota Protocol* ensures that the interests and rights of those most affected by the alleged rights violations are upheld throughout the investigation.

Notes

1 This chapter is dedicated to the memory of Prof. Christof Heyns.
2 Available at: https://www.ohchr.org/en/professionalinterest/pages/remedyandrepara-
   tion.aspx.
3 *International Consensus on Principles and Minimum Standards for Psychosocial Work
   in Search Processes and Forensic Investigations in Cases of Enforced Disappearances,
   Arbitrary or Extrajudicial Executions.* ECAP, Guatemala, 2010.
4 The Inter-American Court of Human Rights has repeatedly recognized the impact of
   enforced disappearances on the individual, family, as well as their life projects. See, for
   example, the 2004 Case: *19 Tradesmen v. Colombia*, which required the State to provide
   "medical and psychological treatment" for the families as a reparation measure.
5 *International Consensus on Principles and Minimum Standards for Psychosocial Work
   in Search Processes and Forensic Investigations in Cases of Enforced Disappearances,
   Arbitrary or Extrajudicial Executions* ECAP, Guatemala, 2010.
6 *Conference Statement: Third Conference on Psychosocial Support in the Search
   for Truth and Justice for Victims of Enforced Disappearance, Torture and Extrajudicial Execution*, Manila, 21 July 2014. Available in: https://www.afad-online.org/
   news/10-statements/194-conference-statement-third-conference-on-psychosocial-
   support-in-the-search-for-truth-and-justice-for-victims-of-enforced-disappearance-
   torture-and-extrajudicial-execution.
7 *Guidelines for the Use of Forensic Genetics in Investigations into Human Rights and
   International Humanitarian Law Violations.* Available in: https://www.icrc.org/en/
   publication/4431-guidelines-use-forensic-genetics-investigations-human-rights-and-
   international.
8 In 2006 the Chilean Medico-Legal Institute was fully restructured on instructions from
   President Michelle Bachelet following the disclosure of the misidentification of at least
   48 out of 96 bodies of the disappeared recovered from the Patio 29 from the public
   cemetery of Santiago.
9 See: https://www.hhri.org/es/organisation/equipo-de-estudios-comunitarios-y-accion-
   psicosocial-ecap/.
10 As an example of this process, see Chapter 3 (Andrea Bleichmar) in this book.
11 See Chapter 12 (Boulanger) in this book on this topic.
12 See: https://www.ohchr.org/Documents/Publications/MinnesotaProtocol.pdf.
13 See: https://www.ohchr.org/Documents/ProfessionalInterest/executions.pdf.
14 See: https://www.ohchr.org/EN/HRBodies/CED/Pages/Guiding-Principles.aspx.
15 Prof. Christof Heyns (January 1958- March 2021) was Professor of Human Rights Law,
   Director of the Institute for International and Comparative Law in Africa at the University of Pretoria and a member of the United Nations Human Rights Committee. He
   served as United Nations Special Rapporteur on extrajudicial, summary or arbitrary executions from 2010 to 2016. He undertook the task of revising and updating of the 1991
   *United Nations Manual on the Effective Prevention and Investigation of Extra-Legal,
   Arbitrary and Summary Executions (Minnesota Protocol)*.
16 *Minnesota Protocol* (supra note), 35–37.

References

Agger, I., Jensen, S.B. (1996). *Trauma y Cura en Situaciones de Terrorismo de Estado.
   Derechos Humanos y Salud Mental en Chile bajo la Dictadura.* Santiago de Chile: Edi-
   ciones Chile América.
Albarrán, J. (2002). "El peritaje psicológico en los procedimientos civiles y laborales." In
   Urra, J. (Comp.), *Tratado de psicología forense.* Madrid: Siglo XXI de España Editores,
   pp. 477–485.

Albertín, P. (2006). "Psicología de la victimización criminal." In Soria, M.A., Sáiz, D. (Eds.), *Psicología criminal*. Madrid: Pearson Prentice Hall, pp. 245–276.

Anderson, M. (Eds.). (2009). *Acción sin Daño: Cómo la Ayuda Humanitaria puede apoyar la Paz o la Guerra*. Bogotá: Ediciones Ántropos. (Martín-Baró, I. 1983, 1984, 1998. Montero, M. 1991, 2000).

Beristain, C. (2010). *Manual sobre Perspectiva Psicosocial en la Investigación de Derechos Humanos*. País Vasco: Universidad del País Vasco y Hegoa.

Berra, J., Grinspon, D., Liwski, N., Tidball-Binz, M. (1986). "Genetical Identification of 'Missing' Children in Argentina." In Brinkmann, B., Henningsen, K. (Eds.), *Advances in Forensic Haemogenetics*, Vol. 1. Berlin, Heidelberg: Springer-Verlag.

Boss, P. (2009). "The Trauma and Complicated Grief of Ambiguous Loss." *Pastoral Psychology*, 59(2), pp. 137–145. https://doi.org/10.1007/s11089-009-0264-0

Boss, P. (2016). "The Context and Process of Theory Development: The Story of Ambiguous Loss." *Journal of Family Theory and Review*, Special Ed. on Ambiguous Loss, pp. 269–286. https://doi.org/10.1111/jftr.12152

Celesia, F. (2019). *La Muerte es el Olvido*. Buenos Aires: Paidós.

Conference Statement: *Third Conference on Psychosocial Support in the Search for Truth and Justice for Victims of Enforced Disappearance, Torture and Extrajudicial Execution*. Manila, 21 July 2014. Available in: https://www.afad-online.org/news/10-statements/194-conference-statement-third-conference-on-psychosocial-support-in-the-search-for-truth-and-justice-for-victims-of-enforced-disappearance-torture-and-extrajudicial-execution.

Díaz Facio, V.E. (2003). *Del Dolor al Duelo: Límite al Anhelo frente a la Desaparición Forzada*. Colombia: Editorial Universidad de Antioquia.

Equipo de Estudios Comunitarios y Acción Psicosocial. (2010). *International Consensus on Principles and Minimum Standards for Psychosocial Work in Search Processes and Forensic Investigations in Cases of Enforced Disappearances, Arbitrary or Extrajudicial Executions*. Guatemala: ECAP.

International Committee of the Red Cross. (2020). Guidelines for the Use of Forensic Genetics in Investigations into Human Rights and International Humanitarian Law Violations. Geneva: ICRC. Available in: https://www.icrc.org/en/publication/4431-guidelines-use-forensic-genetics-investigations-human-rights-and-international.

Lenferink, L., de Keijser, J., Wessel, I., de Vries, D., Boelen, P.A. (2017). "Toward a Better Understanding of Psychological Symptoms in People Confronted with the Disappearance of a Loved One: A Systematic Review." *Trauma, Violence & Abuse*, 20(3). https://doi.org/10.1177/1524838017699602

Mattarollo, R. (1987). *La desaparición: Crimen contra la humanidad, Jornadas sobre el Tratamiento Jurídico de la Desaparición Forzada de Personas*. Facultad de Derecho y Ciencias Sociales de la Universidad Nacional de Buenos Aires, 24 and 25 March 1987, Buenos Aires: APDH.

Perez-Sales, P., Duhaime, B., Méndez, J. (2021). Current Debates, Developments and Challenges Regarding Torture, Enforced Disappearances and Human Rights. *Torture Journal*, 31(2), pp. 3–13. https://doi.org/10.7146/torture.v31i2.128890

Rojas Baeza, P. (2009). *La interminable ausencia, Estudio médico, psicológico y político de la desparición forzada de personas*. Santiago: LOM Ediciones.

Soria, M. (2002). *Manual de Psicología Forense*. Barcelona: Ed. Atelier.

Tidball-Binz, M. (2006). "Forensic Investigations into the Missing." In Schmitt, A., Cunha, E., Pinheiro, J. (Eds.), *Forensic Anthropology and Medicine*. Totowa, New Jersey, pp. 383-407.: Humana Press.

Tidball-Binz, M., Penchaszadeh, V., Vullo, C., Salado Puerto, M., Fondebrider, L., Carlotto, E., Gershanik, A., Villegas Beltran, F., Albertelli, S., Toker, L., Goodwin, W. (2013). "A Good Practice Guide for the Use of Forensic Genetics Applied to Human Rights and International Humanitarian Law Investigations." *Forensic Science International: Genetics Supplement Series*, 4(1), pp. e212–e213.

Weinstein, E., Maggi, A., Gómez, E. (1987). "El Desaparecimiento como Forma de Represión Política." In FASIC, *Trauma, Duelo y Reparación. Una Experiencia de Trabajo Psicosocial en Chile*. Santiago de Chile: FASIC, pp. 151–191.

Chapter 7

Fifty shades of suffering? The wavering international jurisprudence on relatives of disappeared persons as victims of human rights violations[1]

Gabriella Citroni

Introduction

Since the first decisions rendered in the 1980s on cases of enforced disappearance, international human rights mechanisms have recognized relatives of disappeared persons as victims of a violation in their own right, because of the anguish and stress caused by the enforced disappearance of their loved ones, the continuing uncertainty on their fate and whereabouts and the attitude of indifference shown by authorities in the face of their demands and continuing pain. This notion is today enshrined in Art. 24, para. 1, of the International Convention on the Protection of All Persons from Enforced Disappearance (hereinafter, 'ICPED'), which, besides the disappeared person, recognizes as victim 'any individual who has suffered harm as a direct result of an enforced disappearance'.

Albeit the core principle is relatively straightforward, an analysis of the existing international jurisprudence on the matter shows that discrepancies exist on major issues, beginning with who could validly claim the victim status. Does this notion narrow down to the relatives of the disappeared? If so, to which degree of kinship? Could it encompass also persons – including family members – who were not even born when the enforced disappearance begun? Could a collective dimension of victimhood be recognized in contexts where the socio-cultural structure does not revolve around a purely individualistic *Weltanschauung* and a traditional interpretation of 'family' (e.g. indigenous peoples)?

The answers given by international human rights mechanisms to the previous questions depend largely on the position taken on another crucial issue, i.e. the rationale applied to recognize these persons or groups of persons as victims in the first place. Is it because of their suffering vis-à-vis the enforced disappearance of their loved one? If so, how is that suffering assessed? Shall the attitude of the authorities vis-à-vis the demands of the relatives of the disappeared be taken into account to this end? Conversely, is any particularly proactive procedural behavior requested to relatives and persons who wish to effectively claim the recognition of the victim's status?

The burden of proof applied by the international human rights mechanisms concerned weighs significantly on the subjects at stake: some apply presumptions and

DOI: 10.4324/9781003312642-10

revert the burden on the respondent States; others leave it to those claiming the victims' status to prove their suffering and that they have been proactive in approaching the authorities.

Lastly, for those who overcome all the procedural hurdles and are indeed recognized as victims, what is the name given to the violation(s) they endured? Some international human rights mechanisms regard it as inhuman and degrading treatment, others as torture or generic ill-treatment; in some cases, the violations of the rights to family life and to judicial guarantees are also acknowledged.

Moving from an analysis of the relevant rules and provisions of international law and of the jurisprudence on cases of enforced disappearance of international criminal tribunals and of the European and Inter-American Courts of Human Rights (hereinafter, respectively 'ECtHR' and 'IACtHR'), as well as of the Human Rights Committee (hereinafter, 'HRC') and the Committee on Enforced Disappearances (hereinafter, 'CED'), this chapter aims at illustrating the main existing discrepancies and their ramifications, including on the measures of reparation awarded. It is contended that, while each case is certainly unique, there are some common features that should be identified and assessed through fair criteria. This is desirable to avoid troublesome outcomes where the suffering of relatives of disappeared persons – often finding themselves in analogous situations – is evaluated in an opposite manner depending on the interpretative standards applied, ultimately resulting in the denial of the most basic solace of acknowledging the ordeal these women, men and children have to go through on a daily basis.

The first section of the chapter presents the relevant international legal framework and summarizes the jurisprudential benchmarks on the matter. The following section elaborates on the main existing discrepancies in international case law concerning the so-called indirect victims of enforced disappearance, analyzing who can be qualified as such, the rationale behind the different choices made by international human rights mechanisms, the applicable burden of proof and the kind of violations detected. Finally, some conclusions are offered to highlight areas where jurisprudential developments seem to duly recognize the extent of the harm inflicted on persons other than the disappeared, without instances of unwarranted discrimination.

International law and jurisprudence on relatives of disappeared persons

Enforced disappearance is an especially complex crime, characterized by the violation of several human rights, which usually involves various perpetrators and causes a plurality of victims beyond the disappeared person.

Interestingly, even when the legal notion of 'enforced disappearance' had not yet been elaborated, the verdicts of the Nurnberg war crimes tribunals already acknowledged the multiplicity of victims of this heinous practice. Finucane (2010) has noted that, initially, the criminalization of enforced disappearance mostly served 'the humanitarian function of protecting family rights during armed conflicts' and that the 'protected object' was the family and the 'international value' of familial integrity. Arguably, the criminal sanction of those responsible was geared toward the protection of the interests of family members in knowing the fate and whereabouts of those subjected to enforced disappearance – mostly through the application of the Decree known as 'Night and Fog' of 7 December 1941 (*Nacht und Nebel Erlass*)[2] – and toward the provision of retribution for the harm inflicted on the family, besides that suffered by the disappeared. In this context, before the International Military Tribunal at Nuremberg, Marshal Wilhelm Keitel was charged with the implementation of the decree, characterized as a war crime. In particular, the prosecution alleged that the conducts in question (defined as 'murders and ill-treatment') were contrary to, among others, Art. 46 of the Hague Regulations, 1907, which establishes that 'family honor and rights, the lives of persons and private property, as well as religious convictions and practice, must be respected'. In its verdict, the Tribunal found that the implementation of the Night and Fog Decree amounted to a violation of the provision concerned and regarded it as a form of 'mistreatment inflicted upon the missing persons and their families' (Trial of German Major War Criminals, Proceedings of the International Military Tribunal Sitting at Nuremberg, Germany 2, 22, 1946, 453), thus acknowledging relatives of disappeared persons as victims in their own right.

Similarly, in its verdict of 4 December 1947 on the case *Altstötter and Others* (also known as the '*Justice* case'), the United States of America Military Tribunal at Nuremberg held that the implementation of the Night and Fog Decree created an atmosphere of constant fear and anxiety among the relatives and friends of the disappeared and the population of the occupied countries and held that 'cruel punishment was meted out to the families and friends without any charge or claim that they actually did anything in violation of any occupation rule of the army or of any crime against the Reich' (Trials of War Criminals before the Nuremberg Military Tribunals, 1949, 1057–1058). With regard to the relatives of the disappeared, the Military Tribunal found that they

> were in constant distress of mind as to their whereabouts and fate. The *purpose* of the spiriting away of persons under the Night and Fog decree was to *deliberately create constant fear and anxiety among the families, friends and relatives as to the fate of the deportees*.
>
> (para. 1058, emphasis added)

After these precedents, international criminal tribunals did not deal on many other occasions with cases of enforced disappearance. When they did, they mostly focused on the harm inflicted upon the disappeared persons – usually qualifying enforced disappearance as a crime against humanity, in the form of 'other inhumane treatment' – somehow neglecting the families as autonomous victims and rather referring to them as witnesses in the relevant proceedings (*Prosecutor v Kupreškić et al.*, 2000, para. 566).[3] A notable exception is the verdict rendered on 17 January 2005 by the International Criminal Tribunal for the Former Yugoslavia in the case *Blagojević & Jokić:*

... the Trial Chamber is aware that many of the survivors, who lost their relatives under the horrific circumstances described above, are still searching for the bodies of their loved ones and looking for any information which would establish with certainty whether they are dead, and, if so, the exact circumstances of their death. The Trial Chamber is convinced that *the mental harm suffered by these survivors reaches the required threshold to constitute serious mental harm.*

(para. 653, emphasis added)

Indeed, international humanitarian law revolves very much around the rights of the 'families' of missing persons[4] (Finucane, 2010; La Vaccara, 2019). Albeit not elaborating on whether they should be considered victims in their own right, international humanitarian law acknowledges the suffering caused by not knowing the fate and whereabouts of a loved one and the so-called ambiguous loss (Boss, 1999), spelling out what parties to a conflict are required to do to put an end to this condition and to duly assist relatives. In particular, Art. 32 of Additional Protocol I to the Four Geneva Conventions of 1949 establishes that

... the activities of the High Contracting Parties, of the Parties to the conflict and of the international humanitarian organizations mentioned in the Conventions and in this Protocol shall be prompted mainly by the *right of families* to know the fate of their relatives.

(emphasis added)[5]

Similarly, it is a rule of customary international humanitarian law that 'each party to the conflict must take all feasible measures to account for persons reported missing as a result of armed conflict and must provide their family members with any information it has on their fate' (Henkaerts, Doswald-Beck, 2009: Rule 117).

For their part, since the first resolutions concerning enforced disappearance adopted by the General Assembly, the United Nations (hereinafter, 'UN') acknowledge and express concern about 'the anguish and sorrow' caused to the 'relatives of disappeared persons, especially to spouses, children and parents'.[6]

In terms of individual complaints concerning cases of enforced disappearance, the HRC (i.e. the mechanism in charge of monitoring the implementation of the International Covenant on Civil and Political Rights) was the first Treaty Body to be called to pronounce itself. Already in the second decision rendered on the subject matter in 1983,[7] the HRC acknowledged the violations suffered by the relatives of the disappeared person. In particular, it declared that

[it] understands the *anguish and stress* caused to the mother by the disappearance of her daughter and by the continuing uncertainty concerning her fate and whereabouts. The author has the right to know what has happened to her daughter. In this respect, she too is a victim of the violations of the Covenant suffered by her daughter, in particular of Article 7 [of the International Covenant on Civil and Political Rights].

(*Quinteros v Uruguay*, 1983, para. 14, emphasis added)

In the following decisions, the HRC mostly maintained this interpretation, providing clarifications on the underlying reasoning. Nevertheless, as illustrated below, recently, the HRC has arguably undertaken a more restrictive approach.

Art. 1, para. 2, of the Declaration on the Protection on the Protection of All Persons from Enforced Disappearance, adopted through General Assembly resolution 47/133 of 18 December 1992 (i.e. the first international human rights instrument that provides a definition of the practice, hereinafter 'the 1992 Declaration'), recognizes that any act of enforced disappearance 'inflicts severe suffering' on the disappeared and 'their families'. Moreover, Art. 19 provides that 'the victims of acts of enforced disappearance *and their family* shall obtain redress and shall have the right to adequate compensation, including the means for as complete a rehabilitation as possible' (emphasis added).[8] Over the years, the Working Group on Enforced or Involuntary Disappearances (hereinafter, 'WGEID'), i.e. the mechanism that assists States in the implementation of the Declaration, has consistently held that relatives of the disappeared are themselves victims[9] and has issued general comments and thematic studies whereby it delves upon the differential impacts on women, children and migrants victims of enforced disappearance and their relatives. In its 2013 general comment on women affected by enforced disappearances, the WGEID held that 'a comprehensive definition should recognize that family members of the disappeared are also victims because they endure unique forms of suffering as a direct result of the disappearance' (para. 38).

At the regional level, the Inter-American system of human rights is the one that has developed the most innovative case law on enforced disappearance. However, the recognition of relatives of the disappeared as victims of violations in their own right emerges at a later stage in the jurisprudence of the IACtHR. Notably, the first judgments rendered by the IACtHR on cases of enforced disappearance did not analyze this matter, nor was it alleged as an autonomous violation by the petitioners. Similarly, the relevant regional treaty (i.e. 1994 the Inter-American Convention on Forced Disappearance of Persons) enshrines a rather conservative notion of 'victim', referring solely to the disappeared person (e.g. Arts. III and IV). 'Relatives' or 'families' are mentioned only with regard to their right to have access to information on persons deprived of their liberty (Art. XI). It is in the judgment rendered on 24 January 1998 on the merits of the *Blake v Guatemala* case (paras. 114–116), that the IACtHR recognized for the first time that relatives of the disappeared person are also subjected to violations of their fundamental rights pursuant to the American Convention on Human Rights (hereinafter, 'ACHR'), and in particular of Art. 5 (right to humane treatment), read in conjunction with Art. 1, para. 1 (obligation to respect rights). Since 1998, the IACtHR has consistently reaffirmed these findings, further elaborating on the rights violated, the applicable evidentiary criteria, the right-bearers and what are the actual reasons generating the violations.

In the same year (i.e. on 25 May 1998), the ECtHR rendered its first judgment on a case of enforced disappearance (*Kurt v Turkey*) where it also found a violation of Arts. 3 (prohibition of torture) and 13 (right to an effective remedy) of the European Convention on Human Rights (hereinafter, 'ECHR') with regard to the applicant, who was the mother of a disappeared person, essentially due to the authorities' inactivity in the face of her anguish and distress (para. 133). In the judgments rendered in the following years, the ECtHR took a rather unstable stance on the matter, apparently struggling to set sound criteria on which relatives can claim to be victims in their own right, the reasons for doing so and the applicability of presumptions (Baranowska, 2021). To date, the case law of the ECtHR on the matter appears to be the most restrictive one compared to other international human rights mechanisms.

Albeit not specifically devoted to enforced disappearance, the UN Basic Principles and Guidelines on the Right to a Remedy and Reparation for Victims of Gross Violations of International Human Rights Law and Serious Violations of International Humanitarian Law (hereinafter, 'UN Principles on Reparations') represent a crucial reference with regard to the definition of victimhood:

> victims are persons who individually or collectively suffered harm, including physical or mental injury, emotional suffering, economic loss or substantial impairment of their fundamental rights, through acts or omissions that constitute gross violations of international human rights law, or serious violations of international humanitarian law. Where appropriate, and in accordance with domestic law, the term *'victim' also includes the immediate family or dependents of the direct victim and persons who have suffered harm in intervening to assist victims in distress or to prevent victimization.*
>
> (UN, General Assembly resolution 60/147 of 16 December 2005, Principle 8, emphasis added)

The notion enshrined in the UN Principles on Reparations thus goes even beyond the acknowledgment of 'relatives' as victims, adding a specific mention to those who assist victims or are involved in the prevention of violations. Instead, Principle 4 of the UN updated set of Principles for the Protection and Promotion of Human Rights through Action to Combat Impunity (hereinafter, 'Principles against Impunity') establishes that

> irrespective of any proceedings, *victims and their families* have the imprescriptible right to know the truth about the circumstances in which violations took place and, in the event of death or disappearance, the victim's fate.
>
> (UN, Commission on Human Rights resolution 81/2005 of 21 April 2005, emphasis added)[10]

The chosen phrasing seems not to acknowledge families as autonomous victims, albeit recognizing their right to know the truth.

Most of the jurisprudential and legal developments illustrated above are reflected in Art. 24, para. 1, of the ICPED, which explicitly states that 'victim means the disappeared person and any individual who has suffered harm as the direct result of an enforced disappearance'.[11] In the first views delivered on 11 March 2016 on the case *Yrusta v Argentina*, the CED (i.e. the mechanism mandated to monitor the implementation of the ICPED), was called to pronounce itself, among others, on the said provision and its alleged violation and it confirmed a broad and inclusive interpretation, revolving around the international responsibility of the State for not recognizing in domestic proceedings the status as victims of the sisters of a forcibly disappeared man, thus inflicting on them what the CED defined an 'irreversible impairment'.

The fact that the suffering of the 'families' of the disappeared must be regarded as an autonomous human rights violation has been recognized in international law since 1946. Nevertheless, as the following section shows, there are inconsistencies in the interpretation of the notions at stake, especially between the main international human rights mechanisms dealing with individual complaints on the matter.

The main discrepancies

Today the fact that enforced disappearance causes a plurality of victims beyond the disappeared person is undisputed, and the possibility to severely harm a great number of people through one single crime is arguably one of the aims pursued by perpetrators.

However, there remain at least four areas where significant differences exist in international law and jurisprudence, namely who can validly claim the victim status and the underlying rationale for doing so, the applicable evidentiary criteria, and the nature of the autonomous violation(s) suffered by persons other than the disappeared.

Whose harm?

International law and the corresponding jurisprudence are today unanimous in declaring that the harm caused by enforced disappearance goes beyond the disappeared person. However, reference is made indiscriminately to 'families', 'relatives', 'next-of-kin', 'family members', 'dependents' and, in the broader interpretations, to 'friends' and 'any individual who has suffered harm as the direct result' of the crime concerned. While many of these terms may be used as synonyms, there are nuances that are not necessarily captured and they may lead to very different – at times unwarranted – interpretations.

Referring to the notion of 'relatives' of the disappeared person, international humanitarian law applies a broad definition. In this regard, Art. 2, para. 2, of the Model Law[12] on Missing Persons drafted by the International Committee of the Red Cross, refers to the applicable provisions of the Civil Code or Family Law, nevertheless setting forth that the term shall include, at a minimum, 'children born in and out of wedlock, adopted children or step-children; lawfully wedded partner or unwedded partner; parents (including step-mother, step-father, adopter); full or half or adopted sisters and brothers'. While the list aims to be as comprehensive as possible, it would still not encompass anyone beyond the relatives of the disappeared, thus potentially falling short of the real scope of the damage inflicted by such practice. In this sense, friends of the disappeared, or colleagues, fellow trade unionists, members of the same political party, etc. would not be recognized as autonomous victims. The collective dimension of victimhood is not foreseen either.

International human rights mechanisms, having dealt with individual communications on cases of enforced disappearance, essentially agree in recognizing 'relatives' of the disappeared as victims of inhumane treatment. However, even in that realm, differences can be detected and, more in general, there does not seem to be any well-established acknowledgment of persons other than relatives as victims nor of collective victimhood.

On its part, the HRC has so far recognized as victims of a violation of Art. 7 (prohibition of torture and inhumane and degrading treatment), read alone and in conjunction with Art. 2, para. 3 (right to an effective remedy) of the International Covenant on Civil and Political Rights (hereinafter, 'ICCPR') family members of the disappeared, including mothers and fathers, sons and daughters, spouses and siblings. The HRC reaches this conclusion with regard to those relatives who are also formally complainants. In this sense, if the application before the HRC was lodged, for instance, by the wife of a disappeared who is also father of two children and whose mother is still alive and involved in his search, the HRC would assess only whether the rights of the wife of the disappeared were violated and would not look into the situation of the other relatives.

The IACtHR is the international body that has developed the most inclusive jurisprudence also on the matter, and has found a violation of, among others, Art. 5, read in conjunction with Art. 1, para. 1, of the ACHR, with regard to a variety of family members, encompassing cousins, in-laws, and partners or former partners outside the wedlock. Also relatives born after the enforced disappearance took place have been considered victims of a violation of Art. 5 ACHR (*Contreras et al. v El Salvador*, 2011, para. 122). On occasions, it also recognized a collective dimension of the damage inflicted by enforced disappearance, referring to 'society at large' as the victim of a violation of the right to know the truth (*González Medina and family v Dominican Republic*, 2012, para. 251).[13] Seldom, the IACtHR has also referred to the collective damage inflicted on indigenous peoples, especially by the impossibility to perform their rituals and give a dignified burial to members of the community forcibly disappeared (*Bámaca Velásquez v Guatemala*, 2000, para. 161).[14] However, the findings on this matter are not always consistent and, as of today, the IACtHR has failed to analyze in-depth whether, depending on the circumstances, other groups (e.g. political parties, trade unions or school classes) can also be regarded as victims (Citroni, 2020).

The existence of a collective dimension of the damage generated by enforced disappearance – and therefore of a broader scope of the notion of victimhood – has been acknowledged by the WGEID in its study of 9 July 2015 on enforced disappearances and economic, social and cultural rights, whereby it highlighted, on the one hand, as certain individuals (e.g. teachers, human rights defenders and trade-unionists) are targeted and forcibly disappeared with a view at damaging also persons and groups associated with them (UN Doc. A/HRC/30/38/Add. 5 of 9 July

2015, paras. 36–40). On the other hand, with specific regard to the enforced disappearance of indigenous community leaders, the WGEID emphasized that it

...may prevent their communities from exercising their right to hold traditional funerals for the deceased and preserving the language, oral traditions, and religious ceremonies, therefore violating the communities' right to take part in cultural life...

(para. 41)

The unwarranted effects of a restrictive interpretation of the notion of 'victim' of enforced disappearance are shown by the jurisprudence of the ECtHR. As mentioned above, in its first judgments rendered on cases of enforced disappearance, it acknowledged that relatives of the disappeared person who lodged an application to the Court could be victims of a violation of Art. 3 ECHR, but it attached great relevance to the degree of kinship, reaching paradoxical conclusions. While parents of the disappeared – especially if mothers – were seen as victims in their own right without too much trouble, the situation of siblings posed more problems. In the words of the ECtHR:

The Court observes that in the Kurt case, which concerned the disappearance of the applicant's son during an unacknowledged detention, it found that the applicant had suffered a breach of Article 3 having regard to the particular circumstances of the case. It referred particularly to the fact that she was the mother of a victim of a serious human rights violation and herself the victim of the authorities' complacency in the face of her anguish and distress. *The Kurt case does not however establish any general principle that a family member of a "disappeared person" is thereby a victim of treatment contrary to Article 3.* Whether a family member is such a victim will depend on the existence of special factors which gives the suffering of the applicant a dimension and character distinct from the emotional distress which may be regarded as inevitably caused to relatives of a victim of a serious human rights violation. *Relevant elements will include the proximity of the family tie – in that context, a certain weight will attach to the parent-child bond –, the particular circumstances of the relationship, the extent to which the family member witnessed the events in question, the involvement of the family member in the attempts to obtain information about the disappeared person and the way in which the authorities responded to those enquiries...*

(ECtHR, *Çakıcı v Turkey*, 1999, para. 98, emphasis added)

The criteria set forth by the ECtHR to assess which relatives of a disappeared person may qualify as victims do not seem fully persuasive and were criticized by judges Thomassen, Jungwiert and Fishbach in a partly dissenting opinion attached to the judgment concerned. Albeit, in the following years, the ECtHR applied such standards in a rather flexible manner, and the proximity of the family tie does not seem to play a prominent role, the so-called *Çakıcı* criteria are invoked to this very day (Baranowska, 2021). The persistence of the narrow understanding of the ECtHR about who can be considered as victim beyond the forcibly disappeared person is shown by the harshly criticized (Citroni, 2013) judgment rendered on the case *Janowiec et al. v Russia*. In that case, contrary to the findings of the IACtHR in similar circumstances in the case of persons born after the enforced disappearance of their relatives, notwithstanding the efforts undertaken to elucidate their fate and whereabouts and the indifference shown by State authorities, the ECtHR considered that their mental anguish does not fall within the threshold of Art. 3 of the ECHR (*Janowiec et al. v Russia*, 2012, para. 154). With regard to the acknowledgment of a collective dimension of the damage caused by enforced disappearance, the ECtHR once recognized that the failure to effectively investigate on such crimes infringes the right to know the truth of the victims (i.e. the forcibly disappeared persons), their family, other victims of similar crimes and the general public (*El Masri v The Former Yugoslav Republic of Macedonia*, 2012, para. 191). However, as of today, the ECtHR has not analysed in-depth the features and the consequences that a broader notion of victimhood may attract.

Finally, in its views on the *Yrusta* case, the CED found that the sisters of a forcibly disappeared man certainly fall within the notion of 'victim' enshrined in Art. 24, para. 1, of the ICPED and that failing to recognize their legal status as such entails the international responsibility of the State (para. 10.8). Bearing in mind that the notion of victim enshrined in the relevant provision of the ICPED is the most extensive one, the CED has considerable leeway to expand its interpretation in future decisions.

In the light of the above, although international law and jurisprudence recognize that the harm inflicted by an enforced disappearance goes beyond the forcibly disappeared person, there is no unanimity on who the other victims are and how many people – including social groups and communities – can this notion encompass. The described situation suggests a scarce understanding of the aims and ramifications of the crime at stake and may lead to instances of discrimination and re-traumatization. As the subsequent sections illustrate, discrepancies in international case law extend also to the rationale used to identify some individuals as victims, the applicable standard and burden of proof and the rights considered as violated.

Is it the suffering that matters?

If today all international human rights mechanisms dealing with enforced disappearance recognize the multiplicity of victims caused by such a crime, the reasons for doing so are not necessarily the same.

In its first decisions, the HRC focused on the 'anguish and stress' caused by the continuous uncertainty of the fate and whereabouts of a loved one (*Quinteros v Uruguay*, 1983, para. 14). This was the measuring stick to decide whether relatives of the disappeared had been subjected to a violation of Art. 7 of the ICCPR and, to a great extent, remains the main criterion followed by the HRC. In more recent years, the HRC found that to oblige relatives of disappeared person to have a family member declared dead in order to be eligible for social allowances or compensation amounts to inhumane and degrading treatment against the applicant (*Rizvanović v Bosnia and Herzegovina*, 2014, para. 9.6). After decades in which it adopted a rather open approach, in its views of 5 November 2019 on the case *K.K. and others v Russia*, concerning gross human rights violations, including enforced disappearances occurred during World War II, albeit acknowledging 'the tragedy and pain the authors have lived with for many years after losing their relatives' and the fact that the investigations carried out by the Russian authorities 'did not clarify the circumstances of the death of their relatives and rejected their rehabilitation requests', the HRC did not consider relatives as autonomous victims of any violation of the ICCPR (para. 6.7). In this particular case, the HRC considered that more than 60 years after the events concerned, it was unlikely that there could be 'genuine uncertainty in the authors' minds about the fate of their dead relatives' (para. 6.7). Moreover, introducing particularly strict criteria never used before (i.e. requesting the applicants to prove a proactive and intentionally harmful behavior of State authorities), the HRC held that the authors had failed to prove that the attitude shown by authorities 'was manifestly *disrespectful or degrading*, or otherwise *aimed at causing them pain and suffering*' (para. 6.7). These rather uncanny findings seem to suggest that, if relatives know that their loved ones were killed, this should be 'enough' not to regard them as victims of ill-treatment, although they ignore the circumstances of the crimes, cannot obtain the return of the mortal remains to perform their rituals and the authorities reject all their attempts to unveil the truth and obtain justice and redress and show utter indifference in the face of their demands. The reasoning is far from persuasive and actually suggests an 'easy way out' to States that want to elude their responsibility and could be left off the hook by simply answering that a disappeared person 'died'.

Indeed, the ECtHR had reached a similarly disturbing conclusion in its judgment on *Janowiec et al.,* concerning the same events (*Janowiec et al. v Russia*, 2013, para. 182 and 185–187). More in general, the ECtHR has affirmed that the essence of a violation of Art. 3 of the ECHR with regard to relatives of disappeared persons

> does not so much lie in the fact of the "disappearance" of the family member but rather concerns the authorities' reactions and attitudes to the situation when it is brought to their attention. It is especially in respect of the latter that a relative may claim directly to be a victim of the authorities' conduct.
>
> (*Çakıcı v Turkey*, 1999, para. 98)

Indeed, the assessment of the authorities' conduct seems to lack consistency and, on occasions, notwithstanding the failure to adopt effective measures to search for the disappearances and to hold the perpetrators accountable, the ECtHR was satisfied by the existence of domestic judgments generically acknowledging a violation and awarding an (unpaid) amount of money as compensation (*Skendžić and Krznarić v Croatia*, 2011, para. 96). Additionally, the ECtHR attaches certain importance to the involvement of applicants in the attempts to obtain information about the disappeared person, imposing on them the burden to show a degree of proactivity, albeit this criterion is not always applied coherently (Baranowska, 2021).

On its part, since 1998, the IACtHR regards relatives of the disappeared as victims of a violation of Art. 5 (right to humane treatment) of the ACHR, holding that the harm inflicted on their mental and moral integrity is a direct consequence of the enforced disappearance of their loved ones, and finding that 'the circumstance of such disappearances generate suffering and anguish, in addition to the sense of insecurity, frustration and impotence in the face of the public authorities' failure to investigate' (*Blake v Guatemala*, 1998, para. 114). The IACtHR continues to apply these criteria today when assessing the situation of relatives of the disappeared person and, as referred above, it has paid attention also to the specific harms inflicted – especially where indigenous peoples are involved – by the lack of respect for the mortal remains of the disappeared and the failure to return them to the family for a dignified burial or performing last rituals.

Finally, in the already mentioned views on the case *Yrusta v Argentina*, the CED acknowledged the suffering and anguish of the applicants as the source of a violation, however going even further. In particular, the sisters of the forcibly disappeared person, who were also the authors of the communication lodged before the CED, complained that, by refusing to grant their request for legal standing as private criminal plaintiffs (*querellantes*) in domestic criminal proceedings, the authorities of the State concerned essentially denied their status as 'victims' and prevented them from gaining access to relevant information and playing an active part in the investigation into their brother's enforced disappearance and death. The CED held that

> the *anguish and suffering* experienced by the authors owing to the lack of information that would allow clarification of what happened to their brother have been exacerbated by the *de facto failure to acknowledge their status as victims*, which thus becomes a cause of re-victimization that is incompatible with the principles enshrined in the Convention.
>
> (para. 10.8, emphasis added)

When assessing whether there are victims other than the forcibly disappeared person, international human rights mechanisms therefore pay attention – albeit applying different criteria – to the levels of suffering and anguish experienced and to the attitude shown by State authorities in the face of such sentiments. These criteria, however, may be slippery as there is a degree of subjectivity and, as the next section illustrates, the evidentiary standards applied may create insurmountable obstacles.

The applicable burden of proof

Indeed, if, in order to declare a violation of one or more rights of persons other of the disappeared person, international human rights mechanisms focus on the suffering of the individual concerned, their proactivity and the attitude shown in their regard by the authorities, the attribution of the burden of proof and the criteria used to assess the evidence play a crucial role.

The IACtHR, showing a better understanding of the complex features of enforced disappearance and of the ordeal faced by relatives of disappeared persons and others involved in the attempts to establish the truth and obtain justice, applies a rebuttable presumption of a violation of the right to mental and moral integrity of parents, siblings, sons and daughters, spouses and life-partners of disappeared persons (*Radilla Pacheco v Mexico*, 2009, para. 162).

This approach has also been traditionally applied also by the HRC which, however, recently somehow departed from it in the views rendered on 28 October 2020 in the case *F.A.J. and B.M.R.A. v Spain*, where, despite the applicants' repeated attempts to learn the truth about the enforced disappearance of their loved ones, the Committee refused to find a violation of Art. 7, read in conjunction with Art. 2, para. 3, of the ICCPR, surprisingly declaring that the authors had 'not shown that the claim was raised before the domestic authorities' (para. 7.8). The views and the lack of understanding that, to a great extent, the frustration of relatives of disappeared people is caused precisely by the lack of effective domestic remedies, have not escaped the criticism of four members of the HRC who, in their partly dissenting opinion, found the majority's decision 'bewildering' and 'inscrutable', bearing in mind the

> …mountain of uncontested facts that demonstrably reveal the contrary. As painstakingly recounted, despite official denial and their personal severe psychological stress, the authors pursued a variety of legal and administrative avenues in their dogged quest for justice. (…) Any or all of those claims would have provided some accounting for the disappearance of their parents, and in that way assuaged some of the authors' pain and suffering resulting from their lack of knowledge of what happened. But their claims repeatedly floundered because of the uncompromising stance taken by the State party, both during and after the dictatorship, of maintaining a complete wall of silence around the atrocities committed during the dictatorship.
>
> (partially dissenting opinion of Yadh Ben Achour, Arif Bulkan, Ahmed Amin Fathalla and Hélène Tigroudja, paras. 3–4)

The considerations of the dissenting experts, that acknowledge the ordeal of the relatives of the disappeared persons vis-a-vis the callous indifference of the State and do not impose on the relatives an impossible burden of proof, reflect much better the nature of the harm at stake.

These latest developments on the jurisprudence of the HRC seem to go in the direction of the especially restrictive approach of the ECtHR. On the one hand, as already mentioned, the ECtHR considers that if someone was not born when the enforced disappearance of a relative commenced, irrespective of whether these persons have been involved for their entire life in the struggle to establish the truth and to obtain justice and the authorities systematically frustrated all these attempts, such persons cannot be considered as victims. On the other hand, the ECtHR leaves the burden of proof on the applicants, requesting them to 'make proof of a certain amount of diligence and initiative and introduce their complaints without undue delay' (*Gutierrez Dorado and Dorado Ortiz v Spain*, 2012, para. 37). The ECtHR does not seem to attach any relevance, for the purposes of recognizing the violations suffered by relatives of forcibly disappeared persons, to the fact that applicants may be unable to promptly lodge complaints because they are left without effective remedies and are somehow trapped in the lulls of authorities, being these elements among the actual sources of anguish and distress.

Which human right(s) are violated?

The previous sections illustrate that, even if international human rights mechanisms in principle agree on the multiplicity of victims generated by an enforced disappearance, they differ in many respects when it comes to identifying who falls within the category, the reasons for which a person should be considered a victim, as well as the applicable evidentiary criteria. International jurisprudence is equally discordant when it comes to determine which human rights have been violated with regard to persons other than the disappeared.

The HRC would find a violation of Art. 7 (prohibition of torture and inhumane and degrading treatment), read alone and in conjunction with Art. 2, para. 3 (right to an effective remedy), of the ICCPR with regard to the applicants. On occasions, having regard to the specific circumstances of the case, it also found violations of the right to family as enshrined in Art. 17 (*Roy Rivera Hidalgo v Mexico*, 2021, para. 9.10), and, when minors are involved, of Art. 24, para. 1 (rights of the child), of the ICCPR (*Prutina et al. v Bosnia and Herzegovina*, 2013, para. 10).

With regard to relatives of the disappeared, the ECtHR usually focuses on whether there is a violation of Art. 3 (prohibition of torture) of the ECHR, sometimes read in conjunction with Art. 13 (right to an effective remedy). In certain cases, it assessed whether there was also a violation of Art. 8 (right to respect for privacy and family life), but mostly where those responsible for the enforced disappearance also broke into the applicants' house (*Khutsayev et al. v Russia*, judgment of 27 May 2010, paras. 152–155), in cases of enforced disappearances carried out in the form of extra-ordinary renditions (*El Masri v The Former Yugoslav Republic of Macedonia*, 2012, paras. 248–250).

In *Yrusta v Argentina*, the CED found that

> ... the mere fact that it took over a year for a decision to be issued regarding the right of Mr. Yrusta's family members to take part in the investigative proceedings entails, in and of itself, a violation of articles 12 (1) and 24 (1), (2) and (3) of the Convention (respectively on the obligation to investigate, the notion of victim, the right to know the truth and the obligation to search for the

disappeared person). After such a long period has passed, the possibility of playing an active and effective part in the proceedings is lessened to such an extent that the impairment of the right in question becomes irreversible, in violation of the victims' right to know the truth.

(para. 10.9)

Accordingly, the CED requested the respondent State to '*recognize the authors' status as victims*, thereby allowing them to play an effective part in the investigations into the death and enforced disappearance of their brother' (para. 12.a, emphasis added).

With little exception, the three mentioned international human rights mechanisms do not seem to pay any specific attention to the characteristics and specificities of the victim at stake, somehow implying that the 'suffering' would be the same, no matter whether the individual concerned is a woman, a girl or a boy, disabled, an elderly or pertains to an indigenous community.[15] As of today, along with the WGEID, the IACtHR is the only international human rights mechanism that has explored the differential impact on the victim. In general, with regard to relatives of the disappeared, the IACtHR assesses whether there has been a violation of Arts. 5 (right to humane treatment), 8 (right to a fair trial) and 25 (right to judicial protection), read alone and in conjunction with Art. 1, para. 1 (obligation to respect rights), and sometimes 2 (domestic legal effects), of the ACHR (*Garzón Guzmán v Ecuador*, 2021, paras. 66–89 and 90–94). Where minors are involved, it considers Art. 19 (rights of the child) of the ACHR, and, in cases concerning women – and especially pregnant women – it has analyzed the special kind of suffering and anguish imposed on the victim (*Gelman v Uruguay*, 2011, paras. 91–101). As mentioned in a previous section, it has also referred to the specificities of indigenous peoples, in particular with regard to rituals and the respect of the death.

The jurisprudence of the IACtHR is in line with the approach of the WGEID, which recognizes the particular type of harm suffered based on the characteristics of the person involved, be it a woman, a child or a migrant (WGEID, *General Comment on women affected by enforced disappearances*, 2012, paras. 5 and 11). While discrepancies based on unsound criteria such as the degree of kinship are hardly justifiable, a differential approach that takes into account the specificities of the persons concerned, the circumstances and, therefore, the special kind of damage suffered seems much more sensible.

Conclusion

I felt my heart contract and grow small. Pain shrinks the heart. This, I believe, is part of the intention. You make a man disappear to silence him but also to narrow the minds of those left behind, to pervert their soul and limit their imagination.

(Hisham Matar, The Return – Fathers, sons and
the land in between, 2016)

Boss (2017) pointed out that 'ambiguous loss is the most stressful type of loss because there is no proof of finality', because the uncertainty on the fate and whereabouts of a loved one amounts to a 'complicated loss and thus leads to symptoms akin to those of complicated grief', causing 'chronic sorrow and lingering grief' (pp. 521–523). Enforced disappearance causes consequences at the individual level (including anxiety, depressive symptoms, suicidal ideation, addiction or abuse), at the family level (whereby relationships are ruptured and the family as a system becomes fragile) and at the community level (Boss, 2017, pp. 525–526).

Recognizing the features of this particularly serious harm and its multiple dimensions is key to understanding the real nature of enforced disappearance and its consequences. Indeed, it is essential to bear in mind that hitting as many people as possible, spreading terror among them and confining several persons or groups between hope and despair is one of the actual purposes of the crime. The recognition that relatives of the disappeared person, her or his colleagues, friends or social group or ethnic community are targeted since the very beginning as victims of this practice is pivotal to acknowledging the damage purportedly inflicted on them, without instances of discrimination that only perpetuate their victimization. This recognition shall be accompanied by the application of flexible evidentiary criteria and the avoidance of an unreasonable burden of proof.

Persons other than the disappeared – including their relatives – are subjected to inhumane and degrading treatment and, under certain circumstances, to violations of other rights, including the right to family life, the rights of the child, etc. This requires the adoption of different measures of reparation, as well as the cessation of the offence. Further, the community to which the victim belongs can also be subjected to other violations (e.g. of their right to freedom of association, or non-discrimination). In these cases, reparation entails the cessation of the unlawful conduct and measures of satisfaction. Finally, society at large is also victimized and, in this case, the adequate measure of reparation is the establishment of the truth that is equivalent to the cessation of the offence, bearing in mind that the concealment of the truth is an essential element of the crime of enforced disappearance. With regard to communities and society as a whole, without prejudice to whether they are formally parties in the proceedings concerned, reparations – including guarantees of non-repetition – can be awarded *ex officio*, given the extreme gravity of the human rights violation at stake.

However, besides recognizing this plurality of victims of the same kind of violations, it is equally necessary to acknowledge that the characteristics and circumstances of those concerned weigh on the assessment of how the effects of an enforced disappearance are lived and faced by the person concerned. In this sense, age, gender and ethnicity certainly play a relevant role. The recognition of these differential impacts will, in turn, allow the design of 'tailored' measures of reparation, that are directed at better responding to the nature and dimension of the harm suffered by the victims at stake and their communities. Only if conceived on the basis of this differential approach are measures of reparation going to have a meaningful impact, not only returning the individuals and communities concerned to the situation exiting prior to the enforced disappearance, but also transforming pre-existing excluding stereotypes and hierarchies that made the enforced disappearance and the ensuing consequences in terms of marginalization possible in the first place.

Allowing relatives of forcibly disappeared persons, as well as their communities, to go from victims to right-holders is the first step toward their empowerment, through giving due consideration to their suffering and making it the basis to build a different future and prevent similar violations.

Notes

1 The opinions expressed in this chapter are strictly personal and do not in any way reflect the position of the WGEID or any of the institutions/organizations to which the author is affiliated.
2 This decree was adopted by Adolf Hitler and established that, in the context of World War II, people suspected or accused of offences against the Reich were to be transported to Germany secretly and would be prosecuted there by military courts. These measures were conceived with a deterrent effect because prisoners would vanish without leaving a trace (as in 'night and fog', hence the name of the decree), and their relatives would not receive any information as to their whereabouts of their fate, therefore remaining trapped in uncertainty.
3 See also Special Panels for Serious Crimes within the District Court of Dili, East Timor, *Prosecutor v. Rusdin Maubere* (No. 23/2003), Trial Chamber judgment of 5 July 2004; Extraordinary Chambers in the Courts of Cambodia, *Prosecutor v. Nuon Chea and Khieu Samphan* (Case No. 002/01), Trial Chamber judgment of 7 August 2014 and Appeals judgment of 23 November 2016, and Extraordinary Chambers in the Courts of Cambodia, *Prosecutor v. Nuon Chea and Khieu Samphan* (Case No. 002/02), Trial Chamber judgment of 16 November 2018.
4 The notion of 'missing persons', usually applied in international humanitarian law and by the International Committee of the Red Cross (ICRC) is broader than that of 'victims of enforced disappearance'. In this sense, 'missing' includes anyone whose whereabouts are unknown to their relatives and/or who, on the basis of reliable information, has been reported missing in connection with an international or non-international armed conflict, another situation of violence, a disaster, or any situation that may require action by a neutral and independent body.
5 Additionally, see the Model Law on Missing Persons drafted by the ICRC in 2009. In particular, Art. 7 (rights of relatives to know the fate of missing persons) and 10 (right to financial assistance and social benefits for the missing and their relatives). See also ICRC (2014).
6 UN, General Assembly Resolution 33/173 of 20 December 1978 Disappeared Persons, preamble.
7 Notably, in the first views issued on a case of enforced disappearance (i.e. Case *Bleier v. Uruguay*, views of 29 March 1982), the Human Rights Committee did not find any separate violation with regard to the authors of the communication (respectively the daughter and the wife of the disappeared person).
8 Art. 13 of the 1992 Declaration sets forth the right of relatives to lodge a complaint on the enforced disappearance of a loved one and have it duly investigated and the States' obligation to protect them from ill-treatment, intimidation or reprisal and to appropriately punish any such instance.

9 This is reflected in the WGEID's methods of work: 'while the Declaration does not define explicitly the concept of victims of enforced disappearance, a definition may nonetheless be inferred from it and by taking into consideration the evolution of international law. For the purpose of the implementation of its mandate, the Working Group considers that victims include a disappeared person and any individual who has suffered harm as the direct result of an enforced disappearance', UN Doc. A/HRC/WGEID/102/2 of 7 February 2014, para. 9.

10 See also Principle 31.

11 Art. 12 of the International Convention on the Protection of All Persons from Enforced Disappearance (ICPED) sets forth the right of relatives to lodge a complaint on the enforced disappearance of a loved one and have it duly investigated and the States' obligation to protect them from ill-treatment, intimidation or reprisal and to appropriately punish any such instance. Moreover, Art. 15 of the ICPED requires States parties to cooperate with each other with a view to 'assisting victims of enforced disappearances' (thus arguably encompassing relatives); and Art. 18 of the ICPED spells out the core information on persons deprived of their liberty to which relatives, among others, are entitled.

12 A 'model law' is a sort of 'template' designed to assist States when reforming or drafting domestic legislation on a specific subject. In general, the model law deals with general principles and leaves a margin of discretion to States to ensure their applicability and enforcement at the domestic level, taking into account the existing national legislative framework.

13 Inter-American Commission on Human Rights, *The Right to Truth in the Americas*, OEA/SER.L/V/II.152 Doc. 2, 13 August 2014, paras. 15, 19, 81, 108–110 and 120. Moreover, Principle 2 of the UN Principles to Combat Impunity acknowledges the collective dimension of the right to know the truth, which is recognized to 'every people'.

14 On the collective dimension of the damage – and suffering – in cases where an indigenous leader is forcibly disappeared, see, IACtHR, *Chitay Nech and others v Guatemala*, judgment of 25 May 2010, Ser. C No. 212, paras. 141, 159 and 162.

15 Indeed, in some of the cases mentioned above the disappeared persons or some of their relatives were minors, women or indigenous and the international human mechanism concerned did not remark or analyze in-depth this aspect in its judgment or decision.

References

Baranowska, G. (2021) *Rights of Families of Disappeared Persons – How International Bodies Address the Needs of Families of Disappeared Persons in Europe*. Cambridge: Intersentia.

Boss, P. (1999) *Ambiguous Loss: Learning to Live with Unresolved Grief*. Cambridge, MA: Harvard University Press.

Boss, P. (2017) Families of the Missing: Psychosocial Effects and Therapeutic Approaches. *International Review of the Red Cross* 905(99), 519–535. Available from: https://international-review.icrc.org/sites/default/files/irrc_99_905_4.pdf [Accessed 16th February 2022].

Citroni, G. (2013) *Janowiec and Others* v. *Russia*: A Long History of Justice Delayed Turned into a Permanent Case of Justice Denied. *Polish Yearbook of International Law* XXXIII, 279–295. Available from: https://doi.org/10.7420/pyil2013l.

Citroni, G. (2020) La desaparición forzada como violación de los derechos económicos, sociales y culturales en la jurisprudencia de la Corte Interamericana de Derechos Humanos.

In Ibáñez Rivas, J.M., Padilla Cordero, J. & Flores Pantoja, R. (eds.) *Desaparición forzada en el Sistema Interamericano.* Quéretaro, Mexico: Instituto de Estudios Constitucionales del Estado de Querétaro, pp 133–186.

Finucane, B. (2010) Enforced Disappearance as a Crime Under International Law: A Neglected Origin in the Laws of War. *Yale Journal of International Law* 35, 171–197. Available from: https://ssrn.com/abstract=1427062 [Accessed 16th February 2022].

Henkaerts, J.M., Doswald-Beck, L. (2009) *Customary International Humanitarian Law: Rules.* Vol. I. Cambridge: Cambridge University Press. Available from: https://www.icrc.org/en/doc/assets/files/other/customary-international-humanitarian-law-i-icrc-eng.pdf [Accessed 16th February 2022].

International Committee of the Red Cross. (2014) Living with Absence. Helping the Families of the Missing. Geneva. Available from: https://reliefweb.int/sites/reliefweb.int/files/resources/icrc-002-4152.pdf [Accessed 16th February 2022]

La Vaccara, A. (2019) *When the Conflict Ends, While Uncertainty Continues: Accounting for Missing Persons between War and Peace in International Law.* Paris, Oxford: A. Pedone and Hart Publishing.

Case law

Committee on Enforced Disappearances

Yrusta v Argentina, Comm no 1/2013, views of 11 March 2016.

European Court of Human Rights

Çakıcı v Turkey, App no 23657/94, judgment of 8 July 1999.

El Masri v The Former Yugoslav Republic of Macedonia, App no 39630/09, judgment of 13 December 2012.

Gutiérrez Dorado and Dorado Ortiz v Spain, App no 30141/09, decision of 27 March 2012.

Janowiec et al. v. Russia, App no 55508/07 and 29520/09, judgment of 16 April 2012.

Janowiec et al. v. Russia, App no 55508/07 and 29520/09, judgment of 21 October 2013 [GC].

Khutsayev et al. v. Russia, App no 16622/05, judgment of 27 May 2010.

Kurt v Turkey, App no 24276/94, judgment of 25 May 1998.

Skendžić and Krznarić v Croatia, App no 16212/08, judgment of 20 January 2011.

Human Rights Committee

Bleier v Uruguay, comm no R7/30, views of 29 March 1982.

F.A.J. and B.M.R.A. v Spain, comm no 3599/2019, views of 28 October 2020.

K.K. et al. v Russia, comm no 2912/2016, views of 5 November 2019.

Prutina et al. v Bosnia and Herzegovina, comm no 1917/2009, 1918/2009, 1925/2009, 1953/2010, views of 28 March 2013.

Quinteros v Uruguay, comm no 107/1981, views of 21 July 1983.

Rizvanović v Bosnia and Herzegovina, comm no 1997/2010, views of 21 March 2014.

Roy Rivera Hidalgo v Mexico, comm no 3259/2018, views of 25 March 2021.

Inter-American Court of Human Rights

Bámaca Velásquez v Guatemala, judgment of 25 November 2000, Ser. C No. 70.
Blake v Guatemala, judgment of 24 January 1998, Ser. C No. 36.
Chitay Nech and others v Guatemala, judgment of 25 May 2010, Ser. C No. 212.
Contreras et al. v El Salvador, judgment of 31 August 2011, Ser. C No. 232.
Garzón Guzmán v Ecuador, judgment of 1 September 2021, Ser. C No. 434.
Gelman v Uruguay, judgment of 24 February 2011, Ser. C No. 221.
González Medina and family v Dominican Republic, judgment of 27 February 2012, Ser. C No. 240.
Radilla Pacheco v Mexico, judgment of 23 November 2009, Ser. C No. 209.

International Criminal Tribunal for the former Yugoslavia

Prosecutor v Blagojević & Jokić (IT-02-60), Trial Chamber judgment of 17 January 2005.
Prosecutor v Kupreškić et al. (IT-95-16), Trial Chamber judgment of 14 January 2000.

Trial of German Major War Criminals

Proceedings of the International Military Tribunal Sitting at Nuremberg, Germany 2, 22 (1946).

Nuremberg Military Tribunals

Trials of War Criminals before the Nuremberg Military Tribunals under Control Council Law No. 10 (1949).

Working Group on Enforced or Involuntary Disappearances

General Comment on children and enforced disappearances, UN Doc. A/HRC/WGEID/98/1 of 17 May 2013.
General Comment on women affected by enforced disappearances, UN Doc. A/HRC/WGEID/98/2 of 14 February 2013.
Study on Enforced Disappearances and Economic, Social and Cultural Rights, UN Doc. A/HRC/30/38/Add.5 of 9 July 2015.
Thematic study on enforced disappearances in the context of migration, UN Doc. A/HRC/36/39/Add.2 of 28 July 2017.

Bibliography

Needham, A. (2015) Putting the Victim's Families First: The Comparative Analysis of the Inter-American Court of Human Rights and the European Court of Human Rights on the Right to be Free from Torture in Cases of Enforced Disappearances. *Institute of Advanced Legal Studies Student Law Review* 3(1), 33–47. Available from: https://doi.org/10.14296/islr.v3i1.2248.
Vermeulen, M.L. (2008) 'Living beyond Death': Torture or Other Ill-Treatment Claims in Enforced Disappearances Cases. *Inter-American and European Human Rights Journal* 1, 159–198.

Chapter 8

The fight against impunity for enforced disappearances

A historical and personal account

Baltasar Garzón

The victims and the right to exist

As a judge-magistrate of the Fifth Central Court of Instruction of the Spanish National Court, while championing the principle of universal jurisdiction, I found myself dealing with several cases of enforced disappearance, and I thus closely witnessed the pain and the endless effort of the families who never stopped desperately looking for their missing loved ones.

The crime of enforced disappearance destroys the fundamental dichotomy life/ death, by leaving the victim in a non-living-undead state, with the authorities refusing to disclose the fate of the person or take responsibility for the disappearance. In these cases, through lies, cover ups and misleading explanations and excuses, and especially by getting rid of those who seek information about the missing person, the authorities reinforce the terror among families and relatives. On the other hand, the disappeared, and their loved ones, are left alone with their questions and fears. The sophistication of the cruelty becomes, therefore, an indispensable element of those criminal activities aimed at depriving someone of their liberty, by submitting the person to torture, humiliation, death and, finally, concealment, and placing him/her outside the protection of the law. All this, for me, implies the denial of the victims' very "right to exist".

In light of all this, the international jurisprudence considered that the enforced disappearance itself constitutes a form of torture for the family of the forcibly disappeared persons who, therefore, are entitled to knowing the truth, as well as the right to redress and reparation until the whereabouts or fate of the disappeared loved ones has been established, or an independent and effective investigation has been conducted, and a sanction has been imposed (Brody & González, 1997).

In late 1990s, thanks to the application of the principle of Universal Jurisdiction, Spain took a crucial step forward in the fight against impunity for the enforced disappearances, in which I had the honor of taking part in my capacity as investigating judge.

DOI: 10.4324/9781003312642-11

The Scilingo case

Background

On March 24, 1976, a coup d'état was carried out in Argentina by the Armed Forces to overthrow the President, María Estela Martínez, the widow of Argentina's former President Juan Domingo Peron, and form a civil-military government euphemistically called National Reorganization Process (unofficially "The Process"). From then onward and until 1983, Argentina experienced systematic violations of human rights. Official reports indicate that a range from 6,000 to 9,000 people are believed to have disappeared during the dictatorship, while civil society organizations have estimated up to 30,000 cases of enforced disappearances (Robin, 2011).

That year, shortly before Christmas, Adolfo Francisco Scilingo Manzorro, a corvette captain, joined the Navy Mechanics School (Escuela Superior de Mecánica de la Armada-ESMA) in Buenos Aires.

At ESMA, besides having logistic tasks, Scilingo participated in the Task Force 3.3.2., the operational unit in charge of carrying out clandestine detentions, interrogations, tortures, and all kinds of crimes. In addition, he took part in two of the so-called Death Flights, the main and systematic extermination method, in which opponents of Argentina's military regime were sedated and thrown from airplanes into the ocean, disappearing them in the anonymity of its waters.

This deliberate strategy was carefully designed by the authorities to make people disappear without leaving a trace. The truth would however have come to the surface of the River Plate (Río de la Plata) that separates Argentina and Uruguay, as if the river did not want to be an accomplice of this macabre machinery of extermination.

The trial

Argentina's civic-military dictatorship ended in 1983. In 1985, the historical "Trial of the Juntas" saw the prosecution of the leaders of the first three military governments that had ruled the country from 1976 to 1983. However, a later series of amnesty laws were passed, shielding the authors of serious human rights violations: the Full-Stop Law ("Ley de Punto Final", 1986), the Due Obedience Law ("Ley de Obediencia Debida", 1987), together with a series of presidential pardon measures approved by President Carlos Menem (1989–1999).

To overcome the dominant situation of impunity, on March 24, 1996, 20 years after the coup, members of the Spanish Progressive Union of Prosecutors (Unión Progresista de Fiscales, UPF) decided to file a criminal complaint against members of the Argentinian military junta, under a principle of an international law known as "universal jurisdiction", which empowers any nations to investigate serious international crimes regardless of where they occurred, the nationality of the victim, or of the perpetrator. At that time, the law governing universal jurisdiction in Spain (Ley Orgánica del Poder Judicial 6/1985 (LOPJ)) was extremely broad in scope.

The case was assigned by law to the Spanish federal Court (Audiencia Nacional), with jurisdiction over international crimes, and by lot to me as the Fifth Central Court of Instruction of the Spanish National Court. The investigation started on March 28, 1996.

I met Adolfo Scilingo in 1997 when he voluntarily came to Spain and was summoned to court to testify about his crimes.

At that time, he had already appeared on national television in Argentina to recount his involvement the death flights, and also participated in a famous interview with journalist Horacio Verbitsky (Verbitsky, 1996). Immune from prosecution because of the "Punto Final" and "Obediencia Debida", he could trust that his statements would not have resulted in any adverse consequence.

However, in Spain, it would have been another story. In a several days' testimony that produced a massive and detailed statement on the workings of the ESMA, he reported on the criminal activities committed by the armed forces.

I remember that day as clearly as if it had happened just yesterday. There was a tense atmosphere, and then Scilingo began to unravel the facts. We all were astonished and horrified by his confession of deeds of barbaric violence: abductions, clandestine detention centers, sexual abuse, rapes, systematic torture mechanisms, looting of property, mass graves burials, cremations of corpses, and the death flights. For the first time, the repressive machinery was revealed in all its harshness in front of a court of law, even if it was thousands of kilometers far from where these crimes occurred.

Having heard his declarations, I ordered to take him into provisional custody. He was shocked. He hadn't realized that it was different from the public statements he had given before, and above that the amnesty laws adopted in his country would not have protected him in Spain.

His attitude changed completely while on stand during the oral trial, where his collaboration could have been relevant: he retracted all his previous confessions, and faked illness to avoid prosecution, while claiming that he had been pressured to lie under oath. Scilingo never made amends to the victims, on the contrary decided to hide himself behind a barrier of silence.

On April 19, 2005, the Spanish National Court sentenced Scilingo to a total of 640 years of imprisonment for crimes against humanity. Although the defense filed all possible legal remedies, in 2007, Scilingo was finally sentenced by the Supreme Court of Spain which increased his prison sentence to 1,084 years, finding him guilty of murder, illegal detention and torture, not for crimes against humanity which were yet not included in the Spanish criminal code (Andrés Domíniguez, 2006; Fernández, 2002; Gil Gil, 2005; Lamarca Pérez, 2007; Ollé Sesé, 2008).

At the time, the case against Argentine's military officer Adolfo Scilingo was the first and only one based on universal jurisdiction to have resulted in conviction in Spain.

Operation Condor

Among the many proceedings and cumulative past evidence in the Argentinian cases, there was a case that led a life of its own: the Operation Condor or Condor Plan. The amount of information on it was such, that I decided to open a separate procedure to keep the investigation in order. I took this decision on June 5, 1998. At the time, there was nothing to foreshadow the consequences that this decision would have had.

Operation Condor implied the coordination of all South American dictatorships, aiming for the disappearance of their political adversaries (Calloni, 2016). The first formal coordination meeting was summoned on November 25, 1975, in Santiago, Chile, the day on which Chile's dictator, Augusto Pinochet, turned 60. The countries convened were Argentina, Bolivia, Chile, Paraguay and Uruguay. Brazil attended as an observer. The meeting was strictly secret, and its objective was to lay down the foundations for "excellent coordination and better action for the benefit of the National Security of our respective countries" (Calloni, 2015).

The "National Security Doctrine" was based on "the concept of hemispheric protection", which was defined by ideological borders, instead of the limited doctrine of "Territorial Defense" (Calloni, 2015), and was promoted in the Latin American region by the United States. One of its key features was the concept of "Internal Enemy", according to which the armed forces no longer had to fight a foreign enemy, but target those who were considered communists within their own country's population, preventing a possible guerrilla war or a revolution. However, the concept of the "Internal Enemy" included not only potential guerrillas but "any person, group or national institution that had ideals opposed to those of the military governments" (Leal, 2003).

The Condor Operation's purpose was to stop and, possibly eliminate any advance of the communist ideology in South America. For the Operation to succeed, contacts, joint actions, and cooperation among the different intelligence services and the ultra-right paramilitary organizations of the South American countries had to come together. Therefore, a series of tactics were established which came to be termed "Dirty War". This type of tactics also had dedicated support from the president of the United States, Richard Nixon, as well as the Secretary of State, Henry Kissinger, who made their country's interest prevail above all other considerations. It was still the time of the Cold War and the United States was preoccupied that the Cuban example could permeate and be imitated by other countries in the region, so they taught and trained South American military forces at the School of the Americas, then located in Panama, a doctrine aimed at counteracting any subversive activity and which had to be implemented at any cost.

In this "Dirty War", dictatorships systematically resorted to the practice of enforced disappearance. According to recent studies, there were two decisive factors to this. On the one hand, the adoption of the "National Security Doctrine", which offered a theoretical framework to legitimize this barbarism, and on the other hand, the need to cover up the crimes from the increasing scrutiny of the international community on human rights violations (Aguilar & Krovas, 2018). It is estimated that the repression in South America left 50,000 dead, 30,000 missing and around 400,000 imprisoned (Guadichaud, 2003), many of them under Operation Condor.

Pinochet was behind the creation of these criminal networks and their functioning. Therefore, Operation Condor constituted a point of connection between the case of Argentina, which was followed in the Central Court of Instruction No. 5 under my ruling, and the case of Chile, which was followed in the Central Court of Instruction No. 6, under Judge's Manuel García Castellón ruling.

Pinochet's case

The background

Following the same line as Argentina's lawsuit, on July 4, 1996, the Prosecutors Progressive Union (UPF) filed a complaint against the members of the Chilean Military Junta, led by Augusto Pinochet. About the case of Chile, in 1996, Joan Garcés, a Spanish lawyer (and a very close friend and counselor of former Chilean President Allende), issued a complaint representing nearly 4,000 victims in more than 3,000 cases of murder, enforced disappearance and torture.

Around October 13, 1998, Joan Garcés asked for a meeting and informed me that Augusto Pinochet was in a London clinic undergoing surgery, which could be an opportunity to issue a "letter of appeal" to take a statement from him. I was amazed by the news, but even more by the petition since I was the judge of the Court No. 5 and Chile's case was in Court No. 6. With his usual and exquisite formality, Joan Garcés replied: "You already know that it is very difficult for your colleague to authorize it and we would miss the opportunity". Garcés was right, as Judge Manuel García Castellón was very conservative, he had hardly advanced the cause of Chile; he considered that it was a hindrance and that a Spanish judge should not meddle in the internal affairs of other countries. So, I asked Garcés: "Do we have room to carry out that diligence in my Court?" and as if he had already everything planned in his mind, Joan Garcés finished: "You have the Operation Condor process" (Garzón, 2019).[1]

I accepted the challenge in the understanding that it was only a matter of issuing a letter of appeal for the cross-examination, but under the condition that this same request would have been issued to the Central Instruction Court No 6, which was led by Joan Garcés. Shortly afterward, he informed the media that the Spanish Judge García Castellón was about to issue a letter of appeal to the relevant British judicial authorities to take a statement from Augusto Pinochet. The news spread quickly. Fortunately, it did not transpire that I was preparing a similar diligence, which allowed me to act with stealth and without media pressure.

The first thing I did was to send a letter, via fax, on October 14, to the Interpol in London, for the British police to inform me of Pinochet's whereabouts and whether he was able to be interrogated. They answered immediately, although briefly and negatively, indicating that they would not provide any information. As

I was preparing a new request, I received a call from John Dew, the then-acting ambassador of the United Kingdom to Spain.[2]

I had met Dew a year earlier, in 1997, at a conference on International Judicial Cooperation, where I was overly critical of the lack of cooperation by the British authorities on money laundering matters relating to Gibraltar. Following the conference, John Dew contacted me to have a meeting on judicial cooperation between the United Kingdom and Spain, which demonstrated his concern and willingness in such matters.

In 1998, after the initial refusal from Scotland Yard, John Dew called me to tell me to ignore the first response, because in the next few hours I would have received a more appropriate one, given the need for a good relationship of cooperation between our countries. Indeed, that was the case. In this reply, I was asked to provide more data corroborating the reasons for my request. I sent the new response, and the next day they answered back informing me that Pinochet was in a London clinic. I was asked to forward the request around the same time that John Dew called me to ask if everything was in order.

By Friday, October 16, I processed an addendum of the claim, along with the complaints presented by the Association of Relatives of the Chilean Detained Disappeared, Herminia Antequera Latrille, and by the United Left Party (Izquierda Unida), in addition to the one of Joan Garcés. At the end of that Friday, which was a shorter day, a court official handed me an Interpol fax in which I was informed that "the person of interest" (Pinochet) had requested to be discharged and was leaving the country the next day on a special flight. For that reason, they would not be able to interrogate him, "unless an arrest warrant was issued". Until that moment, we had only thought about taking a statement and now, the decision to stop him or let him go was up to me. The challenge became greater.

After thinking it through for a few moments, I returned to my office, closed the door, and started to dictate the resolution with the little data I had at the time. The data was enough to ask for an interrogation, but I recognized that the evidence was not sufficient to substantiate an international arrest warrant. In addition, I did not have the case within my reach because it was kept safe, and the responsible official had already left. Faced with this challenge and with the urgency of the case, even with some mistakes, I stated, as specifically as possible, the facts being investigated, especially those which pertained to the Condor Operation. The proper legal classification was terrorism, torture and genocide. I signed the international arrest warrant against Augusto Pinochet, former President of Chile. Afterward, with the translations, and requests for strict confidentiality from the police, I was informed that the arrest warrant was issued to Interpol in London. The die was cast! There was no turning back! The only thing left was to wait.

Throughout the afternoon, I received several calls from John Dew informing me of the steps that were being taken in the United Kingdom. At about half past eight in the evening, Dew informed me that the judge had signed Pinochet's arrest warrant and that the police were heading to the clinic. A couple of hours later John Dew called me again and confirmed that Pinochet had been arrested and was in detention.

I would like to acknowledge all efforts made by John Dew, who was key to the success of this matter. He must be remembered as an important piece of this operation, for which he has never claimed credit.

The facts

On September 11, 1973, in Chile, the army took total control of the entire state apparatus by exercising censorship. Many went into forced exile and, among those who remained in the country, thousands were arrested and subject to the most horrifying methods of torture, massive and selective murders, as well as widespread and systematic enforced disappearances. According to the Truth Commissions, 3,216 people were the victim of enforced disappearance and arbitrary executions, and 38,254 of political imprisonment and tortures (Observatorio, 2011).

As part of his legacy, Pinochet left Chileans a new political constitution, tailor-made to his belief. This laid out a path that included a referendum that would keep him as the "democratic" President for eight more years. Even more, after that period, he would remain in command of the Army for another eight years, and finally, he would become Senator for Life. His advisers carefully planned this metamorphosis, to go from being a bloodthirsty dictator to a democratic guarantor of the "new institution" to which the country should be ever grateful.

Procedural path

Judge Nicholas Evans, from the Bow Street Criminal Court, signed the arrest warrant, which was served on October 16, 1998. It was a provisional detention order, which should not exceed 40 days, pending the subsequent formalization of the extradition request. However, I was aware that the arrest warrant was very generic and had several weak links. Given that Pinochet was already imprisoned, I decided to work over the weekend on a more detailed substantiation and documentation of each of the specific cases, with the invaluable collaboration of the court officials and plaintiffs. That way, I was able to issue a new arrest warrant by Sunday, the 18th, which was dispatched on early Monday.

To extend the arrest warrant, I included 94 cases of victims of the enforced disappearance of different nationalities having been kidnapped through the ploy created by Operation Condor, which was under my ruling. In addition to the Spanish legislation, cited in the original order, I added a series of international criminal laws, applicable in the United Kingdom.

On October 20, Judge Manuel García Castellón, from the Central Instruction Court No. 6, in charge of Chile's case issued an order by which he recused from the procedure in my favor. Among the arguments that he provided, the most outstanding ones were the crimes that he was investigating were linked to Operation Condor and the legal attributes were coincidental; also, the case I was instructing was older.

The Spanish Prosecutor's Office opposition

As soon as Pinochet's arrest was known, the Prosecutor's Office of the Spanish National Court began to oppose any action aimed toward extradition. Beyond how debatable the position of the Prosecutor's Office could be, from an ethical and legal perspective, what was striking were the arguments, which were long surpassed by the evolution of international law after the Second World War, as well as its inaccuracy over the facts and premises.

On Saturday, October 17, 1998, one day after Pinochet's arrest, Prosecutor Pedro Rubira requested the annulment of Pinochet's unconditional arrest warrant. He argued the lack of jurisdiction of the Spanish courts to investigate Operation Condor. Even more, he pointed out the "lack of courtesy and international reciprocity" since Pinochet was a Senator of the Republic of Chile, with which Spain maintained international relations. He stressed that the cases were already being tried in Chile and that the crimes against him were not even indirectly accredited. Lastly, the prosecutor added a formal argument: he had not been notified of the resolution ordering the arrest, but only of Pinochet's detention.

On October 22, the Prosecutor's Office appealed for the annulment and reform of the extended international arrest warrant on Pinochet's unconditional detention. In addition, to reiterating the arguments of his previous orders, he added that the punishment of the dictator cannot be done without violating the Spanish Constitution itself. He invoked some articles referring to the legality of the actions of the public powers, the inviolability of senators in the exercise of their functions, and the constitutional mission of the Armed Forces. He further mentioned the constitutional principles of the Rule of Law and non-retroactivity of the Criminal Law, adding that:

> As horrendous as the crimes committed by Pinochet are, as much as he deserves to be labelled as a dictator, usurper, murderer, the issue of the matter here is one of a technical-legal nature and focuses on the fact that the Spanish jurisdiction is not competent to rule over these criminal acts, just as it was not at the time they were being committed, despite this being known.[3]

Finally, the prosecution opposed both the international arrest warrant and its extension, requesting that it should be submitted to the Second Chamber of the Supreme Court to rule on the immunity of Senator Pinochet. Under the prosecutor's view, the case should be referred to an International Criminal Court.

The handling of the case in the United Kingdom

Between October 22 and 26, Pinochet's lawyers filed a *habeas corpus* request against Evans and Bartle Magistrates, who had decreed Pinochet's provisional detention at the request of the Spanish justice system to secure his extradition, and against the London Metropolitan Police for having executed the arrest warrants, moreover it requested a review of the precautionary measure.

On that same day, October 22, 1998, Pinochet's defense submitted a request to the Secretary of State for the Home Department of the United Kingdom to not initiate the extradition proceedings and to void the arrest warrant issued under the provisions of the Extradition Act of 1989.

In both cases, Spain's lack of jurisdiction was argued (since the crimes had not been committed in Spanish territory and Pinochet was not a Spanish citizen), as well as the immunity he had been given as a former Head of State. Regarding the second arrest warrant, it was further argued that all the charges brought against him were not criminal offenses, at the time of the acts according to English Law.

The Fourth Chamber of the London Supreme Court (High Court) heard the first appeal on October 26 and 27 and the second one on October 28. The three magistrates, Lord Bingham, Chair, and Judges Lord Collins and Lord Richards, issued a controversial ruling upholding the *habeas corpus* and declaring Pinochet's detention illegal. In addition to other arguments, the main basis was the recognition of his immunity as a former head of state.

According to the chair of the court, the British State Immunity Act, read in conjunction with the 1961 Vienna Convention on Diplomatic Relations, conferred lifelong immunity to a former Head of State for acts committed while in the position. In his view, this immunity was not affected by the UK legislation on genocide, hostage-taking, and torture, since the relevant statutes did not contemplate exemptions to that immunity for such crimes (Woodhouse, 2003).

It must be said that this judgment was rendered against the position held by the Crown Prosecution Service and barrister Alun Jones, who represented the interests of the State for the extradition in Spain. He argued, in line with the instructions given by me and sent to London, that the immunity that protects a Head of State is just related to acts or omissions linked to his duties as Head of the State, and such functions did not include, by any means, acts such as those for which Pinochet was being accused. According to the Prosecutor: "Being these crimes so profoundly repulsive to any notion of morality, to the point of configuring Crimes Against Humanity, such as genocide, torture, and hostage-taking, they could not be protected by immunity" (International Commission of Jurists, 1999, pp. 34–35).

However, despite accepting the *habeas corpus*, the London High Court decided to keep Pinochet under arrest, anticipating an eventual appeal, which indeed was the course of action the Prosecutor's Office followed soon after.

Legal proceedings in Spain

Despite the unwelcome news, Pinochet was still under arrest in London. So, I proceeded to issue the formal extradition request, on November 3, 1998. I did not forget that the United Kingdom was one of the four States that had representation at the Nuremberg Tribunal. So, in the extradition request, I spared no reference to it, such as the *case of Rudolf Hess*, who in 1944 was arrested on British soil and handed over to the Nuremberg Tribunal, sentencing him to life imprisonment.

The next day, November 4, 1998, the Criminal Chamber of the National Court made the order public confirming that the Spanish courts had the jurisdiction over the Argentinian case (including the separate ploy of Operation Condor). On November 5, 1998, the same Criminal Chamber did the same with the Chilean case.[4,5] Both resolutions were adopted unanimously and under the same argument, focused on the application of the principle of universal jurisdiction and on the fact that the legal classification of crimes as torture, genocide, and terrorism was correct.

During those days, other international arrest warrants and extradition requests began to arrive in the United Kingdom from other countries that were willing to exercise extraterritorial jurisdiction in the *Pinochet case*, in case the extradition to Spain was rejected. The first country was Switzerland, followed by France. Also, Human Rights organizations considered the possibility of Pinochet being tried by the United Kingdom itself. Just four days after Pinochet's arrest, three organizations, including Amnesty International, informed Scotland Yard about the case of William Beausire, a British Citizen who disappeared in 1975, after being handed over to the Chilean police. Later, on November 19, the United Nations Committee Against Torture (CAT) reminded the United Kingdom of its internationally contracted obligations as a State party to the Convention against Torture and Other Cruel, Inhuman or Degrading Treatment or Punishment, 1984 (Amorós, 2019). CAT also recommended the United Kingdom try Pinochet for the cases of torture imputed against him in case the extradition was denied to Spain or some other countries.[6]

All this was happening while the verdict of the Lords regarding Pinochet's immunity was still pending, but it would have arrived soon.

A historical verdict

On November 25, the judges of the Judiciary Committee of the House of Lords delivered their verdict. The five Lord Judges communicated their decision with the solemnity and paucity of their great deliberations. Never has a judicial pronouncement captured the attention of so many international actors.

Pinochet was confident of a favorable verdict. Such was the confidence that his collaborators had their suitcases prepared and arranged in an adjoining chamber, ready to embark on a Chilean air force plane whose engines were roaring at the Norfolk Base. Everything had been planned for his departure (Garzón, 2019). That same day, in addition, and by chance of fate, was Pinochet's birthday.

We all remember seeing that moment, in one way or another, because the verdict was broadcasted live everywhere. The Lords decided by a majority of three to two, to revoke the immunity of General Augusto Pinochet. Joy was unleashed in the streets of London, Madrid, Santiago de Chile, and so many other corners of the world, as justice seemed to loom and the impunity of so many years began to crack.

While it is true that International Law recognizes that the responsibilities of a Head of State may include improper, and even illegal, activities, the Lords deemed those acts such as genocide, torture and terrorism were outside the ordinary proceedings of this role. These acts are strongly punishable by international law, as the worst crimes that a state can commit. Thus, it would be a contradiction if international law punished those acts but then offered diplomatic immunity to the Heads of State who perpetrated them, given their position of authority. A lot can be said about this matter, but I just want to highlight Lord Steyn's words criticizing the reasoning of the appeal pointing out that, when Hitler ordered the "Final Solution", these acts should not be considered an official act derived from exercising his functions as Head of State. Lord Steyn stressed that he was not willing to follow that path (Woodhouse, 2003).

On December 9, 1998, the Secretary of State for the Home Deparment, Jack Straw, authorized the extradition process (*Authority to Proceed*), following my extradition request and stating that Pinochet was able to stand on trial. He also added that it was United Kingdom's responsibility to extradite the senator to Spain.

The Chilean government positions

The Chilean government showed its intention, from the beginning, to prevent the extradition of the dictator to Spain. Undoubtedly, the best way to prevent it was for the Chilean justice system itself to request the extradition. This was coherent given that most of the events happened in Chile, and most of the victims and the accused were from Chile. The Chilean State had an unbeatable position to carry out justice. Despite this, there was never an extradition request; just political, diplomatic, and judicial allegations against the extradition and in favor of the release of the dictator, from different Chilean public powers.

On December 11, Pinochet appeared for the first time before Judge Graham Parkinson at the Belmarsh Maximum Security Courthouse. Of course, he did not acknowledge the jurisdiction of the court and called all the facts a "lie."

Advances and setbacks

On December 10, 1998, the day of the 50th anniversary of the Universal Declaration of Human Rights, I issued the corresponding indictment against Augusto Pinochet for the crimes of genocide, terrorism and torture and ordered the seizure of his assets and the restrain of his bank accounts.[7]

The same day, while I was signing the indictment in Madrid, Pinochet's defense, in London, submitted a petition to the House of Lords to invalidate the judgment of November 25, 1998. They challenged Judge Lord Hoffmann for his lack of impartiality since he was related to Amnesty International, which affected his appearance of neutrality. Since 1990, Lord Hoffmann was the director and chairman of Amnesty International Charity Limited (AICL), a charity to raises funds for Amnesty International's campaigns. They also questioned that his wife was an Amnesty International employee with an administrative position in the press and publications departments, since 1977.

Following the petition, an Appeal Committee was set up in the House of Lords, chaired by Lord Browne-Wilkinson and composed of Lords Goff, Nolan, Hope, and Hutton. This action had no precedent as the House of Lords is the Highest Court in the United Kingdom and therefore there was no room for an appeal. On January 15, 1999, the judges voided the ruling and ordered that the trial on Pinochet's immunity had to be restarted.

From January 18 to February 4, 1999, the entire process on Pinochet's immunity was reviewed, and seven Lord Judges were appointed as a new Appeal Committee to hear on this new phase.

After almost two months of deliberations, on March 24, 1999, the Judiciary Committee of the House of Lords decreed, six votes to one, that Pinochet could be extradited to Spain, thus reaffirming the previous verdict, and denying him the immunity, as a former Head of State. Of all the charges brought against him, only those of torture and conspiracy to commit torture, after December 8, 1988, remained in effect, given that the Convention against Torture and Other Cruel, Inhuman or Degrading Treatment or Punishment, was already in effect at that time, in the three countries concerned (Spain, Chile and the United Kingdom).

On March 25, the *Crown's Prosecution Service* sent a note to inform me of the case's deadline and the suggestion that the Lords made to the Ministry of Interior. They advised him to reconsider the authority on the extradition due to the considerable reduction of the charges.

Meanwhile, the investigation in Madrid continued gathering information and evidence with the accusations and the victims' help. On March 25, I was able to issue an order expanding the case with another 85 cases of torture, which occurred between September 1988 and December 1989. On March 26, I added 9 more cases of torture and other related offenses, and on April 5 another 13 cases. It was a race against time. The effort was huge. We finally managed to add 105 more cases, which met the demands of the Committee of Lords. There were more victims, but the material had to be translated and sent, so I set April 5 as the deadline to receive the extensions of the complaint.

On April 14, 1999, Jack Straw, the UK Interior Secretary, issued a new authorization for Pinochet's extradition, thus opening the process.

On April 27, I issued an order to include 12 more cases of torture included in the time fixed, prima facie, by the House of the Lords. Three days later, on April 30, I issued a new order, to include the prosecution of new cases, which exemplified the repression carried out during the dictatorship in Chile. Thus, in addition to the cases identified in the initial indictment, I added new cases, covering the period between 1980 and 1986 (outside the period indicated by the Lords) to show that the tortures between 1988 and March 1990 were part of the same systematic plan, devised from the beginning. Likewise, I included 1,198 cases of enforced disappearance, arguing that this situation constituted until that date (and until today) suffering deliberately inflicted by the accused on these families, without legal justification. This suffering falls within the definition of the Convention against Torture and Other Cruel, Inhuman or Degrading Treatment or Punishment. Later, Judge

Ronald Bartle would accept this interpretation, against the individual perspective of the cases assumed by the Lords.[8]

The extradition hearing before Ronald Bartle, the *Bow Street* Criminal Court Magistrate, took four days, after which the political lobby intensified, with Margaret Thatcher directly entering the scene. She had already issued a statement and allowed herself to be filmed and photographed paying him a visit when Pinochet was under house arrest. She even used the occasion to thank him for his collaboration on the Falkland Islands war against Argentina (Las Islas Malvinas for Argentines). Just two days before the verdict she demanded the immediate release of her friend Pinochet, claiming that he had been treated cruelly and unfairly by the British government.

Finally, on October 8, 1999, the ruling of Judge Bartle was announced, which granted the extradition to Spain of Senator Augusto Pinochet for 34 crimes of torture in which he had authorship, and one case of conspiracy to torture, perpetrated since December 1988. About enforced disappearances, he noted:

> Whether the disappearances amount to torture; the effect on the families of those who disappeared can amount to mental torture. Whether or not this was intended by the regime of Senator Pinochet is in my view a matter of fact for the trial court. Based on my findings I am therefore satisfied that all the conditions are in place which obliges me under the terms of Section 9 (8) of the Extradition Act 1989 to commit Senator Pinochet to await the decision of the Secretary of State.
> (Judgment: *The Kingdom of Spain vs Augusto Pinochet Ugarte*,
> London, 8 October 1999)[9]

The following month, on November 9, the Belgian Public Prosecutor's Office requested the United Kingdom to extradite Augusto Pinochet, in addition to the requests previously filed by Switzerland and France, based on the accusations filed in Belgium by 19 families of victims of enforced disappearance.

Political interference

After Pinochet's arrest in London, the Spanish government headed by José María Aznar maintained a discreet position, due to the belief that the initiative would not prosper. Aznar's position began to change when the extradition process was put on track with Jack Straw's second authorization to proceed. On October 20, 1999, a few days after Judge Bartle's decision on extradition, Abel Matutes, the Spanish Minister for Foreign Affairs, categorically stated that should Secretary of State Straw decide to return the general to Chile on humanitarian grounds, Spain would not appeal. From then on, Alun Jones was forbidden to communicate with me. At some point, the use of faxes was also prohibited, and all communication was controlled by the ministry, except for the stealthy telephone calls. The confrontation reached such a level that it had to be Belgium the one to appeal to the medical opinions on which the decision not to hand over Pinochet would be based. Spain, which had been the country that initiated the procedure, remained passive while others continued the work. In short, what the Spanish government showed is that the resolution was already agreed upon or, at least, they demonstrated that they were not going to do anything to try Pinochet in Spain (Garzón, 2019).

The return of Pinochet

On January 11, Secretary of State Straw gave the interested parties a deadline to present allegations about his intention not to extradite Pinochet due to his alleged illnesses. On January 25, 2000, Belgium filed an appeal with the British Court requesting a judicial review of the Secretary of State for the Home Department's preliminary decision to release Pinochet.

The appeal was heard by Judge Maurice Kay, who did not grant permission to Secretary of State Straw to disclose the contents of the medical reports. This decision was appealed. The appeal hearing was held before a panel of three *High Court* judges: Simon Brown, David Latham, and John Anthony Dyson. On February 15, they ordered Secretary of State Straw to disclose the contents of the reports to the parties involved, namely the human rights organizations and the government of Belgium which had promoted the appeal. Spain was also included to receive the reports, so I sent seven different injunctions, different from the British ones to Secretary of State Straw that established Pinochet´s full capacity to stand trial.

Finally, Secretary of State Straw announced on March 2, 2000, that he would not release Pinochet under the Spanish extradition request on health grounds. He stated that, after an independent medical study, the reports led to the conclusion that the defendant was not able to stand trial. In addition, he did not grant the extradition request to Switzerland, France, or Belgium either.

It was clear that the political agreement between governments could collapse if these reports became known, so on March 2, 2000, Secretary of State Straw quickly ordered Pinochet's departure for Santiago. In my view, the speed with which these procedures were carried out revealed prior coordination.

The entire world witnessed it. Pinochet arrived in Chile, showing himself stiff and cheerful at the airport while receiving military honors. He left his wheelchair, walked, raised his cane to greet the attendees, and after a few hours in the military hospital for a medical check-up he returned home.

Pinochet had lost the court battle, but he had won in the political field. However, once back in Chile, he had to face new trials against him, promoted by the relatives of the victims and their lawyers, until his death. Pinochet died on December 10, 2006, after being subjected to a trial and under house arrest.

The Pinochet effect

I am firmly convinced that the application of universal jurisdiction, as demonstrated in the cases of Argentina and Chile, made an important contribution to the consolidation of the defense of human rights around the world. This has been possible thanks to the efforts of thousands of victims, human rights defenders, politicians, citizens, judges, and prosecutors. Those who understood that the law had to be interpreted as an instrument for the defense of those who suffered the most and as a legal instrument against impunity always respect the standards of a fair trial. Although nothing is set in stone, given that at any time and place, violence, terror, and brutality can ignite and spawn thousands of victims, as we, unfortunately, are seeing again along our time. To deal with these incidents, we must have the instruments granted by the rule of law, among which universal jurisdiction is inalienable.

The Spanish process against the Francoist crimes

The facts

On Friday, July 17, 1936, the troops from the Spanish provinces of Africa began a coup. The next day rebellion started in the peninsula. However, by Sunday 19th, it became clear that the coup against the constitutional government was not going according to plan: several regiments and platoons remained faithful to their oath of honor and respected the legality, while weapons were distributed among civilians who were willing to fight against the plotters. Then, one of the bloodiest wars of the twentieth century began. The Spanish War or Spanish Civil War (1936–1939) arose from this failed coup.

This war was also a sort of prelude to what would later be known as the Second World War. Mussolini's Italy and Hitler's Germany participated on one side of this war and the international brigades (mostly French) on the other. On both sides were the Spanish.

After the end of the war, a civic-military dictatorship, that lasted 40 years, purged and massacred the defeated, leaving a balance of tens of thousands of people imprisoned and tortured, including raped and humiliated women, thousands of children taken from their mothers or handed over for irregular adoptions, some 140,000 disappeared, and more than half a million exiled to avoid persecution or death (Sferrazza, 2014). As well as the mass robbery of the patrimony of the defeated by institutions and individuals related entirely to or partially to the dictatorship. All this is covered by a silence cloak enforced by an official doctrine. This has been called the *Spanish Holocaust* (Preston, 2011).

The procedural path

On December 14, 2006, a group of lawyers, representatives of Associations for the Recovery of the Historical Memory and a Socialist congressperson filed eight complaints requesting an investigation into the disappearances, murders, torture, and forced exiles committed since 1936. Those complaints reached my court. A few months later, on July 18, 2007, various associations of relatives of disappeared persons during Franco's regime filed a new criminal lawsuit.

I began to conduct preliminary procedural verifications, looking for evidence and identifying the potential number of victims. Associations and individual victims sent documentation to the court, aiming at recording the facts related to the crimes. The amount of information provided was overwhelming. It was as if someone had opened a dam through which now the desire for justice, and the recognition of all the pain suffered in silence for decades, could flow. With this help, the first "census of victims" was compiled. It was an immense effort on the part of the victims' associations, something that will forever embarrass the Spanish State institutions, which never took responsibility for this task. Even today there is not a unified victims list that includes the entire Spanish geography.

Initially, the Prosecutor's Office accepted the investigation, but on January 29, 2008, it issued an opposition to it. The Public Prosecutor's Office used the Amnesty Law of 1977 as the key argument to paralyze the investigation of these crimes.

The investigation continued, and thanks to added information and a computer tool, we were able to identify an even greater number of victims: 140,000 disappeared, of which 130,137 were in Spain and at least another 7,000 outside our borders, in concentration camps abroad (in Nazi's concentration camps, among which Mauthausen-Gusen stands out).

After studying the background, and collecting more data, I issued an order on October 16, 2008, in which I declared myself competent to hear the "preliminary proceedings" of these crimes. To state the jurisdiction criteria over this court, I used the precedents of Argentina's and Chile's dictatorship crimes that my court had processed. I also based myself on the resolutions of the different Committees and organs of the United Nations that had repeatedly condemned the impunity of these crimes.

Additionally, I also took the issue of the 1977 Amnesty Law. I maintained that all laws, including the Amnesty Law, should be interpreted, and applied in the light of international human rights law standards. I also stated that the Amnesty Law cannot be applied in the face of so-called "heinous crimes" or any other international crimes.

I demanded, among other things, certain exhumations to be conducted, including the one of Federico García Lorca, the poet, who had also been executed by Franco's repressors.

The head of the Prosecutor's Office of the National Court, Javier Zaragoza, immediately announced that he would appeal the order. He stated that these crimes could not be prosecuted because of the Amnesty Law and that, in any case, the local courts located in the places where the acts were committed should take over these cases. He argued that the facts did not constitute crimes against humanity. A direct appeal was lodged suggesting that I could be held liable. The message was clear; the case could not move forward. The decision to exhume the remains of Federico García Lorca was the most contested.

But not everything was bad. At that time, I received exciting support from prestigious writers such as José Saramago, Ernesto Sábato, Antonio Gamoneda, José

Luis Sampedro, Juan Goytisolo or José Manuel Caballero Bonald. All of them, together with other intellectuals and jurists, drafted a manifesto of support. Ian Gibson, the author of the classic biography of Federico García Lorca, said in the introduction of the manifesto that my claim was the "most chilling" document he had read in years.[10]

Internationally, reactions were unanimously favorable. The United Nations Human Rights Committee stated, in its concluding observations to Spain's report in November 2008, referring to the Amnesty Law:

> The Committee, taking into consideration the recent decision of the National High Court to examine the issue of the missing persons, is concerned about the continued existence of the 1977 Amnesty Law. The Committee recalls that crimes against humanity are imprescriptible and calls on the attention of the State on the general comments No. 20, according to which, the amnesties related to serious violations of human rights are incompatible with the Covenant; and comments No. 31, regarding the nature of the general legal obligation imposed on the States by the Covenant.[11]

There were friends (judges, prosecutors, government ministers) who strongly recommended I close the investigation as soon as possible, as I could suffer severe consequences. But far from it, on November 18, 2008, I issued a new order in which I delved deeper into the arguments, so it would be difficult to disregard them if the process were to be closed.

In the new ruling, I elaborated on facts such as the case of the stolen children during Franco's regime. The need to create a commission (legal experts, anthropologists and historians), and the need to create a police commission to investigate those facts. I requested new exhumations and conducted numerous proceedings through warrants to other courts within Spain to recuse myself. My strategy, however, did not help much; the decision to bury the procedure and extend the cloak of silence was already taken.

The order of the Chamber of Deputies as a whole, whose presence had been assumed by the presiding judge Gómez Bermúdez, was predictable. Fourteen votes were in favor of the closing of the file and three were against it (Judges José Ricardo de Prada, Ramón Sáez and Clara Bayarri). According to the majority, the facts were outside the competence of the National Court, which would be the jurisdiction of the territorial courts. In addition, they ruled that, the crimes had already been prescribed due to the passage of time and had been subject to amnesty due to the Amnesty Law of 1977, by then in full effect.

Afterward, I ordered my inhibition of competence referring the cases to the respective Provincial Courts at the place of the victim's burial. Only a few Provincial Courts tried to keep the cases open, and the prosecutor's offices refused to accept the cases. The Provincial Courts started to close the cases without any investigation resorting to the Amnesty Law.

In May 2009, the Supreme Court opened an investigation against me, because I was investigating Francoism crimes. The complaint came from a Union called "Clean Hands" (an ultra-right organization). The case against me was opened for prevarication (for not applying the amnesty law to Franco's crimes), which led to my suspension from office for almost two years, even though I was absolved from it.

This fact was undoubtedly painful. However, what hurts me, even more, is that the sentence pointed out that my interpretation was indeed wrong, stating that nothing could be adverse to the Amnesty Law of 1977, given its essential role in the foundation of our democracy. In this way, they closed the door for any other judge to dare to investigate such facts. This remains the same to this day. We'll see what happens with the recently approved Democratic Memory Law in October 2022.

Subsequent effects

The principle of universal jurisdiction is the last hope for the victims. When all seems lost, when the doors of justice seem closed, the possibility of going to another court, in a different country, even if distant, is undoubtedly the last resort to prevent that impunity from prevailing. If these serious crimes are universal, if the victims are universal, then the jurisdiction over them must be universal as well.

In the case of Spain, the same issue happened. The Spanish courts had closed their doors to the victims, so, they went to Argentina to claim justice, and an Argentinian Court accepted the case. This is the so-called Argentine lawsuit that arose and showed that the principle of universal jurisdiction can operate in both directions, back and forth. If Spanish justice had helped to end impunity in Argentina, now it was Argentina's turn to return the favor, because Spain was unable to do justice for its victims.

I remember that while Pinochet was detained in London, someone said: why don't you judge Franco's crimes instead? Have you ever done justice, to dare give us a lesson? You do not have any moral authority!

They were right to expose the shames in Spain, which had not been able to end impunity for the crimes committed in their own house. And when there was a judge who dared, you see the results.

Fighting against impunity in its most heinous forms has a price to pay. But we must be clear that it is worth it. Justice as a public good must be the standard for the defense and protection of the victims. Thus, when it acted against them, justice is not being served.

The new Democratic Memory Law promises that there will be changes in Spain. I hope so.

The endless fight against an endless crime

From the beginning, I stated that enforced disappearances are one of the most serious, if not the most serious, of international crimes. The absence of the person is sustained and perpetuated day by day, while the State is indifferent to the relatives' suffering. There is a belief that these issues are things of the past, but they are not. There is a part that happened in the past, but the pain and violation of the right of the victim's relatives are current and the crime continues; until an independent and clear response is given from the State and its institutions, together with all the guarantees of the due process.

When I look back, I feel calm and at ease, because I did the right thing. I did what a judge is expected to do, which is to seek justice and not bow down to political or other interests outside of justice.

This struggle continues and will continue until we find the victims and know the whereabouts and fate of those people from Spain, Argentina, Chile and so many other places. This chapter is a tribute to all the disappeared people and to their families who will continue in their endless struggle because they do not lose hope that, one day, they will be able to find their loved ones.

Notes

1 Pinochet arrived in London on September 22, 1998, intending to undergo surgery in the *London Clinic*, an exclusive hospital located in one of the most elegant neighbourhoods of the city and very close to the Chilean embassy.
2 A digital version of the trade is available in the database *online* of Equipo Nizkor (www. derechos.org).
3 Appeal by the Public Prosecutor's Office against the order of October 18, 1998, which extended the provisional detention of Augusto Pinochet Ugarte.
4 A digital version is available in the database *online* of Team Nizkor (www.derechos.org).
5 The version is available in the database *online* of Team Nizkor (www.derechos.org).
6 See: Concluding observations of the Committee against Torture (A/54/44, para. 77 (f)), (29 August 2021).
7 An electronic version is available in the database *online* of "derechoshumanos.net".
8 The processing order is available in the database *online* of Team Nizkor (www.derechos. org).
9 Judgment: *The Kingdom of Spain vs Augusto Pinochet Ugarte*. In the Bow Street Magistrates' Court Mr Ronald David Bartle, Metropolitan Magistrate. London, 8 October 1999. See: (https://legal-tools.org/doc/b48ec0/pdf).
10 *The Country*, 21 November 2008. See: https://elpais.com/diario/2008/11/21/espana/ 1227222004_850215.html.
11 CCPR/C/ESP/CO/5 Available in: http://undocs.org/sp/CCPR/C/ESP/CO/5.

References

Aguilar, P., Kovras, I. (2018). "Explaining Disappearances as a Tool of Political Terror." *International Political Science Review*, vol. 40, no. 3, pp. 1–16. https://journals.sagepub. com/doi/abs/10.1177/0192512118764410?journalCode=ipsa
Amorós, M. (2019). *Pinochet. Biografía Militar y Política*. Santiago de Chile: Ediciones B.
Andrés Domínguez, A.C. (2006). *Derecho Penal Internacional*. Valencia: Tirant Lo Blanch.
Brody, R., González, F. (1997). "Nunca Más: An Analysis of International Instruments on «Disappearances»." *Human Rights Quarterly*, vol. 19, pp. 365–405.
Calloni, S. (2015). *Operación Cóndor. 40 años después*. Buenos Aires: Centro Internacional para la Promoción de los Derechos Humanos Categoría II UNESCO.

Calloni, S. (2016). *Operación cóndor, pacto criminal.* Caracas: El Perro y la Rana.

Comisión Internacional de Juristas (1999). *Crimen contra la humanidad: Pinochet ante la justicia.* Ginebra.

Fernández Pons, X. (2002). "El principio de legalidad penal y la incriminación internacional del individuo." *Revista Electrónica de Estudios Internacionales*, N° 5.

Garzón, B. (2019). *No a la impunidad. Jurisdicción universal, la última esperanza de las víctimas.* Madrid: Debate.

Gaudichaud, F. (2003). "La sombra del Cóndor. Terrorismo de Estado Internacional y Contra-Revolución en el Cono Sur." *Revista Dissidences.*

Gil Gil, A. (2005), "La sentencia de la Audiencia Nacional en el caso Scilingo." *Revista Electrónica de Ciencia Penal y Criminología*, vol. 7, pp. 1–18.

Lamarca Pérez, C. (2007). "Jurisprudencia aplicada a la práctica. Internacionalización del Derecho Penal y principio de legalidad. El Caso Scilingo." *La Ley Penal; Revista de Derecho Penal, Procesal Penal y Penitenciario*, vol. 34, pp. 69–77.

Law No. 23.492, La Ley de Punto Final [Full-Stop Law], Dec. 29, 1986, B.O.

Law No. 23.521 La Ley de Obedencia Debida [Due Obedience Law], June 9, 1987, B.O.

Leal, F. (2003). "La doctrina de seguridad nacional. Materialización de la Guerra Fría en América del Sur." *Revista de Estudios Sociales*, vol. 15, pp. 74–87.

Observatorio De Derechos Humanos. (2011). *Cifras de víctimas y sobrevivientes de violaciones masivas a los ddhh oficialmente reconocidas por el Estado chileno.* Universidad Diego Portales, Centro de Derechos Humanos. Available at: https://derechoshumanos.udp.cl/cms/wp-content/uploads/2020/12/Cifrasvictimasreconocidas2011.pdf.

Ollé Sesé, M. (2008). "El Principio de legalidad en el Derecho penal internacional: Su aplicación por los tribunales domésticos." In García Valdés, C., Cuerda Riezu, A., Martínez Escamilla, N., Alcácer Guirao, R., Valle Mariscal De Gante, M. (Eds.). *Estudios Penales en Homenaje a Enrique Gimbernat*, pp. 975–1001. Madrid, Edisofer: Tomo I.

Preston, P. (2011). *El holocausto español. Odio y exterminio en la Guerra Civil y después.* Madrid: Debate.

Robin, M.M. (2011). *Cómo la batalla de Argel enseñó a torturar a los militares argentinos*, 2011. En http://www.diasdehistoria.com.ar/content/c%C3%B3mo-la-batalla-de-argel-ense%C3%B1%C3%B3-torturar-los-militares-argentinos.

Sferrazza, P. (2014). *La responsabilidad internacional del estado por desapariciones forzadas de personas. Obligaciones internacionales y atribución.* Tesis Doctoral. Inédita. Disponible en: https://e-archivo.uc3m.es/bitstream/handle/10016/20173/Pietro_Sferrazza_tesis.pdf.

Verbitsky, H. (1996) *The Flight: Confessions of An Argentine Dirty Warrior.* New York: The New York Press.

Woodhouse, D. (2003). "The Progress of Pinochet through the UK Extradition Procedure: An Analysis of the Legal Challenges and Judicial Decisions." In Davis, M. (Ed.). *The Pinochet Case. Origins, Progress, and Implications.* London: Institute of Latin American Studies, pp. 87–106.

Part III

Enforced disappearance in psychosocial and psychoanalytical perspectives

Chapter 9

Memories of enforced disappearance

Psychological need and political aim

Maria Giovanna Bianchi

Traumatic memories

Memory is defined as the faculty and the process of acquiring, encoding, storing, consolidating, and later retrieving information. Over the years, researchers conceptualized several theories and models on how memory works,[1] confirming that memory is far from being a monolithic entity. It is also not a "thing" that can be physically and concretely identified in the brain, rather it consists of a series of parallel, interacting systems, at their turn comprising complex neural pathways that can get stronger or weaker according to several factors ranging from biological disposition to life experiences. Memory related to traumatic events differs from 'ordinary' memory because the amygdala is particularly activated in the fight/flight fear response and in the emotional processing of the event (Ledoux, 1994). In the context of an enforced disappearance, this is true both for the persons who disappeared and for their relatives.

In encoding an event in the memory, emotions are as important as cognition: the event recorded will not be an exact replica of what occurred but an elaboration with a strong affective component. In front of any event, the brain, on the basis of a series of data, memories included, classifies, discriminates and predicts different possibilities and outcomes in order to read reality and choose a course of action: prediction being one of its most fundamental functions (Pally, 2000). To do this, the brain uses what Jung defined "the *process of recognition*"[2] by which it compares and differentiate memory images (Jung, 1919a, par. 290).

Enforced disappearance is affectively charged and lacks any predictability: no 'process of recognition' is possible because it is neither part of normal life experiences nor is based on previous similar events that victims can use as frameworks to retrieve past memories to help comprehension. Once the disappearance has occurred, however, the memories surrounding it are connoted by emotions so strong that they will remain always vivid and alter how future information are received, selected and remembered. Those memories change forever the lives, the worldview and the actions of those who remain.

DOI: 10.4324/9781003312642-13

Memory and trauma in psychoanalysis

The exploration and integration of traumatic memories were at the origin of psychoanalysis itself. In fact it has been argued that psychoanalysis began as a theory of trauma with Freud's attribution of pathogenic qualities to the memories of hysterics (Bohleber, 2007). Before him, Breuer understood that the pathogenic 'ideas' were memories of certain events which he called 'traumatic' (Jung, 1932, par. 62). For Freud, the aim of the analytic treatment was to bring repressed memories to consciousness to be able to work through the conflicts of the past. In doing so he discovered that memory is repeated in the behavior displayed in the transference toward the analyst and that, through what he conceptualized as 'deferred action', memories can be remolded retroactively (Freud, 1950 [1895]). The past experiences can be incorporated in the current life experience, memories are rearranged according to new circumstances and retranscribed (Masson, 1985, p. 207) so that they can be comprehended also as constructions influenced by the present.

Jung, at the beginning of his career, wrote about memory and trauma in terms of cryptomnesia, schizophrenia (*dementia praecox*) and dissociated consciousness, in particular in his first scientific articles now gathered in volumes 1 to 3 of the Collected Works. In his most famous word 'association experiment', he demonstrated how emotions and affects can disturb memory, what he called 'the feeling-tone' complex (Jung, 1905, 1919b). Contrary to Freud's theory of sexual trauma in childhood, he affirmed that the erotic conflict could definitely not account for all causes of trauma (Jung, 1935a, par. 34) "for the simple reason that the trauma was found to be almost universal" (Jung, 1916, par. 599). Jung then defined trauma as an emotional shock "psychic experiences of a highly emotional nature, called traumata or psychic wounds" (Jung, 1955, par. 205) that splits off a bit of the psyche and is at the basis of the creation of the complexes which are in fact "splinter psyches" (Jung, 1934, par. 204). He further noted that "the intensity of a trauma has very little pathogenic significance in itself; everything depends on the particular circumstances" (Jung, 1955, par. 219).

While Jung considered the "memory data" or "a long series of memories" as constitutive of the ego (Jung, 1935b, par. 18), he equally observed that conscious "memory often suffers from the 'disturbing interferences of the unconscious contents'" (Jung, 1939, par. 504). From this remark stemmed Jung's most prominent contribution of the conceptualization of individual memory and of collective memory, the latter conceived as a container for archetypal images of the collective unconscious: a timeless memory, what Yeats described as the "Great Memory passing on from generation to generation" (1959, p. 345). Jung defined the archetypes as primitive, deeper forces and structures of the psyche which constitute, together with the instincts, one of the sources of psychic energy; they are innate, universal and impersonal. He also affirmed that:

> There are as many archetypes as there are typical situations in life. Endless repetition has engraved these experiences in our psychic constitution, not in the form

of images filled with content, but at first as *forms without content*, representing merely the possibility of a certain type of perception or action.[3]

(Jung, 1954, par. 99)

Memory and trauma can then be understood respectively as an archetypal image and as an archetypal situation. On one hand, memory as archetypal image was elevated in Greek mythology to the status of goddess, Mnemosyne, who among other things was also worshipped in the cult of Asclepius, the god of medicine, to ask for help in remembering healing dreams, which is an indication that from an immemorial time it is recognized that memory can play a role in the healing process. Jung explicitly noted the priceless value of such 'prehistoric' memories that "can have a remarkably healing effect in certain cases" (Jung, 1961, par. 593). On the other hand, trauma, intended as one of the reoccurring constructions of human psyche encompassing universal forms of experiences across culture, time, and history, can be considered an archetypal experience, a framework. However, the content of trauma – the trauma complex – is unique and can be understood as the individual constellation of the traumatic experience in cognitive-affective structures located within the Self and its intrapsychic processes (Wilson, 2006).

Adler (1979) observed how the human psyche has a profound need to remember and an equal tendency to forget and how remembering and forgetting are polarities of its total experience. He noted that the essence of memory is to "recollect, to collect what one knew, to collect together into a new whole" (Adler, 1979, p. 121) and that the literal meaning of recollection is to "re-find within" (Adler, 1979, p. 122). The theme of remembrance and recollection is the task of the Self because "memory is memory of the archetypal foundations; true memory is relating to the transpersonal or super personal centre of the psyche – to the self" (Adler, 1979, p. 131). This means that in the dynamics and process of remembering there is a predominance of the Self, rather than a predominance of the ego as in the defense of forgetting or in the decision of letting go.

For Kalsched (1996, 2013), trauma overwhelms the psyche with such an affective and emotional content that the psyche cannot consciously bear and elaborate it. By connecting analytical psychology with contemporary object relations theory and dissociation theory, Kalsched postulates that trauma interrupts and breaks the connection between the Self and life experiences, building a wall along the ego-self axis and resulting in the 'inner world of trauma.' There, archetypal defenses, that is powerful archaic and primitive images mobilized to defend the Self and protect the soul, come "into play to prevent the 'unthinkable' from being experienced" (Kalsched, 1996, p. 1) and assume the connotation of powerful dissociative complexes that result in further trauma for the person.

Memory is always emotionally charged, even more so the memory related to profoundly traumatizing events. For this reason, it may be imprecise and not have a univocal correspondence to what happened. Memory then is important not only as an historic account of the past but also as a means of communicating the nature of self-other relationships. It is the Self that recollects painful memories in a new narrative that needs to be told and shared. The more painful the memories are, such as those related to the enforced disappearance of a beloved one, the more urgent is the need to tell, re-tell, share, repeat those memories over and over, until they are almost consumed: until they don't belong anymore to the individual, rather they belong to everybody and become collective. This is the unconscious mechanism that compels the relatives of the disappeared to demand that the memory of the person *and* the memory of the collective trauma of the society, be kept alive. It is the wounding character of these painful memories that ultimately motivates their political action.

Trauma and memories of those who disappeared

Traumatic memory has the quality of here-and-now as experienced in flashbacks, with a strong somatic component, rather than of a mental recollection or re-elaboration of the past (Pally, 2000; Schacter, 1996). It can be extraordinarily vivid: the emotions and the release of stress hormones render the traumatic experience dramatic and memorable, especially in its central aspect, the one that the victim considers most meaningful (MacNally, 2005). This is the kind of memories that activates in the persons who were assaulted, made disappeared, subjected to torture before they reappeared and that keeps on hunting them over the years, long after they have returned to a 'normal' life.

The persons who were disappeared and subsequently released, with whom I met, describe their trauma in terms of an indelible experience with its component of un-bearable physical pain, humiliation, psychological exhaustion, mental anguish for their own families, and terror of imminent death. These were not clinical encoun-ters and therefore I cannot elaborate on the extent of the psychological damage endured by these victims; however, the way they described their captivity commu-nicated an absolute inner sense of isolation and desolation, where the internal good object broke up and there was no expectation for human empathy. While the full extent of these experiences is incommunicable, the feeling of inner abandonment, accompanied by fear, shame and despair, is recurrent: it is the region of the non-self (Grand, 2000). I met those persons in their quality of 'survivors' because they were literally some of the very few who survived torture and disappearance in particu-larly harsh secret detention centers, while most of their comrades were killed. They were those who had also the strength to let the world know about their experiences through interviews, books and documentaries. Based on my practice, and without scientific evidence, I postulate a particular pre-existent resilience that allowed them to endure the disappearance and, notwithstanding the extent of trauma, far from merely function, be able to meaningfully contribute to the society and engage po-litically. These are the ones who, while in captivity and albeit the harsh punishment that they knew would have followed, organized resistance in the form of hunger strikes, sang loudly when it was prohibited and refused to bargain better treatment against the provision of information (El Bouih, 2008; Mdidech, 2002). Still, they cannot avoid being possessed by flashback memories or sudden gloomy moods and it is possible to perceive their terrified souls behind their apprehended composure. Like when I tried to attract the attention of Ana,[4] victim of enforced disappearance 40 years ago at the age of 22 and one of fewer than 20 who survived out of 2,200 persons disappeared in a notorious secret detention center in Latin American, by touching her shoulder from behind and she jolt suddenly justifying herself:

> they took me from the shoulders at the exit of the metro, they were behind me and I couldn't see them, they blind-folded me, all of a sudden everything was dark. Since then I cannot avoid feeling scared if somebody approaches me from behind.

Or when I accompanied Ali[5] when he enters for the first time after 30 years the room of a former police station, now part of a block of apartments where ordinary families live, where he was repeatedly tortured in a Northern African country. This talkative and engaged man once entered the room cannot hold back the tears and falls in a somber mood, in a thick silence, he literally dissociates, he is elsewhere where it is not possible to reach him for the rest of our time together that day. For trauma survivors connecting to memories, and from memories to their feelings, can be a very frightening process. It takes trust and a long time before an individual can unlock and verbalize the violence suffered.

Trauma and memories of the relatives of the disappeared

For the relatives of the disappeared, whose excruciating experience amounts to psychological torture (Perez-Sales et al., 2021), trauma can be defined as chronic, interpersonal and inflicted by the collective violence of the society, both by the direct perpetrators and by the passivity of the society at large. It consists in a shocking disruption of normal life, distinct from a one-off incident or attainment at one's physical safety: it is a prolonged and ever-growing state of acute anxiety marked by several renewed stressors, for example each time that the expectation to find the beloved disappeared person in a prison or hospital is disappointed. These stressors are targeted attacks on "the coherence, reality testing, and worldview of the victim" (Dalenberg, 2000, p. 14) and end up penetrating and overwhelming the psyche. The disappearance causes psychological, moral and spiritual wounds that result in a trauma which is ever-present, devastating and potentially interminable. This is the most convincing argument that enforced disappearance is indeed a continuous crime as defined in international human rights law.

Rojas Baeza (2009), on the basis of the fieldwork by FASIC that prepared the ground for further researches, distinguished four stages, four periods, during which the 'double bind' (Bateson, 1972, 1999) of the schizophrenic-like message 'they are dead, but they may be alive' evolves for the relatives of the disappeared. During the first period of search there is hyperactivity and at the same time stupor and perplexity caused by the conflicting messages received and false interpretations;

during the second period, there is the acceptance of the occurrence of the disappearance accompanied by guilt, fantasies on the situation in which the disappeared person may be living, and the ever-present question whether they are alive or dead; during the third period, the families start pondering the possibility of the death, but they do not accept it, and enter in a depressive phase of despair because de facto they are asked to assume the responsibility to declare the disappeared dead in the absence of a formal and official recognition of the death; during the fourth period the relatives enter "a heart-breaking permanent uncertainty" (Rojas Baeza, 2009, p. 173).

The memories of the relatives of the disappeared have therefore a different quality, albeit no less painful, from those of the persons who disappeared. It is the quality of imagining what it may be happening, or may have happened, without knowing what it is really happening or has really happened, without any certainty about the truth.

From a neurological viewpoint, the brain does not make a clear distinction between reality and imagination: some cognitive processes display analogous modalities whether we have lived the experience in reality or whether we have only imagined it (Pascual-Leone et al., 1995). We may well remember things that we thought or imagined and never lived: we do not necessarily need real experiences to activate the process of memorization. Indeed, to imagine means to create mental images that reflect our personal knowledge, our unique sensitivity and are rooted in our subjective experience. It is a process that, far from being abstract, creates actual neurophysiological responses: when we think of a danger our heartbeat accelerates, when a relative thinks of the disappeared, the fear, anguish, anxiety, hopelessness and despair, as well as the somatic responses such as the continuous production of stress hormones, are real. Each time that this process is activated, "grossly inhuman and cruel memories"[6] (Neelapaijit, 2024) are created by the families constantly engrossed in, and haunted by, incessant images about the details of the disappearance, their loved ones subjected to torture, the modalities of their killing and the disposal of their bodies. These fabricated images are fantasies that may have no correspondence to the reality of the facts as they occurred but that carry a real psychological suffering. Over time, they engrave in the relatives' psyche as if they were memories because the negative emotions, associated to the trauma of the loss, leave scars[7] that neurologically have strong analogies to memory traces. At this juncture, the unconscious is preponderant and may invade the victims' psyche in targeted attacks on coherence and reality testing. The capacity to distinguish between reality and imagination is lost, introducing schizophrenic-like elements such as inconsistent or contradictory parts in the narrative and in the worldview of the victims, as well as a sense of mental fragmentation.

A woman I met developed fantasies around the disappearance of her husband that well demonstrate the break in narrative coherence, an altered interpretation of reality and the 'inner world of trauma' as Kalsched (1996) conceptualized it. She told me that she was sure that her husband was alive and treated reasonably well in prison: very likely in that very same moment he was reading books and gazing from the window, his preferred pastimes. The problem – she added – is that he was just too lazy to take any initiative to get out of that situation and try to escape. For many years, she remained in that illusion and in an almost permanent state of anger and disappointment toward her husband. It was a defensive mechanism, expressed in the form of a fantasy, that fundamentally altered her behavioral response and her ability to relate to reality. In a way she locked herself up in her own prison, where she could remain under the spell that the husband was too lazy to return, which provided the comfort of not having to face the overwhelming and unbearable reality of the disappearance. In doing so she retreated in an 'autistic territory', splitting off into the abysmal recess of her psyche, where she felt safe. I met her several times in the years, and I could witness a turn approximately ten years after the disappearance when the memories of her husband as a loving partner started emerging again: time allowed for the ability to suffer the pain which at the beginning she did not permit herself to experience for the fear of not being able to survive. Slowly she started re-collecting, not only memories but also parts of her Self and started her healing process. After 20 years from the disappearance, she admitted that initially she was 100% certain of his return, then hope diminished to 80% and now that same 80% transformed in acceptance of reality with a remaining 20% of hope due to "loyalty."

During all the time that it takes to elaborate the reality of the disappearance, the disappeared, beyond their bodies, continue to be more present than ever in the inner experience of those who have loved them. There is an attempt of halting time and preserving the last strands of attachment and physicality through objects that contribute to give a sense of continuity and stability: bedrooms remain unchanged, left exactly as the last time the disappeared persons inhabited them; the jumper that a mother was knitting for her son remains unfinished, the yarn still hanging from the needles 25 years later, because of the untold fear that if spaces are changed or objects thrown away it is as if the disappeared does not exist anymore, even as an inner representation. Memorabilia become transitional objects indispensable to navigate the intermediate area of a unique human experience defined by the dissonance between the imperative, continuous, almost obsessive, psychological presence of the loved ones in the relatives' inner realities and the objective absence of their bodies in the external reality. These objects represent the certitude that the disappeared persons did exist in the physical world, not only as inner presences, and notwithstanding the attempt by the state to destroy any trace of their ideas, their political opinions, and their bodies.

Through those desperate attempts, the relatives make unconscious appeal to memory as one of the elements of the framework of continuity through which human beings build their identity, their narrative Self, their self-perception, and make sense of the present, including through the congruence between their inner representation and the psychosocial context. One of the most harmful consequences of enforced disappearance on the psyche, whether of an adult, an adolescent or a child,[8] is that this congruence is shattered. Rogers (1965) called 'experiential field' the internal frame of reference of the individuals, their private world, which is composed by internal representations, continuously updated through the interaction with the environment, that can be considered as approximated models of reality. A match between internal representations of the psychosocial world and external psychosocial situations in the real world enables efficient adaptive interpersonal relationships while an incoherence or inconsistency between the two may create a cognitive dissonance that could give raise to incoherent, conflictual or maladaptive emotions, feelings and behaviors.[9] In the specific case of enforced disappearance there is inconsistency between the internal representation of the authority and the 'social pact' supposed to provide legality, justice and protection and the external psychosocial reality of illegality, insecurity and abuse. Exactly as for a child, the most pathogenic element of an intrafamilial abuse is the fact that the violence is perpetrated by a person who is supposed to protect, similarly in the case of enforced disappearance the greater trauma is caused by the breakdown of the trust that the State will protect its citizens, through the rule of law and law enforcement, and will not become a perpetrator. In other words, the fact that enforced disappearance is a state crime perpetrated by those who are supposed to protect and defend their citizens contributes to the helplessness of the latter who have no institutional replies to their cries for help, or worse are harassed because of their search activities, and adds to the intensity of the trauma: as Jung (1955) affirmed, circumstances matter when it comes to trauma.

Because of this betrayal of the social contract, the relatives of the disappeared often become bewildered and terrified and their representation of the world in which they live and their adaptation to it, is completely disrupted. However, there are also those for whom the contrary is true and such psychic devastation does not result in a total loss of trust in the world. Or maybe a total loss of trust in the world does occur but is re-established through new relationships built around collective action like those of the associations of the relatives of the disappeared, the creation of which must be guaranteed by the States according to article 24 of the International Convention for the Protection of All Persons from Enforced Disappearance.

Attempts to erase memory and guarantees in international law to preserve it

Memory is powerful: the perpetrators of crimes against humanity know it well and fear it. For this reason, most regimes in the immediate aftermath of their collapse, during the transition from the authoritarian to the democratic state, pass amnesty laws to guarantee the non-prosecution of, and grant forgiveness to, those responsible of horrendous crimes. The etymology of the words amnesty is explicit: it derives from the Greek 'amnesia' which means forgetfulness or oblivion. The aim of amnesty laws is to erase memory; their perverse logic is to wait legally for the statute of limitations (the timeframe within which the prosecution of a crime is possible) and psychologically to wait for the next generations that have no lived experiences of the events, no direct affective link with the disappeared and with the perpetrators. There is a clear attempt to manipulate the collective memory around the facts occurred, for example through the public media that disseminate messages on pardon, national reconciliation, and oblivion as if forgetting would guarantee a promising future. What is really hoped for is collective amnesia.

To contrast the attempts to erase and manipulate memory, there are several provisions in international law, both in its main (covenants and conventions) and secondary (principles and guidelines) sources, that impose on States the obligation to carry out memory processes where violations of human rights and international human rights law have been committed. The updated set of Principles for the Protection and Promotion of Human Rights through Action to Combat Impunity (United Nations, 2005b, E/CN.4/2005/102/Add.1) establishes the duty of States as it relates to memory and their responsibility for transmitting history with a view to "preserving the collective memory from extinction and, in particular,... guarding against the development of revisionist and negationist arguments" (principle 3). In the Basic Principles and Guidelines on the Right to a Remedy and Reparation for Victims of Gross Violations of International Human Rights Law and Serious Violations of International Humanitarian Law, adopted by the General Assembly in resolution 60/147 in 2005 (United Nations, 2005a), memorialization processes are integral part of the right to reparation. In his report of 2020, the United Nations Special Rapporteur on the promotion of truth, justice, reparation and guarantees of non-recurrence considered memorialization processes in the context of serious violations of human rights and international humanitarian law as a fundamental pillar of transitional justice (Salvioli, 2020, A/HRC/45/45). The General Assembly of the United Nations decided to declare 30 August the International Day of the Victims of Enforced Disappearances (United Nations, 2010, A/RES/65/209), starting in 2011, acknowledging the fact that the same day had already been observed in many countries around the world at the initiative of association of families of the disappeared to attract the attention of the international community on the crime and to keep the memory of the disappeared alive.

Only States, the primary responsible for human rights violations and political violence, can mend the extensive damage caused to their citizens because only States can provide the complete truth on the facts, deliver justice and mobilize the necessary financial resources for providing reparation programs (Rauchfuss & Schmolz, 2008). The reality is that in the aftermath of violence, fringes of the old establishments maintain a certain degree of influence within the States and contribute to a toxic and defensive political culture resistant to any activity aimed at inquiring into the past. For this reason, a robust demand by the civil society for truth, memory, justice and the respect of human rights is fundamental and the construction of memory, intended as reparation of great symbolic breadth, cannot be accomplished without the decisive contribution of the families of the disappeared.

The response to enforced disappearance through the construction of a community of memory and the creation of collective memory

Wherever enforced disappearance occurred in a widespread and systematic manner, it ultimately engendered spontaneous resistance.

Individuals who at the beginning interacted casually, usually for the same purpose of searching for the disappeared, progressively formed 'thick relations' (Margalit, 2002): ethical bonds based on collective victimhood and shared memories. Their interaction created a community of memory in which thick relations existed both among those who remain, and between them and those who disappeared. Such community was also accompanied by people with whom there were 'thin relations', those with whom there were no shared traumatic memories, but who joined the fight from all walks of life because of their moral concern for humanity and justice.

On the basis of this initially unconscious mechanism of aggregation, individual and collective political resistance took a variety of forms, for example protest marches, such as those of the Madres and Abuelas de Plaza de Mayo (Bousquet, 1983); covered actions by psychotherapists who collected the testimonies of the victims of authoritarian regimes, such as those by FASIC in Chile; legal battles by courageous judges like Baltasar Garzón who, applying the principle of universal jurisdiction, issued a letter of appeal for the cross-examination of Pinochet which subsequently led to the arrest of the dictator (Garzón, 2024); academic studies and researches; and innumerable creative pursuits in literature, performances and art (López Casanovo et al., 2021; Martínez, 2020; Matar, 2011, 2017),

In the short term, the aim of those actions was to resist and counteract repressive regimes; in the mid-term, to restore legality; and in the long-term to obtain reparation and guarantees of non-repetition. However, an additional and fundamental result of those combined actions was the creation of collective memory in which the individual memories, communicated from person to person, together with the contribution of those different perspectives, permitted the recollection of each episode in one single, shared, version thus allowing the entire community to be connected to it even if not all its members were present (Margalit, 2002). It is memory from the past and not about the past; it is reliving the past, with all the emotions associated to the people and the events remembered, even for those who were not even born yet.

Collective memory is created at unconscious level by the intertwining of personal memory, shared memory and archetypal memory which reinforce each other: it is there that the traumatic material is collected and recollected, that is collected together again in a new whole as Adler (1979) theorized. The result of that elaboration is a collective psyche, cohesive and healed from the destruction caused by the trauma, that needs conscious actions to be preserved and institutionalized through archives, monuments, street names and memorials, so that it becomes the responsibility of the society to remember and not only of the individual citizens.

Memorials displaying the names of the victims are a good example and a tangible result of the confluence of personal, collective and archetypal memory. Their powerful symbolism goes behind the provision of reparation, as foreseen in international law, and generates a catalytic and cathartic power in the daily life of victims, families, communities and entire societies (Vital-Brasil, 2018). For example, the European *stolpersteine* or the Argentinian *baldosas* that display the names of the victims respond to the individual psychological need of the relatives to mourn and care by putting the disappeared person at rest in a place where they can be, symbolically and reliably, found again. At the collective level, it is the public admission of the States of the atrocities committed against those specific individuals and the occasion of remembering and mourning together in a last resort of mourning rituals that were cruelly denied to the relatives of the disappeared because of the nature of the crime. At the archetypal level, the one of the Great Memory (Yeats, 1959), the personal names refer to the essence of human beings in a way that nothing else does (Margalit, 2002): it is as if with the survival of the names, engraved and visible in public spaces, also the essence of the disappeared survives so that the killing of their bodies is not equal to the killing of their names, their ideas, and the values for which they were disappeared.

Memorials carry messages and warnings: while honoring those who are no longer, they are also powerful reminders for those who remain of how inhuman humans can be toward each other. They indicate the ethical duty to be aware of our collective shadow and to assume responsibility for it in order to transform the unconscious transgenerational transmission of trauma into the conscious intergenerational transmission of experiences. Thus, memory is not only the link between past and present but also the link between present and future.

Memory as future

Memory has meaning not as the cult of the past but as the cornerstone on which to build and imagine a different future that, while is certainly marked by previous horrors, is equally shaped by the awareness of the resilience demonstrated by certain parts of the society that in the end prevailed. It is a precious chest where incalculable loss and hope, sufferance and resilience, cowardice and courage, devastation and reparation are stored; the aim is not to keep this incredible human experience amassed for the record, but to renew it and use it to create a future in which the new generations are aware of the risks posed by authoritarian governments and regimes, as well as by the lethal combination of radical evil[10] and indifference. This awareness is paramount because there is no evidence that enforced disappearance, truly evil in one of its worse incarnations, will become obsolete in a near future given that States continue to use it as an effective and efficient way to control society through terror.

Memory in the context of human rights violations means politics of memory because memory on its own is insufficient to prevent similar atrocities from happening again, unless it is actively backed-up by public policies. Exactly as the disappearance of a beloved one creates an indelible memory trace in the psyche of their relatives, so the systematic and widespread practice of enforced disappearance remains located at deeper level in the psyche of the society but in a subtler and more unconscious way. For these collective memory, traces to be made explicit and have a healing function, as well as an impact on public policy, deliberate actions in the form of the reappropriation of public spaces – in the form of memorials, literature, exhibits, movies and other art forms – and of political space is necessary.

It is impossible to keep track of all those actions and initiatives, some however are worthwhile mentioning for their symbolic value. For example, the *siluetazos*, the real-size silhouettes of persons that relatives of the disappeared displayed in streets and public spaces in Latin American countries, sent the message to the authorities that the political space temporarily vacated by the disappeared persons would have been occupied again by those who remained with the same demands for change, freedom and democracy. In the exhibit 'Huellas de la Memoria' (*Footprints of Memory*), the consumed soles of the shoes of the relatives of the disappeared were engraved with messages about the real pilgrimage in search for the loved ones and for the truth to symbolize that the walk will continue. In the initiatives known as 'Bordando por la paz y la memoria' (*Embroidering for Peace and Memory*), people gather in public places in different Latin American countries to sew and embroider one handkerchief per person disappeared, symbolically reestablishing the thread of the social fabric in a stitch-by-stitch process.

The relatives of the disappeared, with their demand for truth, justice and memory, and the activists who support them, play a vital political role in the transformation of their society for the benefit of future generations. In cultivating private memory, they attend to their psychological sufferance; in demanding public policies of memory, they contribute to the integration of the collective psyche of the society that had been previously fragmented by the trauma of collective violence. This is one of the reasons why transitional justice is deeply involved in the ethics of memory.

At the deepest level, and whether we are conscious about it or not, to disappear and be forgotten is one of our biggest fears. We know that a part of us will continue to live in the memories of the others only up to a certain time and until also those will fade away; this is part of nature and a universal experience. Some, however, don't disappear, they *are made disappear*: brutally, tragically, unjustly, ahead of their time and 'against nature.' The search for them will continue, being the search itself a practice of memory.

Notes

1 For example, the multi-store model (Atkinson & Shiffrin, 1968), levels of processing (Craik & Lockhart, 1972), working memory model (Baddeley & Hitch, 1974), Miller's magic number (Miller, 1956); memory decay (Peterson & Peterson, 1959); flashbulb memories (Brown & Kulik, 1977); neural Darwinism (Edelman, 1987).
2 Italic in the original text.
3 Italic in the original text.
4 Fictive name.

5 Fictive name.
6 The author paraphrases the official name of the Convention against Torture and Other Cruel, Inhuman or Degrading Treatment or Punishment.
7 The etymology of trauma is the Greek word for wound.
8 The considerations presented in this chapter refer to a developmentally mature individual, to an adult psyche, whether an adult who was made disappeared or adult relatives of the disappeared. However, many of the disappeared, especially in the context of Latin America, were children, either born in captivity or subtracted to their families, or young adults in their 20s whom, according to contemporary developmental psychology would be rather considered late adolescents. Also, many children and adolescents were either not raised by their biological parents and families or were exposed to the disappearance of a relative in the family. They may have been exposed to a range of traumatic experiences from acts of omission such as lack of care and neglect or acts of commission such abuse. These children are now adults in an age range spanning between late 30s and early 50s; research across disciplines including psychology, psychiatry, general medicine, criminal fields, neurophysiology and neurobiology, have demonstrated the connections between adult pathology and early childhood trauma (Becker et al., 1987; Spermon et al., 2010). While this is not the object of this chapter, as this matter would deserve an entire separate volume, it is worthwhile mentioning the concept of complex Post Traumatic Stress Disorder (Herman, 1992, ; van der Kolk et al., 2005) the consequences of which can include alterations in affect regulation; consciousness; self-perception; perception of the perpetrator; relations with others; and systems of meaning. Even if we can only draw generalizations, we can imagine how these traumatic experiences, and the memories associated to them, affected, penetrated and overwhelmed the undeveloped psyche of children and adolescents who may have well developed different attachment styles (more likely avoidant and disorganized), behavioral problems and dissociation at a later stage as adults. In addition, also children not born yet at the time of the disappearance of a relative, are exposed to the transgenerational transmission of trauma both at family and at social level (Danieli, 1998; Daud et al., 2005; Edelman, 1989; Epstein, 1979; Fossion et al., 2003; Fromm, 2011; Schwab, 2010), as recognized by jurisprudence in the interpretation of article 5 of the American Convention on Human Rights.
9 Monica Luci, personal communication.
10 Enforced disappearance truly is evil in one of its worse incarnations. And while the concept of the 'banality of evil' (Arendt, 1963) may have some relevance when referred to some joiners or sympathizers of violent regimes, it falls short from accounting for the depth of the horrors certain individuals and societies are capable of. Améry (1966), who survived Auschwitz and suffered the consequence of the personification of evil in Eichmann-like characters in the Nazi concentration camps, strongly rejected any reference to banality when referred to violations of human rights. His position was shared by several other authors (Sønnenland, 2021; Stein, 1995; Vidal-Naquet, 2005)

References

Adler, G. (1979). *The Dynamics of the Self*. London: Conventure.
Améry, J. (1966, 1995). *Par-delà le crime et le châtiment. Essai pour surmonter l'insurmontable*. Arles: Actes Sud.
Arendt, H. (1963). *Eichmann in Jerusalem – A Report on the Banality of Evil*. New York: Viking Press.
Atkinson, R. C., & Shiffrin, R. M. (1968). Chapter: Human memory: A proposed system and its control processes. In Spence, K. W., & Soebce, J. T. (Eds.), *The Psychology of Learning and Motivation*, vol. 2, pp. 89–195. New York: Academic Press.

Baddeley, A. D., & Hitch, G. (1974). *Working memory*. In Bower, G. H. (Ed.), *The Psychology of Learning and Motivation: Advances in Research and Theory*, vol. 8, pp. 47–89. New York: Academic Press.

Bateson, G. (1972, 1999). *Steps to an Ecology of Mind: Collected Essays in Anthropology, Psychiatry, Evolution, and Epistemology. Part III: Form and Pathology in Relationship*. San Francisco: Chandler Pub. Co.; Chicago: University of Chicago Press.

Becker, D., Maggi, A., Dominguez, R. (1987). "Tortura y Daño Familiar." In E. Weinstein (Ed.), *Trauma, Deulo y Reparacion: una Experiencia de Trabajo Psicosocial en Chile*. pp. 95–108, Santiago del Chile: FASIC Interamericana.

Bohleber, W. (2007). "Memory, Trauma and Collective Memory – The Fight for Memory in Psychoanalysis." *Psyche*, 61(4), pp. 293–321.

Bousquet, J.P. (1983). *Las locas de la Plaza de Mayo*. Madrid: El Cid Editor.

Brown, R., & Kulik, J. (1977). "Flashbulb memories." *Cognition*, 5(1), pp. 73–99.

Craik, F. I. M., & Lockhart, R. S. (1972). Levels of processing: A framework for memory research. *Journal of Verbal Learning and Verbal Behavior*, 11(6), 671.

Dalenberg, C.J. (2000). *Countertransference and the Treatment of Trauma*. Washington DC: American Psychological Association.

Danieli, Y. (ed.), (1998). *International Handbook of Multigenerational Legacies of Trauma*. New York: Plenum.

Daud, A., Skoglund, E., Rydelius, P. (2005). "Children in Families of Torture Victims: Transgenerational Transmission of Parents' Traumatic Experiences to their Children." *International Journal of Social Welfare*, 14, pp. 23–32.

De la Fuente-Herrera, J.J., Soria-Escalante, H. (2021). "The Ravages of Enforced Disappearance: A Psychoanalytic Perspective of Traumatic Events and Encrypted Mourning." *OMEGA - Journal of Death and Dying*, 87(1). https://doi.org/10.1177/00302228211019208

Edelman, G. M. (1987). *Neural Darwinism*. London: Basic Books.

Edelman, G. (1989). *The Remembered Present*. London: Basic Books.

El Bouih, F. (2008). *Talk of Darkness*. Austin: Center for Middle Eastern Studies at The University of Texas at Austin.

Epstein, H. (1979). *Children of the Holocaust: Conversations with Sons and Daughters of Survivors*. New York: Penguin Books.

Fossion, P., Rejas, M., Servais, L., Pelc, I., Hirsch, S. (2003). "Family Approach with Grandchildren of Holocaust Survivors." *American Journal of Psychotherapy*, 57(4), pp. 519–527.

Freud, S. (1950 [1895]). "Project for a Scientific Psychology." In Strachey, J. (Ed.), *The Standard Edition of the Complete Psychological Works of Sigmund Freud*, vol. 1, pp. 281–391, London: Hogarth Press.

Fromm, M.G. (ed.) (2011). *Lost in Transmission: Studies of Trauma Across Generations*. London: Karnac Books.

Garzón, B. (2024). "The fight against impunity for enforced disappearances: A historical and personal account". In Bianchi, M. G., & Luci, M. (Eds.), *Psychoanalytic, Psychosocial, and Human Rights Perspectives on Enforced Disappearance*. London: Routledge.

Grand, S. (2000). *The Reproduction of Evil: A Clinical and Cultural Perspective*. Analytic Press.

Herman, J.L. (1992). *Trauma and Recovery: The Aftermath of Violence from Domestic Abuse to Political Terror*. New York: Basic Books.

Jung, C.G. (1905). Experimental Observations on the Faculty of Memory. In *Experimental Researches CW*, vol. 2, pp. 272–287. London and New York: Routledge.

Jung, C.G. (1916). Psychoanalysis and Neurosis. In *Freud and Psychoanalysis CW*, vol. 4, pp. 243–251. London and New York: Routledge.

Jung, C.G. (1919a). Psychoanalysis and Association Experiments. In *Experimental Researches CW*, vol. 2, pp. 288–317. London and New York: Routledge.

Jung, C.G. (1919b). Instinct and the Unconscious. In *The Structure and Dynamics of the Psyche CW*, vol. 8, pp. 129–138. London and New York: Routledge.

Jung, C.G. (1932). "Sigmund Freud in His Historical Setting" in *The Spirit in Man, Art, and Culture CW*, vol. 15., pp. 33-40, London and New York: Routledge.

Jung, C.G. (1934). "A Review of the Complex Theory" in *The Structure and Dynamics of the Psyche CW*, vol.8., pp. 92-104, London and New York: Routledge.

Jung, C.G. (1935a). What Is Psychotherapy?. In *The Practice of Psychotherapy CW*, vol. 16, pp. 21–28. London and New York: Routledge.

Jung, C.G. (1935b). The Tavistock Lectures. In *The Symbolic Life CW*, vol. 18, pp. 5–182. London and New York: Routledge.

Jung, C.G. (1939). Conscious, Unconscious, and Individuation. In *Aion CW*, vol. 9i, pp. 275–289. London and New York: Routledge.

Jung, C.G. (1954). Archetypes of the Collective Unconscious. In *The Archetypes and the Collective Unconscious CW*, vol. 9, pp. 3–41. London and New York: Routledge.

Jung, C.G. (1955). A Review of Early Hypothesis. In *Freud and Psychoanalysis CW*, vol. 4, pp. 88–101. London and New York: Routledge.

Jung, C.G. (1961). Healing the Split. In *The Symbolic Life CW*, vol. 18, pp. 253–264. London and New York: Routledge.

Kalsched, D. (1996). *The Inner World of Trauma: Archetypal Defences of the Personal Spirit*. London and New York: Routledge.

Kalsched, D. (2013). *Trauma and the Soul: A Psycho-Spiritual Approach to Human Development and Its Interruption*. London and New York: Routledge.

LeDoux, J.E. (1994). "Emotion, Memory and the Brain." *Scientific American*, 270(6), pp. 50–57. https://doi.org/10.1038/scientificamerican0694-50

López Casanova, A., Melenotte, S., Vallejo Flores, V. (2021). "Art, Memory, and Disappearance in Contemporary Mexico: A Conversation with Alfredo López Casanova." *Violence: An International Journal*, 2(1), 169–192. https://doi.org/10.1177/26330024211003010

MacNally, R. (2005). *Remembering Trauma*. Cambridge: Harvard University Press, Belknap Press.

Margalit, A. (2002). *The Ethics of Memory*. Cambridge: Harvard University Press.

Martínez, I. (2020). *Las Soledades de Olga*. Montevideo: Editorial Planeta S.A.

Masson,J.M.(ed.)(1985).*The Complete Letters of Sigmund Freud to Wilhelm Fliess, 1887–1904*. Cambridge, MA: Belknap.

Matar, H. (2011). *Anatomy of a Disappearance*. New York: Viking Press.

Matar, H. (2017). *The Return – Fathers, Sons and the Land in Between*. New York: Viking Press.

Mdidech, J. (2002). *La Chambre Noire ou Derb Moulay Chérif*. Casablanca: Eddif.

Miller, G. A. (1956). "The magical number seven, plus or minus two: Some limits on our capacity for processing information." *Psychological Review*, 63(2), pp. 81–97.

Neelapaijit, A. (2024). The Curse of ambiguity: The traumatic memory of victims of enforced disappearance. In Bianchi, M. G., & Luci, M. (Eds.), *Psychoanalytic, Psychosocial, and Human Rights Perspectives on Enforced Disappearance*. London: Routledge.

Pally, R. (2000). *The Mind-Brain Relationship*. London: Karnac Books.

Pascual-Leone, A., Nguyet, D., Cohen, L.G., Brasil-Neto, J.P., Cammarota, A., Hallett, M. (1995). "Modulation of Muscle Responses Evoked by Transcranial Magnetic Stimulation during the Acquisition of New Fine Motor Skills." *Journal of Neurophysiology*, 74(3), pp. 1037–1045. https://doi.org/10.1152/jn.1995.74.3.1037

Perez-Sales, P., Duhaime, B., Méndez, J. (2021). "Current Debates, Developments and Challenges Regarding Torture, Enforced Disappearances and Human Rights." *Torture Journal*, 31(2), pp. 3–13. https://doi.org/10.7146/torture.v31i2.128890

Peterson L. R., & Peterson M. J. (1959). "Short-term retention of individual verbal items." *Journal of Experimental Psychology*, 58(3), pp. 193–198.

Rauchfuss, K., Schmolze, B. (2008). "Justice Heals: The Impact of Impunity and the Fight against It on the Recovery of Severe Human Rights Violations' Survivors." *Torture*, 18(1), pp. 38–50.

Rogers, C.R. (1965). *Client-Centered Therapy: Its Current Practice, Implications and Theory*. Boston: Houghton Mifflin.

Rojas Baeza, P. (2009). *La Interminable Ausencia*. Santiago de Chile: LOM.

Salvioli, F. (2020). *Memorialization Processes in the Context of Serious Violations of Human Rights and International Humanitarian Law: The Fifth Pillar of Transitional Justice*. Report of the Special Rapporteur on the Promotion of Truth, Justice, Reparation and Guarantees of Non-recurrence. United Nations: A/HRC/45/45.

Schacter, D-L-(1996). *Searching for Memory: The Brain, the Mind, and the Past*. New York: Basic Books.

Schwab, G. (2010). *Haunting Legacies: Violent Histories and Transgenerational Trauma*. New York: Columbia University Press.

Sønnenland, A.M. (2021). "Survivors' Experiences with Testifying in Trials after Gross Human Rights Violations in Argentina." *Torture Journal*, 31(3), pp. 32–44. https://doi.org/10.7146/torture.v32i3.125118

Spermon, D., Darlington, Y., Gibney, P. (2010). "Psychodynamic Psychotherapy for Complex Trauma: Targets, Focus, Applications, and Outcomes." *Psychology Research and Behavior Management*, 3, pp. 119–127. https://doi.org/10.2147/PRBM.S10215

Stein, M. (ed.) (1995). *Jung on Evil*. London: Routledge.

United Nations. (2005a). Resolution adopted by the General Assembly. *60/147. Basic Principles and Guidelines on the Right to a Remedy and Reparation for Victims of Gross Violations of International Human Rights Law and Serious Violations of International Humanitarian Law*. A/RES/60/147.

United Nations. (2005b). *Principles for the Protection and Promotion of Human Rights through Action to Combat Impunity*. E/CN.4/2005/102/Add.1.

United Nations. (2010). Resolution adopted by the General Assembly.*65/209. International Convention for the Protection of All Persons from Enforced Disappearance*. A/RES/65/209.

Van der Kolk, B.A., Roth, S., Pelcovitz, D., Sunday, S., Spinazzola, J. (2005). "Disorders of Extreme Stress: The Empirical Foundation of a Complex Adaptation to Trauma." *Journal of Traumatic Stress*, 18(5), pp. 389–399.

Vidal-Naquet, P. (2005). *Les Assassins de la Mémoire: Un Eichmann de Papier*. Paris: La Découverte.

Vital-Brasil, V. (2018). "An Ethical and Aesthetic Challenge: Symbolic Reparation and the Construction of Memory." *Torture Journal*, 28(1), pp. 70–83. https://doi.org/10.7146/torture.v28i1.105479

Wilson, J.P. (ed.) (2006). *The Posttraumatic Self: Restoring Meaning and Wholeness to Personality*. London and New York: Routledge. https://doi.org/10.4324/9780203955932

Yeats, W.B. (1959). *Mythologies*. New York: Macmillan.

Chapter 10

Tortured and disappeared bodies

The problem of 'knowing'

Monica Luci

Introduction

This chapter questions the issue of the location of 'knowing' in societies that practice torture and enforced disappearance. These societies are generally characterized by a widespread denial that social violence is taking place. In light of this consideration, this essay intends to pursue the hypothesis that the bodies of citizens who were tortured and then disappeared are the places where such 'knowing' ends up. Such bodies are the 'places' in which the unprocessed social contents are stored and interrogated through the torture by the ruling group, and then, made to disappear, sometimes forever, to represent the impossibility of knowing, the closure of social spaces for a politically self-aware subject.

The combination of crimes such as torture and enforced disappearance perpetrated by states represents an extreme social case that illustrates the processes leading to the social dynamics of a massive and widespread denial of what is happening in a society that has slipped into what I call a *monolithic societal state* (Luci, 2017a, pp. 135–139). This insight comes from the treatment of those who survived torture and were lucky enough to get a psychotherapy. In these psychotherapies, in fact, the patient's body in its post-traumatic suffering and the therapist's body in their countertransference return truths that are not only individual but are linked to the life of the social group. In these clinical cases, individual and collective life become one, personal and political body, and psychotherapy is often aimed at disentangling the two and articulating their relationship in more complex and subtle ways (Luci, 2022).

Torture and enforced disappearance

The term 'torture' describes a crime, a severe violation of human rights, a situation of horrific pain and suffering, physical and psychological, being inflicted on someone mostly in captivity; a cruel and degrading abuse of human beings with the potential for serious lifelong suffering as aftereffect (Luci, 2017a). According to its definitions in several conventions, for the violence to be considered torture, severe pain or suffering, physical and/or psychological, has to be inflicted on the individual by a public official, i.e. a representative of the state, and for some specific

DOI: 10.4324/9781003312642-14

reasons (extortion of information or confession, punishment, discrimination) (for an analysis of definitions, see Luci, 2017a, pp. 3–14). In addition, according to some authors, torture is "much more than a deliberate, systematic, or wanton inflic-tion of physical or mental suffering by one or more persons acting alone or on the orders of any authority to extract information or a confession from an individual" (World Medical Association's Declaration of Tokyo, 1975); it is an "act of ter-rorism aimed at instilling a paralyzing fear not only in individuals but also in the family, the community and society" (Ortiz, 2001, p. 14), keeping this society under strict control. In some (civil or conventional) wars, it is also used as a weapon, an illegal weapon, against civilians.

An 'enforced disappearance' is considered to be the arrest, detention, abduction or any other form of deprivation of liberty by agents of the State or by persons or groups of persons acting with the authorization, support or acquiescence of the State, followed by a refusal to acknowledge the deprivation of liberty or by con-cealment of the fate or whereabouts of the disappeared person, which places such a person outside the protection of the law (Article 2 of the ICPPED and Preamble of the Declaration on the Protection of all Persons from Enforced Disappearance). It is characterized by three cumulative elements (defined in A/HRC/16/48/Add.3[1]): deprivation of liberty against the will of the person; involvement of government officials, at least by acquiescence; refusal to acknowledge the deprivation of liberty or concealment of the fate or whereabouts of the disappeared person.

A disappearance has a doubly paralyzing impact: on the victim, who is removed from the protection of the law, frequently subjected to torture and in constant threat of their lives; and on their families, ignorant of the fate of their loved ones, their emotions alternating between hope and despair, wondering and waiting, sometimes for years, for news that may never come. Enforced disappearance has frequently been used as a powerful strategy to spread terror within societies by authoritarian regimes or parastatal forces. The feeling of insecurity generated by this practice is not limited to the close relatives of the disappeared, but also affects their communi-ties and society as a whole. And the more arbitrary it is, the more threatening and effective it is at silencing society because it is unpredictable who will be the next.

A debate developed around the overlapping of these two crimes and there are strong arguments to consider that enforced disappearance is a form of torture (Huerta Perez & Esgareño, 2021; Perez-Sales, Duhaime, & Mendéz, 2021), since it implies, toward the person disappeared, *intentionality, purpose, suffering, pow-erlessness, absolute deprivation of will* and *attacks to dignity*.

The concept of embeddedness and the disappearance of 'knowing' in perpetrators, bystanders and victims

The concept of embeddedness expresses the notion that social actors exist within relational, institutional and cultural contexts and cannot be seen as atomized decision-makers and embeddedness approaches prioritize the different condi-tions within which social action takes place. This is of crucial importance to understand these crimes, since it implies that torture and enforced disappearances are not the result of a few "rotten apples in the barrel," or of isolated groups, but the precise effect of the establishment of certain socio-political conditions to which many different social actors contribute (Kelman, 1993; Staub, 1989, 1993, 2003). Only a systemic approach to the matter enables to understand deeply the nature of such crimes. This approach makes apparent to what extent we are socially, intellectually and culturally embedded and above all unconsciously imbricated (Cohen, 2001).

From my previous research on torture, it emerged that the disappearance of 'knowing' from 'torturous societies' is the actual pivotal point to every kind of social actor involved, i.e. perpetrators, bystanders and victims (Luci, 2017a).

Perpetrators seem to stage a crime of obedience: torture is not private violence, the action is supported by the authority structure, as long as the perpetrators have good reasons to believe that the action is authorized, expected at least tolerated and probably approved by the authorities (Kelman & Hamilton, 1989, p. 50). Generally, a military or civil chain of command is in place when torture occurs and actual torturers are typically ordinary human beings who perform violent and abhorrent acts under particular socio-political situations and work circumstances, thanks to 'states of absence,' dissociative states – produced through a specific training – that enable them to inflict cruelties on other human beings. Such dissociative states that enable to practice torture and other atrocities are intentionally and carefully fabricated through specific kind of training and techniques which are usually prerogative of the police, the army and the secret services, that is, those sections of the state appointed to manage 'legitimate violence' (on this topic, see Luci, 2017a, pp. 31–49).

At institutional level, in order to perpetrate enforced disappearance, there is need of a wide network of more or less conscious complicity. Under Article 4(1) of the United Nations Convention against Torture and Other Cruel, Inhuman or Degrading Treatment or Punishment (1984), high-ranking officials, who instigated, ordered, authorized, or approved the commission of illegal techniques amounting to torture by their soldiers, are criminally liable of torture for their participation or complicity in the crimes committed by subordinates. In enforced disappearances, we find the same level of institutional complicity, despite all States have an obligation to promptly, thoroughly, impartially and effectively investigate allegations of enforced disappearance to bring those responsible to justice. However, in practice, the prosecution of higher-rank officers and above all political leaders is difficult and always controversial (Bantekas, 1999, 2000; Bonafé, 2007; Martinez, 2007; Meloni, 2010; Mettraux, 2009) and it is not clarified what kind of link there might be between political and military fields. Orders become mini-policies or grand policies as one moves up a chain of command, and policy is logically of a much more general nature than a specific order or the actions carried out in response to it. About torture, Conroy (2000, p. 256) comments that it appears as the perfect crime, perfectly designed to conceal responsibilities in a huge collective collusion: in fact, a puzzling 'natural crime.'

Under different regimes and in democracy, torture is supposed to be clandestine. Nonetheless, the public has to be given enough information to be persuaded that the repression was justified; hence, we can say that there is 'twilight' state of mind in the population. Indeed, torture in the context of enforced disappearances is mostly used as punishment for the victim and as means to terrorize and silence the family and population in general. Indeed, although torture happens in secret and separate spaces, it is also *shown* and news about torture are left leaking in order to paralyze society. In a similar way, although enforced disappearances leave the families in the uncertainty of what happened to their loved one, they instill the idea that he or she must have done something to deserve punishment, and that for this reason, *he or she is somewhere between the prison and the grave.* For this reason, for example, the Argentinean junta generated a richly verbal and sophisticated version of the 'double discourse' in a delicate balance between making state terror known yet hiding or denying its details. The regime denied (by definition) the existence of *desaparecidos*, and simultaneously proclaimed that victims got what they deserved. This double discourse was supposed to be normal – opponents were demonized, repression justified and terror heightened by uncertainty. The regime used language to disguise its true intentions, say the opposite of what is meant, inspire trust, instill guilt in parents to seal their complicity, and spread a paralyzing terror (Feitlowitz, 1998, p. 20). Abductions were 'public' spectacles, but also clandestine and later totally denied. Details of the torture, the killings, the disposal of the bodies remained secret and state violence was enacted behind closed doors, but terror was continually projected on to the public through unofficial leaking of news about torture and disappearance. Life was in two parallel worlds, public and secret: bystanders recognized what they saw, yet avoided this recognition; knew the general facts, yet did not believe them. The political split between closed and open created a state of mind that was expressed afterwards in the common refrain 'we knew but we didn't know.' And even if you did 'really' know, the price for making public knowledge open was too high (Hollander, 2008). Fear generated a state of self-censorship that makes likely that you avoid talking in public or even with your friends, or that you monitor internal thoughts. The Argentinean junta's media communiqué and news addressed the victims' family and friends, who were told to keep quiet about the disappeared person who would only cause them dishonor. The disappearance was surely proof of guilt (Cohen, 2001, p. 155; Graziano, 1992, p. 77). In the population of active and passive bystanders – a position in which an entire population can be put – this 'absence of knowing' can be retraced in the many forms of denial, from passive to active, that allow people to live in a state of 'knowing and not knowing' that torture and enforced disappearance are carried out. 'Bystander' is the term most widely used in literature on collective violence to describe those who are neither victims nor perpetrators (Cohen, 2001; Staub, 2003, 2012). Here the term is used to indicate all those people who share a range of mental states of denial that torture and enforced disappearance is happening. Some authors suggest that the bystander position is crucial to the maintenance of the world of atrocities (Cohen, 2001; Crelinsten, 2003; Hollander, 2008). The passivity or silent acquiescence on the part of the larger society allows the authoritarian reality construction to spread into more and more spheres of political and social life until it is sufficiently anchored in law, custom and discourse to define what is right and what is wrong, what is permissible and what is not.

Silence is often also what characterizes the victims, for those who survive, a tiny minority of those disappeared. Their silence comes from the deep transformations their self has gone through because of the extremely traumatic experience of torture, captivity, incommunicado and physical and psychological abuse. In the frame of an attempt to give a name to the survivors' suffering, concepts have been proposed to classify the longer-term effects in personality and world view (Complex PTSD, Continuous Traumatic Stress Response, Disorders of Extreme Stress Not Otherwise Specified, Enduring Personality Change after Catastrophic Experience) (Herman, 1992; WHO, 2016; Luci, 2022). Trauma of the interpersonal type is more harmful than that caused by natural disasters or accidents, and produces more profound suffering that may crystallize into disorders in the individual's identity and beliefs, like in "complex trauma". In addition to the typical symptoms of post-traumatic stress related to a single event, complex trauma is characterized by alterations of consciousness and dissociative symptoms that disorganize the functioning of the individual at different levels, biological, physiological, behavioral, relational and at level of identity, in direction of a deficit of integration and alteration in the functioning of memory. The alarm responses remain active – like in the PTSD – but are located within the person's self, which in time becomes deeply changed, often fragmented, inconsistent, pessimistic about one's life and future. Not only the psyche, but the bodily self of a person with a complex trauma expresses this disintegration through somatization or physical problems. These somatic reactions and medical conditions may relate directly to the type of abuse or physical damage suffered or they may be more diffuse (Herman, 1992).

The difficulty of survivors in sharing their experience with the rest of humanity is expressed in many forms: post-traumatic avoidance symptoms, feeling that they will be not believed, amnesia, distrust in life, God, and humanity. This is clearly visible in the consequences of torture. All those who endured torture know that they will not be the same anymore. Améry states, "Whoever has succumbed to torture can no longer feel at home in the world" (1980, p. 40). All this does not make it easy to disclose what happened, even in those circumstances in which it would be reasonable or even required, like in psychotherapy, or during an interview for an asylum application, in case they become refugees, or witnessing in a trial, or with family, friends and in close relationships. And the silence in which the families of those disappeared feel themselves entrapped into is something central to their suffering, too.

The contraction of spaces and *monolithic societal states*

Relying on psychoanalytic concepts about the functioning of self, derived from American Relational Psychoanalysis, Object Relations Theories and Analytical Psychology, I elaborated on a specific idea of self and internal objects that might account for the way individuals and groups operate in torturous societies and their institutions (see Luci, 2017a, chapter 4). I called 'reflective triangle,' the self's ability of knowing, resulting from a pattern of interconnections that allow the mental ability of processing at the same time identity and difference in relation to others. Ideally, this reflective triangle keeps together three poles, Me, You and Other and it represents the mental capability to process at the same time identity (Me-You, You-Me) and difference (Me-Other, Other-Me), creating a 'space in-between' (the area of the triangle) that is an empty, not pre-determined potential space for meaning. Whereas the environment 'impinges' on mind the delicate processing of the reflective triangle is interrupted and, we might say, 'the reflective triangle' splinters flattening the creative and symbolizing space in-between. The rests of the splintered reflective triangle are paired and linear horizontal and vertical internalized and external relations that process identity and difference separately, in relation to different others. This is what makes individuals align in monolithic groups, where a leader is taken as ideal (Freud, 1921). In this state, individuals in these groups are in the grip of *states of twoness*: they are aware of identity and not of differences (segment Me-You and You-Me) or are aware of differences and not of identity (segment Me-Other and You-Other), feeling dependent or absolutely independent. Mechanisms like projection, identification and projective identification are used not only as forms of groupal defense but as mental states for the construction of a specific kind of knowledge (Luci, 2017a, pp. 147–148), a specific heuristic attitude.

These psychic dynamics make mental and social spaces 'contract' and this has an interesting effect on the possibility of 'knowing,' on the reflective abilities of mind. Torture and enforced disappearances make their appearance in what I termed *monolithic societal states*, where the tension between the three poles cannot be kept, and the social *in-between space* for transactions, negotiations, meaning making activities among different groups narrows and often collapses. *States of twoness* appears in the social life of *monolithic societal states* characterized, on one hand, by the 'pathology' of unity – *identity* becomes *identi-fication* with peers through a political and/or religious ideology – and, on the other hand, by the 'pathology' of difference – that becomes social fragmentation and individual isolation. In both these conditions, social conflicts cannot be processed in the framework of a shared system of rules – the law – because this implies mutual recognition (Benjamin, 2017) and creative and reflective thinking – which connects body-states, affects and cognition – is largely impeded. In Jungian terms, this is an impairment of the 'soul' function (Luci, 2023).

My hypothesis is that *monolithic societal states* arise as a product of the splintering of this 'reflective triangle' in large group dynamics due to a widespread, uncontained overwhelming dread. Tremendous emotions triggered by a perceived threat to survival make the task of processing identity and difference in group relationships impossible: as a consequence, identity is emphasized as a base for togetherness among those who are perceived as in-group (Me and You, You and Me are together on the base of our similarity and our 'togetherness' cannot be disturbed by possible difference), usually in the majority group. On the other hand, difference is overstated for out-group people, those who are put outside the protection of law

(Me and the Other, You and the Other are separate on the base of our difference, so that we are not disturbed and/or contaminated by difference), usually referred to members of minority groups. This results in a sense of fusion with peers through a unifying principle providing a sense of purity/identity/oneness with the group, merging with its leader giving a sense of triumphal superiority, and separateness from the powerless, the inferiors, those made different, who are placed in a subordinate status. This guarantees some degree of relief from dread and sense of vulnerability.

Monolithic societal states can be identified in different historical and political phenomena such as totalitarianism, fascism, religious fundamentalism, communism, theocracy and nationalism, which often made (in the past) and are making (in the present) use of torture and enforced disappearances. Often torturous societies are characterized by a rigid political and/or cultural context. Although different in their historical and political meaning, they show some similarities: a common delusion of unity (of the nation, people, believers, comrades etc.) while often hiding an extremely fragmented society holds together through a set of principles of identification collectively assumed. This pretended unity becomes the ground to impede a truly democratic processing of multiple opinions, economic interests, political positions, etc. The term 'monolithic' is to signal both this rigidity and the fact that their social and political life relies on fixed positions, a specific ideological thinking, and a peculiar relational style, characterized by an 'adhesive' way to stay together, to form a unique solid social body with no space between people, no mutuality, and very constrained subjectivity. And enforced disappearances are powerful devices to keep such a state of things, to freeze and, if possible, make a social body even more monolithic, solid and still. I do not refer only to totalitarian states but also to democracies entered into a monolithic mode of governance where the social processes of representativeness are in fact constrained, and the space for mutual recognition among different groups become very narrow.

Current psychoanalysis is more and more conceptualizing mind in 'systemic' terms, as an emerging property of multiple self-states in each other interaction. A healthy self is described as a shifting among multiple self states engaged in processing experience and 'allowing' the emergence of new meanings (Bromberg, 1993, 1998; Jung, 1920, 1928; Mitchell, 1993). This systemic metaphor lends itself to comparison with groups and society, and enables to understand the mutual influences between inner and outer worlds. According to relational psychoanalysis, subjectivity is essentially constructed in the context of relationships and is intersubjective at its core. Personal experience is created and re-created at the threshold of the intrapsychic and the social, amid the integration of diverse elements of personal experience and the world of internal object representations and external relationships, such that they are inextricable. According to this view, subjectivity encompasses both 'me-ness' and 'we-ness': the awareness of both interpersonal differentiation and connection in the construction of self and relatedness is thus maintained and coordinated. At the cross-roads of two axes, me-ness/we-ness and difference/identity, we find a different quality of knowledge and different processes of 'knowing.'

The body of victims as location of 'knowing'

Going back to the main point of this chapter, psychotherapy with torture survivors suggests that there is a site where, in case of severe social violence, the social knowing is stored and can be regained: this place is the survivor's body.

The body is always *the* place of an intersubjective encounter, especially in the case of violent encounters. It is the body (and not property or other goods) the place of storage for the worst forms of pain, terror, degradation and suffering. Torture shows that the violence perpetrated is a hideous attempt to expose, penetrate and occupy the material human form. The physical and psychological trauma of torture combined with the experience of displacement causes survivors' therapy sessions to be filled with silence and dissociative mental states (Luci & Kahn, 2021) in which the body is the foreground (Luci, 2017b, 2022). In the case of torture victims, due to their exposure to a severe and relational trauma, the self disintegrates along with the loss of their subjectivity. The person perceives himself as an object in someone's hands, the tormentor, without the possibility of free will. Experiences are terrifying and overwhelm the self which, in order to survive, can only close itself, freeze, dissociating the experiences suffered and distributing them in different parts of the body. A functional break is created during violence between body and mind. Améry writes about torture

> only in torture does the transformation of the person into flesh become complete (…) the tortured person is only body and nothing else (…) The pain is what it was, beyond that there is nothing to say (…) [it marks] the limit of language to communicate.
>
> (1980, p. 33)

Massive trauma is characterized by the absence of mental experience because the mind is unable to process bodily, emotional and cognitive experience of the traumatic events in a coordinated way. Traumatic memories are indelible, sensory, affective, imprinted fragments that lack narrative cohesion and agency. These imprints of visual, auditory, olfactory, kinesthetic and physical sensations and strong affects remain outside a narrative structure, outside personal story, even outside experience as it is remembered, and for this reason, they can continue to exert an influence on unconscious cognitive and emotional processes many years after the original traumatic event. When the empathic other totally fails in the external world of torture, in Laub's words (2017) "the internal empathic 'Thou,' the means for self-dialogue, ceases to exist. The ongoing internal dialogue, the internal 'I' speaking to the internal 'Thou,' which allows for historicity, narrative and meaning to unfold, falls silent" (p. 29). Laub describes this two-part sequence consisting firstly, of the destruction of the internal 'other' and secondly, of the failure of the process of symbolization through internal dialogue, which leads to the absence of conscious experience (it is the splintering of what I called the 'reflective triangle').

However, in psychotherapy, and especially in the unconscious transits within the therapeutic couple, the meaning of the senseless violent experience finds its chance to be traced. Torture survivors' somatic symptoms and with them sensations, physical postures and the entire vocabulary of movements of a person, mirroring and supporting various parts of themselves, are essential for the recognition, the formulation of descriptive hypotheses of the dissociative parts and their functioning. Thus, for example, the subsistence of a 'frightened' part (which functions to contain the need for reassurance and feeling safe) can be inferred from the recurrent wide-eyed presentation and a hypothetical and collapsed posture; or an angry part (which the patient still fails to be aware of) manifests itself in a repeated and stereotyped way with an extreme tension in the jaw and shoulders, typical of those who are always ready to fight to counter the threats. These can be considered dissociated mental and physical states, or autonomous complexes (although here with traumatic origin) according to the Jungian model (Jung, 1934). The physical sensations and the turbulence that accompany them are the tools that allow a first management of the emotion that is still indistinct and free in the field. They often represent something that has a double meaning; it is a voice for the individual, and a voice for their group (Luci, 2018, 2022).

Especially at an early stage of therapy, the possibility to tell the experience is extremely reduced or even impossible, but the meeting is at the same time full of countertransference elements that can be felt by the therapist in their body (Luci, 2017b, 2022). For the therapist to experience in their body this "state of identity" (Jung, 1921) with the bodily states of the survivor is fundamental to record their somatic states that narrate in a basic form – a level that precedes the higher functions of symbolization – the experiences lived by the patient, which cannot be narrated through language. For this reason, bodily-based countertransference takes on a special meaning for interpersonal communication in therapy. These 'body to body' experiences that are generated in the therapeutic dyad occur within a relationship that might be called 'adhesive,' borrowing an expression from Meltzer (1975). I mean by this term a relational style characterized by the lack of interpersonal space and a quality of excessive closeness or stickiness supported by an unconscious or implicit phantasy of sharing partially or totally the surface of the container of self, i.e. the skin (Luci, 2017b, 2021). Although this type of relationship can be unpleasant or annoying for one or both members of the therapeutic couple, nonetheless, this quality of relationship allows the patient to feel supported and to re-establish a sense of self-containment, an epidermal extension, a way of producing a self-generated sense of protection and security, through continuity with the therapist's 'psychic skin.' It is precisely through these body-to-body communications and the conscious and affectively regulated containment of the patient's dissociated parts, and his/her ability to "make them speak" through the therapist's reveries, that the connections necessary for the emergence of meaningful psychic images are restored within the therapeutic relationship (Luci, 2017b, 2021).

So far I have been referring to torture survivors, but what about the bodies of those who were disappeared (often after having been tortured) and killed and whose remains cannot be found?

To disappear a person is not to kill them, but a way to torture and control not only the victim but their group (family or other enlarged group) and even an entire society. It is the application of a perverse logic to a group scale. It is something intentionally made to entrap them in a schizo-paranoid world where 'knowing' is not possible because everything can be made and unmade, as it is typical of *states of twoness* (Luci, 2017a, pp. 100–121). The normal dynamics between opposites cannot occur in the psyche, because opposites become equivalent: life and death, past and present, innocent and guilty. History has no space in this mental state, normal logical thinking cannot happen since cause and effect can be reversed. In this world, subjectivity and responsibility are not viable (Luci, 2017a, pp. 106–108).

The only possible therapeutic journey in this case is made of the social and political efforts to restore a universal law, unearthing the truth. This does not mean that the process in itself will automatically lead to the healing (Sønneland, 2021, pp. 34–36) of individuals, but individual therapies have limited power to reach a good enough result if they are not accompanied at the same time by a process of advancing the awareness about the truth of the small (the family, for example) and large group.

Sometimes this process is accompanied and facilitated by the discovery of the remains of the disappeared person. Regarding the subject of the 'location of knowing,' Morales-Sáez and Espina's study (2021) seems to confirm the hypothesis of this chapter, that it is located in the disappeared's body. Their investigation seeks to understand the experience of family members during the process of bone-remains identification, carried out following the discovery of a mass grave in the commune of Paine (Chile), in which 11 people were identified. The remains belong to a population of 70 men arrested, executed and disappeared between September and November 1973. Researchers focus on the intergenerational effects. In their interviews, the central theme is the identification of bone remains as part of a family process of searching the truth. The analysis of information is carried out through a codification of the data from main thematic categories according to research objectives. Three research questions are particularly relevant for the argument of this chapter: "where are they?", "the meanings of the bone remains" and "the duty to recognize": the three generations of relatives of the disappeared persons give differentiated answers clearly detectable.

About the first question (*where are they?*) the first generation faces a dilemma of a death without a body, without the possibility of performing the funeral rites. This generation has lived constrained by the dispossession of collective networks of protection and sustenance, as well as the social practices of stigmatization and discrimination. The second generation grew up under the silence and stigma of being the *hijo de* (child of). Most were either very young or had not been born at the time of arrest. This generation perceives itself as 'neglected,' since it does not have the testimonial and/or political protagonism of the first generation. This generation has also had to 'support' and 'accompany' their mothers, but at the same time has not been able to reflect on their own bereavements and has received scarce attention from health teams. In the third generation, the family silence is challenged by some grandchildren, either in the form of dreams that reveal the truth about the absent grandfather or in the direct questioning of the story behind the photograph that is treasured in everyday space. Often they find the information outside the domestic space, in the same testimonies that their grandmothers have given in interviews with journalists and researchers. We might summarize the three answers of the three generations as: *disappearance, void* and *claim* of the disappeared person.

About the second question (*meanings of the bone remains*), for the first generation, the bone remains bear the historical burden of the repression experienced by them and by the missing relative. This burden is expressed in the individual imperative of closing a process of suffering. The bone remains are *limited and fragile representation of the body and the person of the disappeared.* Their recovery helps to generate in relatives the feeling of the end of the search and waiting stage, and allows the elaboration of a place for death, "a place to put flowers." For the second generation, the bone remains represent *the materiality of death.* This generation grew up surrounded by stories of detention in which the figure of the father is blurred. This absence can be described more as a *void* than a loss. For this generation, the bone remains are the proof of death as a logical end to the story of detention and repression. This evidence not only brings back the disappeared but also the woman (mother/grandmother) who was absent for many years. The story of the second generation has been built on the self-sufficiency (self-reliance) and accompaniment role of the first generation, usually without taking over their pending grieving process. In the case of the third generation, the bone remains are an *imprint of the raw, unrelenting violence exerted on the missing person.* This generation has built itself between the distance of the facts of suffering (detention and repression) and the account of the demand for truth and justice of its predecessors. Recapitulating, the first generation deals with the *re-appearance* of the remains of the person and with the *completion of the grief,* the second generation deals with the *void filled with the certainty of death,* and the third one with the *claim* for the disappeared person of a *political truth as collective healing.*

It is particularly interesting to observe how these different meanings related to different generations are in relation to the third question, the *duty to recognize.* For the first generation, the 'duty to recognize' is an imperative that has been expressed in the recognition of the skeletons, in the recognition of the bone remains and cultural vestiges, and in the acceptance (with possible objections) of the genetic analysis reports. The second generation silently contemplates how this duty to recognize was instilled in the family. The third generation questions the positions regarding the duty to recognize of previous generations who have sought to give course to the need to continue life, resolve pain, and process grief. This need for recognition is embedded in the working through of collective grief marked by public funeral rituals and tribute ceremonies with the participation of public officials and political leaders.

Looking at the overall results of this research, it becomes apparent how in the passage from one generation to the other in three generations, the discovery and identification of the body of the disappeared assumes different meanings from *disappearance* to *void* to *claim*; from *re-appearance and completion of grief*, to the *void filled with the certainty of death*, to a *restoring of political truth as collective healing*; and about the duty to recognize from a *personal imperative* in the first generation, to a *family imperative* in the second generation, to a *social imperative* in the third generation. We can observe that in the passage from the first to the third generation, the discovery and recognition of the remains means not only the possibility of mourning but also a return of the *presence* of the relative in the family, and the possibility of repairing social ties.

The remains return not only the bones to the family but the possibility for individuals, the family and society to reach a mental state in which 'knowing' is possible and permitted within society. The materiality of whereabouts and remains gives back the possibility of mourning the loss, 'knowing' the truth, repairing the capability of perceiving reality, restoring social meaning and subjectivity for individuals, family and society.

The problem of restoring 'knowing,' subjectivity and a universal law

The issue of 'knowing' and its 'location' within institutions, groups and particular individuals is crucial to process the traumatic experience both at individual and collective levels. The search for truth is a key factor in all those restorative circumstances following torture, i.e. in the trials of perpetrators (when they are held) in truth and reconciliation commissions (when they are set up) and in the rehabilitation of victims (when they are lucky enough to access to medical and psychological care). In all these cases what is constantly pursued is the possibility of 'knowing.'

At collective level, in terms of law and human rights in the post-torture and enforced disappearance period, it poses the delicate questions regarding the allocation of criminal liability, the issue of the reparation for victims, and the problem of how establishing a collective 'truth' about torture and enforced disappearance in society as a whole.

As far as perpetrators are concerned, the problem in the legal field is often posed as whether the abuse perpetrated by ordinary soldiers can be imputed, and to what extent, to the higher military echelon, to the top-level policy makers and legal officers, or even to the political leaders. Pursuant to general principles of criminal law, not only the direct perpetration of acts of torture but also any form of participation or complicity thereto, is criminally relevant, but in practice the prosecution of higher-rank officers and above all political leaders always proves complex and contentious (Crenzel, 2011).

The problem of reparation of victims of torture deals essentially with the dilemma of 'how to redress?' The point about redressing victims seems to concern which is the most effective form of 'recognition' of the damage produced by torture and the disappearance of a relative. This implies that individual reparation goes hand in hand with social recognition, emphasizing the importance of witnessing the 'truth' of what happened and that 'it did happen': in ultimate analysis, a question of restoring 'knowing' and mutuality in society.

Surely truth commissions and tribunals break the silence for society as a whole about the crimes that have occurred and begin, albeit some glaring missteps and failure, to make them thinkable. They constitute a space where, though contested and problematic, survivors can begin to reclaim their history, an essential dimension of the restoration of subjectivity (Hamber, 2009). However, the issue of truth is complex, multifaceted and crucial to link problematic demands of justice and hopes for reconciliation (Knoops, 2006). It is also the arena in which the parties' competing versions of history and politics of memory play themselves out (Thomas, 2010, p. 45). The victims' truth is certainly spoken by their bodies, tortured, disappeared, sometimes their remains found and memorialized or kept as a fantom presence forever.

I like to think of the psychotherapy of victims of torture and enforced disappearance and the collective process of reconciliation as a 'testimony' – the eyes of a witness having the courage to look at traumatic overwhelming events, through what Dori Laub calls a "re-libidinization of fragments." This is a process that at the same time tends to restore an 'I-You' dialogue. Testimony is a process of symbolizing the concrete so that the traumatic experience can become communicable to oneself and known and transmittable to an 'other,' thus producing an experience that can be known, remembered, transmitted and forgotten (Laub, 2017, p. 30), reinstating it in the flowing of history and memory.

The role of the therapist as a witness also serves to guard the epistemic and moral truth about the trauma, about what happened and who is the perpetrator and who is the victim, who is to be protected and who prosecuted, keeping themselves as ethical compass. This function, which must be carried out for some time in a vicarious manner for the patient, must gradually nourish the patient's sense of autonomy and integration so that it can take the place of the survivor's sense of guilt in their response to their trauma (Luci, 2022).

Similarly, but in a reverse logic, testimony in a social process of revealing or discovering the truth may have a therapeutic function for society. Thus, I wonder who is up to this function in a collective process of reparation: prosecutors, the disappeared's relatives, therapists, political activists, citizens in general, the Truth Commissions, who else? Each of them contributes to such a collective work of re-libidinization of fragments in society, 'soul making' in Jungian terms, which, in secular sense, can be seen as a natural consequence of differentiating and assimilating previously unconscious contents, particularly shadow contents (Jung, 1921, par. 781). In this sense, the aim is a moral reparation of a wound to shared humanity inflicted by the torture and enforced disappearances. All the parties need some kind reparation to their trust on humanity and the possibility of a 'just world,' although this does not mean that perpetrators, bystanders and victims have the same responsibilities, nor that the path to reparation is the same.

The only possible reparation for those who have disappeared is to honor their memory with the daily practice of keeping alive our and their individual and collective subjectivity, restoring the truth and respecting a universal law of justice, at the same time taking care that our lives be worthy of their total sacrifice, so that there will be no longer a need for further sacrifice. *Nunca más* is a promise to keep oneself always alive and present to oneself and others, under certain circumstances an *opus contra naturam*, but certainly worth pursuing.

Note

1   Human Rights Council 16th session Agenda, item 3 Promotion and protection of all human rights, civil, political, economic, social and cultural rights, including the right to development. Report of the Working Group on Enforced or Involuntary Disappearances. Retrieved at: https://documents-dds-ny.un.org/doc/UNDOC/GEN/G10/179/54/PDF/G1017954.pdf.

References

Améry, J. (1980). *At the Mind's Limits.* Bloomington: Indiana University Press.
Bantekas, I. (1999). "The Contemporary Law of Superior Responsibility." *American Journal of International Law*, 93, p. 573.
Bantekas, I. (2000) "The Interests of States versus the Doctrine of Superior Responsibility." *International Review of the Red Cross*, 838, pp. 391–402.
Benjamin, J. (2017). Beyond Doer and Done To: Recognition Theory, Intersubjectivity and the Third. Abingdon, Oxon; New York: Routledge.
Bonafé, B. (2007). "Command Responsibility between Personal Culpability and Objective Liability: Finding a Proper Role for Command Responsibility." *International Journal of Criminal Justice*, 5(3), pp. 599–618.
Bromberg, P.M. (1993). "Shadow and Substance: A Relational Perspective on Clinical Process." *Psychoanalytic Psychology*, 10, pp. 147–168.
Bromberg, P.M. (1998). *Standing in the Spaces: Essays on Clinical Process, Trauma, and Dissociation.* Hillsdale, NJ: Analytic Press.
Cohen, S. (2001) *States of Denial: Knowing about Atrocities and Suffering.* Cambridge: Polity Press.
Conroy, J. (2000). *Unspeakable Acts, Ordinary People: The Dynamics of Torture: An Examination of the Practice of Torture in Three Democracies.* New York: Knopf.
Crelinsten, D. (2003). "The World of Torture: A Constructed Reality." *Theoretical Criminology*, 7, pp. 293–318.
Crenzel, E. (2011). *Memory of the Argentina Disappearances. The Political History of Nunca Más.* Abingdon and New York: Routledge.
Feitlowitz, M. (1998). *A Lexicon of Terror: Argentina and the Legacies of Torture.* New York: Oxford University Press.
Freud, S. (1921). "Group Psychology and the Analysis of the Ego." In *The Standard Edition of the Complete Psychological Works of Sigmund Freud*, trans. and ed. J. Strachey, vol. 18, London: The Hogarth Press. (hereafter, *SE*).
Graziano, F. (1992). *Divine Violence. Spectacle, Psychosexuality, and Radical Christianity in the Argentine "Dirty War."* Boulder, San Francisco, and Oxford: Westview Press.

Hamber, B. (2009). *Transforming Societies After Political Violence: Truth, Reconciliation and Mental Health*. New York: Springer.

Herman, J. L. (1992) *Trauma and Recovery: The Aftermath of Violence – From Domestic Abuse to Political Terror*. New York: Basic Books.

Hollander, N.C. (2008). "Living Danger: On Not Knowing What We Know." *Psychoanalytic Dialogues*, 18, pp. 690–709.

Huerta Perez, N., & Esgareño, E. (2021). "Enforced Disappearance as a Form of Psychological Torture: Evidence from the Ayotzinapa Case (México)." *Torture Journal*, 31(3), pp. 19–31. https://doi.org/10.7146/torture.v32i3.125248

Jung, C.G. (1920). "The Psychological Foundations of Belief in Spirits." In H. Read, M. Fordham, & G. Adler (eds.), *Collected Works of C. G. Jung*, vol. 8 (trans. R. Hull). Princeton: Princeton University Press/Bollingen Series XX.

Jung, C.G. (1921). "Psychological Types: Definitions." In H. Read, M. Fordham, & G. Adler (eds.), *Collected Works of C. G. Jung*, vol. 6 (trans. R. Hull). Princeton: Princeton University Press/Bollingen Series XX.

Jung, C.G. (1928). "The Relations between the Ego and the Unconscious." In H. Read, M. Fordham, & G. Adler (eds.), *Collected Works of C. G. Jung*, vol. 7 (trans. R. Hull). Princeton: Princeton University Press/Bollingen Series XX.

Jung, C.G. (1934). "A Review of the Complex Theory." In H. Read, M. Fordham, & G. Adler (eds.), *Collected Works of C. G. Jung*, vol. 8 (trans. R. Hull). Princeton: Princeton University Press/Bollingen Series XX.

Kelman, H.C. (1993). "The Social Context of Torture: Policy Process and Authority Structure." In R.D. Crelinsten & A.P. Schmid (eds.), *The Politics of Pain: Torturers and their Masters*, Centrum voor Onderzoek van Maatschappelijke Tegenstellingen/Center for the Study of Social Conflicts. AK Leiden, The Netherlands: Leiden University, pp. 21–38.

Kelman, H.C., & Hamilton, V.L. (1989). *Crimes of Obedience: Toward a Social Psychology of Authority and Responsibility*. New Haven and London: Yale University Press.

Knoops, G.G.J., "Truth and reconciliation commission models and international tribunals: A comparison". Paper presented at the Symposium on 'The Right to Self-Determination in International Law', organized by Unrepresented Nations and Peoples Organization (UNPO), Khmers Kampuchea-Krom Federation (KKF), Hawai'i Instituted for Human Rights (IHR) (29 September–1 October 2006, The Hague, Netherland). Available at: http://www.unpo.org/downloads/ProfKnoops.pdf.

Laub, D. (2017). "Reestablishing the Internal 'Thou' in Testimony of Trauma." In J.L. Alpert & E.R. Goren (eds.), *Psychoanalysis, Trauma and Community. History and Contemporary Reappraisals*. London and New York: Routledge, pp. 27–42.

Luci, M. (2017a). *Torture, Psychoanalysis & Human Rights*. Abington and New York: Routledge.

Luci, M. (2017b). "Disintegration of the Self and the Regeneration of 'Psychic Skin' in the Treatment of Traumatized Refugees." *Journal of Analytical Psychology*, 62(2), pp. 227–246. https://doi.org/10.1111/1468-5922.12304

Luci, M. (2018). "The Mark of Torture and the Therapeutic Relationship." *International Journal of Psychoanalysis and Education*, X(n1), pp. 47–60.

Luci, M. (2021). "The Psychic Skin between Individual and Collective States of Mind in Trauma." *Journal of Psychosocial Studies*, 14(1), pp. 33–45.

Luci, M. (2022). *Torture Survivors in Analytic Therapy: Jung, Politics and Culture*. Abingdon and New York: Routledge.

Luci, M. (2023). "In Search for Soul: The Contribution of Analytical Psychology to Heal Human Rights Violations." *British Journal of Psychotherapy*. Open Access at: *https://doi. org/10.1111/bjp.12855 (accessed 6 July 2023)*.

Luci, M., & Kahn, M. (2021). "Analytic Therapy with Refugees: Between Silence and Embodied Narratives." *Psychoanalytic Inquiry*, 41(2), pp. 103–114. https://doi.org/10.1080/07351690.2021.1865766

Martinez, J. (2007). "Understanding Mens Rea in Command Responsibility: From Yamashita to Blaskic and Beyond." *Journal International Criminal Justice*, 5(3), pp. 638–664.

Meloni, C. (2010). *Command Responsibility in International Criminal Law*. The Hague: Asser Press.

Meltzer, D. (1975). "Adhesive Identification." *Contemporary Psychoanalysis*, 2, pp. 289–310.

Mettraux, G. (2009). *The Law of Command Responsibility*. Oxford: Oxford University Press.

Mitchell, S.A. (1993). *Hope and Dread in Psychoanalysis*. New York: Basic Books.

Morales-Sáez, N., & Espina, J. (2021). "The Aftermath of Forced Disappearance and Concealment: A Qualitative Study with Families in Paine, Chile." *Torture Journal*, 31(2), pp. 34–49.

Ortiz, S.D. (2001). "The Survivors' Perspective: Voices from the Centre." In E. Gerrity, T.M. Keane, & F. Tuma (eds.), *The Mental Health Consequences of Trauma*. New York: Plenum Publishers, pp. 13–34.

Perez-Sales, P., Duhaime, B., & Méndez, J. (2021). "Current Debates, Developments and Challenges Regarding Torture, Enforced Disappearances and Human Rights." *Torture Journal*, 31(2), pp. 3–13. https://doi.org/10.7146/torture.v31i2.128890

Sønneland, A.M. (2021). "Survivors' Experiences with Testifying in Trials after Gross Human Rights Violations in Argentina." *Torture Journal*, 31(3), pp. 32–44. https://doi. org/10.7146/torture.v32i3.125118

Staub, E. (1989). *The Roots of Evil: The Origins of Genocide and Other Group Violence*. Cambridge: Cambridge University Press.

Staub, E. (1993). "Torture: Psychological and Cultural Origins." In R.D. Crelinsten & A.P. Schmid (eds.), *The Politics of Pain: Torturers and Their Masters*. Leiden, The Netherlands: COMT, pp. 109–123.

Staub, E. (2003). *The Psychology of Good and Evil: Why Children, Adults, Groups Help and Harm Others*. New York: Cambridge.

Staub, E. (2012). "The Roots and Prevention of Genocide and Related Mass Violence." In M. Anstey, P. Meerts, & I.W. Zartman (eds.), *The Slippery Slope to Genocide: Reducing Identity Conflicts and Preventing Mass Murder*. New York: Oxford University Press, pp. 35–52

Thomas, N.K. (2010). "Whose Truth? Inevitable Tensions in Testimonies and the Search for Repair." In A. Harris & S. Botticelli (eds.), *First Do Not Harm: The Paradoxical Encounters of Psychoanalysis, Warmaking, and Resistance*. New York: Routledge, pp 45–63.

United Nations, Convention Against Torture and Other Cruel, Inhuman or Degrading Treatment or Punishment, adopted and opened for signature, ratification and accession by General Assembly of United Nations resolution 39/46 10th December 1984 (entered into force 26 June 1987). Available at: https://www.ohchr.org/en/instruments-mechanisms/instruments/convention-against-torture-and-other-cruel-inhuman-or-degrading (accessed 19 March 2022).

United Nations, International Convention for the Protection of All Persons from Enforced Disappearance. Adopted on 18th December 1922 by General Assembly in its resolution

47/133. Available at: https://www.ohchr.org/en/instruments-mechanisms/instruments/international-convention-protection-all-persons-enforced (accessed 29th April 2022).

Winnicott, D. W. (1958). "The Capacity to Be Alone." In D.W. Winnicott (ed.), *The Maturational Process and the Facilitating Environment*. London: Hogarth Press, 1965, pp. 29–36.

World Health Organization. International Statistical Classification of Diseases and Related Health Problems, 10th Revision, Fifth edition, 2016. World Health Organization. Available at: https://apps.who.int/iris/handle/10665/246208 (accessed 6 July 2023)

World Medical Association, Declaration of Tokyo – Guidelines for Physicians concerning Torture and Other Cruel, Inhuman or Degrading Treatment or Punishment in Relation to Detention and Imprisonment – Adopted by the 29th World Medical Assembly, Tokyo, Japan, October 1975 and editorially revised by the 170th WMA Council Session, Divonne-les-Bains, France, May 2005 and the 173rd WMA Council Session, Divonne-les-Bains, France, May 2006. Available at: https://www.wma.net/policies-post/wma-declaration-of-tokyo-guidelines-for-physicians-concerning-torture-and-other-cruel-inhuman-or-degrading-treatment-or-punishment-in-relation-to-detention-and-imprisonment/ (accessed 6 July 2023)

Chapter 11

Enforced disappearances and its perpetrators

The psychosis of total loss

Richard Mizen

Introduction

Our lives are lived in the shadow of death. On the one hand, we may accept it as an objective fact. On the other, for each of us, the idea of death and our fear of this, takes its own idiosyncratic form. Psychoanalytic clinical practitioners are constantly reminded of the multiplicity of ways in which death is apprehended and its meaning for each individual. Amongst others, for some, it is the idea of being dead; for others dying. What unites these fears, however, is the experience of loss, of which death represents the most inevitable, complete and inexorable example. Death is "The undiscovere'd country, from whose bourn, No traveller returns" (Shakespeare, 1623/2008 line 80, p. 242), providing the blank canvas on which humankind's worst fears are painted. Psychoanalysis is at heart a developmental understanding of human experience and one of its most important discoveries concerns the early life origins of our hopes and fears. Central to this is the understanding that, as we grow, our earliest experiences of separation and loss shape our ideas about death and dying; how aspects of these past experiences come to be re-experienced in the present and also projected into the future.

It may not be immediately obvious how these matters are directly relevant to enforced disappearance but I intend to show that they are central. It is my contention that, although obscured by the more obvious violence involved, it is primarily upon these early anxieties that it depends, in order to intimidate and exercise power, not only over individuals and organs of the state but also over societies as a whole. In particular those affective states that occur before, or in the absence of, the cognitive and emotional developments that bestow an enduring sense of self. These later states of relative integration emerge in later childhood and are grounded in repeated experiences of loss *and* return. But before these develop, the concept of time is lacking along with a sense of object constancy over time. These later serve to mitigate the annihilating qualities of the earliest fears, which have the qualities of being experienced as timeless and unending. In addition, developmentally later anxieties, with roots in the struggles that children have to reconcile the conflicting feelings of love and hostility that inevitably arise in relation to those objects that

DOI: 10.4324/9781003312642-15

a child is most closely attached to and dependent upon, are also played upon and exploited by the users of enforced disappearance.

A caveat here. It is not my intention to negate the more conscious motivations of those individuals, organizations and sections of society who use enforced disappearance as a means of exercising political power and control. But these more instrumental motives are the ones that are more usually thought about. Here, however, it is the affective aspects of enforced disappearance that give it its power to extort, that I will focus on.

In order to illustrate the kinds of affective forces and processes that I have in mind, I want to use a film. The 2017, award-winning, semi-autobiographical, Catalan/Spanish, film *Estiu 1993* (*Summer of 1993*), written and directed by Carla Simón, portrays the months following the death of a six-year-old girl's mother. In the film, it emerges that her father is also dead and that both parents have died of AIDS. The child, Frida, goes to live with her maternal uncle and aunt and her three-year-old cousin, Anna. The film follows, with great sensitivity and lack of sentimentality, Frida trying to comprehend her loss, charting her love, dependence and developing attachment to her new family but also her intense feelings of hostility toward them. In particular, her envy and jealousy in relation to Anna and the antipathy she feels toward her surviving relatives whose presence, daily reminds her, even in their acts of caring for her, of the absence of her mother and the enormity of her loss. Particularly powerful are Simón's evocations of the ways in which Frida tries to defend herself against the pain of her grief and her sense of abandonment. Often she does this by trying to reverse her position, by instead becoming the rejecter and abandoner of a child. On two occasions, Frida leads Anna into potential danger. Once by taking and leaving her into thick woods, lying to her aunt about Anna's location and callously ignoring her distress. Later she encourages her cousin into deep water, where she might drown. The film does not spare the viewer having to grapple with their sympathetic identification with a child who has lost everything, and its demand that they must also face their feelings of hate for a child who is tempted to escape from her own almost unbearable sense of loss, by evoking and locating it in somebody else.

Few of us have not had the experience of a sudden, unanticipated separation between child and carer. In both child and carers, such situations provoke acute, panicky feelings, and overpowering ideas and images of a permanent, catastrophic separation. Most if not all parents are always, to some degree or other, vigilant and on guard against the possibility of their child being lost. This apprehension may diminish as a child grows but may never be entirely absent even into their adulthood. Hardly less painful are those situations in which there is slower dawning of a similarly catastrophic and equally dread filled realization. If such fears are rarely fully realized, the anticipation of them is, I think, universal but if not that, certainly ubiquitous. They are common and powerful enough to have become literary and cinematic tropes and as fact rather than fiction, the subject of enduring and compelling newspaper stories. If such a separation as either an adult or a child is not their worst nightmare, it must be quite close to it.

If in *Estiu 1993* the painfulness of the child's loss is poignant and at times heart-breaking, almost as painful is observing the adults' frequent indifference and apparent obliviousness to Frida's anxiety and distress. Scenes, early in the film, show Frida standing, shocked and frozen, whilst around her the adults, apparently indifferent or taken up with their own sense of loss, dismantle her home; aged six her whole world. As the film develops, Frida's aunt, now her main carer, struggles with her powerful feelings of resentment, irritation and outright anger, evoked in her by her traumatized, cut-off, often rejecting and destructive niece. These emotions oscillate, however, with her equally powerful feelings of concern, sympathy and love for Frida as she tries to contain her pained, angry feelings and make the empathic identifications that might anchor her relationship with Frida in these.

Despite the painfulness of watching Frida grapple with her loss, it is this alternative scenario, in which one is not identified with the victim or as a carer and protector of the victim, but instead left feeling responsible for the victim or their carer's sense of abandonment and loss. This is so much more difficult to identify with, let alone acknowledge or imagine in oneself and the feeling of guilt that such an identification evokes may be close to overwhelming.

Neglecters, abusers and abductors of children, especially when they are responsible for death or serious physical or psychological injury, are uniquely hated. When the events leading to a death or injury are protracted or sadistic and sexualized, they tend to be regarded as unforgiveable. Perpetrators of such crimes are likely to find themselves despised and ostracized even by other criminals. Guilt aside, the fear of such disapproval and in all probability of becoming a pariah, is likely to mean that admitting to such ideas or impulses, even to oneself, is very difficult, regardless of whether there is the least likelihood that they might be enacted.

Freud's psychoanalytic theory is founded on this (Freud, 1914). At its core is the understanding that human beings are inevitably possessed of powerful emotions, especially those of a sexual or aggressive kind and there is the recognition that these feelings are often interacting in complex ways that may be held consciously but also, importantly, unconsciously. Freud further contended that these feelings and impulses, often experienced as ideas and images, are likely to express wishes that are felt by the individual to be relationally or socially transgressive. The painfulness of the emotional conflict that then arises, shame or guilt especially, gives rise to psychological defenses that are intended to banish the offending emotion from a troubled mind: repression in the psychoanalytic idiom (Freud, 1936). But as Freud went on to point out, the unacceptable idea, impulse or feeling does not disappear. It is merely removed from consciousness and from this unconscious state continues to exert its influence.

Literary or cinematic portrayals allow us to consciously identify with the recipients of pain and loss; the vicariousness of the experience mediates, titrates and makes more bearable the pain of the affective experience. By this means, art and literature play their important part in facilitating the integration of our more direct experiences of life and loss. Less obviously, in direct consciousness, is the awareness of the ways in which we might secretly wish for, enjoy or be relieved by the losses we can see other people endure. It leaks out, however, often, as Freud pointed out (Freud, 1905), using humor. At a village quiz-night, recently one of the questions posed was 'What royal loss occurred in 2002?', to which the correct answer was 'The death of the (British) Queen Mother.' The next question was, 'What cause for royal celebration happened in 2002?' One wag called out 'The death of the Queen Mother' provoking laughter (the correct answer being, it was the Queen, her daughter's, Golden Jubilee). I think this demonstration of 'The Queen is dead. God save the Queen' reflects the deep vein of hostility toward those who are ostensibly revered and even loved, existing in tandem with the wish to safeguard and protect.

Affect

Attention to conflicting impulses and emotions is not just the province of psychoanalysis of course nor is it new. Both religion and the law, whatever else they may be, are also concerned with providing ways of trying to think about and manage emotion and its expression. Nor did Freud's discoveries in relation to unconscious processes come as revelation, in their assertion that some motives may be hidden or disavowed. Nonetheless, psychoanalytic ideas have been important because, counter-culturally, they privilege affect over cognition and mind over behavior and in large measure this goes against the prevailing current, since the Enlightenment at least, that has emphasized cognition and rationality often treating emotion as a contaminant or antithetical to these.

Important findings of affective neuroscience (see, for example, Ledoux, 1999; Panksepp, 1998) have thrown a different light on the relationship between cognition and affect, however. There is much that remains to be discovered but affect has come to be understood, amongst other things, as having a deeper and more fundamental role in self-experience. This recognizes emotion not just as something that is experienced by a self but as having a central role in the development of the sense of a self that does the experiencing; that we not only have our feelings; we *are* our feelings (Damasio, 1999).

Freud hypothesized a primary drive, libido, as providing the energetic and motivational substrate of the human psyche. He characterized this initially entirely in terms of sexuality (Eros), (Freud, 1905) but later revised this to include a destructive drive, the Death Instinct (Thanatos) and the tension between these (Freud, 1920) as fundamental. Jung accepted Freud's idea of libido but conceptualized it as a generalized form of psychic energy that acquired form over time (Jung, 1935). Klein proposed an epistemophilic instinct (Klein, 1930/1948). Later still, Bowlby, drawing on Harlow's empirical research into attachment behavior in rhesus monkeys (Bowlby, 1965), placed the drive to make attachments, at center stage. The work of the late Jaak Panksepp both confirmed and disconfirmed aspects of all of these conceptions (Panksepp, 1998). Pankseep identified discrete neurological, affective systems (Panksepp, 2005) as providing the command, motivational and evaluative orientations of all sentient animals, including humans, within their environment. These provide the means by which they can make rough and ready evaluations of the objects they encounter in terms of their capacity to either threaten of enhance body homeostasis (Damasio, 1999).

Panksepp (1998) identified seven basic affective-emotional command and motivational brain systems, which he called the SEEKING, RAGE, FEAR, LUST, CARE, (rough and tumble) PLAY and PANIC systems. Later, he elaborated on this to highlight their command and motivational functions in:

> ... i) seeking resources, ii) becoming angry if access to resources are thwarted, iii) becoming scared if one's bodily well-being is threatened, iv) various sexual desires that are somewhat different in males and females, v) urges to exhibit loving and attentive care to one's off-spring, vi) feelings of panic and distress when one has lost contact with one's loved ones, and vii) the boisterous joyousness of rough and tumble playfulness.
>
> (Panksepp & Watts 2003, p. 206)

Interestingly, these neurological systems can be seen as reflecting some of the basic 'instincts' posited by Freud, Jung, Bowlby and others, albeit each giving primacy to a particular affect type. Experientially, these affective systems operate at multiple levels. Garfield and Lane (2005) describe (subjective) emotional experience in terms of, five levels of emotional awareness, in ascending order, "awareness of physical sensations, action tendencies, single emotions, blends of emotions, and blends of blends of emotional experience (the capacity to appreciate complexity in the experiences of self and other)" (Garfield, Lane, 2005, p. 9), by means of the aversive or attractive hedonic tones that they generate.

These understandings have the capacity to change our understanding of human experience and human behavior in the way that they underline and emphasis the primary role played by affect, both consciously and unconsciously. As Panksepp and Wattts comment:

> all sustained cognition is affectively directed and motivated, often invisibly in a way that promotes the illusion of cognitive autonomy from emotion (Panksepp, Watts, 2003, p. 115).

This is not to say that cognition and rational functioning are not important. As I will go on to describe, the cognization/socialization of affective experience is of central importance in terms of the ways that the affective *potentials* are expressed and represented psychically and the ways that affect is experienced and processed. But initially, the regulation of an infant's emotional and sensation feelings is entirely dependent upon the external interventions made by their primary carers. Over time these interventions (or in their absence do not) facilitate the development of an internal capacity for what has been called *reflective function* (Fonagy, Target, 1996), linked to affective experiences acquiring meaning, as the basis of being able to self-regulate, affect. Central to this is primary carers' capacity to 'read' infants' feeling states and respond in ways that are congruent with the infant's experiences. This bestows the capacity to *mentalize*, which endows the capacity to understand ourselves and others in terms of intentional mental states (Fonagy, Luyten, 2009).

The affective basis of violence

We can use this knowledge about the role of affect and the ways in which feeling states may be represented psychically, acquire meaning and become subject to self-regulation, to also understand what happens if they do not. Violence is one of the ways in which this can be played out (Mizen, 2009, 2019). There are two aspects to this. The first is the way that in the absence of a mentalizing capacity, individuals have an unstable sense of their feelings 'belonging' to them (which in any case, is quite ordinarily felt to be shifting in quality); they are unable of generating a feeling of agency in relation to an object in the environment (Knox, 2011). Instead, feeling may be experienced as having a violating quality and as something that is being forced into the individual by an object in the environment. This leads to the second aspect; in the absence of being able to manage the emotional-feeling as something inside, the individual is likely to try to manage it by controlling the objects that are felt to be responsible for the feeling. The violent and violating quality of the emotional experience results in violent behavior as an attempt to manage externally, what cannot be managed internally.

From this perspective, the conscious rationalizations advanced by perpetrators or observers to account for violence, recedes and what comes to the fore instead are the unconscious, underlying, affective elements. Instead of violent actions being seen as primarily driven by instrumental or opportunistic motives, unconscious affective elements need to be considered. It is common, nevertheless, to think of acts of violence as opportunistic and instrumental: aggressive acts during a robbery; to escape the consequences of committing a crime; to disable a pursuer: aggressive and violent acts resorted to as part of a *crime passionnel* or to intimidate, exploit or control another person. Violence may be 'hot' and enacted by a person who is in the grip of, or overwhelmed by, their affect, or alternatively 'cold.' Here although subjectively cut-off, projecting or dissociated in subjective experience, from the hot qualities, the individual is equally in the grip of them.

More than 80 years ago, Karl Menninger, building on Freud's psychoanalytic understanding, wrote his seminal book 'Man against Himself' (Menninger, 1938). In this, he catalogued and described the ways in which the mode and method of a suicide is not just driven by opportunity and instrumental in the sense of merely being a means of self-destruction. Instead, he describes how each suicide is a carefully, if mostly unconsciously determined communication by the individual intended to convey the underlying, emotional meaning of their act. What is true of violence, at least ostensibly directed against the self, is true also of acts of violence directed toward an external object. Psychoanalytic perspectives reveal the ways in which acts of violence are determined and indeed over-determined by unconscious motives and meaning (Bell, 2001; Hyatt-Williams, 1998). Although conscious intentions may be apparent and the external world provides opportunities and limitations that bear upon the form taken by a violent act, the communicative function has a powerful effect beyond that which is merely opportunistic or instrumental.

These are understandings we can apply to the phenomenon of abductions and enforced disappearances to look beyond the more commonly considered, conscious and instrumental aspects and think about the ways that it is driven and informed by complex motives that have a deeper and wider resonance than those that are immediately apparent. Enforced disappearance is intended to elicit particular kinds of fears that are felt far beyond the individuals who are perpetrators, victims or those who are close to the victims, to exert powerful emotional forces across an entire society or culture, paradoxically in an intensely personal way.

The mediation and representation of affective experience

I referred earlier to Freud's concept of *repression* by which those ideas, images or feelings that for whatever reason are felt to be unacceptable are disavowed. Gathered under the rubric of repression are a variety of psychological mechanisms including *splitting* and *projection*. Since Menninger's work was published considerable progress has been made in understanding the ways in which they operate, not just as psychological defenses that locate unwanted or threatening aspects of the self in the other, but at a deeply unconscious level, also functioning as an early, primitive means of non-verbal communication.

The anthropologist, Lévy-Bruhl's concept of *participation mystique*, was adopted by Jung (Jung, 1923) to describe those states of mind in which there is no clear differentiation between individuals; when, in relation to one another and especially as part of a group, they act as though they are of one mind. Fordham later recognized this phenomenon as active and particularly important in infancy, although following Jung by no means confined to infancy, describing these as *states of identity* (Fordham, 1995). By this means, for example, people (mothers and babies, sexual partners, creative collaborators, analysts and patients) may have experiences in which their sense of being individuals with individual feelings, dissolves. As an example, we might think here of mothers, who in the immediately post-natal period find themselves not just responding to their baby's need for a feed but by anticipating it.

Within another analytic tradition, Klein's developed a slightly different concept, *projective identification* (Bion, 1967; Klein, 1946; Mizen, 2019; Mizen, Morris, 2007; Meltzer, 1986). It was originally conceived as a psychological defense, by which overwhelming, unmediated, threatening or inadequately represented emotional/body states are unconsciously projected, *into*, as opposed to *onto* an object (as tends to be the case with Freud's original concept of projection (Freud, 1936). It involves a process of dividing the sense of self *and* of the other, in a way that enables the individual to divest or distance themselves of those feelings that are expressions of threatening, unintegrated or unwanted emotional-feelings.

Psychoanalysts later came to recognize, however, that splitting and projection (and projective identification) have an original, primary function as primitive, pre-verbal means of communication, particularly of proto-mental (unmentalized) states. Bion gives the example of a mother, seized by the thought that her baby is dying (Bion, 1967). He understands the mother's thought as a consequence of the infant having conveyed to her, a proto-thought-feeling that has the (as yet uncognized/unrepresented) quality of fear-of-death. If the mother responds by attending to her baby with actions that are congruent with the baby's experience and relieve the baby of their anxiety, she conveys both that she understands her baby's fear and that this state can stop. If repeated many times the infant develops a growing sense of the meaning of their own experience and that it may be borne; in Bion's case, he proposes, the development of an ordinary fear of death. Crucial to his understanding is that it is the mother who fears that the baby is going to die, not that she thinks that the baby is afraid. The mother's experience is one in which she has, as it were, her baby's thought *for* it and it is upon this basis that she responds, expressed in the action that she takes: she can have the emotional experience *and* that she can think about it and her response is one that establishes herself and the baby as both subject *and* object.

One of my students described to me, a small child playing on a beach at the sea's edge. An unexpectedly strong wave knocked her over, momentarily submerging her. Panicking, she regained her feet, immediately looking to the mother, sitting a few meters away. After a slight pause, the mother smiled and said "Ah, Sploosh!". The child smiled back and then returned to her play in the water. This brief vignette describes a securely attached child with a mother who can tolerate separation and perhaps because of this, is also closely and empathically, emotionally connected to her daughter. One might imagine this experience as one in which the mother facilitated in her child, a strengthened capacity to mentalize and manage powerful, internal and external forces. Alternatively, a mother might turn away, unable to bear her anxiety; or a mother in the grip of her own panic, rushing over, adding her affective overload to that of the child's. In both situations the child might be left lacking what is needed to make sense of their experience. Despite the ostensible difference, in both cases the primary carers' response to the child may convey they too are overwhelmed by the experience. In circumstances where there is a powerful emotional experience but no reflective, mentalizing dimension or the mediating effect this provides, an infant is likely to dissociate, shutting-down and cutting- off as a means of coping.

A mentalizing capacity is facilitated in infants when they find themselves accurately represented in the mind of the caregiver as a thinking and feeling intentional being (Fonagy et al., 2002). Freud identified the triangulating dynamics of the Oedipus complex, as being central to the structuring of the mind (Freud, 1910), although we may have doubts about whether the 'oedipal' situation is primary or a relatively late manifestation of underlying structures (Mizen, 2019). But it is the experience of being both subject and object; of being as it were in the 'feel' of the emotional experience but also being able to stand back and think about it, that enables meaning to be created and emotion to be regulated. As Bateman and Fonagy (2016) state, "mentalizing is seeing ourselves from the outside and others from the inside" (p. 5) facilitating the transition from an ego-centric to allocentric way of relating to the world.

Separation and loss

In birth, we may imagine the infant as floating in a sea of their own subjectivity, carried along by the currents of body-sensation-feeling and emotional-feelings that are contingent upon its changing, present body state. Infants' survival depends upon the primary carers' capacity to provide the resources required to maintain body homeostasis within relatively narrow parameters: warmth, holding, food, cleaning and so on. Without these, infants' body systems quickly become dysregulated. When this happens changes in the body state activate an affective corollary, a subset of the panic system called 'primitive distress vocalization' (the baby wails!). The affective 'feel' of this is an alarmed and alarming emotional experience for both infant and carers, one that acts on carers to respond, to correct the deficit. Neonates have a parallel lack of psychological resources to draw on. Initially, there is no experience or memory of an absent object returning or, accompanying this, a sense of time. Emotional states change as abruptly as body states, as deficits arise and are then made good. Babies can slide between hellish distress to Arcadian satisfaction very quickly. Only over time does the infant learn that the absence of carers is reliably followed by a return: that objects go away and also come back. A toleration of absence and loss develops that, in tandem with increased physical capacities, endow durability, sustainability and resilience in the growing infant. The experiences of loss, however, need to be carefully titrated, in order to steer a course that exposes the infant to pleasurable and unpleasurable affective experiences, without leaving them at risk of feeling annihilated by overwhelming affect (Carvalho, 2002).

Failure in the mediation and integration of aggression – violent feelings and violent acts

I noted previously that primitive mechanisms of communication may also be used for defensive purposes. If, as a communication, infants' use the projection/evocation of a feeling in their object is part of the processes by which carers metabolizes an emotion so that it acquires representation psychically and creates meaning, this is digestive. By contrast where these mechanisms operate destructively and egestively, they work as a defense against what is felt to be unbearable. The affect, however, along with its complex of associations and internal objects relations, becomes self-dystonic rather than syntonic, and is experienced as, invasive and violating rather than integral aspects of a self.

From this perspective, violence may give the *appearance* of being provoked by a particular set of external circumstances but that is largely illusory. The external situation may be better thought of a being a catalyst rather than a cause. There will of course be precipitating factors, but like the child on the beach, there are quite different ways of experiencing and responding to the same circumstances. Instead, we can understand violence as a defensive structure that drives the perpetrator to compulsively evacuate what is anticipated as being unbearable emotional experience from their conscious, self-experience by means of locating or evoking it in an external object. For this reason, each violent act communicates what it is that is felt to be unbearable and must be evacuated. When we come to consider the unconscious, underlying motivations for abduction, enforced disappearance and similar crimes, as well as the abhorrence in which they are held, we can begin to see how this springs from its potential for evoking primitive, annihilatory affective experiences linked to a loss of agency, identity and an enduring, coherent sense of self (Luci, 2017).

Abduction and enforced disappearance

I earlier described how in infancy, from a cognitive point of view alone, the baby has a very limited conception of themselves and their objects as having a separate existence. An infant's distress on experiencing separation is only mitigated by the appearance of the object. Their capacity to increasingly tolerate separation is as a consequence of the baby's growing understanding and confidence in the object's return. Initially, a baby's experience is of the object vanishing; they have no experience and therefore no conception that it goes on existing elsewhere. Epistemic trust develops gradually as the carers slowly dismantle the baby's illusion of omnipotence. In this way, confidence in the constancy and good-enough reliability of objects, internal and external, develops. They become more firmly established, enabling increased toleration of separation from the objects upon which they were previously entirely dependent as they internalize the various functions, physical and psychological, they need to survive absences. Survival here means not just physical presence but also a sense of the goodness of the object, which will continue to endure, even in the face of the powerful feelings of hate that the absent object evokes. I return here to Frida's loss and the way that her aunt and uncle must bear and not avoid her hatred and hold on to their love for her, in the face of her spiteful and destructive attacks and their intuitive understanding of the importance of this, in order to preserve her capacity to love.

This may perhaps be expressed in the truism that although it is in our relations with other people that we find ourselves, within the same medium, we can lose ourselves, or at least the unwanted parts of ourselves. Abduction, enforced disappearance and similar crimes play upon the anxieties aroused by the earliest and most primitive experiences of separation and loss and the annihilatory, psychotic anxieties that these evoke. These are experiences that precede the establishment of an integrated and enduring sense of self and objects; of time passing and the independent existence of self and other; of absence and return. In enforced disappearances, this is played out, in the absence of the body, in ways that elide imagination and external reality, whilst simultaneously eroding the possibilities available to reinstate these distinctions. The passing thought is treated as though it is the same as the act. The identification with the person who has disappeared, including imagining their loss of the person making the identification, further erodes the capacity for processing the separation and loss and of mourning the lost object. The paradox arises that the manner of the loss increases the difficulty in accepting it; time and space dissolve in ways that makes the experience both more immediate whilst at the same time it feels less real.

These dimensions are reinforced and exacerbated in the absence of a body and the persistence of a forlorn hope of a return. Accepting the loved one as being dead is made more difficult if there is no body, so mourning and actually living a life may be felt to be a betrayal of somebody who perhaps still, somewhere continues to live and suffer. To move on to new relationships and to discover things of value in life may become confused with the idea that person who is lost is unwanted so that the person left behind is responsible for the loss (and this is one of the very many interesting, interwoven threads in Daniel Vigne's 1982 film, *Le Retour de Martin Guerre* (*The return of Martin Guerre*)). Those left behind may come to feel complicit in the disappearance. The apparent indifference of the adults in the immediate aftermath of Frida's mother's death is ambiguous, for example. Is it a lack of empathy and sensitivity to the child's grief? Or is it a more directed, avoidance of her pain? In *Estiu 1993*, in an early scene, Frida grazes her knee in the playground. Another mother, ignoring Frida's hurt, rushes over to remove her child from proximity to Frida. The moment captures the elision of the physical and the emotional. AIDS as emblematic of the 'infectiousness' and 'contaminating' qualities of affect and its capacity to generate fear, evidenced by the guilt of the adults about their hostility toward the distressed child that at times threatening to crystallize into an explicit rejection of Frida or, alternatively, facilitate a more empathic identification with her. This ambiguity compounds the way that enforced disappearances have a particularly violent quality in the way that the equivocal nature of the loss blurs the distinction between imagination as means of *exploring* external reality and what it means and the uses of imagination as a *substitute* for and retreat from external reality. The way imagination can be used to manically fill-up the empty space left by the absent object rather than to create new relationships with the world and the objects in it. The danger emerges that a population may be silenced by an unconscious guilt that an entire society is in some way complicit, which in a vicious circle, the silence then reinforces.

Estiu 1993 draws particular attention to how absence and loss evokes and intensifies feelings of hate, envy and jealousy in ways that are in sharp conflict with the capacity for attachment and love. William Golding was asked what his novel, *The Lord of the Flies*, is about. He replied "grief, sheer grief, grief, grief, grief" (Donoghue, 1983), linking the violence to be found there, with loss that underlies this: small boys without the adult care they need. MacBeth, following the death of his wife and surveying the destruction before him, and his own imminent demise says, "life is a tale told by an idiot, full of sound and fury, Signifying nothing" (Shakespeare, 1623/2021, lines 25–28, p. 288). Strictly speaking it is not the loss that is the problem but the failure or the inability to face it and the destructive psychological defenses that are deployed in order to deny its reality, in particular by attacking and denigrating the unavailable object or an object that is selected to stand in for it. Aesop's fable of the Fox and Grapes is an obvious example of this. While the successful deployment of denigration against the unavailable object may be felt to negate the painfulness of losing something good in the short term, in the longer-term, the capacity to establish faith in enduring good objects, even if one lacks access to them immediately or directly, is damaged. The price of having something good is being able to tolerate the pain of its absence; the cost of being able to have a life is to face the final and immutable loss, the reality of death.

Enforced disappearances immerse all who are (re)exposed to them, in the earliest experiences of loss, where loss is not relative but absolute. Not just the loss of the object but exposure to the psychotic anxieties aroused by the loss of the integrity of the self that experiences. There is a common source of confusion and consequent misunderstanding that often creeps into the literature here, because psychoana-lytic understandings of psychosis are markedly different to psychiatric concepts, even though the same words are used. Most psychiatric theories assume that the symptoms of psychosis: hallucinations, thought insertion, thought stopping, ideas of reference and so on, *are* the illness. Analytic theories, by contrast, understand these (often bizarre) manifestations as *defenses* against psychosis and the illness, the extent that a coherent and enduring sense of a psychological-self is threatened. The individual is beset by anxieties about annihilating, overwhelming affect that threatens to oblate the self (in contrast to neurosis where the anxiety is of being badly hurt; classically castration anxiety). In consequence, power and control take precedence over the capacity for collaboration and creative engagement; projec-tion and splitting replace curiosity and psychological integration. In psychosis the dramatic qualities and floridity of the images and ideas have delusional intensity (disconnected from external realities). This is a defense against underlying preoc-cupations, which are, however, entirely ordinary: loss and separation evoking anxi-eties about an individual's acceptability and value. What is intolerable is the way that these ordinary, painful feelings are experienced, not as transitory and finite, but endless; there is a regression to the stage of development before the sense of time, transition, loss *and* return of the good object is firmly established. Orwell's novel *1984* has, as its ultimate image of despair, articulated by Winston Smith's torturer O'Brien, not just a boot stamping on a human face, but a boot stamping on a human face *forever* (Orwell, 1949). A boot in a face might be painful, but it is survivable and bearable. It is the *forever* quality that renders it *un*bearable.

In enforced disappearance the missing body has the significance of being, not just the loss of the object, but also of the self and its integrity. Perhaps for most people, the apprehension of death carries with it a sense of 'the end of *my* world.' In some circumstances, individuals are prepared to sacrifice themselves on the basis that, even though they will die, this will preserve what is loved and felt to be good. But if the anxiety has the quality of being the end of *the* world and involves the destruction of everything that is good, loved and loving, then death is much less easily accepted. Enforced disappearances play upon such latent, psychotic anxie-ties because they threaten to undermine all that is loved and good and thereby over-whelm or undo the sense of a coherent self.

Hannah Arendts' famously talked about the banality of evil and how Eichmann and other perpetrators of the Holocaust were so often "terribly and terrifyingly normal" (Arendt, 1963). If we can agree with her that they ways in which they presented had the appearance of 'normality,' then her further observations on the stereotypy of their ideas and presentation may perhaps be understood better as arising from a particular kind of identification with the appearance of normality. Perhaps one of the striking things about those people who in one form or another resort to violence is that very often, they are rather boring: their violence may be the most 'interesting' thing about them. I don't use the word 'boring' pejoratively or lightly. One might say (if you can bear with the oxymoron) they have a quality of being deeply superficial. Rather than 'normality,' I think this is as a consequence of their operating in a fixed state of projective (egestive) identification in relation to any kind of deeper affective engagement. I have in mind the concrete, essentially phatic qualities of their communications that reflects a defensive need to maintain a fixed emotional atmosphere that dissociates, splits-off and projects those power-ful, passionate unmediated affective elements that in consequence are anticipated as having a violating qualify that provides the substrate to violence (Mizen, 2009). The crime of enforced disappearance, as a phenomenon, bears the hallmarks of these processes expressed in terms of power and control, by individuals, organiza-tions, states and cultures that appeal to the inability to face change, loss, uncer-tainty, doubt and grief, by evacuating, locating and evoking it in those, who might otherwise demand that these matters must be faced.

References

Arendt, H. (1963). *Eichmann in Jerusalem: A Report on the Banality of Evil*. London: Penguin.

Bateman, A., & Fonagy, P. (2016). *Mentalization-based Treatment for Personality Disor-ders: A Practical Guide*. Oxford University Press.

Bell, D. (2001). "Who Is Killing What or Whom? Some Notes on the Internal Phenomenol-ogy of Suicide." *Psychoanalytic Psychotherapy*, 15, pp. 21–37.

Bion, W.R. (1967) (reprinted 1984). "Attacks on Linking." In *Second Thoughts*. London: Karnac, p. 313.

Bowlby, J. (1965). *Child Care and the Growth of Love*. Harmondsworth: Pelican books.

Carvalho, R. (2002). "Psychic Retreats Revisited: Binding Primitive Destructiveness, or Securing the Object? A Matter of Emphasis?" *British Journal of Psychotherapy*, 19(2), pp. 153–171.

Damasio, A. (1999). *The Feeling of What Happens*. London: Vantage.

Donoghue. D. (1983). "Lecture 4. A Cherishing Bureaucracy." In *The Arts without Mystery: 1983 Reith Lectures*. London: BBC Books, p. 82.

Fonagy, P., & Target, M. (1996). "Playing with Reality: I. Theory of Mind and the Normal De-velopment of Psychic Reality." *International Journal of Psycho-Analysis*, 77, pp. 217–233.

Fonagy, P., Gergely, G., Jurist, E., & Target, M. (2002). *Affect Regulation, Mentalization, and the Development of the Self*. New York: Other Press.

Fonagy, P., & Luytens, P. (2009) "A Developmental, Mentalization-based Approach to the Understanding and Treatment of Borderline Personality Disorder". *Development and Psychopathology*, 21(2009), 1355–1381.

Fordham, M. (1995). "The Model." In R. Hobdel (Ed.), *The Fenceless Field; Essays in Psychoanalysis and Analytical Psychology.* London: Routledge, pp. 69–75.

Freud, A. (1936). *The Ego and the Mechanisms of Defence.* London: The Hogarth Press.

Freud, S. (1905). "Three Essays on the Theory of Sexuality." In J. Strachey, A. Freud, A. Strachey, & A. Tyson (Eds.), *The Standard Edition of the Complete Psychological Works of Sigmund Freud.* London: The Hogarth Press, vol. 7, pp. 123–246.

Freud, S. (1910) "Five Lectures on Psycho-analysis." In J. Strachey, A. Freud, A. Strachey, & A. Tyson (Eds.), *The Standard Edition of the Complete Psychological Works of Sigmund Freud.* London: The Hogarth Press, vol. 11, pp. 1–56.

Freud, S. (1914). "On the History of the Psycho-Analytic Movement." In J. Strachey, A. Freud, A. Strachey, & A. Tyson (Eds.), *The Standard Edition of the Complete Psychological Works of Sigmund Freud.* London: The Hogarth Press, vol. 14, pp. 1–66.

Freud, S. (1920). "Beyond the Pleasure Principle." In J. Strachey, A. Freud, A. Strachey, & A. Tyson (Eds.), *The Standard Edition of the Complete Psychological Works of Sigmund Freud.* London: The Hogarth Press, vol. 18, pp. 7–64.

Garfield, R.D., Lane, A.S. (2005). "Becoming Aware of Feelings: Integration of Cognitive-Developmental, Neuroscientific, and Psychoanalytic Perspectives." *Neuropsychoanalysis*, 7, pp. 5–30.

Hyatt-Williams, H. (1998). *Cruelty, Violence and Murder.* London: Routledge.

C.G. (1923). "The problem of typical attitudes in aesthetics". *The Collected Works VI.* London: Routledge.

Jung, C. G. (1935). "The Tavistock Lectures". *The Collected Works XVIII.* London: Routledge.

Klein, M. (1930/1948). "The Importance of Symbol Formation in the Development of Ego." In M. Klein (Ed.), *Contributions to Psycho-Analysis.* London: The Hogarth Press, pp. 236–250.

Klein, M. (1946). "Notes on Some Schizoid Mechanisms." *International Journal of Psychoanalysis*, 27, pp. 99–110.

Knox, J. (2011). *Self-Agency in Psychotherapy: Attachment, Autonomy, and Intimacy.* London: Norton Publishers.

Ledoux, J. (1999). *The Emotional Brain.* London: Weinfield & Nicholson.

Luci, M. (2017). *Torture, Psychoanalysis and Human Rights.* London and New York: Routledge.

Meltzer, D. (1986). *The Apprehension of Beauty.* Strath Tay: Clunie Press.

Menninger, K. A. (1938). *Man Against Himself.* New York: Harcourt Brace.

Mizen, R. (2009). "The So-Called Mindlessness of Violence: Violence as a Pathological Variant of Aggression." *Global Crime*, 10(4), pp. 416–431.

Mizen, R. (2019). "The Affective Basis of Violence." *Journal of Infant Mental Health*, 40, pp. 1–14.

Mizen, R., Morris, M. (2007). *On Aggression and Violence: An Analytic Perspective.* London: Palgrave.

Orwell, G. (1949). *1984.* Harmondsworth: Penguin Books.

Panksepp, J. (1998). *Affective Neuroscience.* Oxford: Oxford University Press.

Panksepp, J. (2005). "Commentary on 'Becoming Aware of Feelings.'" *Neuropsychoanalysis*, 7(1), pp

Panksepp, J., Watts, D. (2003). "Review of Looking for Spinoza by A. Damasio." *Neuropsychoanalysis*, 5(2), pp. 201–215.

Shakespeare, W. (1623/2008). *Hamlet.* Oxford: Oxford World Classics.

Shakespeare, W. (1623/2008) *MacBeth.* London: Bloomsbury.

Chapter 12

"Can You Describe This?"

United Nations officers and the families of the disappeared

Ghislaine Boulanger

My title, "Can You Describe This?", is taken from Anna Akhmatova's (1957/1993) epic poem *Requiem,* which grew out of the vigil Akhmatova kept outside the Soviet jail where her son was confined. Instead of a preface to this poem, Akhmatova wrote

In the terrible years of the Yezhov terror, I spent seventeen months waiting in line outside the prison in Leningrad. One day somebody in the crowd identified me. Standing behind me was a woman, with lips blue from the cold, who had, of course, never heard me called by name before. Now she started out of the torpor common to us all and asked me in a whisper (everyone whispered there):
'Can you describe this?'
And I said, 'I can.'
"Then," Akhmatova writes, "Something of a smile passed fleetingly over what had once been her face. *Leningrad, 1957.*"

The families of the disappeared who meet with officers working on cases of enforced disappearances are witnesses to the disappearance of their loved ones. For these family members, the possibility, indeed the necessity of mourning is undermined by uncertainty that the disappeared are truly dead. The officers themselves become eyewitnesses to the lot of the witness survivors,[1] as Akhmatova proved to be even as she was also keeping a vigil for her imprisoned son. Like the fleeting smile that passed over the mother's face when she understood that Akhmatova would describe the line of despairing people waiting for news of their family members in the jail, it is not difficult to imagine the relief many of those survivor families experience once they have an opportunity, finally, to speak in person or in a direct telephone call to a UN representative. Here is someone who is listening to them, someone who will become intimately familiar with particulars of their own case. Most importantly, someone who is in a position to bring this crime to the attention of the world, for it is the officers' task to provide a channel of communication between those who have been left behind, the families of the disappeared, and the States ultimately responsible for the search and investigation of the cases. At first glance, it may appear that the final result of the officers' fact-finding

DOI: 10.4324/9781003312642-16

missions is no more than an official report, but the missions serve many less obvious purposes, including allowing the families of the disappeared to feel that their stories have been given weight, the survivors have been seen and heard, and the disappeared are being remembered. Yet gathering the data is a grueling task for the human rights officers. Like Akhmatova with the ravaged mother, the officers who listen to the survivors' stories are eyewitnesses to a particularly sadistic crime. They did not witness the crime itself but they are there to bear witness to those who have been left in agonizing doubt, the families of the disappeared. Inevitably, in their data gathering, these human rights officers expand the circle of witnesses to the crime of enforced disappearance.

The particular losses we are concerned with here fit Lacan's definition of the Real for they cannot be symbolized, they have no equal, they exist only in a place of horror and, quite literally, absence. The disappeared cannot stop *not* being there. The complexity of the loss and the psychic consequences that the survivor families have suffered feel, at times, insurmountable (Bleichner, this volume; Braun et al., 1989; Hollander, 1997; Neelapaijit, this volume). All the previously imagined but unspoken hopes for the future that families and friends shared with the disappeared in a common anticipatory space have abruptly ended. In the vast majority of cases, these hopes cannot and will never be realized, nothing can or will take the place of the disappeared, leaving only empty years, and overwhelming loss. What could have been will not be, cannot be realized. The families left behind, who have survived the sudden disappearance of their husbands or wives, parents, children, dear friends, may have physically survived this catastrophic trauma, but many are uncertain that they have survived psychologically.

In the last 50 years, the field of psychoanalysis has expanded to include an exploration of the psychic costs paid by adult survivors of massive psychic trauma in the aftermath of overwhelming external assaults and crimes against humanity (Boulanger, 2007; Davoine Gaudillere, 2004; Krystal, 1968, 1978; Laub, Auerhan, 1989; Laub 2005, among others). Often this experience has led to profound and long-lasting psychological symptoms, the survivors have exchanged the sense of a more or less continuous self for an unfamiliar self for whom time stands still. Many of them will have lost the capacity to experience a range of feelings, of senses on which they can rely. Their capacity to reflect and to think efficiently has been thrown into doubt. They have forfeited their ability to enjoy familiar relationships, inhabiting instead a world empty of comfort and hope.

Psychoanalytic technique has adapted to this expanded vision of the psychoanalytic field to include an emphasis on the role of the psychoanalyst as witness (Benjamin, 2018; Boulanger, 2012; Eshel, 2013; Felman, Laub, 1992; Gerson, 2009; Gómez, Kovalskys, 2018; Laub, 2014). In a most prescient definition of the witness role, Eshel (2013) describes this work as "withnessing."

Laub (2014) argues that the pressure to testify is instinctive. In effect, survivors are driven to tell their stories as long as the interlocutor can remain sufficiently present to listen. The compulsion to be heard serves two purposes – it gives shape to the narrative and in so doing allows the survivor to make sense of the external and internal experiences. But with each new survivor of a massive psychic trauma, clinicians must struggle to listen carefully to testimony which is often excruciating. Clinicians understand that the story must unfold in its own way, and that it is important to find the discipline and the fortitude to negotiate those times when the details are proving almost unbearable to both parties.

Extreme traumatization demands this different level of therapeutic engagement, one that is beyond professional obligation; it is a moral imperative that requires clinicians to use imagination when recognition is not enough (Boulanger, 2018). Imagination is the engine of empathy, and it is our best guide to entering an experience which is beyond our recognition, an experience that we, as clinicians, may not have and may never come close to sharing with the survivors. Often, the question of psychoanalytic witnessing turns on this act of imagination, on having the courage to join someone whose self has collapsed in the aftermath of interpersonal destruction and hatred.

The therapeutics of witnessing are founded on the understanding that words spoken to an available person who represents society at large have a reparative function. Words carry more weight when they are spoken to someone who can listen intently and empathically. "The most basic necessity for psychic aliveness in the aftermath of atrocity is the active witnessing presence of another," Gerson concludes (2009, p. 1350). As clinicians, psychoanalysts are morally obligated to bear witness when an external event has caused such a profound disruption in the other's sense of self (and frequently self in relation to other) that a witness is necessary to validate the extent of the psychic distress and, occasionally even, to testify publicly.

In the case of the families left behind, whose loved ones have been forcibly disappeared, the need to tell the story is often compounded by an urgency to reach those who can investigate the crime that has taken place. To let go of the hope that the loss might be reversed can feel, for many, like a betrayal of the person who disappeared.

As I was preparing this chapter, I was given the opportunity to speak with several UN officers who are frequently in touch with the families of the disappeared. The families understandably bring this compulsion to be heard to the encounters. I have also read a number of personal accounts from UN officers describing their experiences in the field in general, and recalling particular instances when the burden of listening proved almost unbearable.[2] These officers were part of the Secretariats of the Working Group on Enforced or Involuntary Disappearances[3] and of the Committee on Enforced Disappearances;[4] both mechanisms serve as channels between families of the disappeared and the States responsible for the search. They all have had extensive experience listening to testimony from the families of the survivors. The testimonials are collected in person, in public or private spaces, in hotels or offices or prisons, on the streets or in a church, hospital, or a home. In other circumstances, testimony is collected over telephone calls placed directly to the UN offices. The personal accounts the officers gave me about these encounters were full of anguish and often self-doubt, only very occasionally relieved by the description of one of those rare moments when there was good news to report, when a disappeared person was located. "You are so happy. It is among the best moments in my life…The weight flies off your shoulders. Even if you get one case in hundreds, it is so important." For the most part, however, as they listen to the survivors' accounts, the UN officers absorb the pain these sudden brutal disappearances have caused, and, to return once more to Lacan's realms of psychic experience, they prepare to translate between the Real into the Symbolic, quite literally to render the unbearable bearable in the form of information provided to the public through the annual reports to the Human Rights Council or the General Assembly. Like Akhmatova, the UN officers are witnesses, and, even if in their case their reports do not fully capture the individual suffering they observe, the officers themselves register the pain. Although their role is not described as such, it could be argued that the most significant contribution made by the UN staff in meeting with survivor families may reside as much in actively witnessing the family's suffering, as it does in the official reports they file on returning to headquarters. The officers I spoke to intuitively perform an active witnessing function. They understand that in meeting with the survivors, they are expected to sense what is not being represented in words, to contain what is being said, and they must be capable of imagining the unbearable all the while making it clear that they can and will keep listening. Through this disciplined listening behavior, they acknowledge the survivors' external and psychic realities. For the survivors to be so fully seen, to have both the actual loss, they have sustained and their grief registered by an official, can have profound psychic consequences.

As a clinician who has worked with survivors of massive psychic trauma, when I interviewed the UN officers and read their accounts, I was deeply moved by their sensitivity and struck by their intuitive understanding of what is being expected of them; theirs is an impossible task. They stand as witnesses both to the absence itself and to the survivors who must live with that absence every day. Yet, the officers have had little or no preparation for this impossible task, this immersion in another's grief. As one said to me "You have to be a little bit of a psychologist without having the tools to be. It's quite challenging. And the material can be horrifying." Another said, "You can't imagine the level of cruelty, the level of inhumanity… when you hear about this cruelty, if you read it in the newspaper, it is distant, but you don't have any defense in person." This kind of listening and imagining exacts a heavy price.

The official training that the officers receive for these interviews varies considerably, but little or no attention is paid to the psychological consequences of listening to such painful material. One UN officer told me that the extent of her training in this regard consisted of "informal meetings with colleagues in the places where I was. Nothing formal or institutional." In some cases, a trauma and self-care manual was distributed as part of a more extensive training package on human rights monitoring. One officer described going through a three-day in-person training on data collection, human rights standards, and protection of the identity of the witness. These are obviously crucial safeguards that must be built into any meeting with the families of the disappeared; however, in the course of this three-day training, only one hour was allotted to a discussion about "emotionally difficult situations." Further, the workshop leader for this particular module was not a mental health specialist and he was himself clearly disturbed by his own experiences in the field.[5] Like most of my clinical colleagues who work in the field of massive psychic trauma, I have been deeply affected by the tales of horror and loss I have heard from survivors; sometimes memories of what I have heard intrude into my dreams, suddenly interrupt my thinking in the course of a regular day, or are manifest in mysterious physical symptoms reminiscent of what I had heard described earlier (Boulanger, 2018). But through reading and exchanges with colleagues, I have learned the significance of the work I do. I understand that lending an active witnessing presence can help begin building a sense of community around a survivor. I know that when survivors' experiences go unwitnessed, they feel further dehumanized (Peskin, 2012). Through that understanding, I have also learned to reduce my expectations about the outcome of this work. So, I am struck not only by the lack of adequate preparation the UN officers receive for this significant dimension of their work but also by the lack of any formal channels these officers have been offered to emotionally debrief. Debriefing, sometimes in the form of supervision, sometimes simply being given the time and opportunity to talk informally with colleagues who are also experienced in this particular area and understand the inevitable personal price we pay for making ourselves accessible as witnesses, is a crucial outlet that allows us to continue to do this difficult work and to be available to our patients without burning out.

Burnout can lead those who are expected to witness emotional testimony to listen without empathic understanding, for empathy requires that feelings are being communicated. Instead, an exhausted officer might record details in a rote fashion, creating an emotional distance between themselves and the survivors with whom they are meeting. In the accounts I heard or read from the UN officers, I did not hear one instance of emotional burnout, but I heard of many occasions when officers were concerned that their interactions with the families were not sufficiently attuned. "All I can do is listen," one said. Yet it is that very concern about being sufficiently attuned that wordlessly reassures the other of the witnesses' committed presence. Professionals that they are, the UN staff prepare for these emotionally demanding encounters each in their own way, mindful of the delicate balance between creating hope and appearing indifferent. They instinctively understand the significance of being prepared for this process; they understand the necessity of being fully present to the families as they express their anguish. "The difficulty I have sometimes is giving the right impression, the right reply to the victims. The wrong reply creates expectations or avoids empathy," one wrote.

There are survivor families who "appreciate it very much when you listen to them" but each officer contends with a painful and ever-present awareness of what the survivors "really want." "They want us to give them answers. You know they have expectations that are far beyond your powers. When you can't listen anymore you have done everything you can, you feel so badly."

It is no coincidence that in his book, *The Ethics of Memory* (2002), Avishai Margalit, whose work I cited in the introduction to this chapter, also quotes from Akhmatova's account of her vigil outside the Yezov prison and the meaning her presence had for the faceless old woman when she assured her that she could describe the scene. In his penultimate chapter, The Moral Witness, Margalit argues that the moral witnesses' task is the goal of discovering and exposing evil. But that is not sufficient, he argues: "to become a moral witness one has to witness the combination of evil and the suffering it produces. Witnessing only evil or only suffering is not enough for a moral witness" (p. 148). Finally, he adds one more dimension to this task, the moral witness must be exposed to risk in the act of witnessing. He puts it this way, "The moral witness should himself be at personal risk whether as a sufferer or just [sic] an observer of the suffering that comes from evil-doing. An utterly sheltered witness is no moral witness" (p. 150).

I have been proposing that while it is generally understood that among the UN staff who work with the families of the disappeared, the official tasks are gathering and publishing data about enforced disappearances, whether at the request of individual countries, or from individual survivor families, in so doing these human rights officers are frequently exposed to the consequences of cold-blooded, calculated, sadistic indifference on the part of those in authority. In brief, they are confronted with the consequences of evil, with the political and/or criminal motives behind these disappearances. They are always and inevitably exposed to the suffering these disappearances have caused to those left behind. In this capacity they become moral witnesses.

Before considering the ways in which human rights officers as moral witnesses face risk I want to address one distinction that Margalit is at pains to make, and that is the distinction between political witnesses and moral witnesses. He points out that political witnesses give factual accounts of the events being investigated, whereas moral witnesses capture the pain that results from those events. As human rights investigators, the UN officers and other NGO representatives are obliged to file factual reports, but, as I have argued and as I shall demonstrate, their witnessing presence also serves the purpose of being moral witnesses to the survivors.

To turn to Margalit's insistence that the moral witness must face risk in the process of gathering data: the risks to the officers I interviewed fell into two categories, physical danger and both short-and long-term psychological pain. To address first the physical risks: several of the officers I interviewed described moments of considerable personal danger when they were meeting with the families of the disappeared in their countries of origin, where, despite the presence of UN security forces and the, possibly reluctant, presence of local law enforcement, the forces ranged against them, trying to prevent or at least disrupt the hearings they had arranged or even to hide or deny evidence, were menacing. Two examples stand out.

On one occasion, a senior officer, traveling with colleagues in a jeep in a foreign country, described a sudden feeling of panic as – after the team had received unspecified threats – the vehicle in which he and his colleagues were being driven was cut off by a truck from the traffic flow near a crowded marketplace. While nothing further happened, the anecdote is worth repeating because it conveys the extent to which the officers and the staff working with them are always on the alert. They are aware that the information they are gathering will be dangerous to know, and that unseen forces are looking for opportunities to disrupt or prevent them from receiving this knowledge.

In a second example, another senior officer described the increasing obstacles put in their way as she and a team of experts tried to reach a group of family members to take their testimony. I am quoting at length from her report because it captures the dangerous political stakes and the mounting tension that can build up to a personal meeting with survivor families. Although these events happened some time ago, we should note that the report sent me recently is written in the present tense, a testament to how vividly the officer is still haunted by the experience. Experiences like these are lodged in a traumatic present that does not fade with the passage of time. As this mission became increasingly threatening, for this officer there was a frightening parallel between the physical danger she was facing and her almost unmanageable fear that, in following through with this meeting, she herself would be harmed and unable to return to her family.

This mission is going to be stressful, we have been asking for the permission to enter the country for a long time and when we finally receive it, we have to enter as soon as possible, before the authorities change their minds. We have less than two months: we remove one obstacle at a time but many more will be in our way. The number of disappeared persons in the country is in the order of several tens of thousands. Notwithstanding the official invitation, and as is always the case, among the state officials there will be some who want to cooperate, some who won't, and some who will actively oppose us.

The schedule spans three weeks during which only a couple of nights we will sleep in the same hotel, for the rest we will be always on the move, trying to speak to as many people as possible and at all levels: from Ministers to Governors, mayors, judges, army, police, activists, academics, journalists, shelters managers, charity organizations, non-governmental organizations and, of course, victims.

The negotiations continue in parallel with the security department of the UN. They advise against visiting certain areas of the country and one city in particular, that particular year this city ranked as the most dangerous town in the world.

After two weeks in the country, we finally receive the agreement from the State authorities and the UN security department to visit the most dangerous city in the world but for one day only and no overnight stay is possible. We will land at 8 am and must leave by 6 pm; ten hours to see it all, record all, listen to all those who want to talk to us. We are six: three independent experts and three UN human rights officers and we are accompanied by six bodyguards: one from the UN, the other five assigned by the State authorities.

When we land on the tarmac, we are welcomed by a dozen unleashed Do-bermans and Pit-bulls and heavily armed military. The intimidation starts im-mediately and it works very well. Later that morning, while on the way to one meeting, our convoy is suddenly joined by hooded policemen heavily armed and in official vehicles: they "escort" us for a while. Nobody speaks in the convoy and I can feel the alertness of our protection officers. When we arrive at our destination, I ask whether the escort was foreseen and the bodyguards provided by the host country reply that it was to show us who rules the town. The most violent town with the most corrupted authorities!

We go from meeting to meeting. We are frustrated: one moment we see mi-nors in a pre-trial detention cell, and a moment later they have been moved, and when we ask to talk to them the police deny that the cell has ever been oc-cupied. Blatant lies. If they lie so shamelessly to us, international experts and UN officers, what chances do the families have to receive honest replies on the whereabouts of their disappeared beloved?

We finally reach the hotel in which we booked rooms to meet the relatives of the disappeared. I do not remember what the hotel looked like. The body guards wait for us outside the premises, we do not want to enter with armed personnel

In these two descriptions, the physical danger to the human rights officers and the staff working with them is clear, but more difficult to capture and much harder to quantify are the psychological risks that these officers face as they meet with the families and open themselves up to listening to their painful testimony. Preparing for the process of receiving testimony, knowing they are probably going to listen to shocking details from family members who are themselves overcome with grief and confusion, each of the officers is aware that they need to strike a balance be-tween being open enough to hear the details but sufficiently defended not to be overwhelmed themselves or to overwhelm the survivor with their own reactions. As one officer put it, "You need to create distance but at the same time, you cannot become a robot, the risk is not feeling anything or feeling very little, a defense I suppose." One officer describes this as a

state of automatism … I'm recording what is being said, but at a distance from what I see and hear. It's like I'm two people, there is the "me" who is present in the room, taking note without memorizing or visualizing what is being said, and the "me" who is in the distance.

The discipline to be present and to carefully track what is being said with-out breaking down or feeling overwhelmed leads many of us in the position to dissociate affect in the moment as a way of being present without overwhelming the survivor with our immediate reaction to what we are being told. Nonetheless the affect is there, waiting to emerge when it is safe to do so. The officer continued, "after I read the notes, I think, 'Did I really listen to this? Did the person really say that? How did I manage to listen to this without crying?'"Another UN officer spoke of being haunted by these feelings for a lifetime.

Margalit writes that the moral witness can suffer "vicarious victim-risk that comes from witnessing the suffering of people who are near and dear to you." In fact, vicarious trauma is not limited to witnessing those who are near and dear. Trauma is contagious, its powerful affect can be transmitted within families, across generations, between a therapist and patient, or, in the situation we are considering here, between a UN officer charged with gathering details about the disappeared and the survivors he or she is closely following (Boulanger, 2018). Following closely the details of a massive psychic trauma, in this instance, the sudden disappearance of a family member, tracking the scene in one's imagination, breaks down the barrier between self and other, leading some witnesses to experience the loss vicariously.

Sometimes, disconcerting physical manifestations of fear emerge as the listener is vicariously infected by the material from the family. "I get cold. Sometimes my legs start shaking in a way that I cannot control. And the stomach aches or burns." Other times, tears arrive. "You realize you cannot cope anymore. You need a break. But feel guilty about interrupting the session to take a sip of water."

Among the meager instructions that some UN officers receive before meeting with the families of the disappeared are warnings against showing strong feelings or crying. These are complicated instructions. How to handle one's own feelings in the moment depends on many factors, but specific injunctions against showing strong feelings without further guidelines are inhibiting and lead those who find they are unable to listen further to blame themselves for being inadequate, when, on the contrary, the fact that they are moved by the testimony can sometimes be validating to survivor families.

Several of the officers I spoke to described a particular moment when the emotional cost of listening to the survivors was very high, when the words they were hearing and the survivors' anguish led them to think and fear for their own families and continuing to listen or respond proved almost too difficult.

One officer described "urgent action requests," signaling a need for immediate intervention, that arrive over the phone or by email to the offices in Geneva. In these instances, the officer will routinely copy and paste such emails into a longer document to forward to the authorities, but on one occasion, a poorly written narrative from someone who was barely literate had to be rewritten in order to make sense of it. In re-writing this email, in effect, putting herself in the subject position in order to convey the family's desperation, the officer found herself increasingly identified with the desperation she was conveying in the official document she was writing. At other times, this officer described receiving calls from families begging for material aid. Knowing that she can do nothing, she is sometimes tempted not to answer the call, but she feels that if she doesn't reply, she is betraying the family, although she cannot offer them the concrete help they so badly need. These calls permeate her life, her behavior, and her emotions far beyond the office.

In the above example, the officer came to identify with one survivor family as she took it upon herself to rewrite the family's emails in the first person, but when the disappearance of a family member mirrors too closely a reporter's family constellation, when there is a possibility of identifying with the disappearance of a particular family member, the investigators are even more susceptible to being indelibly affected by the scene that plays out in their mind's eye as they listen to the testimony.

I have chosen to reproduce the following account verbatim because the officer takes us step by step through his listening process, demonstrating where imagination comes into play, making the scene even more vivid to him. He goes on to describe the impact of this meeting when he has returned to his hotel and reassured himself that his own family is not in harm's way.

A few ago, we carried out a mission to one of the countries with the highest number of disappeared persons in the world. While in the country, we met hundreds of families, among which several relatives of individuals had disappeared during an internal conflict. One of these stories was particularly heart-breaking. One afternoon, an elderly couple entered the office where we were having our interviews…I will never forget their faces, their sad eyes though deep sight. The couple was carrying the pictures of a younger couple and two very young kids, one boy and one girl – around 4–5 years old. They explained to us that the younger couple in the picture were their son and his wife, while the two children were their grandchildren. They told us that at the end of the conflict, the son was asked to surrender to the army. The last he was seen, he was getting on a military vehicle with his wife and children, after which they disappeared.

I still remember shivers running through my legs as they were telling this story with the pictures of the children in their hands. I imagined the scene – the whole family being loaded on the vehicle and vanishing…I imagined the suffering of the elderly couple, the anguish every single day. I imagined the fear and suffering of those disappeared. I felt so deeply sorry for them I wanted to yell, I desperately wanted to do something for them. But I did not know what and how – I felt completely powerless and frustrated. The only thing I could do was listen to them, recognize their suffering, and show my respect and compassion.

When I went back to the hotel, I looked at my phone and started searching for the pictures of my children… Then, once I somehow felt reassured that they were fine, I started crying. I cried desperately for few minutes. I could not stop.

In another instance, a different officer described a scene that proved unbearable, leaving her shaken and doubting her capacity to do her job. On this occasion, a mother came forward holding a photograph of her missing daughter, similar in age to the officer's young daughter. As she described this scene to me, the investigator exclaimed,

In talking about it, I can see it is even bigger than I thought… I was telling myself I was totally useless. Every mission is a confirmation of your limitations. I blame myself for not being humane enough. I felt I had done some wrong. When they are so dignified, so composed what right do I have to cry?

At the conclusion of this particular interview, the mother threw herself on the floor at the officer's feet

I have no defense against her despair. I am powerless. I can do nothing; I can say nothing. I perfectly know that we will never find her daughter. How can I explain that we are not a searching team but we are just collecting information and within a few hours we will leave the town not to return again? How can the fact the State is about to pass a law on disappearance ever compensate what this woman is going through?

Should a moral witness be guided by hope? Margalit asks (p. 151). Hope for what and hope for whom? A sense of hopelessness seems to pervade these last accounts from the human rights officers as they confront the survivors' despair and their own powerlessness to reverse the losses that the families of the disappeared have suffered. Margalit goes on to answer his question by pointing to the frequently cited passage from Akhmatova's preface where she assures the distraught mother that she can describe the scene that is unfolding around them. He suggests that for the survivor, there is hope in finding someone who will describe her plight. A moral witness brings hope that "there exists or will exist a moral community that will listen to their testimony." In a similar vein, in describing her concept of the "moral third," Benjamin (2018) maintains that "Speaking the truth that has not been spoken to someone who listens and hears this truth is a vital form of restoring the moral third, the belief in a lawful world, is restored … even in the face of evil" (p. 121).

This chapter emphasizes the crucial role played by UN officers and others who work for intergovernmental, nongovernmental, or humanitarian organizations who meet, often face to face, with the families of the disappeared. In addition to gathering data for their official reports, I argue they play an equally important, if not more important unofficial role, for these officers answer the question posed in the title of this chapter: "Can You Describe This?" In their meetings with survivor families, they absorb not only the "hard" facts for their reports, but, in addition, their profound and compassionate listening skills allow the survivors to feel that their anguish is being seen and heard. It is in the combination of their unofficial and official roles that the officers meet Margalit's definition of moral witnesses.

Notes

1   *A note on some of the language used in this chapter.*
   I have been asked to comment on my choice of the word *survivor* rather than *victim* in describing the families of the disappeared. This is an important distinction for those words reveal the tension that frequently exists between psychoanalysis and human rights

law. I do not use the word *tension* in a negative sense, but rather to imply that the words survivor and victim stem from our different professional obligations to the people we represent, how they should be represented, and how we envision our work on their behalf. I hope it is clear that this is not a competition, rather it reflects my understanding that the work of human rights lawyers and psychoanalysts complement one another. I understand and respect the necessity in human rights law to use the word *victim* in describing the legal subject. If there is no victim, then there is no crime, no human rights violation, no perpetrators, no trial, and no possibility of reparation.

To me as a relational psychoanalyst, however, the term victim is only a fraction of the psychoanalytic subject I engage in my clinical and written work. My reasoning is based on the understanding that the psychoanalytic subject contains many selves all with relationships to other subjects. As a psychoanalyst I bear in mind that each self has a complex past, a present being constructed in the here and now, and an uncertain future that will grow out of that past and present as they interact in a new and different context. In other words, the psychoanalytic subject is constantly in process.

Survival too is a process; it implies a subject who is going on being, whereas a victim is an object fixed in time, which is imperative for a legal procedure, but which, in itself, contradicts the very notion of the constantly evolving psychoanalytic subject with whom I work.

2 I am deeply grateful to the anonymous UN officers who trusted me with verbal and written accounts of their psychological struggles in meeting with the surviving families.

3 The Working Group receives cases of enforced disappearances and treats them according to one of the following procedures: urgent procedure, urgent appeal, standard procedure, prompt intervention, and general allegations. Once classified, the cases are sent to the State concerned with a view to open a channel of communication between the families of the disappeared and the State. Annual follow ups take place. Additionally, the information and data on the cases are presented in an annual report to the Human Rights Council. The Working Group also produces thematic reports and carries out country visits. For more information of the work of the Working Group see: https://www.ohchr.org/en/special-procedures/wg-disappearances.

4 The Committee has two main tasks: the examination of reports submitted by the States that have ratified the treaty and the analysis of individual cases, either through an Urgent Action request (through which the immediate action of the State is required), or through the casi judicial procedure of "individual complaints" that alleged families can present once they have exhausted all internal remedies. In these three mechanisms, the Committee adopts recommendations that are directly shared with the State concerned and with the victims. The final decisions are made public and are also compiled in annual reports to the UN General Assembly. For more information on the work of the Committee see: https://www.ohchr.org/en/treaty-bodies/ced.

5 In describing their preparation to handle such inevitably emotionally charged meetings with the families of the disappeared, the officers added that there is more sensitivity around mental health care and vicarious trauma today than there has been in the past. They noted, however, that there is a disparity in the attention paid to the staff's mental health between different UN departments and agencies and other intergovernmental or non-governmental organizations. Clearly, further improvement is necessary in providing preparation before, support during, and systematic psychological follow-up after particularly difficult missions.

References

Akhmatova, A. (1957/1993). "Requiem". In Carolyn Forché (ed.), *Against Forgetting: Twentieth Century Poetry of Witness*. New York, NY: Norton, pp. 101 ff.

Benjamin, J. (2018). "How Therapy with Victims of Political Trauma Repairs the Moral Third." *Psychoanalytic Dialogues*, 28, pp. 115–121.

Boulanger, G. (2007). *Wounded by Reality: Understanding and Treating Adult Onset Trauma*. Mahwah, NJ: The Analytic Press.

Boulanger, G. (2012). "Psychoanalytic Witnessing: Professional Obligation or Moral Imperative." *Psychoanalytic Psychology*, 29, pp. 318–324.

Boulanger, G. (2018). "When Is Vicarious Trauma a Necessary Therapeutic Tool?" *Psychoanalytic Psychology*, 1, pp. 60–69.

Braun, J., Dunayevich, D., Pujet, J. (1989). "State Terrorism and Psychoanalysis." *International Journal of Mental Health*, 18(2), pp. 98–112.

Davoine, F., Gaudilliere, J.M. (2004). *History Beyond Trauma*. New York, NY: Other Press.

Eshel, O. (2013). "Patient-Analyst "Withness": On Analytic "Presencing," Passion, and Compassion in States of Breakdown, Despair, and Deadness." *Psychoanalytic Quarterly*, 82(4), pp. 925–963. doi: 10.1002/j.2167–4086.2013.00065.x.

Felman, S., Laub, D. (1992). *Testimony: Crises in Witnessing in Literature, Psychoanalysis, and History*. New York, NY: Routledge.

Gerson, S. (2009). "When the Third Is Dead: Memory, Mourning, and Witnessing in the Aftermath of the Holocaust." *International Journal of Psychoanalysis*, 90(6), pp. 1341–1357.

Gómez, E., Kovalskys, J. (2018). "Reencounter with History and Memory through a Therapeutic Process." *Psychoanalytic Dialogues*, 28, pp. 102–114.

Hollander, N. (1997). *Love in a Time of Hate: Liberation Psychology in Latin America*. New Brunswick, NJ: Rutgers University Press.

Krystal, H. (1968). *Massive Psychic Trauma*. New York, NY: International Universities Press.

Krystal, H. (1978). "Trauma and affects." *The Psychoanalytic Study of the Child*, 33, pp. 81–116.

Laub, D. (2005). "Traumatic Shutdown of Narrative and Symbolization: A Death Instinct Derivative?" *Contemporary Psychoanalysis*, 41(2), pp. 307–326.

Laub, D. (2014). "A Record that Has Yet to Be Made. An Interview with Dori Laub." In C. Caruth (Ed.), *Listening to Trauma: Conversations with Leaders in the Theory and Treatment of Catastrophic Experience*. Baltimore, MA: Johns Hopkins University Press, pp. 47–80.

Laub, D., Auerhahn, N.C. (1989). "Failed Empathy—A Central Theme in the Survivor's Holocaust Experience." *Psychoanalytic. Psychology*, 6, pp. 377–400.

Margalit, A. (2002). *The Ethics of Memory*. Cambridge, MA and London: Harvard University Press.

Peskin, H. (2012). "'Man Is a Wolf to Man': Disorders of Dehumanization in Psychoanalysis." *Psychoanalytic Dialogues*, 22, pp. 190–205.

Chapter 13

Traumatic traces of enforced disappearance through generations

From psychoanalytic theory to a family case study

Manon Bourguignon, Muriel Katz, and Alice Dermitzel

Introduction

Transmission is the inexhaustible fact that provides the continuation of generations and civilizations. Transmitting means being in contact with past generations. In a concrete way, it allows the circulation of things such as family recipes or cultural traditions. Without transmission of knowledge, stories, culture, we would have to start from scratch with each generation. According to psychoanalysts, the human being is also characterized by psychic transmission, which is the basis of the psychic construction of any individual. Whether conscious or unconscious, psychic transmission concerns beliefs, identifications, and myths but also anxieties and defense mechanisms. It has the particularity of linking the members of the same family, and this through several generations. In front of manifestations of collective violence, such as genocide, forced migration, torture, enforced disappearances, mass deportation, and colonial violence, that have always existed but of which we became more aware during the course of the twentieth century, many psychological studies have dealt with transmission of trauma between survivors of political persecutions and their offspring (for example see Grand & Salberg, 2017). As Granjon (2010, p. 37) states, "nothing escapes transmission". How can the transmission of trauma among the relatives of a person who disappeared in the context of political repression be described?

Cases of enforced disappearances throughout history are numerous and typical in situations of state violence. This crime constitutes a fundamental violation of human rights according to the International Convention for the Protection of All Persons from Enforced Disappearance adopted by the General Assembly of the United Nations in 2006. In a few cases, the disappeared returned; in other cases, their remains are found, but mostly, this crime remains unclear and without resolution for a very long time, often forever. It should be noted that victims of enforced disappearance are not limited to the disappeared persons. Article 24 of the International Convention for the Protection of All Persons from Enforced Disappearance states that "victim" means the disappeared person and any individual who

DOI: 10.4324/9781003312642-17

has suffered harm as the direct result of an enforced disappearance. Thus, families are considered direct victims as well. Relatives of disappeared persons have to endure lifelong psychological torture, living without information about their loved ones and their fate (Adams, 2019; García Castro, 2011). The disappearance of the body deprives the relatives of the funeral rites which socially frame the mourning (Blaauw & Lähteenmäki, 2002; Boss, 2002; Bourguignon et al., 2021; Schaal et al., 2010). Losing a loved one due to enforced disappearance implies coping with uncertainty, but also with legal, economic, and social problems that can be overwhelming for the family of the disappeared (Blaauw & Lähteenmäki, 2002).

Insofar as it is perpetrated by agents of the State, this crime forms part of what Puget et al. (1989) termed "state violence". Official institutions are no longer the guarantors of socially shared points of reference regarding the founding prohibitions (e.g., murder, incest, or cannibalism) (Katz, 2012; Kijak & Pelento, 1986). The State denies any traces of the custody of the victim and their possible subsequent murder, until the denial of the very existence of the disappeared person (Lira, 2016; Strier, 2014). Thus, this barbaric crime is part of what some psychoanalysts call a *social catastrophe* (Amati Sas, 1991; Kaës, 1989): the meta-social framework breaks down, hindering the support of intra- and inter-subjective psychic reality of the guarantors. The trauma[1] induced by enforced disappearance has a psychosocial impact. The psychic repercussions are simultaneously individual and collective.

Despite the importance of the transmission to the future generations, few studies have been carried out to understand the after-effects of enforced disappearance over generations. What is the impact of enforced disappearance on family relatives through generations? How is the memory of the disappeared loved one passed on from generation to generation? What is the nature of the traces transmitted to the next generation? In this contribution, we will explore these questions based on the result of our qualitative study[2] of relatives of disappeared persons and their descendants. The research focuses on enforced disappearance during the dictatorships in Latin America. We interviewed 20 participants from two generations (e.g., the close relatives of the disappeared person and their children) living in Western Europe.

Inscribed in a psychoanalytic epistemology, this investigation was built on the many conceptions of the psychic transmission of unelaborated traumatic material that remain from those experiences (Abraham & Torok, 1978; Ciccone, 1999; de Mijolla, 1981; Eiguer, 1987; Faimberg, 1987; Kaës, 1993). We focus on the manifestation of unelaborated objects in subsequent generations: missed acts, repetition of symptoms, chaotic relational patterns, and even serious mental disorders. In contrast with intergenerational transmission,[3] *transgenerational transmission* – also qualified as "negative" or "hollow" transmission – hinders the process of elaboration of the psychic heritage. Indeed, the heir cannot protect themselves from the shameful traumatic traces because they are unaware of them.

To illustrate this issue, we present a case of relatives. We separately met Emily[4] and her daughter, Carolina, for narrative interviews. Data were collected through individual face-to-face interviews.[5] Emily lost one of her brothers, Miguel, during her adolescence in her home country in Latin America. Involved in political activism, Miguel was arrested a few times after the military coup. With no news of him, his mother did everything she could to find any trace of her son. The conditions of life under the dictatorship and the threat to the family of the disappeared led Emily and some of her siblings to leave the country and seek refuge in Europe. Ever since, Emily has looked for her brother by any means: searching for people who could give testimony, going to places where he had been seen for the last time, and being witness to trials to fight against impunity and oblivion in the society. Emily's daughter, Carolina, was born in exile. She is the heir of this family history, which was disrupted by the disappearance of her maternal uncle. We will highlight the possible repercussions of an ambiguous loss caused by enforced disappearance on the second generation.

This contribution focuses on three themes related to psychic transmission from one generation to another. At the beginning of each section, we will present a brief psychoanalytic theory as introduction to the theme. We, then, proceed to illustrate the most relevant results of our current study with the family case study, commenting with the literature and research on the specific issue.

Passing on the story of a loved one's enforced disappearance

The family story is an important element of identification within a family group. In this sense, each subject can recognize himself as a link in a genealogical chain. Family and collective history also conveys the "foundational statements" (Aulagnier, 1975), which highlight the values, principles, norms, ideals and myths carried by the family group. The story that depicts the origin of the family group plays the role of a *foundational family myth*, which supports family identity. Investigation in clinical psychology emphasizes the importance of knowing one's family history to promote the process of subjectivation. In fact, the parents usually tell their children the romance of the origins and generations that preceded them. These oral stories are not reduced to narratives of historical events. They are closely interwoven with the affects mobilized by the work of remembering. *What may or may not be said about a disappeared relative within the family?*

At the beginning of the narrative interview with Carolina, we first asked her about the impact of enforced disappearance on her life. She stated:

> The impact on my life is that I've always heard about Miguel, one of my uncles, stories about him, his character, his political involvement. I've always seen pictures of him at home. I haven't met him physically but it's like he's always been there actually. For me, I've always had this feeling of having known him. It's pretty weird actually.[6]

Carolina's family is a typical example of a family for whom the disappeared person stays present in his absence. In her family, the missing uncle has an important place in family narratives as well as inside the home space. For example, many photographs of him are scattered in the house. For the relatives of the loved one, these visual traces testify his presence despite of his absence. Authors point out the symbolic meaning of having photographs of the disappeared at home or carrying them during street protests (Adams, 2019; Faúndez et al., 2018). Photographs make it possible to embody the disappeared ones to make them present and reintegrate their physical presence within the family and social group.

The presence of the disappeared uncle seems so significant in Carolina's life course that she has the *feeling of having known him*, of having met him, when in fact she was born after his disappearance. The story of Miguel's disappearance forms part of the *foundational family myth*. Transmitted through generations, it promotes values of justice and social commitment inside the family group. She argues that it is *weird* for her to feel closer to her disappeared uncle than to her siblings with whom she used to live. Hence, the disappeared person continues to be psychically present even when physically absent, especially because Carolina's mother continues her search for her brother's body or any information about his disappearance. This illustrates the impact of *ambiguous loss* which is "a situation of unclear loss that remains unverified and thus without resolution" (Boss, 2016, p. 270). Fifty years after his disappearance, the missing one remains in the narratives and in the minds of his relatives, even of the following generation.

In Carolina's family, talking about the past in the same way with everyone is not possible, as she explained: "The rest of my family has a completely different relationship with my uncle, with his disappearance. One of my aunts really put it all in a little box and she kept it in a corner." The expression 'little box' in relation to one of her mother's siblings illustrates Abraham and Torok's (1978) concept of the crypt. This model is highly representative of the pathogenic dynamics that characterize transgenerational transmission of trauma: an unthinkable secret is unconsciously buried in the psyche of a person and cut off from elements of a shameful past that freezes the process of symbolization.

Carolina continued by sharing her feelings about this heavy silence: "I don't think that's the solution because I think leaving the truth aside makes it even heavier, because it is unspoken. It's like the circumstances of the disappearance become family secrets." Following Abraham and Torok's (1978) lines of thinking we can consider Carolina's cousins the carriers of 'ghosts.' The second generation of relatives are the heirs of *unspoken family secrets* that surround enigmatic raw objects. As these authors state, "A buried saying of a parent becomes in the child a dead person without burial" (p. 297). The ghosts represent traces of the trauma transmission that causes "work in the unconscious of another's shameful secrecy. Its law is the obligation of nescience" (Abraham & Torok, 1978, p. 391), the duty of ignorance. In this case, when Carolina's cousins seek answers to various questions, she becomes the storyteller to the second generation, a smuggler who secretly conveys family stories that have remained hidden from a segment of peers in her family. The 'silence law' is transmitted here through the generations. It is related to the concept of a *denial pact* proposed by Kaës (2009) in the sense that a part of history seems to be condemned to silence by a common and unconscious tacit agreement in the family group. This form of defensive psychic alliance guarantees the locking up of certain elements of the past to save the family's balance.

It is impossible to talk about the family silence that can surround the disappearance of a loved one without establishing a close link with the socio-political context. In fact, the law of silence was first of all imposed by the dictatorial regime in place with the aim of sowing terror (Puget et al., 1989). This silence aimed to generate and potentiate a feeling of threat among the relatives (Escalante et al., 2014). In this sense, the silence of relatives concerning the missing loved one can be seen as an echo of the silence about enforced disappearance that reigned and partially continued to reign in institutions.

For Carolina, the silence that surrounds Miguel's fate in part of her family could mean that they are forcing themselves to grieve, which is considered by Carolina as *denying the disappearance.* On the contrary, talking about Miguel's disappearance could be a way to participate in the memory work. In fact, narratives contribute to fighting against the impunity, not to condemn her uncle to oblivion, as well as to request more recognition of the relatives' experience. In contrast, keeping the disappearance aside, not talking about him, would contribute to believe the loved one dead or even denying the existence of the disappeared person himself and his or her sufferings. Some mental health professionals have noted that if family members consider the disappeared dead, they feel that they are "killing" him (Blaauw & Lähteenmäki, 2002). Believing him dead would be experienced as a way to make the person disappear again. By saying "forcing oneself to grieve," Carolina points out the complexity of the grieving process for relatives. Grieving someone without the certainty of his fate or his death is considered impossible according to some authors (Féres-Carneiro & Da Silva, 2010) or, at least, as a major factor of complexity (Bourguignon et al., 2021).

Without remains and proof of death, families are faced with an impossible choice: believing that the missing one is still alive or considering him already dead (Kajtazi-Testa & Hewer, 2018). This hard choice can have significant repercussions that stiffen the family dynamic and may even contribute to its collapse (Faúndez et al., 2018). In the case presented, Emily and her husband transmitted to their children that all possibilities remained open. Carolina expresses it as follows:

I have the feeling that all my life I could imagine all the scenarios because, luckily, I think that my mom, she never expressed a specific possibility to me. In fact, she never told me "he's dead" or "he has completely lost his memory, he's somewhere else". She has always taught me the fact that because he is disappeared, all of these possibilities are valid, the sordid as well as the joyful.

This extract aligns with Cerutti's (2017) idea that factors which could explain the different types of transmission inside a family are the hopes and beliefs concerning the fate of the disappeared loved one. What is the impact for the second generation who inherits scenarios that can ambiguously be as *sordid* as *joyful*? What are the implications of being confronted with multiple versions of the story without being able to choose? Believing that everything is possible also implies that a family is overwhelmed by fantasies of what could have happened to their relative (Díaz & Madariaga, 1993; Lira, 2016). This ambivalence – between believing them dead or alive – is maintained until they find traces of them. The uncertainty remains and persists over generations. The most distressing thing for the relatives is to realize that the hope of finding them depends on their willingness to look for them and to believe them alive; as if the death of the loved one was a decidable private fact, nullifying reality and the responsibility of perpetrators, ultimately the state (Lira, 2016). We can see here the extent of the responsibility of the relatives to keep him "psychically" alive.

When we asked Emily about the way she speaks to her children about the disappearance, she explained that she never hides the family past. Nevertheless, she realizes today that stories of the past are also violent: "When I found out that my family past is a weight for my daughter, Carolina, this hurt me because we want the best for our children and then giving them such a weight made me angry." Emily pointed out the difficulty of finding the right balance, as parent, in the transmission of the family past: on one hand, the transmission of a principle of justice and social values, and on the other hand, the desire to protect her children from the violence of the past.

Authors claim that, generally, silence seems to prevail within families (Brinkmann et al., 2009; Haq, 2020; Hofmeister & Navarro, 2017; Kordon & Edelman, 2007; Kordon et al., 2011). In this case, no single type of communication was observed: Carolina's close family openly talks about their disappeared relative, whereas in the extended family, silence seems required. However, due to the ambiguity of the loss caused by the enforced disappearance – as well as the sorrow and the fear relatives have experienced – communication may be troubled within the family group differently and over several generations.

The traces of trauma in the family and collective history

When we focus on the transmission of enforced disappearance through generations, we must consider the context in which this terrible crime has happened. The context of state violence induced by political repression generates feelings of fear, threat and persecution anxiety in families as well as in society. These anxieties spread within the family and across generations. *Which traces of this traumatic past are passed down within a family group that experienced political repression?*

In our qualitative study, most of the descendants reported having witnessed strong persecution anxiety in their parents, such as fear of being spied on, fear of being prosecuted, fear of uniforms and soldiers, general mistrust towards strangers, and a general feeling of insecurity. Carolina shared examples of persecution anxiety in her daily family life:

> I realize that in many Latin American families who have experienced repression, there are some strange customs. For example, while speaking normally,

all of a sudden, my parents and my grandparents start whispering to say, "So you see they were communists". Still here and now! And it's crazy because it's really customary, it's so entrenched! I figured it out quite late. For me it was normal to lower my voice like that. I grew up like this.

Having to whisper within family when naming certain terms such as 'communist' is a trace of the dark past which persists, even in exile. Present and past seem to merge, to overlap in a confusing way: the family remains immersed in the terror of yesterday. Its actions reflect the degree to which they are haunted by the unelaborated traces of the persecutions suffered under the dictatorship. Enforced disappearance seems to petrify the trauma experienced by the relatives and heirs to equal degrees as impunity prevails.

Carolina directly pointed out the link between parents' anxieties and their experiences of political repression under dictatorship. Parents who are victims of collective violence demonstrate an attitude of mistrust and insecurity in the family home; it is as though they were still dealing with the traumatic past which, if not carefully elaborated, does not pass; instead, they live a form of "unpast" in the words of Scarfone (2012). Carolina described her mother as psychically absent – engaged in a continuous search for her disappeared brother – and injured by her traumatic past: "She's very involved in her investigations, which I leave to her completely. I support this because I feel she needs it a lot". This continually sustained search for whatever trace of a disappeared relative to explain to oneself their absence is something very demanding and impacts the quality of life. The investment in the disappeared says that the process of mourning is undermined, hindering at the same time the investment in the present life. As Carolina expresses it, her mother has been so absorbed in the search of her brother that it is possible she was distant with her own children. According to Lira (2016), when parents are consumed with investigating the disappearance of a person, it is difficult for them to provide an adequate protective environment for children's physical and emotional development. The investment in parenthood is therefore undermined. The perception of the anguish, helplessness, and desolation of adults usually has also emotional effects on children, and in many cases, it has traumatic effects (Lira, 2016). The psychic absence of a parent and the depressive nature of the family circle participate in the transmission of the trauma in the families of a disappeared person (Edelman & Kordon, 2006).

Many relatives of the disappeared were also direct victims of political repression (kidnapping, arbitrary detention, torture, threats). It was the case for Emily, Carolina's mother. This double experience – having a relative who disappeared and having directly endured political repression – can trouble the ability of parental figures to provide the security and holding capacity necessary for children's development (Winnicott, 1971). This may be mediated by psychic suffering due to the loss and the traumatic experiences (Bourguignon et al., 2021). In this sense, for the second generation, the trauma can be considered double: the one linked to the traumatic experiences endured by their family and the one experienced directly through the parents, i.e. living with a distressed parent. This highlights the continuous character of the crime. Even though it happened 50 years ago, the impact of enforced disappearance has left its mark on what is passed down through the generations, but also on parent-child relationships in the present. In this case, Carolina's mother seems to struggle with the haunting past: searching for traces of her brother and fighting against her anxieties coming from the dictatorship.

Carolina explained that this past "puts a certain tension in the body and also in private life". The tension in the body mentioned by Carolina, which is the burden of the collective and family history, reminds us of the break-in of the "protective shield" which produces the psychic traumatism (Freud, 1920, p. 29). When the event is unthinkable, the body can then take over to welcome the traces of what cannot be thought, as for example the death of a close relative which is not certified. This formulation shows how the trauma of the enforced disappearance spreads in different spaces: in the psyche, in the body and in the social group.

About her anxieties and those of her parents, Carolina also tells us: "I think there is still this fear that it can happen again, as it's often said. I mean, memory work is there so that it may never happen again." The *memory work* for all the disappeared persons involves, among other, participating in street protests, making documentary, biography, and so on. It is seen by this heir as a way to struggle against these anxieties, and therefore against the risk of repetition. Moreover, being active in the memory work could also be seen as a reaction against the passive position in which the repression could relegate. In fact, at the emotional level, the feeling of guilt in victims of trauma is frequent (Ciccone & Ferrant, 2015). In the case of enforced disappearance, authors point out the *survivor guilt* (Biedermann, 1991) expressed by the relatives: guilt for not having been able to protect and preserve the lives of the loved ones ("What could I have done to prevent this from happening?") (Féres-Carneiro & Da Silva, 2010) or even the guilt for having angry feelings towards the disappeared (Lira, 2016; Pelento, 2009).

In the context of social violence, the feeling of guilt also propagates in society generating *social guilt* (Puget et al., 1989). Because state authorities deny responsibility for the disappearance or deprivation of liberty of the disappeared person, impunity creates scapegoats (Kaës, 2000). Those close to the disappeared bear a guilt that is not recognized by the authorities.

Taking an active position in the social sphere through the memory work can help relatives to deal with these paradoxical feelings of guilt of uncertain origin which may also be the consequences of impunity.

Importantly, some authors point out that are not only the memories of the traumatic event, but the responses to a traumatic event to be passed down through the generations (Waintrater, 2011). Carolina went on to express her astonishment about some family customs. Since childhood, she has been used to this particular way of doing and living of other family members not asking themselves questions. In reference to her family past and the political repression they suffered from, Carolina tells us:

> When you grow up in exile, you don't imagine that it is possible. I think there are traumas that follow the life of these people. It's a way of functioning: 'You

have to survive, hang on and move on no matter what.' I grew up with this stuff and, it's funny, I figured that out because I do the same in my adult life.

As an adult, Carolina became aware of the content of this traumatic family in-heritance of which she is the guardian. She gradually realized she reproduced her mother's survival *modus operandi* that comes "from all this violence that happened during the dictatorship." The reproduction of defense mechanisms as a kind of fixed temporality is common in a 'surviving family' (Waintrater, 2004). The frozen past in-vades the present. We observed that participating to creative activities (the making of documentaries or the writing of auto-biographical books) is a helpful resource both for the first and the following generations: it can be a powerful tool to communicate when content is difficult to share within the family group.

The second generation can express anxieties that stem from the extreme experi-ences endured by their parents under dictatorship, among which the *ambiguous loss* of a relative, but they may also be related to other traumatic events (before the coup, or in exile) that belong to the family history (Bourguignon, 2020). What other objects of transmission from the family and collective past are transmitted to the next generation?

The transmission of values and duty to the memory of the disappeared

For psychoanalysis, the baby inherits a double mission: as the bearer of parental narcissism, the child is responsible for making it last, but they also carry the mission of 'fixing' the history of their parents, which may be dotted with parents' unrealized desires and dreams (Ciccone & Ferrant, 2015). This inheritance – which could be sometimes a heavy burden aggravated by trauma – becomes the basis of the child's psychic constitution. Thus, the subject's subjugation to the ascending group ensures the transmission of fundamental prohibitions and, at the same time, offers *identifi-cation markers* (Kaës, 2009) for the subject. These markers are foundational state-ments, values, ideals, and myths. They are signs of recognition, a means to 'identify others, be recognized by them and self-identify' (Kaës, 2009, p. 76). Thereafter, each subject has an active role in trying to take their place in the family group and to give meaning to these determinations which precede them. Through these mutual movements of recognition (to be recognized and to recognize oneself as a member of a group), the identification markers define the boundaries of a group. In the psy-chic transmission, each subject thus tries to make their unconscious identifications coincide with the requirements demanded by belonging to the family group, on the one hand, and their socio-cultural group, on the other. Transmitting values within the family contributes to the identification with the family group.

In the context of enforced disappearance, what kind of values are transmitted?

In Carolina's case, family narratives highlight various values and principles re-lated to the commitments and the beliefs of her parents, but also the militancy of the disappeared relative and their fighting attitude for social justice. Regarding the transmission of values in her family, Carolina told us: "Having heard from my parents and grandparents all the values that Miguel had, that triggered in me the need to defend certain causes." She then shared her questions about the reasons for her commitment and the links with the disappearance. Is it a mark of loyalty to her parents' struggle or to her disappeared uncle? Is it a duty to honor Miguel's memory and make him alive through her personal values? About this topic, she said, "I think that all my political notions are based upon his disappearance. I've never really thought about this before actually, but it's true." The interview led this descendant to realize that her uncle's disappearance shaped her way of thinking and acting. This takeover testifies to Carolina's ongoing appropriation of her uncle's values in the process of subjectivization. Our observations converge with other studies on this topic: passing on the memory of the disappeared can also involve passing on their political ideology (Díaz & Madariaga, 1993) and passing on role models – a set of rights and obligations – within the family (Biedermann, 1991).

The various objects of transmission that evoke the disappeared person raise questions. First, there is the question of the representation that the descendants form of the disappeared person without having met them. Second, we can question the impact of these objects of transmission on their psychic development and their identification. In Emily and Carolina's family, the similarities between Carolina and her uncle Miguel were often highlighted: "My grandparents often said that I look like Miguel in my way of being, in the character rather, in banging my fist on the table while defending my ideas." In addition, Carolina added with a laugh, "It's very odd to talk about this with someone I don't know at all because I've never told anyone actually." Carolina gradually became aware of the content of the pact in which she is involved; that is, the pact to pass on the memory of her uncle to keep him alive in everyone's mind. While the members of the family search in vain for his physical traces or documents that objectify the facts regarding his disappearance and his death, Carolina tries to honor his memory as a way to respect family principles. This is in line with Cerutti's (2015) work on the duty the second generation feels to transmit the memory of the disappeared. We see how much the research interview can be a place of elaboration where the subject becomes aware of the alliances in which they are caught, and they realize what they are reproducing from their ascendants as well as the links that bind them to the former generations. In this way, the network of implicit connections within the family context is brought to light.

Beyond the family's discourse, the legacy of the family's traumatic past is observed. According to Bekerman et al. (2009), the resumption of the fight is in connection with the idealization of the disappeared person. Many studies focusing on the process of construction of the figure of the disappeared person[7] point out a risk of idealizing them (Alvis Rizzo et al., 2015; Díaz & Madariaga, 1993; Lira, 2016). Idealization is common for children of disappeared persons (Bekerman et al., 2009), and it could be an obstacle in their psychic development (Busch & Robaina, 2006). In our case, Carolina seems to idealize the fighting figure of her uncle Miguel. As the disappearance shapes the foundational family myth, it can be one of the causes of the idealization of the disappeared. Although she is not the daughter but the niece of the 'disappeared,' we note that a similar psychic process is underway. In our view, this shows the extent of the transmission through generations, even in exile.

Some children – consciously or unconsciously – feel that following their parents' investigations is their mission. Emily is still deeply involved in the search for any trace relating to her brother. She tries in vain to respond to questions that have haunted her since her brother's disappearance: *Where? How? Why?* This commitment is part of her personal and familial life; every free moment during weekends and holiday is devoted to find clues. It seems important to highlight the role played by families: by continuing the investigations, relatives allow the disappeared to continue to exist in the social environment (García Castro, 2001). On the contrary, giving up the investigations could be experienced as a murder of the loved one. Even if Carolina understands her mother, she realizes that her mother's investigation and the family past invade her private sphere. The shadow of the past seems to overwhelm the space of intimacy; which raises questions about her possibility of individuation.

Carolina shared her wish to find answers to these questions:

> I just wish I will have some news someday. Whether it's from him, from others or from a piece of bone or whatever. It's not so much for me but more for my mom and my grandparents. Funny but, it's like a duty but I don't take it as a burden or something heavy. It's not at all. I really think it's a matter of memory work, common to society. Some people have to take care of that. So, that's also why I don't take it lightly. It's gonna be a full-fledged job.

She asks for answers not so much for herself, but for previous generations and for society. The memory work is a principle for which to fight in her family, and in being part of it, she will pursue this struggle. According to Faúndez et al. (2018), "The unsuccessful investigation for the disappeared relative is a painful burden that is constantly passed on to subsequent generations" (p. 98). Carolina underlines the pride felt in having such parents – who are in exile but continue their commitment to fight against political repression – but she also points out the fear of not corresponding to the ideal conveyed by her parents, of not being up to it.

Carolina expressed that she feels invested in such a mission: "I always have the feeling that, one day or another, it is me who will take the torch, and I must not be unprepared." She believes she must *take up the torch* by taking over the investigation that aims to shed light on Miguel's disappearance, for which her mother is currently the guarantor. When Emily is no longer there, Carolina will make it her mission to ensure the continuity of these investigations. Caught in an unconscious pact – which she does not question – this heir considers that perpetuating such a work of memory goes without saying. She therefore considers herself a link in her family's struggle against injustice and impunity. She has to work in turn against the pact of common denial (Kaës, 2009) and of silence established within the social body.

Our observations attest to the shadow that enforced disappearance casts over the second generation as well as the descendants' identification movements towards the family identifying marks. In a 'surviving family' (Waintrater, 2004), differentiation is a threat to the survival of the group. This is also the case for the second generation of relatives of a disappeared person. What is the possibility of differentiating oneself from the family group when the mission of perpetuating the memory of the disappeared is established in the family?

Considering the articulation between a single traumatic event and collective history sheds light on the complexity of trauma transmission in the case of the family of a disappeared person. In fact, as mentioned above, transmission links us to others and it connects an individual story with the history of a group and society.

Conclusion

Enforced disappearance blurs the boundaries between presence and absence, life and death, past and present. In absence of a body, the relatives of a disappeared person are endlessly confronted with uncertainty which is exacerbated by impunity. Moreover, this crime takes place in a context of state violence – a climate of political repression and confusion, in which families face not only the disappearance of their loved ones but also the threat against their lives, as well as other traumas (Haq, 2020). This highlights the pervasive traumatizing effect of criminal politics perpetrated by its leadership on a society. The denial of deprivation of liberty of the disappeared person by state authorities is an integral part of the legal definition of the enforced disappearance (International Convention for the Protection of All Persons from Enforced Disappearance, 2006). Without a trial, the truth, even relative, cannot be re-established and the relatives face with a denial of justice (Kaës, 2000). This deprives the family of the support of those institutions that are supposed to set and ensure the founding legal framework of basic guarantees and prohibitions.

During social disasters, the collapse of the *social meta-frameworks* destabilizes *meta-psychological formations*, which are both the conditions for psychological life and well-being, and for its transmission (Kaës, 2009). The mutation of the meta-framework reverberates through the relationships in the familial, social and institutional contexts. Within these contexts, the psychical transmission from one generation to another is divided into both a positive and structuring slant, but also a negative and desubjectifying slant. The latter concerns the elements that could not be symbolized (Kaës, 2002). These negative objects of transmission can be passed on through generations.

We illustrated the multiple faces of trauma transmission by means of a family study: Emily, the sister of a disappeared person during a Latin American dictatorship, and her daughter, Carolina. Traces of the dramatic past can be expressed through various paths: the complexity of communication, anxieties and identifications. First, we presented the complexity of the transmission story concerning the disappeared loved one and the familial alliances at stake. This family case illustrates two opposite types of relationship with the past: on one hand, an open sharing of memories of the disappeared relative with in the family, on the other hand, imposing the law of silence. Traces of the traumatic past are also manifested as persecution anxiety in the second generation, who realizes they reproduce the same survival-based mode of functioning of their parents. Concerning identifications, we observed that Carolina identifies herself with her uncle's political values and commitment, but also with her parents': she feels it is her mission to follow their investigations to search for the disappeared loved one. In that way, the second generation finds itself as guarantor of the memory work for the disappeared.

The second generation's difficulty in elaborating this kind of ambiguous loss may be linked to the impunity that persists to this day. Not prosecuting and punishing the perpetrators hinders, not only the recognition of the crime, but also the work of recognition and reparation for victims and relatives (Kordon & Edelman, 2005). Time remains suspended. Moreover, impunity can also be considered a form of retraumatization and a source of fear, mistrust, demobilization, and social exclusion (Bekerman et al., 2009; Busch & Robaina, 2006). It would be interesting to explore further the impact that living in exile has on the relatives of a disappeared person: to what extent does living in exile support loss and trauma elaboration? Or does living away from one's family accentuate the feeling of threat and exclusion?

We consider that the 'ambiguous loss' (Boss, 1999) due to enforced disappearance in the context of state violence generates a traumatic effect on the close relatives (spouses, siblings, and parents) of the disappeared which is transmitted through generations. The second generation tries to find their place in the family chain through an awareness of certain dynamics in adulthood, or through the choice – being it conscious or not – to follow the mission of pursuing research and/or the struggle for justice. This struggle may, however, be colored by the traumas of the past. Concerning the impact of enforced disappearance on the second generation, most of the studies have been conducted on children of the disappeared person. In this family case of a niece of a disappeared person, we show that enforced disappearance can travel farer through family relationships. Our investigation could benefit from exploring other family cases to consider the impact of exile, as well as the relational bond of the close relatives with the disappeared. How does the degree of kinship (be a mother, a child, a sibling, etc.) and the type of relationship one had with the disappeared affect the transmission of trauma to the second generation? Through the generations, traumas and questions are passed on, as well as the task to struggle for the right to truth and justice in memory of the disappeared.

Notes

1 In the context of enforced disappearance, loss and trauma can be combined given the sudden loss (Mormont, 2009), the complexity of the 'complicated' grieving process (Bourguignon et al., 2021) and the traumatic context of state violence in which the loss is experienced.

2 The project "From enforced disappearance of persons to the victims' relatives' complicated grief: Observing the historicization process" was conducted by the authors at the

Institute of Psychology of the University of Lausanne (Switzerland) and was funded by the Swiss National Science Foundation. The project was approved by the UNIL Investigation Ethics Commission (CER-UNIL).

3 We make here a distinction between *intergenerational* and *transgenerational* transmission that relies on the definition formulated by Granjon (1987). *Intergenerational* transmission concerns psychically integrable elements (stories, novels, family myths, objects, fantasies,) that favour the processes of identification and integration. This transmission is accompanied by the process of psychic transformation. The heir can take an active position in front of the past by integrating and transforming this heritage by processes of distancing and/or subjective appropriation. The *transgenerational* transmission concerns the transmission of raw objects (Granjon, 1989), of negative and un-representable objects (secrets, unspoken). These objects are transmitted as they are, without transformation or symbolization; they can then become more or less pathogenic for the heir. The prefix *trans* thus refers to objects that pass through the generations.

4 The names as well as some data have been modified to respect confidentiality.

5 Interviews consist in life narratives according to a method inspired by Rosenthal (1993, 2004) and using semi-structured questions.

6 In this article, the extracts from our family case are entirely translated by the authors.

7 We will not develop this topic here, but it would be interesting to explore further the movements of construction and deconstruction of the figure of the 'disappeared' in the life course of the second generation.

References

Abraham, N., & Torok, M. (1978). *L'Écorce et le Noyau* (Vol. 2). Aubier: Flammarion.

Adams, J. (2019). "Enforced Disappearance: Family Members' Experiences." *Human Rights Review*, 20(3), pp. 335–360. doi:10.1007/s12142-019-0546-6

Alvis Rizzo, A., Duque Sierra, C.P., & Rodrìguez Bustamante, A. (2015). "Configuración identitaria en jóvenes tras la desaparición forzada de un familiar." *Revista Latinoamericana de Ciencias Sociales, Niñez y Juventud*, 13(2), pp. 963–979. doi:10.11600/16927 15x.13229270614

Amati Sas, S. (1991). "Souffrance, douleur et cadres sociaux." *Revue Française de Psychanalyse*, 55(3), pp. 945–956. Available at: https://www.cairn.info/revue-francaise-de-psychanalyse-1991-3-page-945.htm [Accessed 20 September 2021].

Aulagnier, P. (1975). *The Violence of Interpretation. From Pictogram to Statement*. London and New York: Routledge, 2001.

Bekerman, S., Pezet, Y., Oberti, C., Soutric, L., Mazur, V., & Lagos, M. (2009). "Terrorismo de estado: Segunda generacion." In B. Brinkmann (Ed.), *Daño transgeneracional: consecuencias de la represion politica en el Cono Sur*. Santiago, Chile: LOM Ediciones, pp. 141–246.

Biedermann, N. (1991). "Detenidos desaparecidos: Consecuencias para la segunda generación." In B. Brinkmann, J.M. Guzmán, C. Madariaga, & S. Ruy-Pérez (Eds.), *Derechos humanos, salud mental, atención primaria: desafío regional. II seminario de la región del Maule*. Santiago, Chile: CINTRAS- El Centro de Salud Mental y Derechos Humanos, pp. 170–176.

Blaauw, M., & Lähteenmäki, V. (2002). "Denial and Silence 'or 'Acknowledgement and Disclosure." *International Review of the Red Cross*, 84(848), pp. 767–784. doi:10.1017/S156077550010416X

Boss, P. (1999). *Ambiguous Loss: Learning to Live with Unresolved Grief*. Cambridge: Harvard University Press.

Boss, P. (2002). "Ambiguous Loss: Working with Families of the Missing." *Family Process*, 41(1), pp. 14–17. doi:10.1111/j.1545–5300.2002.40102000014.x.

Boss, P. (2016). "The Context and Process of Theory Development: The Story of Ambiguous Loss." *Journal of Family Theory & Review*, 8(3), pp. 269–286. doi:10.1111/jftr.12152.

Bourguignon, M. (2020). "Les destins de l'héritage traumatique au cœur du processus de parentalité: à propos de la transmission entre les générations chez les descendants d'exilés politiques chiliens vivant en Suisse." PhD Thesis, Université de Lausanne, Lausanne, Suisse. Available at: https://serval.unil.ch/fr/notice/serval:BIB_B3FA716F9624 [Accessed 18 August 2021].

Bourguignon, M., Dermitzel, A., & Katz, M. (2021). "Grief among Relatives of Disappeared Persons in the Context of State Violence: An Impossible Process?" *Torture Journal*, 31(2), pp. 19–37. doi:10.7146/torture.v31i2.127344

Brinkmann, B., Guzmán, J.-M., Madariaga, C., & Sandoval, M. (2009). "Daño transgeneracional en descendientes de sobrevivientes de tortura." In M. Lagos, V. Vital, B. Brinkmann, & M. Scapucio (Eds.), *Daño Transgeneracional: Consecuencias de la Represion Politica en el Cono Sur*. Santiago, Chile: LOM Ediciones, pp. 15–146.

Busch, S., & Robaina, M.C. (2006). *Una Ausencia Tan Presente*. Available at: http://www.psicosocial.net/historico/index.php?option=com_docman&view=download&alias=253-una-ausencia-tan-presente&category_slug=experiencias-y-propuestas-de-accion&Itemid=100225 [Accessed 2 September 2021].

Cerutti, A. (2015). "La desaparicion forzada como trauma psicosocial en Chile: Herencia, transmision y memoria de un daño transgeneracional." *Multitemas*, pp. 35–47. doi:10.20435/multi.v0iespecial.157

Cerutti, A. (2017). "Fils et filles de disparus en Argentine et au Chili: identité (s), mémoire (s) et résilience." PhD Thesis, Études Ibériques et Ibéro-américaines, Limoges.

Ciccone, A. (1999). *La Transmission Psychique Inconsciente*. Paris: Dunod.

Ciccone, A., & Ferrant, A. (2015). *Honte, Culpabilité et Traumatisme*. Paris: Dunod.

de Mijolla, A. (1981). *Les Visiteurs du Moi: Fantasmes d'Identification*. Paris: Les Belles Lettres.

Díaz, D., & Madariaga, C. (1993). *Tercero Ausente y Familias con Detenidos Desaparecidos*. Santiago: CINTRAS.

Edelman, L., & Kordon, D. (2006). "Efectos psicológicos multigeneracionales de la represión durante la dictadura." *Revista de la Asociación Argentina de Psicología y Psicoterapia de Grupo: Subjetividad y psiquismo*, 29, pp. 67–87.

Eiguer, A. (1987). *La Parenté Fantasmatique. Transfert et Contre-transfert en Thérapie Familiale Psychanalytique*. Paris: Dunod.

Escalante, H.S., Guzmán, M.O., Peñaloza, J.L., & Ruiz, S.R.S. (2014). "Condiciones violentas de duelo y pérdida: Un enfoque psicoanalítico." *Pensamiento Psicológico*, 12(2), pp. 79–95. doi:10.11144/Javerianacali.PPSI12-2.cvdp.

Faimberg, H. (1987). "Le télescopage des générations. À propos de la généalogie de certaines identifications." *Psychanalyse à l'Université*, 12(46), pp. 181–200.

Faúndez, X., Gatica, B.A., Morales, C.B., & Castro, M.C. (2018). "La desaparición forzada de personas a cuarenta años del golpe de estado en chile: Un acercamiento a la dimensión familiar." *Revista Colombiana de Psicología*, 27(1), pp. 85–103.

Féres-Carneiro, T., & Da Silva, M.R.N. (2010). "Transmission, honte et mémoire dans l'histoire familiale... des disparus du régime militaire brésilien." *Dialogue*, 4, pp. 93–106. doi:10.3917/dia.190.0093

Freud, S. (1920). "Beyond the Pleasure Principle." In J. Strachey (Ed.), *The Standard Edition of the Complete Psychological Works of Sigmund Freud.* London: Hogarth Press, pp. 1–64.

García Castro, A. (2001). "Le tiers témoin. Pouvoir, disparitions, représentations." *Diogène,* 193(1), pp. 86–99. doi:10.3917/dio.193.0086.

García Castro, A. (2011). *La Muerte Lenta de los Desaparecidos en Chile.* Chile: Cuarto Propio.

Grand, S., & Salberg, J. (Eds.) (2017). *Wounds of History: Repair and Resilience in the Transgenerational Transmission of Trauma.* London and New York: Routledge/Taylor & Francis Group.

Granjon, E. (1989). "Transmission psychique et transferts en thérapie familiale psychanalytique." *Gruppo,* 5, pp. 47–58.

Granjon, E. (2010). "La famille: un lieu pour s'approprier son histoire." In P. Delion, S. Missonnier, & N. Presme (Eds.), *Quelles Transmissions Autour des Berceaux.* Toulouse: Érès, pp. 23–47.

Haq, S. (2020). *In Search of Return: Mourning the Disappearances in Kashmir.* London: Lexington Books.

Hofmeister, U., & Navarro, S. (2017). "A Psychosocial Approach in Humanitarian Forensic Action: The Latin American Perspective." *Forensic Science International,* 280, pp. 35–43. doi:10.1016/j.forsciint.2017.08.027

International Convention for the Protection of All Persons from Enforced Disappearance 2006, Ga Res 61/177, 20 December 2006, Un Doc A/Res/61/177 (2006), 14 Ihrr 582 (2007), Opened for Signature 6 February 2007, Entered into Force 23 December 2010 ('Disappearances Convention'). Available at: https://www.refworld.org/docid/47fdfaeb0.html [Accessed 4 June 2021].

Kaës, R. (1989). "Ruptures catastrophiques et travail de la mémoire. Notes pour une recherche". In J. Puget, R. Kaës, M. Vignar, L. Ricón, J. Braun de Dunayevich, M. L. Pelento, S. Amati-Sas, M. Ulriksen-Vignar, & V. Galli (Eds.), *Violence d'État et Psychanalyse.* Paris, France: Dunod, pp. 169–204.

Kaës, R. (1993). *Transmission de la Vie Psychique Entre Générations.* Paris: Dunod.

Kaës, R. (2000). "Postface. Traduire les restes, écrire l'héritage." In J. Altounian (Ed.), *La Survivance. Traduire le Trauma Collectif.* Paris: Dunod, pp. 181–188.

Kaës, R. (2002). "Le problème psychanalytique du générationnel: objets, processus et dispositifs d'analyse." *Filigrane,* 11(1), pp. 109–120.

Kaës, R. (2009). *Les Alliances Inconscientes.* Paris: Dunod.

Kajtazi-Testa, L., & Hewer, C.J. (2018). "Ambiguous Loss and Incomplete Abduction Narratives in Kosovo." *Clinical Child Psychology and Psychiatry,* 23(2), pp. 333–345. doi:10.1177/1359104518755221

Katz, M. (2012). "Interdit de l'inceste, du meurtre et cannibalisme sauvage : une trilogie fondatrice?" In M. Vaucher, D. Bourdin, M. Durrer, & O. Revaz (Eds.), *Foi de Cannibale! La Dévoration, Entre Religion et Psychanalyse.* Genève: Labor et Fides, pp. 76–96.

Kijak, M., & Pelento, M.L. (1986). "Mourning in Certain Situations of Social Catastrophe." *International Review of Psycho-Analysis,* 13, pp. 463–471.

Kordon, D., & Edelman, L. (2005). "Efectos psicosociales de la impunidad." In D. Kordon, L. Edelman, D. Lagos, D. Kersner, et al. (Eds.), *Efectos Psicológicos y Psicosociales de la Represión Política y la Impunidad.* Buenos Aires: Asociacion Madres de Plaza de Mayo, pp. 125–139.

Kordon, D., & Edelman, L. (2007). *Por-Venires de la Memoria: Efectos Psicológicos Multi-generacionales de la Represión de la Dictadura: Hijos de Desaparecidos.* Buenos Aires, Argentina: Asociación Madres de Plaza de Mayo.

Kordon, D., Edelman, L., Lagos, D., & Kersner, D. (2011). *Sur, Dictadura y Después...: Elaboración Psicosocial y Clínica de los Traumas Colectivos.* Buenos Aires, Argentina: Psicolibro Ediciones.

Lira, E. (2016). "Desaparición forzada trauma y duelo: Chile 1973–2014." In Á.M. Estrada Mesa & C. Buitrago Murica (Eds.), *Recursos Psicosociales Para el Post-Conflicto.* Chagrin Falls, OH: Taos Institute Publications, pp. 131–168.

Mormont, C. (2009). "Deuil et traumatisme." *Revue Francophone Stress et Trauma,* 9, pp. 218–223.

Pelento, M.L. (2009). "Mourning for "Missing" People." In G.L. Fiorini, T. Bokanowski, & S. Lewkowicz (Eds.), *On Freud's Mourning and Melancholia.* New York: Routledge, pp. 56–70.

Puget, J., Kaes, R., Vignar, M., Ricón, L., Braun de Dunayevich, J., & Pelento, M.L., et al. (1989). *Violence d'État et Psychanalyse.* Paris: Dunod.

Rosenthal, G. (1993). "Reconstruction of Life Stories: Principles of Selection in Generating Stories for Narrative Biographical Interviews." *The Narrative Study of Lives,* 1(1), pp. 59–91.

Rosenthal, G. (2004). "Biographical Research." In C. Seale, G. Gobo, J. F. Gubrium, & D. Silverman (Eds.), *Qualitative Research Practice.* London: Sage, pp. 48–64.

Scarfone, D. (2012). "Moments de grâce: Présence et élaboration de 'l'impassé.'" In M. Gagnebin & J. Milly (Eds.), *Michel de M'Uzan ou le Saisissement Créateur.* Paris: Champ Vallon, coll. L'Or de l'Atalante, pp. 31–41.

Schaal, S., Jacob, N., Dusingizemungu, J.-P., & Elbert, T. (2010). "Rates and Risks for Prolonged Grief Disorder in a Sample of Orphaned and Widowed Genocide Survivors." *BMC Psychiatry,* 10(1), p. 55. doi:10.1186/1471-244X-10-55

Strier, R. (2014) "Fatherhood in the Context of Political Violence: Los Padres de la Plaza." *Men and Masculinities,* 17(4), pp. 359–375. doi:10.1177/1097184x14539965

Waintrater, R. (2004). "La famille survivante: familles et traumatismes." In P. Angel & P. Mazet (Eds.), *Guérir les Souffrances Familiales.* Paris: PUF, pp. 365–371.

Waintrater, R. (2011). "Héritage de la violence, violence de l'héritage." *Revue des Sciences Humaines,* 301, pp. 225–234.

Winnicott, D.W. (1971). *Playing and Reality.* London: Penguin Books.

Chapter 14

Names without bodies and bodies without names

Ambiguous loss and closure after enforced disappearance

Pauline Boss and Simon Robins

Introduction

We begin from the observation that there is a fundamental tension between the goals of the legal framework that defines enforced disappearance, namely, to prosecute perpetrators and to end the violation by revealing the fate or whereabouts of the disappeared, and the immediate versus long-term experience of most families of the disappeared. Here we present the psychosocial and psycho-therapeutic approach of ambiguous loss—that those who were psychologically attached to the disappeared are confused and immobilized by the uncertainty, emphasizing the subjective experience of families and a family-centered approach, in contrast to the legalist narrative of enforced disappearance, which is violation- and perpetrator-centered. We acknowledge that much of what we write emerges from work with families of those missing from soldiers missing in action, to children kidnapped by strangers, to loved ones who disappear in natural disasters (Boss, 1999, 2006, 2022). The impacts, as well as the supports that families need early on, are often very similar. Thus, we present the psychosocial intervention model here as useful also for the ambiguous losses caused by enforced disappearance, even as it has been developed in a broader context of "missing persons".

Our assumption here is that enforced disappearance, where a State is responsible, may have similar impacts on families to other situations where persons go missing, such as migration, natural disaster, or the action of non-State armed actors, notably in the experience of ambiguous loss. For other aspects, the impact can be very different, because the relatives of a disappeared person cannot rely on authorities for their personal search and can even be threatened by them.

We recognize, however, that where the State is the perpetrator there may be additional and different impacts on and needs of families. For example, there may be greater social stigmatization, a greater sense of helplessness, and betrayal, as well as external threats if a family seeks to address an enforced disappearance as opposed to when they search for a member who went missing on a mountain hike. State involvement in disappearance enhances negative impacts on families. It notably shapes the construction of social meanings that emerge from relationships in which families are enmeshed and that are necessarily impacted by the highly visible presence and perspectives of the State.

DOI: 10.4324/9781003312642-18

With enforced disappearance, multiple ambiguous losses result: one resulting from a loved one's disappearance; others from the loss of power, agency, and safety. Given the involvement of the State, families often no longer have the choice between continuing the search or stopping. Most important, rather than putting their lives on hold while waiting for a definitive answer or justice, families need help to find ways to cope with the confusion and to discover meaning and new hope to live with their ambiguous loss (Boss, 2004, 2006; Boss et al., 2003; Robins, 2013).

How can individuals and families function if they are waiting for truth and justice? Do the methods of intervention demand a choice between a human rights focus on truth and accountability and a focus on the well-being of families, or can we address both simultaneously? As we address these questions in this chapter, we present the ambiguous loss framework as an example of such an approach for easing the distress of families of the disappeared.

The theory of ambiguous loss

Definition

Ambiguous loss is defined as an unclear loss that has no resolution because the family lacks definitive information about the fate and whereabouts of the lost person. As a result of the ambiguity, grief is frozen and the lives of those attached to the lost person are put on hold.

There are two types of ambiguous loss, one physical and the other psychological. *Physical ambiguous loss*, the topic of this book, occurs when loved ones are physically gone, with no certainty about their whereabouts or status as dead or alive. Because family and friends do not know if the loss is permanent, the absent person is kept psychologically present in the minds of those who wait for news. In contrast, *psychological ambiguous loss* occurs when a loved one is physically present, but psychologically absent, e.g., loved ones who have dementia, brain injuries, or addictions.

Premise

The premise of ambiguous loss theory is that ambiguity about the absence or presence of a missing or disappeared person is immensely stressful and traumatizing for those who experience it. For individuals or families, and indeed for communities as a whole, the ambiguity freezes the grief process (Boss, 1999), prevents cognition, blocks decision-making processes, and immobilizes people, holding them in a painful limbo of not knowing. With such losses, and until certainty emerges, the source of pathology lies in the family's social context. The culprit is the ambiguity. The theory of ambiguous loss not only names this unique kind of loss but also provides a psychosocial map for increased understanding, thus leading to more effective and early support and intervention for the myriad of families around the world suffering with it.

Core assumptions

To fully understand the ambiguous loss framework, it is essential to know the assumptions underlying it.

First, ambiguous loss is a relational disorder, not individual pathology. It assumes attachment to the person that disappeared (Bowlby, 1982). It is the social rupture of a close relationship.

Second, this approach differs from the most common approaches for post-traumatic stress disorder (PTSD) to treat physical integrity violations (e.g., Quirk & Casco, 1994). While PTSD characterizes the impact of disappearance as individualized and arising from the incident of disappearance as a specific event of trauma, ambiguous loss presents the traumatic event as a family systems stressor, external, and ongoing. That is, the confusion and anxiety expressed by families is about the physical absence of the disappeared person, the systemic "missingness," more than the event of disappearance by itself.

Third, "ambiguous loss is an uncanny loss—confusing and incomprehensible" (Boss, 2010, p. 138). As a result, we assume that resolution of loss is impossible because the possibility of life remains. With ambiguous loss, those left behind must construct a resolution symbolically. For example, when there is no body to bury, the family may decide to bury a missing man's guitar or garment. Or they may join an organization in honor of the lost person to prevent what happened from happening to others.

Fourth, when one member of the group disappears, the ripple effect of loss is felt by the whole system. Since a system is greater and more powerful than the sum of its parts, we ideally intervene with more than the individual—a family, multiple families, community peer groups. We recommend self-definition of "family" so that people can also bring as family their clergy, friends, or neighbors. In the absence of facts, however, views about the disappeared will differ. Conflict often results and may lead to family alienation. Early on, therefore, interventions are needed to normalize divergent views of the loss in order to prevent splintering families or communities.

Fifth, in the case of ambiguous loss, resilience means increasing one's tolerance for ambiguity and unanswered questions. Instead of a goal of closure, we assume it is possible for people to move forward with life in a new way without the missing person. Instead of waiting for a return of their lost person or evidence of remains, we focus on building individual and family resilience to stabilize and function by acknowledging the contradictions of ambiguous loss: he is *both* likely dead, *and* maybe not. Until truth is found, this way of thinking has been helpful for those left behind (Boss, 1999, 2006, 2022; Robins, 2013).

Sixth, instead of the usual epistemological question about truth, we ask, "How do individuals and families manage to function despite not knowing?" (Boss, 2007, p. 106). After ambiguous loss interventions, many have done this, and we learn from them (Boss et al., 2003, 2007, 2016; Boss & Ishii 2015). Because there tends to be a natural resilience in most families, we assess these positive reactions as much as we assess medical symptoms. While symptoms may resemble prolonged or complicated grief disorders, the families have an inexplicable loss, thus challenging coherence and meaning making (Antonovsky, 1979, 1987; Boss, 1999, 2006, 2022; Frankl, 2006; Neimeyer et al., 2011).

Seventh, an assumption of ambiguous loss theory is that while death is a universal experience, ambiguous loss is not. This theory assumes that it is a loss beyond human expectation, unique because it lingers, all too often without finality. Until certainty is achieved through finding remains confirming identity, the family's grief is frozen and complicated. Due to the ambiguity, there is confusion, and feelings of helplessness; trauma often results. Families' processes of decision-making and grief are blocked. Without certainty, frozen grief can be prolonged for a lifetime, even across the generations (Boss, 2022). Instead of seeing symptoms of prolonged grief as psychic weakness, professionals must acknowledge the external context of ambiguity that causes these symptoms. Naming the problem as "ambiguous loss" allows people to know that it's not their fault and to better understand how to cope until more evidence emerges. Having a name for this unique kind of loss increases one's ability to cope with it (Boss, 2006; Lazarus, 1966). Knowing what the stressor is, families can move forward in a new and more functional way—while waiting for proof.

Effects of ambiguous loss from the perspectives of psychoanalysis, sociology, and psychology

The effects of ambiguous loss, however, may be viewed differently depending on our professional discipline and training. From a *psychoanalytic* perspective[1], ambiguous loss is viewed as an uncanny loss which causes a "traumatic anxiety produced by a combination of the known and the unknown …The intellectual and relational uncertainty of living with someone both here and not here produces a terrible anxiety of bizarre human experience" (Boss, 2006, p. 5). Referring to her husband who suffered a psychological ambiguous loss due to a massive brain injury, Feigelson, a psychoanalyst, wrote, "The anxiety of the uncanny involves something on the border of what we both know and don't know, both cognitively murky and affectively alarming" (Boss, 2006, p. 4 cited Feigelson, 1993). While Feigelson was referring to *psychological* ambiguous loss, such both/and reactions also follow *physical* ambiguous losses.

From a *sociological* perspective, the focus is on family boundary maintenance, knowing who is in or out of the family system, knowing who performs what roles and tasks to make the family function. If the family continues to wait for the disappeared person to return, essential roles and tasks are left undone; the family's functioning is compromised.

Finally, from the *psychological* perspective, the focus is on the rupture of the attachment to the lost person. Most important is the inability to grieve for a person when there is no proof of death or a body to bury. Religious rituals may be withheld, grief is frozen (Boss, 1999), and disenfranchised by the community (Doka,

1989). As a result, families of the missing are isolated, and left on their own to cope with a loss that heretofore, has had no name. Our perspective in this chapter is influenced by all three disciplines.

Individual effects from ambiguous loss

Without having the facts about a loved one who disappeared or is missing, individuals exhibit symptoms of sadness, depression, anxiety, helplessness, hopelessness, and frozen grief (Boss, 1999). There is also confusion about one's identity (who am I, now that my loved one is gone?). Symptoms are similar to those of complicated grief but here, the complication comes from the ambiguity surrounding the individual. People do not acknowledge their loss as permanent because there is no proof of it. In the case of ambiguous loss, then, the pathology lies in the context of not knowing and not in the individual's psyche (Boss, 2007, 2017, 2022).

A range of studies (Boss, 1977, 2004, 2006) indicate that situations of ambiguous loss predict symptoms of depression, anxiety, and family conflict. In many family members, disappearance gives rise to repeated thoughts and dreams about the disappeared, disturbed sleep, depression, somatization, hypervigilance, and generalized anxiety disorder (Boss, 1999, 2006; Isuru et al., 2019; Kennedy et al., 2019; Robins, 2013). Most studies indicate that families of the disappeared suffer from normal emotional distress, rather than psychiatric disorders, with only a small minority seeing significant impacts on functioning that require specialist intervention.

Family effects from ambiguous loss

As discussed above, families experiencing ambiguous loss predictably argue with one another about the missing person, where they might be, who caused their disappearance, how to help, when to stop searching. Our task early on is to normalize such disagreements to prevent family rifts that could become permanent and further weaken the family system, and its resources. Also, the families of the disappeared experience isolation when they have no access to the usual rituals of mourning because no death has been verified and there is no body to bury. Neighbors and friends do not know how to support them. They are left alone by their community because no one knows how to respond to ambiguous losses (Boss, 2004, 2010; ICRC, 2020; Robins, 2011).

In families defined by unequal power relationships, notably between men and women, and/or between mothers-in-laws and wives of the missing in patrilocal family structures, a man's disappearance can further reduce the status of his wife. She is neither wife nor widow, no longer considered contributing financially to the family and generally having a weaker connection to it. This typically leads to family conflict plus stigma and discrimination against such women from their in-laws (Robins, 2013).

Community impacts of ambiguous loss

The relational aspect of ambiguous loss is seen clearly in impacts at the community level, where meaning and identity are constructed socially in ways that can be highly negative for families of the disappeared. Since the disappeared are most often men, they leave behind families headed by women whose identity as wives or widows remains unclear. In many contexts, particularly those where women's status is low, this leads to stigmatization as women without men in the extended family and community, and a perception they are sexually available (Robins, 2011). Families of the disappeared are typically characterized as subversive due to their link to the disappeared, reinforced by State narratives about those they have taken that justify their action. This results in the family being stigmatized and potentially being targeted by State security forces, often leading to physical, psychological, and social threats.

Intervention using the ambiguous loss framework

Because enforced disappearance is externally caused, and the ambiguity creates stress and anxiety, therapy and interventions are based on stress management— managing the stress of ambiguity and building the resilience to live with it, whilst seeking the truth. The primary focus becomes one of strengthening people's resilience to live with the ambiguity long term.

Because most cases of disappearance remain unsolved, with truth or justice unattained, both/and thinking becomes helpful to lower stress levels. Holding two opposing ideas in one's mind simultaneously is the closest family members may get to their truth. "He is both gone and may come back." "I both think he is dead, and hope he is not." People living with ambiguous loss understandably have doubts, so encouraging absolute thinking about their lost loved one as being *either* alive *or* dead is not the goal of therapy.

The myth of closure as a therapeutic goal

While "closure" is a popular term used by the media to describe the end of grief that follows loss, it is not the therapeutic goal with either ambiguous loss or the clear loss of death. In both cases, seeking the absolute of closure only delays a normal grieving process. If people are to move forward with their lives in a new way—without the lost person—they need to know that the pain of loss has no timeline, but hopefully is balanced with some joy in life.

Closure, however, may be a misnomer for what families want. They want certainty, not closure. They want facts about whether or not their loved one is alive or dead; they want remains to bury, and this is what international human rights law seeks to deliver. The people left behind do not want to close the door on remembering the lost person. Rather, they want to keep them symbolically and psychologically present while still hoping and struggling for proof. Instead of closure, what they yearn for is certainty, the certainty of death which would allow them to begin grieving and moving forward with life in new ways (Boss, 1999, 2022). Because most families of the disappeared never achieve certainty of death, resolution of loss is impossible because the impact of the loss remains. People want to remember those they have loved and lost. The goal, then, in working with families is not closure but helping them to remember, honor, and memorialize the lost person, individually, and as part of the larger community (Boss, 2022; Robins, 2014).

An ambiguous loss driven practice with families of the disappeared: Guidelines

The six recursive guidelines that emerged from ambiguous loss theory and research shape interventions that are highly relevant for families of the disappeared and can be framed such that they reinforce rather than are in tension with demands for truth and justice.

Finding meaning

While ambiguous loss is a severe rupture in meaning, finding a measure of meaning even in such an absurd loss is essential. The meaning of most ambiguous losses is that they will never make sense, but that too is a meaning. Both/and thinking helps: people can indeed live with contradictions about absence and presence. Many find meaning or purpose in their ambiguous loss by working for a cause that prevents such losses for others; or they may honor the missing person with some memorial in the community; or simply decide to have a life well lived without them, raising their children, and keeping their family moving forward. With ambiguous loss, the resiliency to find meaning without certainty means being able to increase one's tolerance for ambiguity. This requires culturally based interventions to support people as soon as possible after a loved one disappears. Indeed, the goal early on is to strengthen individual and family resilience in order to live with unanswered questions until, or if, evidence emerges to clarify their loss. For families, however, where facts are not yet available, meaning can be derived from learning to live with the paradox of ambiguous loss: "He is both dead and maybe not; she is both gone and still here in my heart and mind." Such early intervention does not impede the search for justice, but rather, maintains family functioning until further evidence is forthcoming. Meaning is constructed relationally and is best achieved through interaction with others in the same position and this drives the importance of solidarity in building resilience.

While the associations of families of the disappeared drove the contemporary legal framework that codified the violation, and are remembered for their activism, their first value to families was as a source of solidarity and understanding, because those who shared the experience of disappearance were best placed to offer support to others (e.g., Bosco, 2006). This represents the creation of a space where family members could construct positive meanings together that help them live with the ambiguity. As such, an important element of reparation is support to structures that allow such solidarity among victims and with community members. (For details on community meetings as a route to easing the stress of ambiguous loss, see Boss, 2006; Boss et al., 2003; Boss & Ishii, 2015; ICRC, 2020; Robins, 2016).

The model of ambiguous loss indicates that the meanings families give to disappearance are crucial to their ability to cope with it and are constructed relationally, through social interaction in family and community (Berger & Luckman, 1966). This may include religious communities.

Adjusting mastery

Mastery is the ability to control one's life and to find answers to problems; it is considered a consistent moderator of stress and trauma (Boss, 2006; Pearlin & Schooler, 1978). The effects of having mastery, however, depend on people's value of always being in charge of what happens, or having little or no control over what happens to them. For people with less agency and power, e.g., women in patriarchal societies, the therapeutic goal is to increase their level of mastery. For them, empowerment is the goal, e.g., group meetings with peers (Robins, 2014). Being unable to solve the problems that come with long-term disappearance requires increasing mastery in other aspects of life, with for example, meditation, prayer, peer support, or working for change on a different problem that has a high possibility of solution, thus lowering feelings of helplessness. In the end, all families of the disappeared need something in their lives that they can master. To live with the unanswered questions of disappearance, at least until facts are found, people need something to master in order to balance what they cannot.

Reconstructing identity

People with ambiguous loss experience a confused identity: "Who am I now?," "Are we still parents if our only son has disappeared?" Reconstruction of identity is a priority for all families of the disappeared for two reasons. *First*, since identity is a relational concept, it becomes a problem psychologically when your relationship to the missing person remains unclear: a woman not knowing if she is a wife or a widow is both inherently stressful and challenging to her relationships with the rest of the family, particularly in patriarchal cultures. *Second*, when the State has disappeared a family member, the social and political identity of the rest of the family is challenged. That is, the violation represents a systematic marginalization of the disappeared and their family by the State, a traumatic message of exclusion, including potentially from a broader social realm. At the socio-political level, disappearance aims not just to kill and ensure bodies are not found, but to dehumanize both its victims and their communities. Identity is lost. The "political trauma" (Hamber, 2009) of disappearance demands not only psychosocial approaches but sees families articulating a broader socio-political need for recognition. The socio-political component of reparation demands both guarantees of non-repetition, i.e., that the State has changed, and a renegotiation of the relationship between the State and (at least some of) its citizens. The ultimate resolution of ambiguity, most obviously through exhumation, creates new identities for both the missing person and their family, and gives new meanings emotionally, socially, and politically to the disappearance.

Understanding the normality of ambivalence with ambiguous loss

Social ambivalence is a typical outcome of ambiguous loss (Merton & Barber, 1963). It is expected. Long term, the ambiguity is wearing, and people left behind begin wishing it were over, and then feeling guilty for wishing the disappeared relative dead. Or they begin grieving and then feel guilty because their loved one may still be alive. Both wishing it was over and grieving when you are not certain of death brings on feelings of guilt and ambivalence—sorrow/hope; resignation/defiance, etc. This is especially true with ambiguous losses as the external social context around those left behind creates "an 'uncanny' union of opposites" (Boss, 2006, p. 4 cited Feigelson, 1993). That is, when loved ones are missing or disappeared, conflicted feelings result from the social context of confusion and not knowing (Boss, 2006). Such feelings with ambiguous loss are typical, but it is important to talk with others about those feelings. Understanding the normality of this ambivalence means acknowledging its source as sociological more than psychological (Boss, 2006). Resilience grows from acknowledging these ambivalent feelings and then learning to manage them. For families of the disappeared this implies accepting that their relationship to the disappeared, and to other family members, will be shaped by the ambiguity of their loss. This requires professionals to understand that conflicted emotions are an outcome of the uncertainty that follows ambiguous loss. Assessing the ambivalence in people left behind demands that it be viewed as caused by the external social situation—the ambiguous loss, and not their psychic weakness. This realization enables people to make a distinction between accepting their feelings as "normal"—given the situation—and developing a more and more conscious attitude toward what came and possibly still comes from the external social situation, e.g., threats, no response, denial (M. Luci, personal communication, April 6, 2022).

Revising attachment

Many families and communities impacted by disappearance construct tributes to the disappeared. Even where families cannot accept the death of the disappeared, many are keen to see memorials of a type that typically honor the dead. Such tributes are a way of revising attachment by making the loss more symbolically real when formal death rituals are impossible (Boss, 2006; Robins, 2013). Memorials become especially important where the State is a perpetrator, as the very presence of a memorial challenges a narrative of seeking to make invisible the disappeared and deny the fact of their having ever existed. While bonds of attachment can continue for the missing or the dead, they need to be transformed. Because a psychological or spiritual bond continues even when a loved one disappears, or is found dead, the therapeutic goal is not closure.

Discovering new hope

Discovering something new to hope for is an essential element for families of the disappeared to sustain their resilience. Because "hope" may be construed by families as maintaining the possibility of the disappeared returning, well-being is best advanced with new hopes and dreams. Families of the disappeared talk of hopes for their children and their wider families for continued peace. In many contexts, however, the greatest barrier to realistic hopes for the future is an obsession with closure (by finding remains, or the return alive of the disappeared) and searching for the disappeared above anything else. For some, their lives revolve entirely around searching, with no route to new hopes, representing immobilization. This emphasizes the importance of tempering a discourse of closure by supporting families to hold two opposing ideas simultaneously: to *both* hold out hope for some certainty *while also* discovering new sources of hope and purpose in life.

Having now described the six guidelines, we re-emphasize that they are to be used flexibly, as needed for a particular case or culture, and *in no prescribed order*. They are intended to support those who are helping families to be customized to the context and nature of the loss, but not seen as a prescription or checklist. The ultimate goal for those left behind is to find meaning and new hope while living with ambiguous loss (Boss, 2006).

An ambiguous loss lens does not imply that families cease their struggle for truth and justice but provides intervention that supports them as long as they are denied truth. The theory of ambiguous loss allows a discursive analysis of enforced disappearance in terms of how it shapes families' perceptions of their loss and the extent to which it supports positive coping and resilience (Robins, 2016).

Resolving disappearances, typically in terms of confirming the death of the disappeared, demands both political will and significant human, technical, and financial resources to support the infrastructure required to locate, exhume, and identify the bodies of the dead. While there have been a number of visible successes, the vast majority of families have received no answer, often after decades of suffering, and have little prospect of ever receiving one.[2]For the many families with no answer around the fate of their loved one, ambiguous loss theory tells us that the therapeutic goal is to support them to live well despite ambiguity, by finding meaning, adjusting mastery, reconstructing identity, understanding the normality of their ambivalence—wishing for a body to bury, while having no certainty of death, thus feeling guilty for mourning prematurely—revising attachment, and discovering new hope and purpose for living a life without the absent person.

Ambiguous loss as a lens on disappearance

While the legal framework of enforced disappearance is constructed around the potential for case closure, the ambiguous loss model focuses on how to live with the ambiguity, at least until proof is found.

Temporally, disappearance in law is framed as something that is ongoing, but the principal goal is to reach a point where the violation is ended. This framing precisely contradicts the therapeutic goal of ambiguous loss to not focus on closure, but to learn to live well despite ambiguity. The very binary nature of knowing/not knowing that the law constructs counters the need for both/and thinking that positive coping demands. Most families of the disappeared never receive an answer, and, even where an answer is eventually received, this typically demands that families have suffered not knowing for many years. If the focus of human rights work with families of the disappeared emphasizes only the need for truth, it encourages negative coping, e.g., when a focus on searching for the missing person becomes obsessive to the point where surviving family members neglect their own well-being (Robins, 2013). Families go deeply into debt to fund travel in search of the disappeared; a wife or mother cannot allow herself to find joy as long as her disappeared loved one may be suffering. This valorization of suffering is a common but extreme emotional response to having a missing family member—and an example of an inability to think flexibly (both/and) to revise one's attachment, a therapeutic approach rooted in ambiguous loss.

The complementarity of legal and psychosocial approaches

Organizations of relatives of the disappeared are rightly lauded as the lens of ambiguous loss sees such family associations as not only crucial in campaigning for justice, but essential to support the well-being and resilience of family members. Especially where families of the disappeared are characterized by the State as subversive and subject to harassment and threats, a family association or community meetings represent a space where families can share perspectives—the basis of finding meaning and new hope. As such, the family association becomes a *therapeutic space* (see Robins, 2016). This value of associations for families of the disappeared demonstrates that the demand for truth and justice need not be in conflict with the need for psychosocial support for affected families (Robins & Bhandari, 2012).

In this chapter, our thesis is that neither law nor psychosocial support alone are sufficient when addressing impacts of disappearance on families and communities: it is necessary to use *both* frameworks. We propose that the dominant lens of international human rights law for disappearance also be informed by the lens of ambiguous loss that centers on the *immediate* experience and needs of the families of the disappeared. Ambiguous loss represents a tested and effective model for professional and family understanding of this unique kind of loss. Giving it a name begins the process of coping and guides therapeutic approaches (Boss, 2007, 2016; Boss & Ishii, 2015; Hollander, 2016; Robins, 2011).

Families of the disappeared suffer traumas that leave their mark across generations. Children will remember the terror around the disappearance of relatives, especially parents, or entire communities targeted by State violence. Where individual therapy is culturally challenged, unavailable due to the lack of expertise and resources, or impossible due to the scale of needs, the collective trauma of ambiguous losses in conflict and political violence has been eased with community meetings using the approaches described in this chapter (Boss et al., 2003, Boss & Ishi, 2015). Similar approaches have been used with families of the disappeared in Nepal (Robins, 2016), Sri Lanka (Andersen et al., 2020) and in contexts where the International Committee of the Red Cross (ICRC) accompaniment approach to families of the disappeared and missing has been used (ICRC, 2020).

The box below provides an example of how community meetings can be organized and implemented after ambiguous losses occur. After the terrorist attacks on New York's World Trade Center on September 11, 2001, this outlines how meetings were organized by mental health professionals for the families of missing workers who maintained the World Trade towers. Many of the missing were immigrants who shunned individual therapy as well as grief therapy.

Box: Organizing community meetings of families of the missing (Adapted from Boss et al., 2003)

Goal: Community meetings are organized to build resilience and new hope after collective ambiguous losses; see Boss et al. (2003), for specific directions on how this was done for families of the workers who went missing in the terror attack on the World Trade towers in New York on September 11, 2001.

1   Gather the families together (where family is self-defined) in a safe community setting.
2   Give a name to their experience and normalize their reactions: "What you have experienced is ambiguous loss; it is the most stressful kind of loss there is because there is no certainty of death and thus no possibility of resolution; it is not your fault."
3   Have families sit together; help them find as much information as possible (including accessing those working on DNA identification).
4   Help them share perceptions and normalize differing views even within the family.
5   Manage family conflict to avoid family breakups.
6   Reconstruct important family rituals, roles, rules, so people can move forward despite the continuing ambiguity.
7   With the entire group, encourage story telling: telling one's own story and listening to others tell theirs. This ancient narrative tradition helps people find meaning in their suffering, and it is an essential tool for living with ambiguous loss. These stories may change over time, but overall, the telling and listening is best done in the company of others.
8   Externalize the blame, normalize the guilt, memorialize the lost persons, imagine something new to hope for.
9   Continue meeting and talking together even when the professionals leave. Find local leaders. Focus on support for each other that is informational, emotional, and also recreational.

For details about implementing meetings for the families/community of the disappeared after 9/11, see Boss et al. (2003), Boss (2004), (2006), and ICRC (2020). For more references, see www.ambiguousloss.com.

Conclusion

Enforced disappearance has become an all too effective instrument for authoritarian regimes to punish targeted persons and communities and to deter resistance. In the face of such State crimes, families, and friends left behind need to be empowered *both* to enhance their coping *and* to pursue justice, two goals that are in fact, mutually reinforcing. Yet, because families are also victims of disappearance, they also need a human rights-based approach. Finding justice and family survival are not mutually exclusive goals.

With neither verification of death or access to human remains, nor the rituals and religious support that make loss bearable, families become dysfunctional and thus weaken communities, even larger society. While the search for justice may take time, families need support right away. The theory of ambiguous loss provides useful tools and guidelines for both early humanitarian support, and for long-term support needed during the search for justice.

We began this chapter with the observation that there is a fundamental tension between the goals of the legal framework that defines enforced disappearance and the psychosocial approaches that support families. We conclude that the lens of ambiguous loss can help the understanding and shaping of interventions for both—seeking well-being and seeking justice. With this more inclusive theory, both endeavors can benefit.

Notes

1 Monica Luci, PhD, writes about understanding torture using psychoanalytic thinking. See Luci (2017).
2 There are, of course, disappearances that are resolved with the reappearance of the disappeared alive, but this is—unfortunately—rare.

References

Andersen, I., Poudyal, B., Abeypala, A., Uriarte, C., Rossi, R. (2020). "Mental Health and Psychosocial Support for Families of Missing Persons in Sri Lanka: A Retrospective Cohort Study." *Conflict and Health*, 14(1), pp. 1–15. https://doi.org/10.1186/s13031-020-00266-0

Antonovsky, A. (1979). *Health, Stress and Coping.* San Francisco: Jossey-Bass.

Antonovsky, A. (1987). *Unraveling the Mystery of Health. How People Manage Stress and Stay Well.* San Francisco: Jossey-Bass.

Berger, P.L., Luckmann, T. (1966). *The Social Construction of Reality: A Treatise in the Sociology of Knowledge.* New York: Doubleday.

Bosco, F.J. (2006). "The Madres de Plaza de Mayo and Three Decades of Human Rights' Activism: Embeddedness, Emotions, and Social Movements." *Annals of the Association of American Geographers*, 96(2), pp. 342–365. https://doi.org/10.1111/j.1467-8306.2006.00481.x

Boss, P. (1977). "A Clarification of the Concept of Psychological Father Presence in Families Experiencing Ambiguity of Boundary." *Journal of Marriage & the Family*, 39(1), pp. 141–151. https://doi:org/10.2307/351070.

Boss, P. (1999). *Ambiguous Loss: Learning to Live with Unresolved Grief*. Cambridge, MA: Harvard University Press.

Boss, P. (2004). "Ambiguous Loss Research, Theory, and Practice: Reflections after 9/11." *Journal of Marriage & Family*, 66(3), pp. 551–566. https://doi.org/10.1111/j.0022-2445.2004.00037.x

Boss, P. (2006). *Loss, Trauma, and Resilience: Therapeutic Work with Ambiguous Loss*. New York: W. W. Norton.

Boss, P. (2007). "Ambiguous Loss Theory: Challenges for Scholars and Practitioners." *Family Relations*, 56(2), pp. 105–111. https://doi.org/10.1111/j.1741-3729.2007.00444.x

Boss, P. (2010). "The Trauma and Complicated Grief of Ambiguous Loss." *Pastoral Psychology*, 59(2), pp. 137–145. https://doi.org/10.1007/s11089-009-0264-0

Boss, P. (2016). "The Context and Process of Theory Development: The Story of Ambiguous Loss." *Journal of Family Theory & Review*, 8, pp. 268–286. https://doi.org/10.1111/jftr.12152

Boss. P. (2017). "Families of the Missing: Psychosocial Effects and Therapeutic Approaches." *International Review of the Red Cross*, 99(2), pp. 519–534. https://doi.org/10.1017/s1816383118000140

Boss, P. (2022). *The Myth of Closure: Ambiguous Loss in a Time of Pandemic and Change*. New York: W. W. Norton.

Boss, P., Beaulieu, L., Wieling, E., Turner, W., LaCruz, S. (2003). "Healing Loss, Ambiguity, and Trauma: A Community-Based Intervention with Families of Union Workers Missing after the 9/11 Attack in New York City." *Journal of Marital and Family Therapy*, 29(4), pp. 455–467. https://doi.org/10.1111/j.1752-0606.2003.tb01688.x

Boss, P., Ishii, C. (2015). "Trauma and Ambiguous Loss: The Lingering Presence of the Physically Absent." In K. E. Cherry, (Ed.), *Traumatic Stress and Long-Term Recovery*. New York: Springer, pp. 271–289. https://doi.org/10.1007/978-3-319-18866-9_15

Bowlby, J. (1982). *Attachment*. New York: Basic Books.

Doka, K. (1989). *Disenfranchised Grief: Recognizing Hidden Sorrow*. Lexington, MA: Lexington Books.

Feigelson, C. (1993). "Personality Death, Object Loss, and the Uncanny." *International Journal of Psychoanalysis*, 74(2), pp. 331–345.

Frankl, V. (2006). *Man's Search for Meaning*. Boston, MA: Beacon Press (Original English publication, 1959).

Hamber, B. (2009). *Transforming Societies after Political Violence*. Heidelberg, London and New York: Springer. https://doi.org/10.1007/978-0-387-89427-0

Hollander, T. (2016). "Ambiguous Loss and Complicated Grief: Understanding the Grief of Parents of the Disappeared in Northern Uganda." *Journal of Family Theory & Review*, 8(3), pp. 294–307. https://doi.org/10.1111/jftr.12153

ICRC. (2020). *Accompanying the Families of Missing Persons: A Practical Handbook* [online]. Geneva, ICRC. Available at https://www.icrc.org/en/publication/4110-accompanying-families-missing-persons-practical-handbook [Accessed 29 March 2022].

Isuru, A., Hewage, S.N., Bandumithra, P., Williams, S.S. (2019). "Unconfirmed Death as a Predictor of Psychological Morbidity in Family Members of Disappeared Persons." *Psychological Medicine*, 49(16), pp. 2764–2771. https://doi.org/10.1017/s0033291718003793

Kennedy, C., Deane, F.P., Chan, A. (2019). "In Limbo: A Systematic Review of Psychological Responses and Coping among People with a Missing Loved One." *Journal of Clinical Psychology*, 75(9), pp. 1544–1571. https://doi.org/10.1002/jclp.22799

Lazarus, R.S. (1966). *Psychological Stress and the Coping Process*. New York: McGraw-Hill.

Luci, M. (2017). *Torture, Psychoanalysis, and Human Rights*. London and New York: Routledge, Taylor and Francis Group. https://doi.org/10.4324/9781315694320

Merton, R.K., Barber, E. (1963). "Sociological Ambivalence." In E.A. Tiryakian (Ed.), *Sociological Theory, Values, and Sociocultural Change*. Glencoe: The Free Press, pp. 91–120. https://doi.org/10.4324/9781315129976-5

Neimeyer, R.A., Harris, D.L., Winokuer, H.R., Thornton, G.F. (Eds.) (2011). *Grief and Bereavement in Contemporary Society: Bridging Research and Practice*. Routledge/Taylor & Francis Group. https://doi.org/10.4324/9781003199762

Pearlin, L.I., Schooler, C. (1978). "The Structure of Coping." *Journal of Health & Social Behavior*, 19(1), pp. 2–21.

Quirk, G.J., Casco, L. (1994). "Stress Disorders of Families of the Disappeared: A Controlled Study in Honduras." *Social Science and Medicine*, 39(12), pp. 1675–1679. https://doi.org/10.1016/0277-9536(94)90082-5

Robins, S. (2011). "Towards Victim-Centred Transitional Justice: Understanding the Needs of Families of the Disappeared in Post-Conflict Nepal." *International Journal of Transitional Justice*, 5(1), pp. 75–98. https://doi.org/10.1093/ijtj/ijq027

Robins, S. (2013). *Families of the Missing: A Test for Contemporary Approaches to Transitional Justice*. New York: Routledge. https://doi.org/10.4324/9780203517079

Robins, S. (2014). "Constructing Meaning from Disappearance: Local Memorialisation of the Missing in Nepal." *International Journal of Conflict and Violence*, 8(1), pp. 104–118.

Robins, S. (2016). "Discursive Approaches to Ambiguous Loss: Theorizing Community-based Therapy after Enforced Disappearance." *Journal of Family Theory and Review*, 8(3), pp. 308–323. https://doi.org/10.1111/jftr.12148

Robins, S., Bhandari, R.K. (2012). *From Victims to Actors: Mobilising Victims to Drive Transitional Justice Process*. Kathmandu: NEFAD.

Chapter 15

An art work for the *Jardin des Disparus* in Meyrin, Switzerland

"Question Mark"

Anne Blanchet

In 2009, the city of Meyrin asked me to compete for the creation of an art work for the *Jardin des Disparus* – the Garden of the Disappeared, located on its territory (Figure 15.1).

> The Garden of the Disappeared is a memorial, in honor of the disappeared persons. A place for contemplation for the families around the world who can neither mourn the death of their loved one, nor place a flower on a grave in the cemetery.
>
> In memory of all the disappeared persons, we ask for TRUTH AND JUSTICE (brochure of introduction to the *Jardin des Disparus*)[1]

The *Jardin des Disparus* is part of the Parc de la Ferme de la Golette. It is a kind of clearing surrounded by tall trees and bushes of native species. A place slightly set back. The traditional architecture of a farm, the old wall and the pebble paving have a rural character, which gives the place a conducive calmness suitable for reflection and meditation.

Figure 15.1 Opening of the "Question Mark" catalog at the *Jardin des Disparus*, Meyrin (CH) June 9, 2011. Photo by Anne Blanchet.

DOI: 10.4324/9781003312642-19

However, the park is not cut off from its urban environment which remains perceptible through the tree trunks and bushes. The effect of depth towards the homes and the schools, that encircle the park, makes it a place apart, but very close to active life. Children, adolescents and young mothers come and sit there for a moment, sometimes joyful, sometimes grappling with all kinds of issues.

Creating an art work on the theme of disappearance is a delicate undertaking. Disappearance is not a death confirmed. We cannot be sure that the disappeared persons died, we cannot consider them resting in peace. As Louis Joinet[2] said, during the tenth anniversary of the *Jardin des Disparus* and the inauguration of the "Question Mark", in Meyrin: "We must consider as alive those who may no longer be. We have the obligation to claim them, one by one, until the answer finally brings the truth".[3]

Designing a sculptural work as a tombstone or a monument would have been impossible: it would have obscured the notion of disappearance with all its weight of the unknown, suspended time, possible reappearance and lack of understanding.

For this reason, I chose to create a place and not an artwork. A place for the sorrow to be expressed and a place for action. A space that is simultaneously private and public in nature.

In the face of the pain of the families and of the loved ones, it is a place to gather oneself, to commemorate the disappeared, to find their presence beyond their absence, to give them a place. It is also a place to meet and comfort each other, to move forward; in the face of human rights violations, it is a place of reflection, of exchange, a place turned outwards, towards the demand for truth and justice.

A disappearance raises innumerable questions: about life and death, about justice, trust in humankind, possibilities and means of action. The lack of response, the uncertainty and the doubt are particularly heavy and led me to mark these questions in the earth.

The "Question Mark"

The "Question Mark" imposed itself upon me as the link between all the families of the disappeared, of all eras and in all continents. The nagging questions about what the disappeared persons endured; where they are; the reasons and the precise conditions of their disappearance; their death or the remainder of their lives; the possibility of finding information and an acknowledgment of the facts: all these questions are highlighted by this large question mark.

This sign is used in countless languages. For us, it comes from Latin (it would be the graphic representation of the word *qo* derived from the name *quaestio*), but it is found in Chinese, Japanese, Korean, Arabic, sometimes turned upside-down.

To draw a question mark is to start with a circular shape that does not close in on itself, but opens and continues with a straight line and a full stop affixed below.

A large question mark of 52 linear meters, made up of a low wall 40 cm high and 30 cm wide, lies on the slope of the park. Its inclination is slightly greater than that of the ground. In its upper part, the low wall seems to retain the earth to a height of

40 cm; at its lowest point, it disappears into the grass. All around the outer rim, the grass is flush with the top of the wall.

At the center of the question mark, in the upper part of the curve, the earth has been hollowed out to create a level difference of 40 cm, making it possible to sit on the low wall. This difference steadily decreases until the end of the straight line, which gradually sinks into the grass. At the bottom of the curve, six meters from the end of the wall, the full-stop itself is a circular concrete slab of two meters in diameter flush with the surface.

The wall and the slab are made of extra-white concrete with aggregation of Greek marble. The glitter of the marble reflects the light.

The question mark is an offset in the slight slope of the park. This cut in the flatness represents for me the never closed wound of disappearance.

The upper part of the question mark constitutes an open hemicycle, a kind of *agora*. This circular area offers a welcoming place, like open arms, where to find and comfort each other, to keep hope. It is a place where you can feel protected. At the same time, this circular shape is not closed in on itself, it is open and soaring towards the world: at festivals, it is a kind of theater for speakers and musicians, and it stimulates debate and encourages to look outward, towards action.

Claiming is a strong gesture. In this artwork, it is represented graphically by the full-stop. Just as we tap on paper to affix a full-stop, so we demand an acknowledgment of the facts, an explanation. We want the TRUTH to be known and JUSTICE to be done.

Figure 15.2 "Question Mark" view from the air, 2011. Photo by Anne Blanchet.

One could have also imagined a 20-meter question mark erected vertically in the park. But I did not want an artwork developed at height, a crushing emblem. It is the absence, the break, the questioning that I wanted to bring to life. It's not about arousing emotions, but giving them a place to talk.

The earth that carries us all, the earth that keeps the imprints of our lives is broken by this questioning. It is from the earth that I want to let the absence scream.

The white question mark is clearly legible on the grass by Google Earth or from the planes landing or taking off from the Geneva airport. The perception of this installation is gentle, its inscription in the grass clear, but without violence. Nothing is closed, the form is open, the question is thrown at all the decision-makers who fly over Geneva, it wants to take them to task (Figure 15.2).

Notes

1 See http://www.jardindesdisparus.org/index.php?id=28.
2 Louis Joinet (1934–2019), French judge, founder of the French Union of Judges, member for 17 years of the then United Nations Human Rights Sub-Commission on the Prevention of Discrimination and the Protection of Minorities, member of the United Nations Working Group on Arbitrary Detention, United Nations Independent Expert on the human rights situation in Haiti. Louis Joinet devoted most of his life to the fight against enforced disappearance. He was among those who drafted the United Nations Declaration on the Protection of All Persons from Enforced Disappearances, adopted by the General Assembly in 1992. Later, he was one of the masterminds behind the drafting, negotiations and subsequent adoption by the General Assembly in 2010, of the International Convention for the Protection of All Persons from Enforced Disappearance.
3 Statement by Louis Joinet, see documentary *Un jardin des disparus* part 3, starting as 4'17" at the following link: http://www.jardindesdisparus.org/index.php?id=33.

Index

Note: *Italic* page numbers refer to figures and page numbers followed by "n" denote endnotes.

For Product Safety Concerns and Information please contact our EU
representative GPSR@taylorandfrancis.com
Taylor & Francis Verlag GmbH, Kaufingerstraße 24, 80331 München, Germany

www.ingramcontent.com/pod-product-compliance
Lightning Source LLC
Chambersburg PA
CBHW050341270326
41926CB00016B/3550

9 7 8 1 0 3 2 3 2 0 5 7 1